BALTIC
SEA

EAST
PRUSSIA

POLAND

Hamburg

PRUSSIA

VISTULA R.

Warsaw

N

W E

S

LAUSITZ
+1526-1635

SILESIA
+1526

AN EMPIRE

Breslau

ODER R.

furt

ELBE R.

Prague

BOHEMIA
+1526

MORAVIA
+1526

HUNGARY
+1526

DNIESTER R.

BAVARIA

DANUBE R.

Augsburg

Linz

AUSTRIA
+1278

Vienna

Budapest

TURKISH HUNGARY
+1699

nnsbruck

+1507

STYRIA
+1278

Graz

Mohacs

MAROS R.

Bucharest

CARINTHIA
+1335

TISA R.

BANAT
+1718

nt

+1518

+1382

CARNIOLA
+1335

DRAVA R.

OLTUL R.

Venice

Trieste

SAVA R.

SLOVENIA
+1718

Belgrade

WALLACHIA
+1718-1739

DANUBE R.

PO R.

CROATIA
+1526

DALMATIA

NORTH SERBIA
+1718-1739

Sofia

Florence

ADRIATIC SEA

OTTOMAN

Constantinople

TUSCANY
+1737

PAPAL
STATES

Rome

NAPLES
+1516-1735

EMPIRE

Naples

SEA

Athens

Palermo

SICILY
+1516-1735

Tunis

0   Miles   300

The Habsburgs

THE HABSBURGS

by Dorothy Gies McGuigan

*Die Könige der Welt sind alt
und werden keine Erben haben.*

(The kings of the world are old
and they will have no heirs.)

Rilke

Doubleday & Company, Inc.
Garden City, New York
1966

Grateful acknowledgment is made for the use of excerpts which appeared in the following publications:

Briefe Kaiser Franz Josephs an Frau Katharina Schratt, edited by Jean de Bourgoing. Reprinted by permission of Dr. Robert Rie. A translation of this book by Robert Rie and Evabeth Miller Kienast has been published by the State University of New York, in cooperation with Antioch Press.

Maria Theresa of Austria by Margaret Goldsmith. Reprinted by permission of the publisher, Arthur Barker Ltd.

Emperor Charles V by Karl Brandi, translated by C. V. Wedgwood. Reprinted by permission of the Estate of the late Karl Brandi and the publisher, Jonathan Cape Ltd.

King of Rome by André Castelot, published by Harper & Brothers. Reprinted by permission of Harper and Row, Publishers, and Hamish Hamilton Ltd. (which published it under the title of *Napoleon's Son*).

The Bourbons of Naples by Harold Acton, published by Methuen & Co. Ltd. Reprinted by permission of David Higham Associates, Ltd.

The Revolutionary Emperor Joseph the Second by Saul Padover. Copyright 1934. Reprinted by permission of Nannine Joseph for Dr. Saul K. Padover and the publisher, Jonathan Cape Ltd.

Francis the Good: The Education of an Emperor, 1768–1792 by Walter Consuelo Langsam. Reprinted by permission of the publisher, The Macmillan Company.

Maria Theresa by Mary Maxwell Moffat. Reprinted by permission of the publisher, Methuen & Co. Ltd.

Mary of Hungary by Jane de Iongh. Copyright © 1958 by W. W. Norton & Company. Reprinted by permission of the publisher.

Charles V, Father of Europe by Gertrude von Schwarzenfeld, translated by Ruth Mary Bethell. Reprinted by permission of the publisher, Henry Regnery Co.

Elisabeth, Die Seltsame Frau; Mensch und Herrscher; Der Alte Kaiser Franz Joseph I; and *Vom Kind Zum Kaiser* by Egon Caesar Count Corti. Reprinted by permission of the publisher, Verlag Styria and Renata Puteani.

"Erzherzogin Leopoldine, das Leben einer Leidgeprüften" by Siegfried Weyr, from *Neues Österreich*, January 17, 1960. Reprinted by permission of Dr. Helene Weyr.

*To my mother
and to the memory of my father*

Foreword

No FAMILY in European history has been so closely bound up with the earth-shaking events of our Western world as have the Habsburgs. For six and a half centuries they dominated the map of central Europe, passing on from one to another that extraordinary set of heirlooms: the vast realm, the assortment of crowns, the medieval palace in the heart of Vienna, the unique set of family traits that marked members down to the end of the Empire.

To those of us who went to school between the two world wars the image of the dynasty was, on the whole, an inimical one. The Spanish Habsburgs continued to live in the shadow of the *Leyenda Negra;* the Austrian Habsburgs suffered not only the bias of nineteenth-century Protestant historians, but the lingering bitterness of nationalists who presided at the dismemberment of the monarchy in 1918.

Nearly a half century has passed since their departure as kings and emperors. New sources of scholarship—but perhaps even more, time itself and the movement of history—enable us to view them in a clearer light, to measure on a fairer scale their successes and failures as human beings and as monarchs.

It is with the Habsburgs as human beings that I am concerned in this account; my aim is to tell the story of men and women in a family of kings. I have recounted only so much of history as has been needed to provide the stage for their movements, and I have given space to legends, to human details and human trivia that could have no possible place in a political history.

A large part of the material is drawn from secondary sources, but wherever possible I have preferred to allow individuals to speak with their own voices, as those voices come down to us in letters and personal records.

ACKNOWLEDGMENTS

I am grateful to the reference staff of the University of Michigan library, and to the staff of the Nationalbibliothek in Vienna. Dr. Erwin Auer, Direktor of the Kunsthistorisches Museum, Reproduktionsabteilung, and the staff of the Bild-Archiv und Porträt-Sammlung in Vienna have been unremittingly helpful in locating illustrations.

While the larger number of translations appearing in the book are my own, and I must take responsibility for any flaws in them, I acknowledge gratefully advice and help from Hedy Cardinaux, of Bern, in translating certain of Maximilian's letters to Prüschenk; from my mother, Jane Gies, in translating from the Latin and Dutch; from Dr. Clarence Pott, of the University of Michigan Department of Germanic Languages and Literature, for reviewing certain passages. Elisa Ross, of Oslo, located and translated some of the material on Queen Ysabeau of Denmark.

In the writing of this book I owe a special debt of gratitude to Dr. Arno Bader, of the University of Michigan Department of English, who gave me encouragement in the crucial beginning; to my friend Thilde Müldner of Vienna, who across many years has stimulated my interest in the Habsburgs; to my aunt, Gretchen Rasmussen, and to Hedy Tsacoyannis for technical assistance.

Dr. Margaret Sterne, of the Wayne State University Department of History, read the manuscript in its final form and offered valuable suggestions and criticism.

And finally my deepest debt of all: to my husband and children, who endured the writing of it.

Contents

Illustrations

GENEALOGICAL TABLE I
From Maximilian I to Maria Theresia.

MAXIMILIAN I d.1519
1. Marie of Burgundy (Daughter of Charles the Bold)
2. Bianca Maria Sforza

PHILIP I d.1506 — Juana of Spain   Margaret d.1530

SPANISH LINE   AUSTRIAN LINE

CHARLES V d.1558   **FERDINAND I** d.1564
Isabella of Portugal   Anna of Bohemia and Hungary

Eleanor d.1558   Mary d.1558 — Lajos of Hungary

Ysabeau d.1525   Catherina

PHILIP II d.1598   **MAXIMILIAN II** d.1576
1. Mary of Portugal (Mother of Don Carlos)
2. Mary Tudor   Maria — Maximilian II
3. Isabella of Valois
4. Anna, daughter of Maximilian II

                           Ferdinand of Tyrol d.1595
                           Philippina Welser

                           Karl of Styria d.1590
                           Maria of Bavaria

PHILIP III d.1621   **RUDOLF II** d.1612
Margarete, daughter of Karl of Styria

                           MATTHIAS d.1619

                           Maximilian d.1618

                           Albert d.1621

                           YOUNGER TYROLEAN LINE
                           Leopold d.1632
                           Claudia de Medici

PHILIP IV d.1665   **FERDINAND II** d.1637
                           1. Mary Anne of Bavaria
Maria Anna, daughter of   2. Eleanor of Gonzaga
Ferdinand III

CARLOS II d.1700   **FERDINAND III** d.1657
                           Maria Anna

                           LEOPOLD I d.1705
                           1. Margarita Teresa
                           2. Claudia Felicitas
                           3. Eleanor of Pfalz-Neuburg

JOSEPH I d.1711   **CHARLES VI** d.1740
Amalia Wilhelmine of   Elizabeth Christine of
Brunswick-Lüneburg   Brunswick-Lüneburg-Wolfenbüttel

Maria Antonia   **MARIA THERESIA** d.1780
m. Maximilian Emmanuel of Bavaria

Prince Joseph Ferdinand
(claimant to throne of Spain)

Maria Teresa
m. Louis XIV of France

Louis the Dauphin

Philip of Anjou
(King Philip V of Spain)

GENEALOGICAL TABLE II
The House of Habsburg-Lorraine

MARIA THERESIA 1736 **FRANZ STEPHEN** of Lorraine
d.1780 (Emperor Franz I) d.1765

Marianna

Elizabeth

JOSEPH II
d.1790
1. Isabella of Parma
2. Josepha of Bavaria

Marie Christine
d.1798
Albert of Saxony-Teschen

LEOPOLD II
d.1792
Maria Louisa of Bourbon-Spain

Caroline
d.1814
Ferdinand of Bourbon-Naples

Marie-Thérèse
(m.Franz II)

Ferdinand
d.1806
Beatrix of Modena-Este

Maria Ludovica
(m.Franz II)

Amalia

Marie Antoinette
d.1793
Louis XVI of France

Louis XVII
"The Lost Dauphin"
d.1795

Maximilian
Prince Elector of Cologne d.1801

Marie Thérèse
m. Duke of Angoulême

FRANZ II (1)
d.1835
1. Elizabeth of Württemberg
2. Marie-Thérèse of Bourbon-Naples*
3. Maria Ludovica of Modena
4. Karoline Augusta of Bavaria

Ferdinand III
of Tuscany d.1824
1. Louise of Bourbon-Naples
2. Mary of Saxony

HABSBURG-TUSCAN LINE

Karl
d.1847
Henrietta of Nassau-Weilburg

Joseph
d.1847
1. Alexandra of Russia.
2. Hermine of Anhalt
3. Maria Dorothea of Württemberg

LINE OF ARCHDUKE JOSEPH

Johann
d.1859
Anna Plochl (Countess of Meran)

Rainer
d.1853
Mary Elizabeth of Savoy

LINE OF ARCHDUKE RAINER

Ludwig
d.1864

Marie Louise d.1847
Duchess of Parma
Napoleon I

"King of Rome"
d.1832

FERDINAND I
d.1875
abdicated 1848
Marianna of Savoy

Franz Karl
d.1878
Sophie of Bavaria

Leopoldine
m. Dom Pedro of Brazil

Albrecht
d.1895
Hildegard of Bavaria.

Karl Ferdinand
d.1874
Elizabeth, daughter of Archduke Joseph

FRANZ JOSEF I d.1916
Elizabeth of Bavaria

Maximilian Emperor of Mexico d.1867
Charlotte of Belgium

Karl Ludwig d.1896
1. Margaret of Saxony
2. Maria Annunciata of Bourbon-Naples*
3. Maria Theresa of Portugal

Ludwig Victor d.1919

Gisela d.1932 m. Prince Leopold of Bavaria

Rudolf d.1889 Stephanie of Belgium

Marie Valerie d.1924 m. Archduke Franz Salvator

Franz Ferdinand d.1914 Sophie, Countess Chotek, Duchess of Hohenberg

(Dukes of Hohenberg)

Otto d.1906 Mary Josepha of Saxony

Ferdinand (renounced title 1911)

Elizabeth d.1963 1 Otto, Prince of Windischgrätz 2. Leopold Petznek

KARL I d.1922 Zita of Bourbon-Parma

Otto Regina of Saxony-Meiningen (Heir to present Habsburg claims)

Adelheid

Robert Margaret of Savoy

Felix Anne, Duchess of Arenberg

Karl Ludwig Jolande de Ligne

Rudolf Xenia, Countess Tschernitschew

Charlotte George, Duke of Mecklenburg-Strelitz

Elizabeth Henry of Lichtenstein

* Mother of children listed

I

Habsburg Ancestor

WHEN IN THE YEAR 1273 the electors met in the town of Frankfurt in Germany to put an end to the Terrible Times of no emperor, that nightmarish interregnum that dissolved middle Europe in violence and anarchy, the princes were at pains to choose an agreeable and a mediocre man, one on whose neck they might keep a collective foot. Above all they wanted a ruler who would not make the most precious of all crowns hereditary.

For these reasons they passed over the obvious choice—one of their own number, King Ottokar of Bohemia—to name for Holy Roman Emperor a provincial nobleman of no particular renown, Count Rudolf of Habsburg.[1]

If the world was astonished at the choice, no less was the lucky candidate—or so the chroniclers relate. When the news was brought to Count Rudolf in his tent in the middle of a September night—he happened just then to be warring with the Bishop of Basel—Rudolf thought at first the emissary was joking.

"It would be farthest from my thoughts to joke with you, mightiest of all lords," the Burgrave replied.[2]

Rudolf made peace at once, released his prisoners, journeyed north to Aachen to receive the crown of Charlemagne. His recent enemy, the Bishop of Basel, who knew him better than the electors, muttered, "Now sit tight, Lord God, or Rudolf will have your throne!"[3]

The electors had, of course, underestimated their man. Rudolf had all the attributes of the fast riser. A superb politician, a master of conniving and maneuver, a gambler and a bargain-driver, he knew perfectly how to turn his stroke of fortune to account. He may already have bribed three of the electors with what came to be his family's most useful bargaining tool—marriageable daughters.

One foot in the door of history, Rudolf was quick to shoulder it open.

He set out to take possession of the rich Austrian duchies in the middle Danube region, lands which had been seized by his rival, King Ottokar, after the death of the last legal heir. When Rudolf reached Vienna, he found the gates locked against him. Judging shrewdly the temper of the Viennese, he threatened to destroy their vineyards and the whole year's wine crop. They opened the gates.[4] Ottokar was persuaded to betroth a pair of his children to a pair of Rudolf's and retire to Prague.

A year or so later, in 1278, the two kings met on the Marchfeld near the Danube to settle their score once and for all. Rudolf won the day. Ottokar, who had dismissed Rudolf a few years earlier as a "poor little count"—*armes Gräflein*—lost the battle and his life.

Rudolf invested his own sons with the Austrian duchies as a family possession. The Holy Crown was more elusive.

We know how he looked from his tomb image at Speyer: the great hawk beak of a nose, the piercing eyes, the deep-graven cheek lines— a face with both harshness and humor. Like a sharp handprint on the margin of history, legend has clung to him. "By God, let any man who will come in to me!" he cried. "I have not become King to live hidden in a closet!" He was not too proud to sit down and eat turnips with his soldiers in the field, and he was so careful with money that he mended his own clothes.[5]

He had the wit to laugh at his nose himself. Once, riding along a narrow mountain road, he encountered an ill-tempered rider who would not give an inch of the way. Staring insolently at Rudolf he demanded, "Now just where would I go to get out of the way of a great giant nose like that?"

Rudolf smiled agreeably, pushed his nose to one side with a finger, and said, "*Nicht wahr, nun geht's?*" It will work out all right now, won't it?[6]

And when the proud tough old man who had had his horse killed under him on the Marchfeld found himself approaching the end of his earthly reign, he mounted his horse for a final journey, saying only:

> I will journey now to Speyer, where so many of my forebears lie
> who were also kings. And so that no one need bear my body
> thither I will go now while I can yet ride.[7]

The world of the Habsburg ancestor was a world from which magic and miracles had not yet vanished. It was told that before he became Emperor, he had ridden out to hunt one day and encountered a poor priest on foot carrying the Sacrament to a dying man. Rudolf had dismounted instantly, saying, "It is not meet that I should ride while the servant of my Lord and Saviour goes on foot." Nor would he have the steed returned to him; it would not be right to use it again for the common services of life. The winning of the crown came to be thought a reward for his act of piety.[8]

It was said too that when he had knelt in Aachen to receive the crown, he had arisen a changed man. "I am not he that once before ye knew," the poet Grillparzer has him say.

Although the Holy Roman Empire in the time of Rudolf was already an uncertain collection of states over which the Emperor exercised only a shadowy power, he continued to carry in his person more than the ordinary divinity of kings. A golden nimbus hovered over the wearer of that great glittering archaic crown, among whose enormous uncut jewels was set the invaluable Stone of Wisdom, of which the poet Walther von der Vogelweide had sung.[9] He ranked above all other monarchs. A king of kings, he stood at the very summit of the feudal world. He was Kaiser, Caesar, heir of Roman greatness. He alone could create a new king in Europe; he alone could be addressed as Majesty.[10]

It was the only supranational secular office in the world, and any prince of Christian faith might be a candidate. In fact, a Spanish and an English king had been elected awkwardly and simultaneously just before Rudolf. In theory an emperor was chosen by the people of the realm; and if the choice had become invested in the seven most powerful German princes—a mystical seven for the Sacraments and for the Stars and Lamps of the Apocalypse—nevertheless the voice of the people and the voice of God were presumed to work infallibly in the balloting.

Nor was the crowning of an emperor like the crowning of an ordinary king. He wore garments fashioned after a bishop's, took Communion like a priest "in both kinds"—that is, both bread and wine. At the moment of his consecration, when he had sworn the oath on the Book of Gospels written in letters of silver and gold, and on the casket of earth soaked with the blood of Stephen the Martyr, the Archbishop of Cologne turned to the assembled throng to ask their consent:

Will you have this king as Emperor and King of the Romans, and will you be obedient to him according to the Words of the Apostle?[11]

The crowd cast a vote in their shouted response, *"Fiat!"* So be it!

For centuries longer the Holy Roman Empire kept alive in the minds of men the concept of a unified world bound together in Christian peace. In the European imagination the Emperor was the only symbol of supranational oneness in the secular realm.

After the death of Rudolf's son, Albrecht, there was an ebb in the tide of family fortune, and the imperial crown passed out of Habsburg hands for a century. An emperor from the rival Luxembourg family, Charles IV, published the Golden Bull in 1356 which excluded the Habsburgs from membership in the electoral college. But another energetic Habsburg, Rudolf IV, had a trick or two of his own. He uncovered in his chancellery a set of documents exalting his family above all other princely families, and consequently above the electors: all Habsburgs, he declared, were archdukes and archduchesses from birth. The documents were denounced as clear forgeries—the poet Petrarch was particularly vehement about the fraud. But the Habsburgs wore their new title with such aplomb and complete conviction that no one really ventured to deny it; eventually one of their own number, Friedrich III, became Emperor and confirmed the title.

From that time on they clung to the imperial crown, wore it almost continuously until the Empire itself flickered out.

II

Habsburgs in the Marriage Market: Maximilian I

1. The Wedding in Burgundy

> For a living and indestructible love bound them
> one to another in such sweet and loving harmony
> that only the mortal sting of death could divide
> them.[1]
>
> *Jean Molinet, Court Chronicler of Burgundy*

IN THE LIFE of a family as in the life of a person, there occur from time to time moments of grave peril, of mortal threat, when survival seems to reckon without our will or our plans, to hang on a trifle, a nod of fate. Such a moment happened to the Habsburgs in the year 1477, when the crucial marriage of a last son and heir, Maximilian, came within a hairsbreadth of failing.

The Emperor Friedrich III, his father, was not a gifted man. A whole string of misfortunes had reduced the power of his family to a fraction of what it had once been.

He had been harassed from within and without, forced to war and divide with a quarrelsome brother, forced to give ground steadily before his intrusive and energetic neighbor, Matthias Corvinus, the Crow-King of Hungary. Twice the people of his own city of Vienna had besieged him and his family in the Hofburg, where they had endured hunger so cruel they had devoured the dogs and cats and even the vultures that came to rest on the roof. When they fled the city, that holiest of monarchs, the only emperor in the Western world, had had to endure jeering and catcalls, and see his wife's baggage wagons plundered.[2]

He had watched the warmth and bright southern grace of his young wife, Eleanor of Portugal, turn to cold bitterness. He had seen their children die one by one, until only the two remained: the boy, Maximilian, and his sister, Kunegunde.

Friedrich had, however, one singular quality of temperament, a stolidity of soul, a tough staying power, that enabled him to survive blows of fortune that might have broken a more impatient or a more sensitive man.

Through all that happened to him Friedrich—impassive, phlegmatic —clung to his absurd conviction of dynastic mission. He collected books on magic and the occult, studied astrology, held to his deep belief in the peculiar power of royal blood—particularly his own. He traced his lineage back to Caesar Augustus, and even farther, to King Priam of Troy. If God had raised his house above all other princely houses, it must surely be for some lofty purpose in this world. He would simply hang on, outwait his evil fortune. Striding like a sleep-walker through the wreckage of his life, through lost battles, lost lands, lost hopes, through disappointment and defeat and personal tragedy, Friedrich was yet so sure of final victory that he invented a curious device and had it engraved on everything he owned:

A E I O U

It signified, he explained, *Austriae Est Imperare Orbi Universo:* The house of Austria is destined to rule the world.[3]

As for the single son, the cherished heir on whom all those stubborn hopes rested, Maximilian was of very different temper from his father, all flash and quicksilver where his father was leather and lead; restless, curious, eager, where his father was deliberate, cautious, slow.

It was true that at first under the sorrow of his mother's early death and under a harsh schoolmaster who did not hesitate to flog him, the boy had learned so slowly that his father feared he was retarded. Then quite suddenly, when he began to fence, tilt lances, and hunt superbly, his bright, gifted mind unlocked of itself.[4]

He was still a child playing siege with his companions in the castle courtyard when his father began to think about a bride for him. Was there, after all, a cheaper or simpler solution for mending the family fortune than the right marriage for his son? It was probably Friedrich's old friend and former chancellor, Aeneas Silvius, now Pope Pius II, who suggested Marie, the only child of the Duke of Burgundy, who stood to inherit on her father's death the richest and most powerful single state in Europe.[5]

But the match was far from easy to arrange. Through the years, as the two children grew to maturity far apart from one another at the opposite ends of the European world, it was discussed and dropped and discussed again. For one thing countless suitors jostled each other for Marie's hand. For another, her father, Charles the Bold ("Rash" would be an apter translation of his French sobriquet *"le Téméraire"*), was a difficult man, driven by inordinate ambition and pride; he asked a preposterous price for this most precious piece of merchandise. Charles had two passions: love for his duchy, and hatred of France. Now he asked in exchange for his daughter a price that would satisfy both passions: elevation of Burgundy to the rank of a kingdom the equal of France, and designation of himself to succeed Friedrich as Holy Roman Emperor, so that he would outrank the King of France.

The two fathers met at Trier in the autumn of 1473 to outbargain each other for the marriage of their children and the perpetuation of their family lines.

In fact that moment might have seemed a plausible one for the extinction of both houses.

Over the times—that century that bore "the mixed smell of blood and of roses"—hung a pervasive melancholy, a sense of weariness, of things coming to an end. Great families were going down in tragedy and decay—the house of York in the Tower and on Bosworth Field. The capture of Constantinople by the Turks and their slow, steady push up the Balkans lay like a pall on the Christian world. In the paintings and woodcuts Death danced over the joys of earth; the poets sang of death and of the snows of yesteryear. *"O misérable et très dolente vie . . ."* Still in the womb of the century lay the unknown wonders to come: Michelangelo, Copernicus, Luther; Columbus, a bored youth bent over the looms in his family's weaving room.

And in Trier the fourteen-year-old Habsburg heir, Maximilian, gazed in wonder at the dazzling magnificence that might be his future.

Charles the Bold appeared just then at the very pinnacle of his career. He made no bones about flaunting Burgundian wealth in the face of the newly-poor Habsburgs. With four hundred wagonloads of precious tapestries, with gold and silver and Flemish paintings and a company of the finest musicians in Europe, he turned the Abbey of St. Maximin into a luxury palace.

He himself made a grand entrance into the city, glittering like a sun king in a mantle his Flemish weavers had contrived out of pure gold thread heavily sewn with jewels; he carried a sword that had the entire *Pater Noster* inscribed in diamonds on the hilt.

When the Habsburg father and son knelt in the chapel in prayer,

it was before an altar loaded with Burgundian treasures—all twelve
apostles in gilded silver, ten saints in massive gold, candelabra and
reliquaries that sparkled with gems, and a single enormous diamond
in the shape of a lily enclosing a nail of the True Cross.

At the opening banquet Charles arranged to have the impoverished
emperor sit facing an enormous credenza on which were loaded eight
hundred pieces of silver and gold plate, and three unicorn horns.

It was not so much that Charles wanted a son-in-law ("I might as
well turn myself into a beggar monk," he told one of his followers),
but he did want passionately that royal crown, and the promise of the
imperial one.

Charles was so sure of his success that he ordered a king's crown
made to his measure in a workshop of Trier.[6]

The Emperor's appearance was far more austere. He had managed
through all his adversity to hang on to a small collection of jewels.
With these, with his title and ancient name, he made Charles appear
ever so slightly *parvenu*. Graciously he handled the daily bouts of
etiquette, refusing to allow his hands to be washed by Charles as his
vassal.

At first the conferences behind closed doors seemed to be going
well. Exactly what happened then no one knows. Did Friedrich fear
the rapprochement through secret messengers of Charles with his
enemy, Matthias Corvinus? Did he take seriously the threats of the
King of France? Or did he simply find Charles's asking price too
high? Certainly some of the powerful German nobles in Friedrich's
company opposed Charles's ambition. And certainly Friedrich had less
power over the electors' votes than Charles imagined.

In any case, just before the day set for Charles's elevation and
coronation, Emperor Friedrich simply departed by boat without fare-
wells, down the Moselle toward Cologne, leaving the conference up
in the air and the Archbishop of Trier to settle his bills. Charles the
Bold was left fuming with anger and frustration, an unbetrothed
daughter and a half-finished crown on his hands.

It was from Trier that Charles set out on that doomed path of impossible conquest, plummeting down toward disaster in a kind of
anguished rage, through one lost battle after another: Granson, Morat,
Nancy.

Friedrich's delaying tactics paid off. In 1476, with so many hands
turning against him, Charles agreed to betroth his daughter to the
Emperor's son, with no price at all demanded. The young pair exchanged rings and portraits, and Maximilian wrote Marie that he

would be wearing her colors. In the difficult journeying of that day, Ghent lay a world away from Vienna; they would not see one another until they married.

But while Marie waited in the palace in Ghent for her father to return home to set the date of her wedding, a handful of Charles's followers searching a frozen pond near Nancy, on a bitter cold January night, turned up the body of the great Duke, naked and half gnawed away by wolves.[7]

And now in the weeks that followed the lost battle of Nancy, as news of the Duke's death made its way across Europe, a drama of conquest and intrigue and bloodshed spun around the person of the young Duchess Marie.

King Louis XI of France, the shrewdest politician alive—the "universal spider," his enemies called him—was the first to jump. It looked very much as if he would swallow up Burgundy, heiress and all. In the felicitous phrase of his historian Commynes, "surprised with joy" at news of Charles's death, Louis immediately called for celebrations and ordered the French army to march into Burgundy, occupying all of Bourgogne and the border regions of Picardy and Artois. As for Marie, his beloved cousin, he announced that he would take her under his protection—the spider guarding the fly—and marry her to his own son, the nine-year-old Dauphin.

Nor was this all. In her own country Marie, a gentle girl whose sheltered life until now had concerned itself chiefly with music, embroidery, falcon hunting, suddenly found herself ruthlessly hurled into a political maelstrom. The court put on official mourning, but the cities of Flanders, which had felt the harsh weight of her father's scepter, could scarcely contain their joy at his death. The townspeople of Ghent rose in revolt, sent away the person most dear to Marie, her clever youthful stepmother, Margaret of York, made Marie a virtual prisoner in her palace, and wrung her consent to a privilege granting them virtual self-rule. For obeying her orders two of her own councilors were put to death, though Marie ran alone out of the palace through a surging mob to beg for their lives. Her courtiers and her subjects wrangled over which suitor should have her—whether the Dauphin of France, or the brother of the English queen, or the son of a Burgundian lord.[8]

In Vienna, Emperor Friedrich, that slow, ponderous man, summoned as much energy as he could possibly summon to push through his own son's marriage. He dispatched an embassy to Burgundy to try to confirm the marriage, and to inquire as discreetly as possible into the amount of the Burgundian revenues. He set about collecting money for the wedding journey, and he sent off invitations to all the great princes of the Empire to accompany his son to his marriage in Burgundy.[9]

In the matter of her marriage Marie showed remarkable firmness and purpose. In March of that year—1477—a trusted messenger went posting out from the palace in Ghent bearing a secret letter to Maximilian:

> Most dear and friendly lord and brother, from my heart I greet you. . . . You must not doubt that I will agree to the treaty made between us by my lord and father, now in glory, and will be a true wife to you. . . . The bearer knows how I am hemmed in. May God grant us our heart's desire. I pray you not to linger, as your coming will bring help and comfort to my lands . . . but if you come not, my lands can look for no aid . . . and I may be driven to do that which I would not, by force against my will, if you forsake me.[10]

What the nineteen-year-old princess feared she would be driven to do, by force against her will, was to marry the nine-year-old Dauphin, a thin, peaked child with hollow chest and crooked legs.

Emperor Friedrich's embassy arriving in Burgundy found civil war still raging, and confusion within the ducal palace. Their courier hurried back to Vienna to implore the Emperor to make haste, for "they would gladly give their bodies and all their worldly goods" to have the Archduke on his way.[11] They added that, so far as the Duchess Marie was concerned, she would only choose Maximilian: "Him she would have and none other upon this earth."[12] Whether she could hold her own against the pressure, the intrigue, the bribery of the French king no one could say.

The imperial emissaries hastily arranged a proxy wedding. Consulting no one, Marie went through with it, lying down before witnesses on a bed of state, while the proxy groom, Duke Ludwig of Bavaria, lay beside her, a sword between them, the right half of his body clad in armor "in token that the bridegroom would avenge her enemies."[13]

Nobody, however, was fooled. Proxy weddings counted for little except as propaganda weapons, and the machinations of the French king, and the advances of her other suitors continued almost as before. As late as June, King Louis was telling the citizens of an occupied Burgundian town that if they permitted their princess to marry Maximilian he would carry her away to his far-off country, "a land both primitive and rude where she would be far from all consolation."[14]

In Vienna an embarrassing dilemma delayed the departure of the real bridegroom. There was simply no money in the imperial treasury. The Emperor's son could not go posting across Europe like a common messenger; he must make an appearance impressive enough to win over the worldly Burgundians who were used to the fantastic magnificence of their own dukes. There was besides a papal dispensation to pay for—the young people were distantly related; and there were jewels to be bought for the bride.[15]

Begging and borrowing wherever he could, squeezing advance revenues out of the imperial cities, collecting an old due bill from the Jews of Ulm, Friedrich managed to scrape together nearly enough for the journey. On the very eve of his son's departure, on May 21, the Emperor was still mortgaging estates, borrowing ducats.[16] In the end there was only enough gold to last to Cologne. To make matters even more difficult, there was Friedrich's old enemy, Matthias Corvinus, sword-rattling again at the gates of Austria.

Maximilian's journey from Vienna to Ghent took nearly three months. Added to the frightful condition of fifteenth-century roads, and the scarcity of accommodations for large groups of travelers, were all the delays attendant on a political journey—receptions and banquets and official presentations of wedding gifts. All the villages and towns along the way turned out to honor the Emperor's son. Mile by mile the wedding procession swelled: bishops and abbots in horse-drawn litters, princes with companies of armed knights, and bringing up the rear, the wedding gifts—live sheep and oxen and horses, wagons loaded with casks of wine.[17]

Maximilian wrote his father joyfully that the city of Augsburg had given him a goblet filled with gold pieces.[18] Nevertheless by the time the party reached Cologne his money was nearly gone. There the whole party halted and waited nearly through the month of July. Not until Marie's determined stepmother, Margaret of York, dispatched her chamberlain with a hundred thousand ducats and an escort of Burgundian knights did the party get underway again. Hardly less valuable than the ducats was their bearer, Olivier de La Marche, courtier, poet, man of the world, who was to be Maximilian's invaluable guide through the intricacies of Burgundian court etiquette.[19]

Intrigue pursued the youthful bridegroom almost to the threshold of Marie's palace. The father of one of her suitors, the Duke of Cleves, tried to delay the party in Cologne and again in Brussels. The French king insisted that Marie could not marry without his consent, since he was her nearest male relative and the lord to whom she owed homage for some of her lands. At the very end, as Maximilian was crossing the border of Burgundy, his father's ambassador sent word that the place and date of the wedding had been quietly changed, and he was cautioned not to reveal it.[20]

At last, at sunset on August 18, Maximilian came riding into Ghent, looking, it was said afterward, "like an archangel," in armor of silver gilt, on his blond head in place of a helmet a garland of pearls and precious stones, on his breast the black velvet cross of Burgundy. Behind him, his impressive following, nearly a thousand strong, princes, barons, bishops, knights, had doffed the mourning they had worn out of courtesy to the dead Duke Charles, and appeared now in polished armor and wedding finery, with plumed helmets, banners flying, foxtails jauntily fixed to their lances. They rode into the city through the circle of great windmills that surrounded it, through streets jammed with people, under banners that spelled out "Most glorious prince, defend us or we perish!"[21]

Late that night the two young people met by torchlight in an inner court of the ducal palace. Marie waited with her ladies on a flight of stairs leading up to the great hall. When Maximilian had made his way through the immense crowd and greeted the ladies with a kiss, the young pair stood gazing at one another in silence "as pale as if they were dead."[22]

Marie must have appeared that night much as she is depicted in the miniature painting in her father's prayer book, handsomely gowned, her dainty, dark-eyed face smiling ever so slightly under the tall, pointed, white-veiled *hennin* with which fashionable court ladies were coiffed. As for the eighteen-year-old Archduke, with his lively, humorous brown eyes and high-arched Renaissance nose, everyone agreed he was delightful.

Neither bride nor groom spoke the other's language; all evening they had to address one another by signs. But a charming expedient had been found to break the ice. The prince was told that, according to an ancient Flemish custom, he must seek and find a flower which the princess had hidden on her person. Hesitatingly the youth began to grope for the flower, "modestly, with two fingers," according to

a German chronicler, while the onlookers smiled and nodded. Presently the elderly Archbishop of Trier standing nearby spoke to the
boy: "Unlace the lady's bodice; perhaps then you will find it." With
trembling hands he obeyed and withdrew a flower—a pink, whose
pretty meaning was instantly comprehensible to the courtly gathering: in the medieval language of flowers it signified the pure love of
marriage.[23]

Marie's councilors interrupted the poetic scene with some concrete
questions about financial arrangements—especially the Morning Gift,
that present of gold which the bridegroom customarily presented
to the bride on the morning after the wedding in compensation for
the loss of her virginity. Maximilian cut the discussion short—he would
agree to everything. The wedding pact was witnessed and signed, he
presented his betrothed with a suitably magnificent diamond, and
the meeting ended with a banquet in the great hall of the palace.

The following morning at daybreak, having managed a bare four
hours' sleep, Maximilian was awakened and brought to the castle
chapel, where the young couple knelt to make their vows, to break
with the papal legate the blessed bread, share the wedding goblet,
and receive the kiss of peace. Marie appeared then as her father's
child, a golden princess in gold-embroidered gown, a golden girdle
set with jewels about her waist, on her head the golden crown of
Burgundy.[24]

The whole company was bidden to a feast with music and dancing
that lasted all day. At nightfall a company of his knights led Maximilian to the bridal chamber, where the young pair were merrily bedded
down together in the lusty custom of the day. One of the Saxon
knights who had accompanied the wedding cortege across Germany
left an account of the journey, ending tersely at the chamber door:
"Wie es da ganngen ist wais ich nit." How things went in there I know
not.[25]

The court chronicler of Burgundy, Jean Molinet, was more explicit. Though he promised to remain tactfully silent on the subject of
the consummation, he did add that the Duke proved to be

> a begetter and a true man and well loved by our Lord God who
> sends generation; for our noble Duchess and natural princess
> conceived and found herself pregnant with a living child . . .[26]

Certainly the whole wedding had come about by a combination
of astonishing luck and the will of Marie and her father-in-law. Barely

three weeks after Maximilian had left Vienna, the Hungarian army
pushed into Lower Austria, to the very gates of the capital. Emperor
Friedrich fled up the Danube; he never set foot in Vienna again. A
threadbare emperor living in semiexile, he could yet take comfort:
however much he had lost, his children's children had secured the
magnificent heritage of Burgundy.

As for Louis XI of France, the universal spider, he counted it the
great blunder of his career to have let the Habsburg marriage come
to pass. Already in his castle of Plessis-les-Tours, he cogitated ways
to recover the prize he had unaccountably let slip from his grasp.

2. The Dowry

> If only we had peace we'd be sitting in a rose garden.
>
> *Letter of Maximilian from Burgundy*[1]

THE FIRST DAYS after his wedding unfolded for Maximilian like one of those chivalric romances of which he was so fond. Each morning he found laid out in his chamber a magnificent new suit of apparel: one day, cloth of gold with silver filigree work; another day, pure white satin adorned with a heavy golden chain; on another day, a suit of finest black velvet; and on another, brown velvet lined with sable.[2]

Philippe de Commynes, the friend and historian of the French king, declared that when Maximilian came to Burgundy "he didn't know anything."[3] It was true that he hadn't a notion of the practice of *Realpolitik*. He had, however, any number of pleasant talents to make him an agreeable bridegroom to a princess who had barely escaped marriage with a sickly nine-year-old boy.

All the knightly accomplishments he performed with enormous dash and vigor; he could bend a horseshoe with his bare hands, a feat he got directly from his Polish grandmother, Cymburga, who was said to have driven nails into the wall with her fingers. He danced well, played the lute, sang with a pleasant voice, painted a little, wrote verse a little. He was accomplished in the arts of love, which he had learned through the generous offices of an Austrian mistress named Rosina, whom he had left behind in floods of tears on his departure from Vienna. (From time to time even in Burgundy he would think of her nostalgically and write inquiring about her from his old friend, Sigmund Prüschenk, his father's chancellor.)[4]

As for the bride herself, he was well content with her. With disarming frankness he compared her to his former mistress:

I have a fair, devout and virtuous wife . . . slenderer in body than Rosina and white as snow, with brown hair, small nose, dainty little head and face, brown eyes flecked with gray, fine and clear, her mouth a little high but red and pure.[5]

Marie looked very charming in the fine gowns she had made for her wedding from stuff she got from the Florentine merchant of Bruges, figured damask and satin, fine velvet in tawny and crimson, white and violet.

Though they had grown up distant lands apart and spoke different languages, yet within the common bond of their courtly education they found a hundred pleasures to share. Each set about teaching the other his language. Years later Maximilian had the scene of those lessons painted: in a charming summerhouse the princely pair sit smiling, a book open on their knees, while pairs of lovers wander hand in hand through the garden.

Sometimes in the evening they played chess on a set made of rock crystal and gold. Or they read together out of the fine manuscript books in the ducal library—the Books of Hours, and the tales of Troy which Marie's father had had collected and written out for him, and the romances of Lancelot and of Perceforest and Mélusine. Or they listened to the palace choir of twenty-four voices, all sweet as angels, who sang intricately woven music such as Maximilian had never heard before. Their voices were kept pure, so Olivier de La Marche told him, by a diet of raw meat.[6]

When they sat at supper with Marie's stepmother (*die alte Frau,* the old lady, he called her in his letters, with the graceless impudence of the young, for Margaret of York was at that time exactly thirty-two), they ate from vessels of gold and vermeil. The food was far more varied and delicate than he had ever tasted, for the kitchen gardens of Flanders grew fine herbs, artichokes, and salad greens unknown elsewhere in Europe, and from the great, well-ordered palace kitchens emerged exquisite sauces, pastries, honey cakes and sweetmeats—the late Duke Charles had particularly fancied a *confiture* of crushed roses.

In no court north of the Alps was the art of graceful living practiced with more deliberate elegance than in the ducal court of Burgundy, where medieval culture was just then enjoying a last Indian summer blossoming.

After the chilly and comfortless family castle in Vienna, more fortress than palace, the warmth and luxury of the palaces of Ghent and Bruges and Brussels were a source of endless wonder to Maximilian. On the walls hung bright paintings by Flemish masters, Van Eyck and Roger van der Weyden; when Maximilian found time he would hurry to the Red Cloister to watch the painter Hugo van der Goes create masterpieces between bouts of madness. Even the royal escutcheons, the holy candles and banners, and the most intimate pieces of palace furniture had been designed by the greatest of artists.

He could never weary of examining in exquisite detail the great tapestries on the walls, on which were recounted scenes from the chronicles. Of special interest to Maximilian were the famous Troy tapestries—he believed as his father did that the Habsburgs were descended from King Priam. The Troy tapestries had been woven on the high looms at Tournai and presented by the city of Bruges to Marie's father, "our much-feared lord and prince upon his instant prayer and desire."[7]

In the elaborate palace household the dukes had set up for themselves, dozens of noble court officials and hundreds of beautifully trained servants executed the complicated steps of a daily ceremonial charade. Four servants were appointed merely to care for the ducal bed: one to open the curtains and fold back the coverlet in the mornings, another to beat and air the feather bed, another to hold the torch for the master when he climbed into bed, and a fourth to close the curtains around the bed. Still another had the sole job of moving the ducal chair, while another held a saucer under his chin each time he lifted his goblet to drink. A nobleman had the honor of cutting his lord's meat—and the privilege of keeping for himself that portion of the meat on which his hand had rested during the cutting. After each course at table a silver basin filled with perfumed water was passed to rinse the fingers, and each guest was handed a golden toothpick pointed with a diamond and headed with a pearl.

There seemed no end to the wonders the palaces held. In the treasure chambers were collected not only great quantities of gold and silver plate (though less, far less than had been piled there by Marie's avaricious grandfather, Philip the Good, for her father had already begun to dip into his capital), but the treasury held also all manner of things beautiful and strange: the pale lavender bowl of agate said to be the very vessel from which Our Lord drank at His last supper, cunningly wrought jewels of many kinds, the largest diamond known to Europe, and the famed unicorn sword of Marie's father, which carried in the hilt a piece of the magical horn that could protect the wearer from all harm.[8]

Singing birds hung in cages all about the palaces, and in the menageries were curious beasts that the Austrian prince had never laid eyes on before—lions and leopards, elephants, bears, camels, monkeys.

But of all the rich possessions in his wife's dowry, what most delighted Maximilian was the hunting gear of her father. Duke Charles had kept four thousand hounds and three thousand falcons trained for his pleasure. Marie too adored hunting. Her favorite falcon lived on a perch above the chimney piece where she fed it with her own hand that it might be tamed to her person. "My wife is a superb huntress with falcon and hound," Maximilian boasted in a letter home. "She has a white greyhound that is very swift. It sleeps almost every night by our bed."[9]

Side by side Maximilian and Marie rode out to hunt whenever they could, wild game on the wide Flemish plains, deer browsing in the forest of Soignes, heron and crane and wild goose in the marshes outside Bruges.

"If there were only peace, and if I had our lord and father here with me for two weeks," Maximilian said again, "I'd be in paradise."[10]

Long before the sweetness was pressed out of the brief honeymoon, long before he had exhausted the pleasures of his wife's inheritance, Maximilian had to take up that one deadly gift in Marie's dowry: the quarrel with France.

The old power struggle between the French kings and their cousins, the Burgundian dukes, smoldering through the Hundred Years' War, had exploded violently in double murder, when Marie's great-grandfather, John the Fearless, had had Louis of Orleans, quasi-Regent of France, killed on a dark Paris street, had himself been slain a few years later by forces of the French Dauphin on the bridge at Montereau.

The feud had simmered through the reign of Marie's grandfather, Philip the Good, and of her father, Charles the Bold. Now assumed by Maximilian along with the defense of his wife's inheritance, and fed by countless economic and political factors, the quarrel would evolve into the long tormented struggle between Habsburg and France for domination of Europe.

Marie demanded now the return of her lands which the Spider King had occupied: the duchy of Bourgogne, with the city of Dijon where her ancestors were buried, and the provinces of Picardy and Artois. A month after his wedding Maximilian was writing vehemently to Prüschenk, "There is no greater scoundrel in the whole world than the French king."[11]

Against the shrewdness, the cunning, the seasoned political genius of the Spider King, Maximilian brought only the naïve optimism of a guileless eighteen-year-old whose brain was full of the outworn furniture of chivalry. In his father's castle he had studied and played at all the feudal forms of warring and siege. Of Louis' kind of warring he knew nothing. It was a new kind of war, a miser's war: a war of nerves and attrition, a war of bribery, of espionage, treason, infiltration, of border sallies and burning of crops, of the sinking of the herring fleet on which the Low Countries depended for food.

Bitterly tedious, that miser's war, and not in the least like the tilting and jousting of great feast days in the courtyard of the Hofburg in Vienna:

> While you're having fun jousting and tilting and dancing [he wrote home], think of me and wish me a share . . . for my only pipers are the French gunners with culverins. They've almost piped me to death three or four times.[12]

The ducal army of Burgundy had been broken at Nancy; Maximilian had to put together and train a new one. For weeks and months he was away in the field rebuilding the Burgundian defenses.

And though he had imagined he would put all money woes behind him once he had married his heiress, he found to his dismay that the war was not easily financed. The rich, self-made merchants of the cities held tightly to their purse strings; they wanted their wars fought at bargain prices. Almost from the beginning his letters home to his father's chancellor are filled with money troubles.

To pay their hired army, Maximilian and Marie began to pawn. First went the glittering golden mantle Charles the Bold had worn at Trier, together with their personal jewels. Next went a great golden salver, prize of the ducal collection. Again and again plate from the palace treasure chambers was melted down for cash. And finally the young couple parted with thirty-two of the finest Flemish paintings from the palaces. They were pawned to the Medici Bank in Bruges with the hope of redeeming them, but a little later Maximilian wrote in great distress that "the said bankers sold the paintings to Certain Englishmen."[13]

Life even in the midst of the miser's war was not without brightness. The summer after their wedding, in June of 1478, while Maximilian was in the field training his troops, a little son was born to Marie in the palace in Bruges. He wrote his friend Prüschenk that he was

> awaiting every day a fine son from my wife, who ought to be brought to bed any day; all the women and doctors say it will be a little duke.

Before the courier had departed he could add a further message:

> I am very happy that I have a boy, and if it were only peace, so I could tilt and joust . . .[14]

The precious Habsburg heir, Philip, was christened in great style. His grandmother, Margaret of York, held him at the font, and later, because the French king was spreading unpleasant rumors that the babe was a girl, his godmother brought him to a balcony of the palace, removed the child's swaddling clothes, and held him up before the crowd that all might see he was indisputably a prince.

Maximilian, who was still in the field with his troops, could not attend the christening. The following month, however, when he signed a truce with the French, he returned home, and his little son was brought to him at the gate of the city. The proud father descended from his horse, took the child in his arms, and carried him on foot through the streets to the palace. The sight touched the town fathers in their most sensitive spot, and they bestowed on Philip a baptismal gift of fourteen thousand gold crowns.

No more powerful counterpoise to the French king's claims could there be than what the Burgundians called Philip: their *prince naturel*, an heir born on their own soil.

In that same summer of 1478, Maximilian, on the advice of the invaluable Olivier de La Marche, checkmated another move of the French king by placing himself at the head of the Order of the Golden Fleece. The twenty-four noblemen who comprised that most exclusive of chivalric orders—"*gentilshommes de nom et d'armes et sans reproche*"—swore to defend the Christian faith, to uphold virtue, to be unswervingly loyal to their sovereign, and to wear the insignia of the order conspicuously at all times: a collar of golden links, representing flints, from which was suspended the symbolic fleece.[15]

Several of the knights had died with their old chief, Charles the

Bold, on the field at Nancy, so that when they marched on a day in April of 1478 to their chapel in Bruges, two of them led by the bridle Charles's white horse; on a black velvet cushion on the empty saddle lay the collar of the Grand Master. In the chapel Maximilian was initiated, clothed in the gold-embroidered vestments of a knight, and given the collar of Grand Master. From that time on, the knights of the order, comprising the aristocracy of Burgundy, would give him their allegiance, serve as a kind of privy council to him, and even a private confessional. Once a year the faults of each member, including the sovereign, were reviewed, and praise or blame allotted.

The Golden Fleece remained closely bound to the Habsburg family; from Maximilian's time a Habsburg would always serve as Grand Master.

That summer of 1478, the year after their wedding, when their son was born and a brief truce made with France, the young ducal couple enjoyed a golden interlude of peace and pleasure. In a day when married love in palaces was not only rare but downright unfashionable, the deep devotion that had blossomed out of a purely political match became something of a legend. On her great seal Marie had chosen for her motto: *En vous me fye*—I trust in you.

At gay little supper parties Maximilian took a hand in the menu, ordering fresh vegetables and rare preserved fruit, seeing to the entertainment, often those mimes and charades in mask and costume, in which he delighted to take part.

But the truce was short-lived, and before long the wearisome miser's war broke out again, only occasionally the mortal tedium broken by a pitched battle, such as that fought at Guinegate in 1479. In that battle Maximilian distinguished himself for valor, leaping recklessly from his horse to lead his foot soldiers to victory against the French infantry.

The following January of 1480 Marie bore a second child, a daughter named Margaret for her much-loved English stepmother. But in autumn of 1481 the first sorrow shadowed the happiness of the couple. Their third child, a boy, died a few weeks after birth. The young mother grieved so bitterly it seemed she would find no comfort for her loss. Not until the long winter had passed, and she found herself again with child, did her spirits begin to revive.

On a day in March of 1482, one of those bright days that break through the frozen crust of a harsh northern winter, Maximilian and

Marie rode out with a party to hunt heron in the marshes near Bruges. Marie must have looked much as she is depicted on her great seal, mounted on her favorite high-spirited steed, the graceful folds of her riding cloak falling about her, her falcon on her wrist, and her favorite greyhound running beside her.

Maximilian, leading a troupe of hunters, beat the brush of the marshland to raise game. Suddenly a heron flew up. Marie loosed her falcon, her eyes on the game. At the same moment her horse, about to leap a ditch, stumbled over a fallen tree trunk; horse and rider tumbled in a heap in the ditch. Grievously hurt, Marie was lifted and carried to the nearby château, next day borne on a litter back to her palace in Bruges.

Through the anxious and terrible days that followed, while courtiers and servants went whispering through the corridors, while her frightened young husband walked in a procession with ashes on his head to pray for her recovery, her young life slowly ebbed away.

Physicians conferred helplessly outside her chamber; it was said that out of womanly modesty Marie refused to allow them to examine her.

Toward the end she called together those dear to her, bade her children good-bye, sent her husband from the room to spare him, saying gently, *"Nous serons, hélas! bientôt séparés!"* To her councilors and to the Knights of the Golden Fleece gathered at her bedside, she said, *"Adieu, chevaliers.* My lords, I know that death is near me. Forgive me, I beg you, if I have ever caused you displeasure." Marie was barely twenty-five when she died on March 27, 1482.[16]

Though Maximilian would marry again, he never recovered from the loss of his young first wife. He told the Estates General of Burgundy that "he had never had either by day or by night an hour of pleasure or of repose in that land except when he was beside her."[17]

For years he could not speak her name without tears starting to his eyes.

There is a story that some years later, when he had become Emperor, he begged the Abbot Trithemius of Würzburg, a clever man known for his skill in working magic spells, to conjure up Marie's spirit from the realm of the dead. The Abbot agreed to do so, on condition that Maximilian would on no account speak to her. But when the image of Marie appeared out of the shadows of the room, wearing, it was said, the same blue dress she wore on the day of her fatal fall, Maximilian could not restrain himself; he cried out a single endearing word and she vanished from his sight.[18]

3. Troubles and Glory

> With such a prince the Golden Age must return.
>
> *Sebastian Brant, on Maximilian's*
> *election as Emperor*

Louis XI lay in a dark chamber of his castle at Plessis-les-Tours. He had suffered stroke after stroke; he lay half paralyzed, seeing no one, an old sick spider waiting for death. But that spring of 1482 the news of Marie's unexpected death brought him one last spurt of joy; he roused himself to greet the delegation of dissident burghers from Ghent, headed by an astonishing shoemaker named Coppenolle. He drew up with them a treaty that gave France nearly everything she wanted at the moment; he filled their pockets with French gold and sent them back to Burgundy. He was so far gone that he had had to lay his left hand rather than his right on the Gospel to swear to the treaty; when he died a little later it was surely with a smile on his face.

In Burgundy, in the wake of Marie's death, a tide of misfortune had engulfed Maximilian. No strong national bond yet united the differing regions, though for a time they had united in fighting the encroachments of France. But they had continued to bicker among themselves, to resent the cost of the war and the troublesome presence of Maximilian's mercenary troops among them. The cities of Ghent and Bruges, stubborn and strongly separatist, had little feeling of kinship with the rest of Burgundy. Marie was barely laid in her tomb in the church of Bruges before her subjects made it clear to Maximilian that he was a foreign nobody now, only the widower of their princess and the father of their prince, whose welfare they would see to themselves.

In one of the bitterest hours of Maximilian's life he was forced to set his signature to the Treaty of Arras, presented to him by the men of Ghent. By the treaty France would be allowed to keep all the lands she had occupied. And as a seal of peace Maximilian's tiny daughter, Margaret, was to be delivered over as bride of the French Dauphin, bringing with her as a dowry yet more of Burgundy. Still in the arms of her nurse the little girl was brought to Amboise in France, where a marriage ceremony united her with the same Dauphin Charles—now thirteen—who had once been intended as her mother's bridegroom.

As matters fell out Margaret—"the little queen," the French called her—did not fare badly. She was carefully brought up in the castle of Amboise under the tutelage of the Dauphin's gifted older sister, Anne de Beaujeu, whom the late King Louis had called "the least foolish woman in France."[1]

Just when matters seemed to be at their worst, Maximilian began to recoup his fallen fortune. The other provinces of Burgundy rallied to his support. With their aid, and with his army of mercenaries he suppressed the Ghent rebellion, recovered custody of his little son, Archduke Philip, who was taken to the town of Malines to be reared by his stepgrandmother, Margaret of York.

Emperor Friedrich, meanwhile, had been watching from afar how the events in Burgundy transpired, but he himself was fully engaged by the encroachments of Matthias Corvinus in Austria. In the summer of 1485 Vienna fell to the Hungarians, and the Crow-King entered in state and took up residence in the Hofburg.

The embittered Viennese who had suffered and hungered through four long months of siege joked now that their Emperor's proud device, A E I O U, really signified: *Aller Erst Ist Österreich Verloren* —in the first place, Austria is lost. Through all of Germany a whisper ran, then a cry, that a new emperor was needed, and desperately, someone young and filled with spirit. From his exile in Linz, stubborn, slow-moving Emperor Friedrich agreed at last to have his son elected and crowned King of the Romans.[2]

In the autumn of 1485 both set out for the city of Charlemagne— Friedrich from south on the Danube, and Maximilian from the Netherlands. Father and son had not met for eight long years—not since Maximilian's departure on his wedding journey—when they met again on the road outside Aachen that winter of 1485. The father was an old man now, an old king of seventy, with little left in the world to him except his son and his hoard of jewels. Maximilian, who had left home eight years before, an eighteen-year-old with much of the child still in him, appeared now a man and a leader of men, stamped with the scars of battle and of the sorrow and joy of his marriage. A little later, when he spoke before the assembled German princes, his listeners were spellbound and described afterward how the words like molten gold had poured out of the mouth of the young prince.

An emperor and a prospective emperor could not meet as any father and son; the encounter had to take place within the ornamental framework of courtly etiquette, and as publicly as on a stage. As Maximilian approached Aachen with his brilliant company—each knight wearing on his left sleeve the white, blue and red of the Archduke's livery—two envoys rode up from his father bringing word that the Emperor wished more than anything in the world to see his child again and was even now on his way to meet him. Maximilian forthwith dispatched a noble envoy of his own back to his father with the message that it was also *his* greatest desire in the world to behold his father, and that only the wars in which he had been engaged had kept him from doing so long ago. Moreover, he humbly begged His Imperial Majesty not to advance one step farther, but permit *him* to close the gap between them. Despite the courteous entreaties of his son's ambassador, the Emperor continued on his way to meet Maximilian. He dispatched another envoy, however, to beg his son to remain where *he* was, and begged him further not to dismount to make his reverence to his father.

Maximilian, says Molinet, was *fort esbahi*—completely overcome— by the Emperor's magnanimous courtesy; he had no choice but to obey. When they rode in sight of one another at last, the Emperor halted and permitted his son to approach. Maximilian made his reverence, bowing as low as it was possible for him to do in the saddle, both father and son, says our chronicler, "shedding many a tear for the joy that filled their hearts."[3]

They passed the twelve days of Christmas together at Aachen and then journeyed on to Frankfurt, stopping along the way for tournaments and jousts and festivities. Maximilian had brought with him his chapel choir of accomplished musicians—all dressed in scarlet tabards lined with different colors according to the parts they sang—who were called upon again and again to entertain the assembly.

Early on the morning of February 16, 1486, Maximilian and the prince-electors appeared at the lodging of the Emperor in Frankfurt, and all proceeded on foot to the church of St. Bartholomew for the balloting.

After the Mass of the Holy Spirit had been sung, the electors drew near the altar and swore on the Gospel that

> not moved by favor, by love, by nearness of kin, by loss or hatred, or fraud or deception, they would elect the best possible of princes, of noble blood and virtue, powerful and renowned in arms, to be King of the Romans.[4]

Actually they were all susceptible to bribes. On this occasion the new king of France, Charles VIII—Maximilian's rival for the hand of Marie of Burgundy and at the moment his prospective son-in-law—had offered fat bribes to all seven if they would hinder the choice of Maximilian. Nevertheless, the whole thing went off smoothly. When the assembly had knelt and sung the *Veni, Sancte Spiritus,* the electors retired to the sacristy to weigh Maximilian's qualifications, and in hardly more than an hour returned, made him a low reverence, invited him to join them, and presented him with his selection by unanimous ballot.

A few weeks later he was crowned in Aachen, and, seated on the throne of Charlemagne, given possession of the Empire, "to hold the monarchy of the world" after his father's death.

When the coronation was over and the dizzying round of festivities, of tournaments, banquets, and ceremonies, Maximilian rode back to Burgundy with the sound of trumpets and clarions, huzzas and cheers, praise and flattery still sweetly echoing in his ears.

He brought back with him a company of thirty thousand *Landsknechte*—German mercenaries—a rough-and-tumble lot, who had a habit of helping themselves freely to the hospitality of the countryside, particularly when they were not promptly paid. He intended to settle things once and for all with France.

But again the burghers of one of those difficult Flemish cities—this time, Bruges—blocked his way. He arrived in Bruges one day with a small company of his mercenaries who began to drill in the main square. The townspeople were troubled, on edge, and a sullen crowd gathered to watch. Somehow a drill order was misunderstood; someone thought the soldiers were ordered to charge. In the twinkling of an eye the great alarm bell was rung, the guildsmen of the town were called to arms, the city gates clapped shut. Before Maximilian could gather his wits, he was surrounded, marched off a prisoner, and locked up in a stout mansion facing the square.

For four long months the proudest young monarch in Christendom

[1] Crown of the Holy Roman Empire, now in the Treasury of the Hofburg, Vienna. (*Kunsthistorisches Museum, Vienna*)

[2] Maximilian I as a child, with his mother, Eleanor of Portugal, about 1464. From the illuminated prayer book of Empress Eleanor. (*Bildarchiv des Österreichische Nationalbibliothek, Vienna*)

CLEOPHAS FRATER CARNALIS IO=
SEPHI MARITI DIVAE VIRG MARIÆ

IACOBVS MINOR EPVS MARIA CLEOPHÆ SOROR
HIEROSOLIMITANVS VIRG MAR PVTATIVA MA
TERTERA D N

IOSEPH IVSTVS SIMON ZELOTES CONSO
BRINVS DNI NRI &

[3] Emperor Maximilian and his family, by Bernhard Strigel. Probably painted
in 1515 at the time of the Habsburg-Jagellon double wedding in Vienna. Left
to right, rear: Maximilian, Philip the Handsome, Marie of Burgundy. In front:
Archduke Ferdinand, Archduke Charles, Prince Lajos of Hungary.

Marie of Burgundy had died thirty-three years before the painting was
made. Nor had Strigel ever seen Philip, who had died in 1506, nor young Ferdinand, who was growing up in Spain, but he doubtless made use of existing
portraits. (*Kunsthistorisches Museum, Vienna*)

POTENTISSIMVS MAXIMVS ET INVICTISSIMVS CÆSAR MAXIMILIANVS
QVI CVNCTOS SVI TEMPORIS REGES ET PRINCIPES IVSTICIA PRVDENCIA
MAGNANIMITATE LIBERALITATE PRÆCIPVE VERO BELLICA LAVDE ET
ANIMI FORTIDVDINE SVPERAVIT NATVS EST ANNO SALVTIS HVMANÆ
M CCCC LIX DIE MARCH IX VIXIT ANNOS LIX MENSES IX DIES XXV
DECESSIT VERO ANNO M D XIX MENSIS IANVARII DIE XII QVEM DEVS
OPT MAX IN NVMERVM VIVENCIVM REFERRE VELIT

[4] Emperor Maximilian I, by Albrecht Dürer, painted at the Diet of Augsburg in 1519. (*Kunsthistorisches Museum, Vienna*)

[5] Eleanor, Charles, and Ysabeau, three of Maximilian's grandchildren, by an unknown Flemish artist in 1502, when Charles was two and a half, Eleanor four years old, and Ysabeau, fifteen months. *(Kunsthistorisches Museum, Vienna)*

[6] Juana of Spain, known as "Juana the Mad," mother of Charles V, in the last years of her life, about 1555. *(Bildarchiv des Österreichische Nationalbibliothek, Vienna)*

lay in captivity in the heart of his recalcitrant city. It was true his jailers raised their hats to address him; he was allowed to keep twelve servants to wait on his person; some of the best Flemish artists were sent to decorate the walls of his apartment.

But a prisoner he remained, while all Europe quivered with the news, while the prince-electors protested violently, while the Pope thundered threats to excommunicate the entire city of Bruges, while the King and Queen of Spain began to arm a fleet for his rescue.

Legend ascribes the most audacious attempts to free him to his friend and jester, Kunz von der Rosen, who tried to cross the castle moat with a swimming belt for his master before he was attacked and driven back by vicious swans. (He remarked ruefully that the swans "must certainly be good Frenchmen.")[5]

Next Kunz learned how to tonsure heads, disguised himself as a monk come to hear the prisoner's confession, and once inside his master's quarters, tried to persuade him to allow his head to be shaved, change clothes with him, and so escape. Maximilian adored masquerades, but this one he declined.

In the end, to obtain his freedom, he promised to abide by the Treaty of Arras and keep peace with France. A week later his father marched into Burgundy with a sizable imperial army. Maximilian disclaimed his promise, declaring it had been got from him by force, and at the head of his father's army he proceeded to subdue the rebellious cities. Most of Burgundy supported him, Bruges and Ghent again surrendered.

Burgundy, which history began to call the Netherlands, remained a prickly possession.

4. Brides Lost and Won

OLD EMPEROR FRIEDRICH had been living out the closing years of his life in Linz on the Danube. He had been driven out of Vienna by the Hungarian king, Matthias Corvinus, in 1485. He knew by comparing their horoscopes—his own and Corvinus'—that he would never best the latter in open battle, must wait out instead the ascendancy of Saturn.

But in April of 1490 the Hungarian king died in the Hofburg in Vienna. He had outdone Emperor Friedrich in all ways save one, and that one happened to be the most important: Matthias left no legitimate heirs. To him is ascribed that envious, witty *mot* on the Habsburgs:

> *Bella gerant fortes; tu, felix Austria, nube:*
> *Nam quae Mars aliis, dat tibi regna Venus.*[1]

> (Let the strong fight wars; thou,
> happy Austria, marry:
> What Mars bestows on others, Venus
> gives to thee.)

By an old treaty the Habsburgs were to inherit Hungary if Corvinus died without sons, but now instead the Hungarian magnates chose Vladislav of the Polish Jagellon family to be their ruler. Friedrich called upon his son to drive the Hungarians out of Vienna, out of Lower Austria, and far back within the borders of Hungary.

With Corvinus dead and the Habsburg crownlands once more in his possession, old Friedrich might have returned to Vienna. He stayed on in Linz, however, giving less and less thought to the Empire, and more to the mysteries of the universe.

He manufactured, it was said, a very passable gold by combining quicksilver with orpiment and certain other substances, and from the filings of his homemade gold he made a healing potion for a dozen diseases. He could read the lineaments of people's faces and the small maps written in their hands. He studied mathematics avidly, and the works of the learned astronomers Purbach and Regiomontanus, who had been at Vienna in his time. He built little observatories that faced in each direction and spent half the night studying the heavens. He was careful to let no one come near; the townspeople, half fearful, half angry, called his watchtowers "mousetraps," joked that their emperor spent his time collecting mouse dung. Friedrich shrugged, having that large indifference to trifles of men who at the end of their lives come to live among the stars.[2]

In the spring of 1493 a gangrene developed in his foot. Maximilian sent his most skilled physicians to his father; he himself came to Linz in June, stood by while they cut off the old man's leg. Friedrich was seventy-eight when he lost his leg; his greatest fear was that posterity would nickname him "Friedrich the Lame." He survived the amputation, was recovering nicely, so it seemed, when toward the end of that summer he gorged on unripe melons, got a stomach colic, and died.

Maximilian, King of the Romans, moved up to his father's place: Emperor of the *Reich*, of that secular imperium of Christ which medieval men had dreamed would one day embrace the world.[3]

The shape of the Habsburg future, only dimly grasped by young Kaiser Max, was in some respects already quite clear. Rooted in central Europe, Habsburgs would wage a two-fronted war: in the west, against France; in the east, against the Turks, slowly and stubbornly hacking a path up the Danube until they would stand one day at the gates of Vienna.

As a family the Habsburgs would reflect the character of sinewy old Friedrich. Lacking military gifts, lacking money, in any real sense, or the means of raising it, lacking all the components that were just then forging powerful national monarchies in England and France (the Golden Bull of 1356 having effectively crippled imperial power forever), they would make extraordinary use of the weapons at hand. They would build fortune and power on marriageable children, and like Friedrich, know how to play a waiting game. They would cut their losses time and again, compromise, adapt to circumstances, possess the will to hang on, to endure, to survive. Valois, Orleans, Bourbon, Tudor, and Stuart came and went; Habsburgs remained.

The focus of Maximilian's life had shifted.

The province of Tyrol was deeded over to him by an elderly, child-less cousin. He came to love the Tyrol above all places in the world, its villages and proud mountain folk, its pine forests and crisp streams, the towering mountain sides scrawled over with the coarse handwriting of glaciers. He called it his peasant's smock.

In the town of Innsbruck, set like an eagle's eyrie among snow-topped peaks, he set up his permanent court and made such home as he had from this time on. He added an extravagant ornament to the old ducal residence in the town square: a double balcony, de-lightfully sculptured, and roofed over with gilded copper tiles. Under the Golden Roof he stood with his court to watch strolling players and musicians perform in the square. From Innsbruck he rode out to fish in the dark tarnlike mountain lakes, and to hunt chamois on the highest crags, wearing the short green loden coat of the mountaineers and the broad-brimmed green Tyrolean hat.

Maximilian was a widower; he began to look once more for an advantageous match.

In March of 1490, a month before the Hungarian king's death, Maximilian had brought off another matrimonial coup, or so it seemed; he had become betrothed—by long distance, to be sure—to Anne of Brittany, heiress to the sturdy, independent duchy that lay to the west of France, the single important adjoining duchy, excluding Burgundy, which an expanding France had failed to absorb.

Unable to appear in person to claim his bride, for he was engaged just then in driving the Hungarians out of Lower Austria, Maximilian sent his ambassador, Wolf de Polhein, to place a naked leg in young Anne's bed in the concrete symbolism of the proxy rite. Everything seemed settled.[4]

But he had counted without another Anne—Anne de Beaujeu, Regent of France, the shrewdest feminine brain in Europe. Her young brother, Dauphin Charles—the same boy who had nearly married Marie of Burgundy and was now considered the husband of Maximilian's little daughter, Margaret—was dispatched to Brittany at the head of an army to besiege Duchess Anne in her capital of Rennes.

While Maximilian pleaded before the Imperial Diet in Frankfurt for money and troops to hurry to the rescue of his bride, the fifteen-year-old duchess held out heroically in her besieged city. But the German princes had no interest in Brittany; they voted Maximilian only two thousand foot soldiers against the French army of thirty thousand. At last, her people famished and winter approaching,

Duchess Anne surrendered, and Dauphin Charles took possession of both duchy and duchess. He lost no time in consummating the match, before the Pope had even decided on a dispensation.

Maximilian smarted under the double humiliation: his betrothed wife seized—and married—to his bitter rival, and his own daughter Margaret, who had spent eight years in France as their prospective queen, sent back like a rejected parcel to Burgundy.

When Maximilian came into his father's inheritance not long after, he found it long on prestige and majesty, very short on cash. He got the precious hoard of jewels his father had clung to through years of austerity as the outward symbol of his kingliness. Maximilian too refused to part with them; he would pawn the treasure, or part of it, again and again, but he passed it on in the end, nearly intact, to his grandchildren.

Meanwhile he needed money desperately, and again he took the easiest way of remedying his need; he married a rich bride. In the eyes of courtly Europe, it was a scandalous mésalliance: he married Bianca Sforza, niece of the Duke of Milan, who had sprung not too long before from peasant stock. Her magnificent dowry—three hundred thousand golden ducats, plus another hundred thousand in jewels and apparel—nearly made up for the lack of ancestors. The proxy wedding in Milan was suitably extravagant; Leonardo da Vinci designed the festivals.

From the beginning the bridegroom was notably unenthusiastic. While the bride on horseback made the harrowing crossing of the Alps in the dead of winter—her mule train loaded down with plate, jewels, altar fittings, household goods (including even a silver bed warmer and chamber pot, and three thousand golden embroidery needles)—reaching Innsbruck on the eve of Christmas, Maximilian, who was staying in Vienna, did not arrive to consummate the marriage until March.[5]

A few months after the wedding Maximilian was complaining to the Milanese ambassador that while Bianca was as fair as his first wife, she was greatly "inferior in wisdom and good sense," though, he added hopefully, "perhaps she might improve in time."[6]

But Bianca seemed to be incurably giddy, hopelessly extravagant, and given to all sorts of curious follies. Once the Milanese ambassador had to remonstrate with her for eating all her meals from the floor; another time Maximilian wrote the Duke of Nassau that, while trav-

eling through a poor region of the Netherlands, Bianca insisted on
being served goose tongues.

She was even more carefree about money than Maximilian. When
in the summer of 1494, soon after their marriage, they journeyed to
the Netherlands to take part in the coming-of-age of his son, young
Archduke Philip, the Emperor complained that Bianca had spent in
a single day the entire sum of two thousand florins the city of
Cologne had given her as a wedding gift. On that same journey
Maximilian himself was so short of money he had frequently to leave
a jewel in pawn for one of their inn bills. The joke that went the
rounds of Europe was that the impoverished Emperor was leaving his
brand-new wife as collateral.[7]

Though she had brought a queen's ransom in jewels from Italy,
still Bianca regularly spent her whole household allowance on personal adornment, often buying jewels on time with a promise to pay.
In 1496 the Emperor's councilors wrote him urgently from Worms
begging that he send money immediately, because

> the Queen and her ladies have provision for only three or four
> days longer; and if within that time no money comes, even their
> supply of food will come to an end.[8]

Bianca herself wrote her husband about that time that she had been
forced to pawn her underlinen, and would he please send cash forthwith to redeem it.[9]

The Women's Court in the Innsbruck Palace was constantly in a
turmoil, and some of Bianca's Italian ladies in waiting did not hesitate
to bring their complaints to the Emperor.[10] Maximilian found it increasingly convenient to travel abroad—without his wife—for long
periods of time.

Bianca's dowry evaporated quickly. In 1494, the first year of their
marriage, the French king marched into Italy. Basing his conquest
on an old and tenuous family claim, he toppled one after another of
the city-states, proclaimed himself King of Jerusalem and Sicily, proceeded to have himself crowned King of Naples. Indignantly—for had
not Italy once been the very heart of the Holy Roman Empire?—
Maximilian joined a league to drive the French out of Italy. Again
and again during the ensuing years Maximilian poured what money
he had, what troops he could wheedle out of the Imperial Diet, into
fighting the French king in Italy. Sometimes one side won; sometimes
the other; racked Italy was the permanent loser.

5. *Kaiser Max: His Image*

WITHIN A DECADE of the time he came to reign as Emperor the image of Maximilian as a kind of ballad hero had taken possession of the minds of his people. He had the personal charm and incautious daring, the lively good humor out of which legend is made. He helped legend along by himself writing up his exploits later on in a pair of vividly embroidered memoirs, *Der Weiss Kunig* and *Theuerdank*.

Tilting and jousting were meat and drink to him. He was the best archer, the best horseman, the best gunner of his time. At the first Diet of Worms when the huge French knight Claude de Barre hung his shield out of the window of his lodging challenging all Germans present to single combat, it was the Emperor himself who took up the challenge, fought and bested him.[1]

He molded his mercenaries into a powerful and dreaded fighting component—quite possibly more dreaded in peace than in war. They had discarded medieval armor and heavy shield to march on foot in parti-colored garments, carrying huge ash lances eighteen feet long. Often Maximilian took pike on shoulder and marched with them. It was said that more than once in the thick of a battle he was seen to spring lightly from his saddle, lift a wounded man in his arms, and mount again.

He was more than likely a bit of a show-off. Once, so he claimed, he entered a lion's cage in Munich, forced open the beast's jaws, and pulled out its tongue, whereupon it lay down and licked his hand. Another time he climbed the highest ledge of the church tower in Ulm, and out onto the iron bar that held the beacon lantern. There he perched on one foot like a circus acrobat, holding the other toe aloft in the air.

Tyrolean mothers for generations have pointed out to their children the lofty crag high up in the Alps where Kaiser Max nearly lost his life out chamois hunting, and was saved by a friendly angel—or perhaps the clever mountaineer Oscar Zips.

He had a passion for exploring, for experimenting. Something of a poet, something of a philosopher, something of a painter, an inventor, a musician, he was one of those extraordinarily versatile men, the type of *uomo universale,* who were so brilliant a product of the Renaissance. He planned dozens of books; twenty-two still exist that he wrote or dictated on all sorts of subjects from hunting and falconry to genealogy and building and cooking. His carefully chosen musicians went with him wherever he traveled. He encouraged art, helped design the magnificent tomb in the Hofkirche in Innsbruck whose bronze figures are masterpieces of late Gothic.

His friend Albrecht Dürer painted his portrait, decorated his private book of prayer, made in a series of magnificent woodcuts a triumphal procession in which all Maximilian's ancestors, real and imaginary, appeared.

Once, when the Diet was in session in Augsburg, Dürer was painting a mural high up on the wall of the great hall. Maximilian called to a nobleman standing near and asked him to hold a ladder for the painter. The nobleman refused, declaring huffily that such an act was beneath his dignity. The Emperor said, "I can make a nobleman out of a peasant any day, but out of no nobleman can I make such a painter as he," and he raised Dürer to noble rank.[2]

He loved feasting and dancing and mumming; he delighted in entertaining his guests himself in mask and costume. In Cologne he gave a great feast after his coronation. When dinner was over, the tables were whisked away and a bright taffeta pavilion set up in the hall, out of which issued singers and players of instruments, and a man and woman in Turkish dress, each carrying on his shoulder a child dressed as a monkey, "making meows and grimaces and very strange things." At the climax Maximilian himself emerged from the silken tent, in a short doublet of cloth of gold and parti-colored shoes tied with golden bands. With him appeared a veiled lady in velvet and jewels, who danced with him a French dance for the pleasure of the assembled guests.[3]

He enjoyed the company of women of all ranks of society, could charm the Lady Abbess of the Convent of the Eleven Thousand Virgins in Cologne quite as beguilingly as he did the burghers' wives of Augsburg, with whom he danced the torch dance on St. John's Eve around a towering bonfire.

Once, visiting the Margrave Frederick in Nürnberg, the ladies be-
seeched him to stay on after dinner, though he was expected at
another castle by evening. Finally his fair entreaters hid his boots and
spurs. Laughing, he agreed to stay, danced with them all through the
afternoon and through the night till dawn, only riding on next day to
Neumarkt, where he had been awaited since the previous day.[4]

Another time a bevy of prostitutes were locked out of Regensburg
just as the Diet was about to begin. The *Fahrenden* or traveling
ladies, as they were called in that day, from their habit of traveling
in groups from city to city, wherever a great feast or meeting was to
be held, took their plight to the Emperor, explaining that they were
certain their company would be greatly appreciated at the Diet.
Good-naturedly Maximilian agreed to smuggle them into Regensburg
if the first girl would hang on to his horse's tail, the second to the
skirt of the one before, and so on. It was thus, in the retinue of the
Emperor and much appreciated by the amused onlookers, that the
traveling ladies got to attend the Diet.[5]

He managed to disseminate the precious Habsburg blood with a
good deal of liberality and left numerous bastards behind. At least
seven were recognized and supported by his grandsons;[6] still others
are imputed to him, including Matthias Lang von Wellenberg, later
Archbishop of Salzburg.

If Maximilian saw himself much of the time as the romantic hero
of a *chanson de geste*—as he pictures himself in his memoir, *Theuerdank*—still he could do what no ballad hero and few real monarchs
could do: he could laugh at his own mishaps and failures, at the
jousts where he ended up on his back on the ground, and the carnival
seasons in which no ladies yielded up their favors:

> I have danced a great deal, and tilted lances and enjoyed carnival
> [he wrote once to Prüschenk]. I have paid court to the ladies
> and earned great thanks; for the most part I've laughed heartily.
> But in tilting I've fallen so often that I could scarcely take courage
> again; no lady will love me from the heart alone. . . . Now it is
> Lent and I know not what to confess, for all I've done in this
> carnival confesses itself.[7]

And if he was a gay and humorous emperor, he was also a profoundly thoughtful and religious man. "Why," he asked the Abbot
Trithemius once, "should witches have power over evil spirits, while
an honest man cannot get anything from an angel?" And he wished
to know of the learned Abbot: "Since Christendom comprehends only

a small part of the globe, should not everyone who believes in a God be saved by his own religion?"[8]

All his life he contemplated a crusade to drive the Turks out of Europe and free Constantinople; to the very end he was endeavoring to enlist the other Christian rulers in the cause.

Perhaps the single event of his life about which most legend accumulated was his discovery beneath the altar of Trier cathedral of the seamless coat of Christ. According to a popular song written in 1512, the year of the discovery, an angel visited Maximilian in Cologne and bade him ride to Trier. There in the cathedral fifteen candles suddenly appeared mysteriously burning on the altar. When the altar was moved, the seamless robe of Christ was found beneath it, together with the dice the crucifiers had used to gamble for Christ's last garment.[9]

The seamless coat became a symbol of the Holy Empire, the undivided Christian world, eventually of the Habsburg realm.

6. The Spanish Marriage:
Philip the Handsome and Juana the Mad

> *Une rage d'amour, qui est une rage excessive et inextinguible . . .*[1]

HIS SECOND WIFE, Bianca, remained childless.

Once more the future of the dynasty was staked on a single son and daughter—Philip, growing up in Malines in the Netherlands under the guidance of his grandmother, Margaret of York, and his sister, Margaret, the little ex-queen of France, who had rejoined her brother now in the household in Malines.

Philip was a handsome boy, blond and blue-eyed (history would name him *Philippe-le-beau*). His long, slender straight legs in the tight-fitting hose and pointed shoes of the day were a significant mark of male beauty. He had more than a little of his father's outgoing charm; women from his doting grandmother on would conspire to spoil him.

He was not quite sixteen when he was declared of age and freed from his father's regency. In a vivid ceremony before the Estates General gathered in the church in Malines, the seals of the regency were broken by blows of a hammer, to be replaced by the seals of Philip, their native-born prince. That summer, the summer of 1494, Maximilian came with Bianca to the Netherlands, where father and son took part in the ceremonial Joyous Entries into the cities and regions of the land.

Just at that point King Charles VIII of France was crossing the Alps on his way to his short-lived conquest of Italy. The following year, in a plan to dislodge France and to encircle it, Maximilian joined in an alliance with the Catholic Majesties of Spain, King Ferdinand and Queen Isabella: "a total and perpetual alliance," read the terms of the treaty. And as a pledge to its perpetuity Philip and his sister Margaret knelt in the church of Ste. Gudule in Brussels in December of 1495, and pledged themselves in betrothal to Juana and Juan, children of the royal house of Spain.

When Philip journeyed to the Tyrol the following summer to visit his father, it became suddenly evident that he had a mind of his own. He was now independent sovereign of the Netherlands; he flatly refused to join his country's interests to his father's anti-French policy. It was a quarrelsome summer. At one point, in a terrible burst of rage, Maximilian ejected his son's Burgundian tutor, Busleyden, and forbade him to appear again in his presence.[2]

Philip must have been relieved when a courier reached him in Linz in early October to inform him that his bride, Princess Juana of Spain, had landed in the Netherlands and was even now awaiting his arrival.

Philip set out at once, burning up the last stages in his eagerness to see her and intercepted the Spanish bridal party at Lierre.

It was a tinderbox encounter. Juana was not pretty, but her dark hair, olive skin, and sea-green eyes—"yeux verts de mer," the Flemish described them—and the inward, closed look of her seldom-smiling face held something exotic and exciting for Philip. He could not wait to possess her. He insisted on having the bishop of the diocese perform the marriage that very afternoon so that he might sleep with her that night. His grandmother and sister were hastily summoned from Malines, the rite was performed, and while the guests enjoyed a hurriedly prepared feast, the bridal pair retired to a borrowed mansion near the river.[3]

From the night of their marriage Juana gave to her husband a singlehearted passion that devoured her, body and mind. Whether she bore a taint of mental illness from her mother's mother, who had died insane, or whether as a child she had been ignored by her beautiful and busy mother, Queen Isabella, who nicknamed her "la suegra," the mother-in-law, Juana had grown into a brooding and introverted adulthood. She had been devoutly religious; after her marriage she found no time for pious pursuits. Nor did she enjoy the gay life that Philip did, the banquets and balls and hunts that engaged the youthful ducal court. Her only interest in life was that "rage of love" for her husband. Such love can grow burdensome to the one loved; Juana's consuming passion began to irritate, finally to bore Philip.

From the beginning the royal ménage knew scarcely a moment's peace. Neither seemed to have a talent for domesticity. Philip enjoyed flirting and the flattering attention of women in a day when the amours of princes stirred no comments save envy. Bitter quarrels broke out between them, stormy scenes of jealous anger and recrimination. The Venetian ambassador who knew the couple declared that "the princess tormented her husband so much that he had reason to be little satisfied with her."[4] It was said that Philip could only control her rages by denying her the marriage bed.[5]

Meanwhile the second Habsburg-Spanish marriage had taken place. The same convoy of Spanish galleons that had carried Juana to the Netherlands sailed back to Spain with Philip's sister, Margaret, who was to be bride of the Spanish throne heir, Juan. On the voyage the ships were buffeted by a terrible storm. It was said that Margaret had bound to her wrist a purse filled with gold pieces for a royal burial, in case the ship foundered, together with the witty two-line epitaph:

> Cy-gist Margot, la gentil' damoiselle
> Qu'ha deux marys et encore est pucelle.[6]

(Here lies Margaret, the gentle girl,
Who had two husbands, and is virgin still.)

But Margaret reached Spain safely and the wedding took place.

The same unbridled sensualism smoldered in both brother and sister: Juan fell as passionately in love with the blonde Habsburg princess as Juana had with Margaret's brother. Fearful for her son's health, Queen Isabella tried to separate the young couple; she advised her daughter-in-law to be more reserved toward her husband lest he burn out his strength. Eighteen months after their marriage Juan died of a fever in his young wife's arms. In Spain it was said that he died of love.[7]

Juan's death was the first of a series of mortal accidents that conspired to bring the greatest of all prizes into possession of the Habsburgs. Within a year after Juan's death, his elder sister died, then her small son, leaving Philip's wife, Juana, heiress of the throne of Spain.

In the Netherlands Juana had meanwhile borne children to Philip —Eleanor, Charles, Ysabeau—but she showed no more interest in them than in anything else outside her husband.

In November of 1501 Philip and Juana journeyed to Spain, so that

Juana might give the required oath before the *cortes* (the Spanish equivalent of the *parlement*). To Maximilian's keen displeasure Philip chose to accept the invitation of the French king to travel through France rather than by sea. The journey was a long progress of festivals and entertainments, with gay, lively Philip the center of attention, and Juana, silent, wretched, apart. When the French king offered her a gallant kiss on the cheek, she rebuffed him sharply; she angered the French queen by cold-shouldering her and taking precedence.

In Spain Juana's parents observed with alarm the change in their daughter, the fits of passion and rage, the long periods of brooding silence. The necessary oaths were taken, but when the autumn of 1502 approached, Juana found herself far advanced in pregnancy and unable to make the voyage home. Philip, however, declaring he could not endure the climate of Spain, and relieved perhaps to be free of his wife's disturbing company, journeyed back without her, crossing France once more, feted all the way and ending with a friendly treaty signed with the French king.

Left behind in Spain, Juana sank into deeper melancholy. The birth of a second son, Ferdinand, in March of 1503 did nothing to lift her spirits; she waited only for the day when she might rejoin Philip.

When she discovered late that autumn that her mother had withheld a letter from Philip asking for her return, "she behaved like an African lion," according to the chronicler Petrus Martyr.[8] The season of storms had begun again, making sea travel impossible. Her mother sent her to the fortified castle at Medina del Campo.

One wild, stormy night that winter Juana ran out of the castle half dressed, and hurrying to the gate begged the guards to open that she might hasten to rejoin her husband. When the guards refused she wept, pounded on the great doors, sat shivering through the night and next day, refusing the warm garments her servants brought her, until at last her mother, Queen Isabella, was sent for from Segovia. The Queen wrote her ambassador in Brussels that

> She spoke so disrespectfully and so little as it beseemed a daughter that if I had not been aware of her mental state I should never have suffered such speech.[9]

At last in spring Juana was able to take ship for the Netherlands, leaving her small son Ferdinand behind in Spain.

Philip's affection for his wife had cooled even further, to say nothing of his patience with her difficult moods. One day Juana discovered—or believed she had discovered—that Philip had taken as his mistress a fair-haired beauty of the court. Frantic with jealousy, Juana attacked the girl with a pair of shears, cut off the golden hair, slashed at the pretty face.[10]

Outraged, Philip locked his wife in her apartment in the Brussels palace. More than once, it was rumored, he had to resort to blows to control her. He called her "the terror"; she called him "the fairest of all husbands."[11] She tried to escape and defended herself from the charge of madness, writing lucidly to a friend:

> I ought not to marvel that false testimony is brought against me, since it was brought against our Lord.[12]

Even now there were brief periods of reconciliation. In September of 1505 Juana bore their fifth child, a daughter named Mary.

Soon afterward news came from Spain that Queen Isabella had died and, believing her daughter incompetent to rule, had left the regency of Castile in the hands of her husband, King Ferdinand. Ambitious Philip bridled at this; he and his wife set out again for Spain to claim Juana's inheritance.

Philip quarreled with his father-in-law, King Ferdinand, who had remarried in indecent haste after his wife's death a very young and very pretty French princess, Germaine de Foix, which might even threaten the succession of Philip's children. Philip's well-known charm and his political skill paid off, the Castilian *cortes* supported Juana and Philip, King Ferdinand resigned the regency and sailed off to Naples with his new wife.

Juana was even more difficult, however, during this second sojourn in Spain. They had barely arrived before she sent back to the Netherlands all the ladies of their company except for one very old serving-woman whom she allowed to remain. Juana kept to her chamber much of the time, wore only black, refused to take part in official ceremonies.

Maximilian's envoy in Spain wrote the Emperor at this time:

> The greatest enemy our gracious Lord of Castile [Philip] has to deal with is, apart from the King of Aragon, the Queen, His Grace's wife; she is worse than I can describe to Your Majesty.[13]

On a burning day in September of that year, 1506, Philip played a game of pelota with friends in Burgos. Afterward he drank a quantity of iced water, and the following day came down with a low fever, followed by a chill. Presently he was seized with severe cramps and spat blood. His physicians bled him on the opposite side from the pains. On the fourth day he rose and dressed, but his fever suddenly mounted, his tongue and throat swelled so that he could barely speak or swallow. On the fifth day his physicians applied cupping glasses to his shoulders and neck, and administered purgatives. He grew worse; they bled him again and again. He became confused in his mind, sweat heavily, fell into a lethargy. On the sixth day he died.[14]

The doctors of the Spanish court declared Philip had died from doing what no southerner would dream of doing—drinking iced water in a state of great heat. The whisper that spread through Philip's Flemish suite, and thence through all the courts of Europe, was that Philip had died of poison. Some said it had been given at the order of his father-in-law, others by his jealous wife.[15]

Cold as ice, silent as the grave, Juana had watched at her husband's bedside, tasted all his medicines before she gave them, cooled his fever-hot forehead while his life ebbed away.

When the body had been embalmed and laid in the coffin, a fierce wild grief racked her. She could scarcely bear to be parted from the corpse, and when after the funeral the coffin had been brought to a nearby monastery, she would go every day and have it opened so that she might embrace her beloved dead. She had elaborate mourning outfits made in order to wear a new gown each time she visited his tomb.

In January she thought she would bring her husband's body to the royal crypt in Granada. She started southward in a great funeral cortege, the coffin on an open bier before her carriage, journeying only at night by the light of torches, for, she said, "A widow who has lost the sun of her own soul should never expose herself to the light of day."[16]

Once, stopping to rest overnight at a religious house, Juana discovered it was a convent of nuns rather than monks; instantly she had her husband's coffin brought out to the open fields far from the company of women, and there she watched over it through the night.

In the town of Torquemada Juana was seized with labor pains; refusing the help of midwives, she gave birth alone to a little daughter whom she named Catherina.

The gloomy procession never reached Granada. Juana turned aside to meet her father, King Ferdinand, returning from Naples. Not long after he had her confined to the castle of Tordesillas.

Once a monk told Juana of a prince who had returned to life after fourteen years. Patiently like a child Juana waited for the years to pass until Philip would return to life. Like a child she wept when the fourteen years had passed, and the corpse of her husband withered and moldered in the coffin.[17]

7. The Children of Malines

THE FOUR CHILDREN whom that tragic pair, Philip and Juana, had left behind in the Netherlands, grew up under the watchful eye of their aunt, Philip's sister Margaret, among a bevy of cradle-rockers, governesses, tutors. The brother and sister born in Spain grew up in Spain, without ever encountering—for many years—the Netherlands brood: Ferdinand at the court of his grandfather, the King of Spain, and little Catherina, the child of sorrow and death, in the grim confines of Tordesillas Castle with her insane mother.

Maximilian's daughter Margaret had married again after the premature death of her young Spanish bridegroom, but her second husband, Philibert of Savoy, died young and left her a widow once more. Her father tried to persuade her into another helpful political match, with the elderly and ailing King Henry VII of England. Margaret demurred; she had performed her matrimonial duties for her family; she preferred widowhood to another royal marriage.

A woman of wide interests and cultivated tastes, Margaret was less given than Maximilian to flights of fancy; she was more practical, down-to-earth, with a firm notion of the value of a golden guilder and how hard it was to come by. Named Regent of the Netherlands during the minority of her nephew Charles, Margaret performed efficiently. In the quiet town of Malines she brought up her dead brother's four children with care and devotion, a precious nest of Habsburg fledglings for whom Maximilian was already hatching great plans.

The Emperor and his daughter were very close; no other woman was so close to Maximilian during the last decade of his life. Messengers posted from Constance, from Düsseldorf, from Fribourg and Cologne, from Frankfurt and Innsbruck, bringing letters to the shrewd young woman in widow's weeds in the Malines palace.

Maximilian's letters, often dashed off in his own hand, in French and Latin with an occasional German word thrown in, a bit garbled and frequently misspelled, were addressed to "My good daughter" and signed "Your good father Maxi." Margaret's salutation to her father was "My very dreaded lord and father."

He sends his pastry cook to be trained in her kitchen, for he well knows that nowhere in the world are such delectable pastries made as in Flanders. She sends him from Malines a packet of the sweets and *confitures* to which he is so partial. Another time she sends fine underlinen that she has made with her own hand; it reaches him in Bolzano, where he is making ready for another Italian campaign:

I have received [he writes] . . . the fine shirts and linen which you helped make with your own hand, and with which we are overjoyed, chiefly because . . . you have taken thought for our person; and when this year we are wearing our armor, which is hard and heavy, then our heart will be comforted with the good feel and gentleness of that fine cloth which the angels of paradise might well be using for their garments.[1]

Later, from camp in Italy, he writes telling her where to find the jewels he has had to pawn to pay his soldiers, for, should he be killed in battle, he wishes her to redeem them "for our very dear and very much loved grandchildren."[2]

Often his letters are brusque. He commands her peremptorily to bring the children to Brussels where he is shortly to be, for he wishes to see them. Again and again he asks for money—he needs it desperately to pay his troops—can she raise it somehow, anyhow? In high spirits he writes that he has received the ten thousand golden florin she has sent through her *maître d'hôtel*, and will she come and join a hunting party that promises to be very gay?

For her part, Margaret complains that his letters have been rude, and he replies sweetly that "to make our peace together" he is sending a fine carbuncle that belonged to his dead father, Emperor Friedrich, and which he has just found "in an old coffer in Augsburg."[3]

In 1510, as winter approaches, he writes of the grave illness of the Empress Bianca and wishes his daughter to consult several of the best doctors she knows, in secret, and send him "the means of remedying this sickness."[4] But Margaret replies that, while the doctors believe that Bianca's illness is "very strange and dangerous," they cannot remedy it without more information.[5] A little over a year later he must write to inform Margaret that Bianca has died, having received all

the Sacraments, and is now "with the blessed in the kingdom of
Paradise."[6] Maximilian was far away in Fribourg when Bianca died in
Innsbruck; he sent his court marshal to attend to the funeral arrange-
ments.

A few months after Bianca's death Maximilian unfolds to his
daughter a startling plan that has just come into his head:

> And not finding it for any reason good that we marry, we have
> resolved never again to lie beside a naked woman. And are send-
> ing tomorrow [the Bishop of Gurk] to Rome to the Pope to find
> a way . . . to take us as coadjutor, so that after his death we can
> be assured of having the Papacy and becoming a priest and after
> that a saint, and so after our death you will have to adore me.[7]

He adds that he is beginning to work on the cardinals, and that two
or three hundred thousand ducats would be most helpful in con-
vincing these gentlemen. He signs the letter, "from the hand of
your good father Maximilian, future Pope."

It was a marvelous and simple solution, that of uniting Papacy and
Empire under a single head—himself; at one stroke he could reform
the Church, which needed it badly, defeat the Turks, settle his
quarrel with the King of France, and at the same time balance his
sadly depleted budget. But Pope Julius II was uncooperative; he
obstinately refused to die, lingered on in the Vatican a venal and
troublesome man.

Luther once wrote that when someone asked Maximilian why he
laughed so hard, he replied that it made him laugh "to think that God
had so arranged the spiritual and temporal realms that the first was
under the rule of a drunken and dissolute Pope, the other under a
chamois hunter."[8]

The grandchildren in Malines were still in the cradle when Maximilian began to give thought to their marriages. The eldest grandson,
Charles, heir to the enormous realm of both parents—Netherlands,
Spain, the Austrian crownlands—was betrothed several times during
his childhood as part of changing political plans. Eleanor, the eldest
of the children, was destined for an especially brilliant match. Maximilian wrote his daughter Margaret quite frankly that he was waiting
for one of Europe's great queens to die, so that Eleanor might take
her place.

First of the grandchildren to be married was Ysabeau, a gentle,

blue-eyed child of thirteen, whom Maximilian betrothed to the King
of Denmark in April, 1514. The marriage treaty was signed in Linz
and the Danish party immediately rode off to Malines where the
proxy ceremony was to take place. Aunt Margaret would have preferred to postpone the wedding a bit, the child was so young, and
time so short for suitable preparations. But the Danish embassy was
extremely pressing, and nothing would do but for Margaret to manage
a wedding, complete with banquets, tourneys, dancing. In the evening
the whole party gathered to witness the child Ysabeau in her wedding
finery lie down obediently on the ceremonial bed, while the Danish
ambassador, one leg bared, lay beside her, "as it is accustomed to
happen with great princes," Margaret wrote in the account to her
father.[9]

The reason why the Danish king was in such haste to acquire a
royal bride was certainly not made clear to Ysabeau's family.

Some years previously King Christian had taken as mistress a pretty
Dutch girl named Duyveke ("the little dove"), whom he had found in
a cake shop in Bergen and moved into the Copenhagen palace. Along
with the girl came her mother, a formidable woman, more vulture
than dove, named Siegebritte, who was soon running the palace,
deciding who would see the King and who would not, in general
making things extremely disagreeable for the nobles of the court.
Some went so far as to accuse her of witchcraft. Things had reached
such a pass that the Danish king could hardly hope to maintain his
throne unless he married an acceptable bride.

A few months after her proxy marriage Ysabeau sailed off to
Copenhagen, escorted by the Bishop of Schleswig, who had written
warningly to his king:

Her Highness deserves that you receive her well, because she is
noble, wise, virtuous, and wonderful! . . . I beg Your Majesty
humbly that you receive her with the greatest processions and
festivals, and let all the Burgundians and Danes see that she is
very dear and welcome to you.[10]

And then he adds:

And have Your Majesty's beard cut off at once for many reasons!

Unfortunately King Christian did not heed his bishop's good advice.
The beard remained; so did the Little Dove and her domineering
mother.

Before long gossip and rumors began to reach the ears of Aunt

Margaret in the Netherlands and grandfather Maximilian in Innsbruck. Gentle Ysabeau, trained for the queenly career for which all Habsburg daughters were destined, barely allowed an intimation of her wretched homesickness to escape her. Soon after her arrival in Denmark she wrote her aunt in August of 1515:

> Madame, if I could choose for myself I would now be with you. For to be parted from you is the greatest sorrow which can happen to me, especially as I do not know when I may hope to see you again.[11]

When Maximilian got wind of the state of affairs in the Copenhagen palace, he dispatched an envoy to Denmark to persuade the King

> to abandon his disordered life and to persuade him to make more faithful companion of our daughter.[12]

To Ysabeau's brother Charles in the Netherlands, Maximilian wrote in January of 1516:

> The displeasing and shameful life which our brother and son-in-law the King of Denmark leads with a concubine, to the great sorrow and displeasure of our daughter, your sister, is blamed by all her relatives.[13]

But Christian did not change his ways. When children were born to Ysabeau, they were turned over to the overbearing Siegebritte to rear. In the end an uprising of nobles deposed the King; Ysabeau and her three children fled Denmark with him. In her aunt's peaceful household in Malines, Ysabeau died very young—at twenty-four—in 1525, leaving her children, a new generation of quasi-orphans, for her Aunt Margaret to bring up.

At approximately the same time as Ysabeau's proxy marriage, another matrimonial project of far greater import to the Habsburg family future was underway. The youngest child in the Malines household, little Mary, a child of eight, was dispatched on the long journey across Europe to Vienna, where she was to marry Prince Lajos, heir to the Hungarian throne.

By the peace treaty Maximilian had signed with King Vladislav of Hungary in 1491, it was agreed that if Vladislav left no male heirs the Hungarian crown of St. Stephen would pass to the Habsburg dynasty. Vladislav's first child was a girl, Princess Anna; Maximilian immediately proposed that she be betrothed to one of his grandsons, Charles or Ferdinand. A strong party of Hungarian nobles, however, had a candidate of their own: János Zápolya, Prince of Transylvania. Now when word leaked out of another pregnancy in the royal palace in Budapest, Maximilian lost no time at all. In 1506 he betrothed his infant granddaughter, Mary, still in a cradle in the Malines nursery, to the unborn child of the Hungarian king.

By good fortune the child turned out to be of the proper sex, Prince Lajos, but his premature birth cost the Queen her life, and the frail child's life clung by a thread, while Hungarian court physicians improvised an incubator out of freshly killed carcasses of animals to keep the babe warm. A momentous marriage agreement was signed in 1507, by which Princess Anna of Hungary was to wed either Charles or Ferdinand, and Prince Lajos, little Mary. Maximilian's clever ambassador Cuspinian, who knew how difficult and complicated the marriage agreement had been to bring off, considered it such a vital accomplishment that his sole entry in his journal for that year was simply: *Captus Ludovicus*—Lajos captured.[14]

But Maximilian knew too well from experience that marriage treaties were nothing to performance; and though the children were too young for marriage, a wedding ceremony performed before witnesses would be far more binding than a paper contract. For this reason he sent for his granddaughter Mary, and through the winter and spring of 1515 made preparations for a great and festive wedding.

The tremendous hurdles in the way of that double wedding would have discouraged a lesser man than Maximilian. He was short of money, short of health, short a bridegroom.

His financial woes, instead of easing, had become more desperate through the years. He had long ago taken to borrowing from an accommodating banking family of Augsburg, the Fuggers, who were quite willing to lend to the Habsburg Emperor at usurious interest rates, and against the security of Habsburg silver mines in the Tyrol, Habsburg estates and rents. Again and again he lost control of a mine or an estate when a debt fell due.

Now in the spring of 1515, with the crown of Hungary as the stake, he simply did not have enough cash to pay the cost of the magnificent and showy wedding it had to be. Though already deep in their debt, he finally succeeded in extracting a loan of 54,000 florins from the Fuggers, who needed protection for certain mines they owned in Hungary.[15]

Emperor Maximilian was ailing, besides. He lay so ill that spring of 1515 that the date of the wedding had to be postponed; when summer came he could no longer mount a horse, and had to be carried in a litter.

But neither of these hurdles was so serious as the shortage of a bridegroom. Princess Anna had been promised one of Maximilian's two grandsons, but Archduke Charles was betrothed to the English princess Mary—an agreement of import to the economic interests of the Netherlands—while Archduke Ferdinand was growing up in the court of Spain, the favorite and namesake of his grandfather, the Spanish king, who had not the slightest intention of dispatching young Ferdinand to Vienna for the purpose of further enlarging Habsburg power.

Yet even in these straits the political situation in Hungary was so pressing that Maximilian did not dare delay the wedding a single month. In July of 1515 King Vladislav of Hungary and his two royal children, his brother, King Sigismund of Poland, and a great company of Hungarian and Polish lords crossed the border into Austria and were met by Maximilian a few miles east of Vienna.

Even then, on the very eve of the wedding, the whole project came within an ace of collapsing. Maximilian received the kings seated in a litter, surrounded by five hundred armed knights. When he invited the royal brothers to ride with him into Vienna, some of the Hungarian nobles suddenly objected, saying that the whole thing might well be a trap. The Cardinal of Gran whispered in Vladislav's ear that he might be delivering himself unprotected into the power of a man with whom he was warring only a few short years ago.[16]

In the nick of time King Sigismund of Poland spoke up, declaring that he for one trusted the honor of the Emperor, and he would ride into the city with him. Thereupon King Vladislav too consented, and the whole great company moved on into Vienna.

Even the weather, however, turned against Maximilian. The borrowed money he had poured into a grand ceremonial entry went for nothing: a drenching downpour ruined the day, plumes dangled and dripped, fine raiment got a soaking, musicians could not play.

Finally Maximilian had to dig deep in his bag of tricks to solve the most difficult problem of all: the absence of a bridegroom for Princess Anna.

He was equal even to this. On July 22, in the Cathedral of St. Stephen, the gray-haired Maximilian in his imperial robes knelt beside the twelve-year-old princess and spoke the marriage vows. According to a carefully worded agreement, if either of his grandsons did not appear to claim Anna within a year, then Maximilian himself would consummate the match and make her Empress in fact. Together with Maximilian and little Anna, the two nine-year-olds, Mary and Lajos, promised to take one another as rightful wife and husband.

A brilliant round of festivals, balls, and ceremonies accompanied the double wedding of 1515; the three child participants no doubt enjoyed most of all the great tournament during which a hundred noble boys were raised to knighthood, and least of all, the long-winded Latin speeches of greeting by twenty-two members of the University faculty, which, bound later into a book, made a stately volume.

As for Maximilian, he took the greatest pleasure in the acquaintance of King Sigismund, delighted to find in the Polish king an intellect as lively as his own, and a deep interest in humanist scholarship. He would never forget that without Sigismund's good offices, Princess Anna would never have married into the Habsburg family,

> for the Hungarians [he wrote his daughter], who hold their king for nothing . . . would have given this lovely princess to her servant and subject, to the perpetual shame . . . of the house of Austria and of God.[17]

The "subject and servant" to whom Maximilian referred was the rival suitor, János Zápolya.

In typical Maximilian fashion, the Emperor tried his best to reward Sigismund too with a Habsburg bride. When the Polish king lost his wife a little later, the old matchmaker wrote to his daughter Margaret, proposing Sigismund as a husband for his eldest granddaughter, Eleanor, describing the Polish king enthusiastically as

> handsome, rather stout, with very white hands.

He added, moreover, the valuable information:

> He told me with his own mouth, which is beautiful and red, that his age is forty-six or forty-seven.[18]

Margaret and her niece seemed something less than enthusiastic, though a tactful reply was sent. The Polish marriage, however, never came off, and Eleanor was saved for the King of Portugal.

A few months after the double wedding of 1515, two events occurred which proved how foresighted Maximilian had been in pressing the wedding through against all obstacles. King Ferdinand of Spain died in January of 1516, leaving his grandson, Ferdinand, free to take Maximilian's place as Princess Anna's bridegroom. He remained in

Spain for the time being to complete his education, but a proxy marriage took place within the stipulated time.

In March of 1516 King Vladislav died, and the anti-Habsburg party in Hungary made strong gestures to nullify the marriages. So dangerous and unpredictable did the situation seem that Maximilian had the two princesses, Anna and Mary—*Reginulae,* little queens, they were now called—hurried out of Vienna and brought to the safety of his palace in Innsbruck to finish their studies, and to await the coming of their bridegrooms.

8. Dürer's Last Portrait

Innsbruck, ich muss dich lassen.
ich fahr dahin mein Strassen,
in fremde Land dahin.
Mein Freud ist mir genommen,
die ich nit weiss bekommen,
wo ich im Elend bin.

Song attributed to Maximilian

(Innsbruck, I must leave thee.
I go my way hence to strange
lands. My joy is gone from
me, and I can have none, here
where I am in misery.)

IN THE SUMMER of 1518 the Emperor attended his last Diet.

High up in a little room in the palace in Augsburg that summer, Albrecht Dürer painted his last portrait of Maximilian, the magnificent portrait of a king grown old. The eyes still crinkle with humor at the corners, but the hair under the beaver hat has gone gray. There is a look of immense weariness in the face. He holds in his hand an open pomegranate, as if it were the world he had bitten into, and found it, after all, sour fruit to his taste.

The old conjurer was engaged in performing just one more trick. At the Diet that summer he was busy buying the electoral votes needed to assure the imperial succession for his grandson, Charles, and he was buying them with money he did not possess.

Toward the end of September, just as the Diet was coming to an end, a pushy young Augustinian monk named Martin Luther appeared in Augsburg, to defend before the papal legate, Cardinal Cajetan, the ninety-five theses he had published the year before, challenging the sale of papal indulgences. Maximilian had granted the monk a safe conduct to Augsburg; he did not stay to hear the confrontation. He had no patience with such gadflies as Luther; that the Church needed reforming and needed it badly, everyone in the Empire knew. He himself had had Jacob Wimpheling study and draw up for him a list of the worst abuses a few years previously. To prod the Church into reform was a task for an emperor, not for a monk; and an emperor must choose his time and place.

At the moment other business had priority. The Turks were more menacing than ever, and the Pope had once more appealed for a Crusade. When Maximilian opened the Diet, the papal legate had presented him with a consecrated sword to be used in recapturing Constantinople and Jerusalem. Maximilian had worked out a plan for conquering the Turks within three years; he sent a copy of his proposal to all the Christian monarchs in Europe.

But the most pressing business of all was the choice of the next emperor.

He had had in the last year the gravest intimations of mortality. The Pope had confided to the Venetian ambassador the previous year that

> the Emperor had had a fit of apoplexy—that the stroke was slight, but when once such attacks commence, those who experienced them did not usually outlive the year.[1]

It was long now since Maximilian had leapt into the saddle, danced a *morisco* or a fast *Koralle* with a pretty partner. Worn out by the hard life of camp and battle and journeying year in and year out across the face of Europe, his magnificent constitution was breaking down. He traveled by litter now, and it was said that the chest borne in his equipage contained a coffin in practical readiness.

His only son, Philip, was dead years before. It was essential for his eldest grandson, Charles, to succeed him as Emperor, and to be named King of the Romans while Maximilian yet lived. Six of the seven electors were members of the Diet; the seventh, the King of Bohemia, in the person of his grandson-in-law, young King Lajos of Hungary, was not a member of the Diet, but Maximilian felt confident he could manage that vote. The votes of the German prince-electors came expensively, and that of the Elector of Saxony, Frederick the Wise, he could not get for love or money. Maximilian managed to wring promises out of the other five; and though deep, deep in debt to the Fuggers already, he promised 600,000 gulden in bribes, to be payable after the election. He could hardly be anything but annoyed by Luther's impolitic stand just then, for three of the five bought electors were the three German Archbishops of Mainz, Trier, and Cologne—and it was against the Mainz Archbishop's sale of indulgences that Luther inveighed.

Having finished the important business of securing the election, Maximilian left Augsburg before the Diet was over. During that summer, it was said, he had asked the pretty burghers' wives, who customarily wore veils at public balls, to leave off their veils that he might enjoy once more the sight of their faces.

He traveled southward over the well-known mountain road to Innsbruck, that town of all in the world most dear to him. Times without number he had ridden down from the mountains into town, from hunting deer and chamois, from journeying the length and breadth of the Empire, from warring in Italy, to glimpse from far off the Golden Roof that shimmers in sunlight, glistens in rain.

In November of 1518 he rode into Innsbruck for the last time, an old man and ailing. He longed for the cheer of the Advent season, the warmth and brightness of candlelight, of fires crackling in the porcelain stoves of his New Palace, of good wine, of the sweet voices of his choir—the best in the world, he might brag—and the company of the two little queens, Anna and Mary, to turn winter into spring for a king growing old. In the three years since the young girls had come to Innsbruck to live, Maximilian had looked in on them whenever he could, and when he was absent, sent them gifts—a dozen white feathers, velvet and jewels for fine Renaissance hats.

Maximilian had always been generous when he had anything to give. His own needs had been astonishingly simple for an emperor —his only personal indulgences, fine armor and fine music. For years half the town of Innsbruck had lived off his bounty.

But now at last his debts caught up with him. The Austrian Estates meeting that year had been deeply concerned, had tried to force the Fuggers to disgorge some of the profitable Tyrolean rents and the silver and copper mines they had taken over.[2] Now it was the innkeepers of Innsbruck who dunned the Emperor for an old bill he could not pay. They refused to put up his followers again, the town fathers would not spend a florin on the grand reception he customarily got; it was said that even Maximilian's horses were left unstabled all night in the street.

Stung with the insult, weary, ill, perhaps suffering another stroke, Maximilian ordered his servants to carry him away. On he went, out of Innsbruck, borne by litter and by boat to the town of Wels on the Danube, where he was too sick to travel farther. Doctors were sent for from Vienna, but he who was himself learned in the medical arts knew there was nothing to be done.

He lay very quietly in Wels, waiting for death to come for him, his favorite hound by his bed, cages of singing birds in his chamber, musicians to play for him when he called, and his old friend Dr. Mennel to read aloud during the long sleepless nights from the history of his Habsburg ancestors.

He dictated his last will, with its curious and explicit instructions: his body to be shaved completely, all his teeth pulled, and to be clothed not merely in a shroud but in underlinen (to the very end, Cuspinian said later, *omnium mortalium vericundissimus*—the most modest of men).[3]

When death came on January 12, 1519, Maximilian was not after all carried back to Innsbruck to lie in the grand tomb in the Court Church among the bronze figures of the kings he claimed for kin. He was brought instead to the town of his birth, Wiener Neustadt, and buried near the high altar, so that the priest elevating the Host would be standing above his breast.

He asked that his heart be carried back to Bruges and placed in the tomb with the wife of his youth, Marie of Burgundy.

III

The One World of Charles V

1. Heir to the World

THE ELDER Habsburg grandson, Charles, had grown up with his three sisters in Malines in the Netherlands, a solemn little boy and hardly prepossessing to look at. The fair hair, cut straight like a page boy's, did little to soften the thin sharp face with its long pointed nose and angular protruding jaw—the famous Habsburg jaw in its most exaggerated form. It protruded so far that his mouth hung open, giving him the appearance of being not quite bright, and, together with a short thick tongue, made it difficult for him to articulate well.[1]

Charles learned to regard his uncomforting face with wry humor. Years later, urging the King of France to a meeting, Charles wrote that it was true his mouth often hung open—"but not to bite people," so the French king need have no fear.[2]

Charles had a single trait of his father's exceptional good looks: a pair of fine straight legs that never bowed even after years in the saddle, as most aristocratic legs did in that day.

Charles was six when his parents left the Netherlands on that last tragic journey to Spain—the dashing young father, whom the children had glimpsed from time to time on his way to a hunt, or a feast, or a Joyous Entry into one of his towns, and their mother, dark of mood, who had passed like a stranger through their young lives. On the day in October of 1506 when Charles's governor, the Sieur de Chièvres, broke the news of Philip's death in Spain, he wrote the children's grandfather, Maximilian, that "they had grieved according to their age, and more than I thought they would."[3]

It is not, perhaps, surprising that Charles was a nervous child and given to fits of melancholy.

The children's court was a miniature of the grandiose court of their Burgundian forebears. No fewer than ninety-three persons waited on

them—cradle-rockers, nurses, governesses, tutors, physicians, cooks, butlers, footmen, cellarers. A swarm of grownups worried and fretted
over his education.

At six Charles was made head of the Order of the Golden Fleece.
At seven he was signing state documents, at eight composing diplomatic letters in Latin to the Pope. By ten he was sitting in the
Council of State, a grave little figure in black, setting down the minutes
in a meticulous script.

It is difficult to imagine Charles V romping, even as a child; yet
despite the grandeur that pursued him unrelentingly, there were such
pleasures as a small chariot "painted with pleasant pictures," a sleigh
that skimmed over the snow in the shape of a ship with masts and
standards and banners, and a pair of knights in jousting postures that
a child could manipulate with cords. There were banquets and
hunts and trips to the gayer, larger towns of Brussels, Antwerp, and
Louvain.

The English ambassador gives us a picture of such a visit to Brussels
in 1512, when a great bonfire flamed outside the palace gate on St.
John's Eve, and "the Prince and his sisters and the young folk danced."
The French embassy, observed the Englishman acutely, could not
have been much pleased at sight of the four little Habsburgs:

> the sight of whom (as I deem) was neither much pleasant or
> comfort to the said ambassadors; for, blessed be God, they be all
> right fair and tall, and go right up upon their joints and limbs.[4]

Charles's fragile physique was deceptive: he had that kind of
tensile strength born of a formidable will; he did everything as if it
were absolutely necessary even as a child to prove his fitness to rule.
He learned to ride and joust and fence superbly. His grandfather,
the old chamois hunter, was enormously pleased with Charles's love
of the chase, and he wrote to his daughter:

> We were very joyous that our son Charles takes so much pleasure
> in the chase; otherwise one might have thought he was a bastard.[5]

Like his grandfather too, he had a passion for music. He sang
well, played the flute, and as a child could hardly be dragged away
from the spinet. Later on, his beautifully trained choir traveled with
him wherever he went. He could instantly detect plagiarism in a
newly composed Mass, and though when he was a monarch the most
devastating political crises failed to shatter his composure, he could
lose his temper when a chorister hit a flat note.

Music was a refuge for a child who had no privacy. Charles's thoughts, his opinions and prejudices were a matter of profound international concern. His governor slept in his room, awakened him at odd hours of the night to examine a late dispatch and write his opinion in the margin. When he was thirteen his two grandfathers, Maximilian and King Ferdinand of Spain, together with their ally, Henry VIII of England, solemnly agreed that each would furnish one "good personage" to act as gentleman in waiting to Charles, each to possess a key to his apartment and take turns sleeping in his chamber.

It was perhaps that total lack of privacy that taught Charles early the trick of withdrawing into himself. In his whole life very few persons, either kin or courtiers, would unlock the inner doors of his mind. And it was no doubt the arduous discipline in his growing-up that turned a sensitive child into an instrument of devotion and duty, to whom kingship was the highest calling, prayer his instant reaction to each significant event in his life. That prickly hair shirt of a conscience would give him no peace, would drive him finally to that last incredible scene near the end of his life, in the great hall of the Dukes of Brabant in Brussels.

Charles must have been very young indeed when he first examined the charts and globes in the schoolroom, traced out with his fingers on one of those early maps the lands over which he was to rule. His realm had none of the neat compactness of England or France that a king might almost hold in his hand; it sprawled across the map of Europe from the eastern borders of the Austrian duchies to the Netherlands, south to embrace the kingdom of Naples, Spain, and now across the ocean the vast New World that ended God alone knew where.

Eight years before Charles's birth, his grandmother, Queen Isabella of Spain, had sent Columbus on his voyages of discovery. When Charles's parents, Philip and Juana, had made their last journey to Spain in 1506, the old admiral, Columbus, crippled with gout, had written them courteously, begging their Graces' pardon that his infirmities kept him from paying his respects, but promising his future services to them. Those services were never tendered, nor, as it turned out, needed; both the old explorer and the young Prince Philip died in the same year.

It was a seafaring world into which Charles was born in Flanders, never far from the smell of the sea and the sight of great sailing ships. The excitement of voyaging was in the air. During Charles's lifetime the cartographers of Amsterdam and Nürnberg, of Venice and Lyon and Strasbourg would be kept busy in their workshops enlarging and detailing and printing new maps, so rapidly were explorations going on. Charles too would bend over the latest maps of earth and heaven, would learn to use the instruments of mariners and astronomers—the astrolabes and compasses, and an orrery of pure gold that took the astronomer Petrus Apianus ten years to make.

He himself would journey as no monarch had ever journeyed before.

His first voyage was to Spain when he was seventeen, to claim his inheritance after the death of King Ferdinand, his grandfather.

The royal fleet of forty vessels hoisted sail at daybreak on September 18, 1517. In the King's ship went Charles, his sister Eleanor who was to marry the King of Portugal, the Knights of the Golden Fleece, their secretaries and personal servants, Charles's musicians and his bodyguard of twenty archers—in all three hundred persons.

An observant young wardrobe assistant named Laurent Vital went along on that voyage and kept a gossipy journal, and it is to him we are indebted for the details.[6]

As the royal fleet made its way proudly into the Channel, all the vessels in Flushing harbor followed, each to pass Charles's ship and make a reverence to the King in farewell.

For a long time watchers on the shore could discern the King's vessel, for it bore his banners on the main mast and on the bellying sails bright pictures—Christ on the Cross, the Holy Trinity, the Blessed Virgin and Child, with the moon under her feet and on her head a crown with the seven planets. On the main sail appeared the Columns of Hercules—the farthest southern reaches of Charles's new domain, and the device he had just chosen for himself: *Plus Oultre*—Yet farther.

The young king left sorrowful hearts behind him, says Vital:

Truly, they had good reason to love him and to pray God for him, noble and brave prince that he was; he had between him and death only a half-foot of wood fixed with a nail or a peg . . . he was at the mercy of so many and such divers dangers that only to think of them was a frightening thing.[7]

It was true that all the perils of the sixteenth-century seas plagued Charles's first voyage. Between Dover and Calais a pirate ship pursued them, probably one of the English freebooters that often lay in wait for rich Flemish ships. It was driven away unceremoniously with a few cannon shots.

Charles had given strict orders in writing governing safety measures for the fleet. Against the danger of fire all passengers were ordered to go to bed without candlelight; only he, his sister, and a few highly placed personages were provided with iron lanterns. Despite all these precautions one of the ships caught fire at night. Like a great torch on the dark water the craft went up in flames while the rest of the convoy watched helplessly, hearing across the water the terrible cries for help: *"Jésus! Miséricorde!"* All hundred and fifty men and women on board perished that night.

The Sieur de Chièvres had given orders that Charles and his sister were not to be awakened. When news of the tragedy was brought to Charles in the morning, he declared that he would rather lose all his treasure than *"tant de gens de bien"*—so many good people.

In between adventures life on board the little floating palace was a microcosm of courtly life on land. Trumpets broke the dawn; music attended every meal. When Charles awakened he went first to greet his sister on deck, and together they made their devotions before a crucifix in the open air. With their friends they passed the day reading chronicles, playing chess, conversing, joking with Charles's fool. In the evening at sundown all gathered on deck to sing the *Ave Maria* and the *Salve Regina*.

When they reached the Spanish Sea the water changed from blue to clear green, the wind shifted and dropped, and the ships lay becalmed, unable to approach nearer to the coast of Castile. Next a thick black fog settled over everything, so that the pilots could not see their way. The fog was followed by a gale so frightful that waves like mountains tossed the ships about. Everyone was deathly ill. Young King Charles, bowed in prayer, promised processions, fasts, and alms if only God would grant him a safe passage to his kingdom.

At last the storm abated, and twelve days after they left Flushing Harbor they came in sight of land. They had, however, been blown off their course, and instead of landing on the Biscayan coast, it was the barren shore of Asturias they sighted, whose mountains rose sharp and steep straight out of the sea. Charles, fearing another change in the weather, ordered his own craft to land; a barge brought the little company to the lonely shore, while the rest of his fleet sailed on to Santander.

It turned out that Charles's adventures had scarcely begun, for the mountaineers on that savage shore, never dreaming their king was among them, mistook them for Turkish pirates and prepared to make short work of the party. Not until they observed the number of ladies among them did they put away their daggers and pikes.

Borrowing mules and carts for their baggage, Charles and Eleanor and their friends made their way across the wild country of north Spain toward the Castilian capital of Valladolid. Some barely escaped death when they forded swollen mountain torrents, others when they lost their footing on the dim mule track that led along steep mountain sides. Icy rain and snow soaked them, they sickened on the coarse food and drink the poverty-stricken villages offered them. Several died of fever with no help near.

Charles himself became ill, and the whole party had to halt in a desperately poor village, where no spot clean enough for the King's bed could be found inside the stinking huts crowded with livestock. Finally in an outdoor shed a little tent was made, lined with the finest Flemish tapestries from the baggage wagons, hung with master-pieces of Flemish painting. While the wind raged and the rain poured down outside, Charles slept inside his bit of transported Flemish luxury, until he had recovered his health and could continue the journey.

Two months after he had set foot on the coast of Spain Charles rode into Valladolid.

His whole life would be consumed by such journeys, on horseback over the primitive sixteenth-century roads, by ship at the mercy of wind and storm, by litter, from one end of the vast realm to the other. For a long time his youth and his formidable will would keep him going. His device remained *Plus Oultre*.

In Valladolid a few weeks after his arrival, the Bishop of Burgos brought two strangers to see the young king: one a sinewy, sun-burned seaman, the other a nervous, irritable astronomer. They had brought along as proofs of their authenticity a pair of dark-skinned slaves, and as a model of their plan, a globe, on which they pointed out the line the Pope had drawn in 1493, cutting the world in two as neatly as one splits an orange, bestowing all the undiscovered lands west of the line on Spain, and east of the line on Portugal. The Spice Islands, declared the seaman, Magellan, were certainly Spain's—if one could reach them by sailing west. Turned down by the Portuguese king, they wanted Charles's backing. He agreed to pay three quarters of the cost of the voyage, in March of 1518 set his signature, *Yo el Rey*, to the document. Delighted with the whole enterprise young Charles could hardly wait for the ships to be built and provisioned; in August of 1519 Magellan's five vessels dropped down the Guadalquivir from Seville on the first lap of the journey around the world.

Three years later the single surviving ship, the *Victoria,* put into Seville harbor. Magellan lay dead in the far-off Philippines; the tiny remnant of the crew, eighteen survivors, gaunt specters, walked barefoot in white shrouds with lighted candles in their hands to give thanks in the little church of Santa María de la Victoria.

With pride and joy Charles wrote his aunt, Regent Margaret in the Netherlands that one of his ships had encircled the globe and brought him back ginger, cinnamon, muscat, and sandalwood.[8]

2. Family Matters

ALTHOUGH THE SIX CHILDREN of Philip and Juana never in their entire lives spent so much as a single night under one roof, yet strangely deep ties of loyalty and affection bound them one to another. Their parents' stark tragedy and the proud eminence of their birth set them apart from the world at large; it was as if that lonely distinction knit them together far more closely than ordinary brothers and sisters.

To the others Charles was lord as well as brother; absolute head of the family as he was absolute head of state. Reticent by nature, trained by courtiers to mask his spontaneous feelings under a set of flawless manners, Charles kept scrupulous guard over his emotions. Only rarely, in some inconspicuous family drama, might a close watcher glimpse the inner man beneath the bearing of the King, a flash of struggle between private feelings and his strict concept of public duty.

On that first voyage to Spain Charles met the mad queen, his mother, whom he had not seen for eleven years. And he met for the first time in his life his only brother, Ferdinand, and his littlest sister, Catherina.

But there had been a family problem to deal with even before he embarked for Spain.

On the shores of Middelburgh in the Netherlands, in the summer of 1517, Charles, his sister Eleanor, and a youthful court dallied through the pleasant August days, waiting for their fleet to be readied. There was feasting and dancing, music, games, excursions aboard the unfinished vessels. Eleanor, on her way south to marry the King of Portugal, was not exactly beautiful, but she was an attractive girl, blue-eyed, fair-haired, with a delicate rosy complexion.

One of the courtiers, the Count Palatine Frederick, unwisely fell in love with her, and she with him.

Eleanor was older than her brother by a year or two, but Charles did not hesitate to tear from his sister's hands an incriminating letter, a passionate declaration of love beginning *"Ma mie, ma mignonne"*— my love, my darling. In it Frederick promised to dare anything for her sake; he called on God and the Holy Virgin to help them; he demanded nothing less than that "he belong to her and she to him."[1]

Fully master of the situation, Charles forced the lovers to swear before witnesses that they had not married secretly, that they would renounce one another forever. Count Frederick was banished from court; before a year was over Eleanor was delivered over as bride to the elderly King of Portugal.

Eleanor understood. Her devotion to Charles remained undiminished to the end of her life when she went with him into exile. While Charles addressed his other sisters in his letters as "Madame, my good sister," to Eleanor alone he wrote always, "Madame, my best sister."

A little later, in November of that year, 1517, Charles and Eleanor, newly arrived in Spain, turned aside before making their ceremonial entry into the capital to visit their mother in Tordesillas. What the two young people knew of their mother's mental state can only be guessed. Neither could have had any clear recollection of her: Eleanor had been seven, Charles not yet six, when Juana had sailed off on that last tragic journey to Spain. A single word and gesture betrayed the dread and anxiety Charles felt on that first visit.

Some years earlier the Bishop of Málaga had reported on a visit to Tordesillas, that the Queen had grown quiet, no longer screamed at her servants:

> But since I came she has not put on a clean shift, nor combed her hair, nor washed her face. They tell me she sleeps on the floor, eats from a plate on the floor, does not go to Mass.[2]

She suffered also, added the Bishop, from *incontinentia urinae*.

Charles's visit to his mother was political as well as personal. The Castilians, her mother's people, continued to look upon Juana as their rightful queen—bewitched perhaps, but not insane. Charles was, in fact, only to be joint ruler with her so long as she lived. And that first visit was attended with all the propriety and etiquette due a ruling queen, mad though she might be.

Charles's ubiquitous wardrobe assistant, Laurent Vital, was con-

sumed with curiosity to watch the meeting between so unusual a
mother and son. When Charles and Eleanor and a few intimate
courtiers who had known Juana in the early days of her marriage
approached the threshold of her apartment, young Vital ostentatiously
seized a torch from a servant and made as if to light the young king's
way to his mother's chamber. But Charles brushed Vital aside,
brusquely and firmly, "for the King wanted no light."[3]

Charles had always lived in the glare of a prince's public life; his
most personal encounters, even his first meeting with his betrothed
bride, would take place under the eyes of a hundred witnesses. But
this meeting he would have in private: he wanted no light. He and
his sister entered their mother's chamber and the door was swiftly
shut. Vital was left outside, forced to salve his curiosity later with
secondhand reports from the few eyewitnesses.

With Eleanor on Charles's left and a step behind him, as the rules
of precedence demanded, brother and sister approached the mother
whom they had not seen for so many years. They made her three
reverences, each one deeper and more courtly than the one before,
the third time "making her honor to the ground." Charles lifted his
mother's hand to kiss, but she withdrew it quickly and embraced
them both.

Charles spoke the few words of formal greeting, which he had no
doubt prepared:

> Madame, we, your humble and obedient children, happy to see
> you in good health, God be thanked, have long wanted to make
> you reverence, to offer our honor, service, obedience.

The mother gazed at them without speaking, only smiling, nodding
her head. Presently she asked, as if in wonder:

> Are you really my children? That you have grown so big in so
> short a time!

Then, as any mother might, she said:

> Certainly, children, you've had a long and exhausting journey.
> It isn't surprising if you are worn out. Because it is late now, it
> would be a good thing for you to go to bed early and rest until
> tomorrow.[4]

The young people nodded, bade her good-bye, and took their leave.

Charles's astute councilor, Sieur de Chièvres, remained behind. He
had business to transact: he suggested it might save the Queen great

trouble if she were to give over her lands entirely to Charles to rule. He got her signature on the document.

Again and again, whenever he was in Spain, Charles returned to visit his mother in Tordesillas; of what they talked on those visits no one can say. The shadow that lay on Charles's temperament, the strain of melancholy and pessimism was surely from his mother. And it was no doubt of Juana he was thinking, and of the passion that had burned out her brain, when he advised his own son Philip years later "to be reasonable in matters of love"—*d'être raisonnable dans les choses d'amour*.[5]

It was on that first visit to Tordesillas in 1517 that Charles and Eleanor first encountered their youngest sister, Catherina, the child born to Juana on the somber funeral journey across Spain with her husband's body ten years before. The "solitary and humble princess," as Vital calls her, had shared her mother's prison during all those childhood years. She lived in a single room behind her mother's chamber, a bare little room with matting on the floor and without entry save through her mother's room. Catherina had not even had a window until her mother's *chevalier d'honneur* had thought, a short time before, of having a window cut through the wall so the child might look out and see

> passers-by going to church or out walking; to see horses drinking at a trough; and often, at her request, children came to play; so that they would more willingly return there to play, she would throw down a piece of silver.[6]

Vital describes her as a delightful little girl, very gentle and graceful and pretty. Of all the Habsburg children, Catherina most resembled their handsome father, Philip, particularly when she laughed. She could not have laughed very often, seeing no one save her mother, two ancient serving-women, and a priest. The little girl's lonely life had set its mark on her: she spoke very little.

When her older brother and sister came to visit her, she was dressed like a serving-maid, a garment of leather such as Spanish peasants wore over her coarse gray dress, her fair hair tightly braided down her back in a single pigtail.

Her plight touched them deeply; they worried too that she was growing up with none of the careful training in deportment and etiquette needed to prepare her for the only possible career of a Habsburg daughter—marriage to a prince or king.

Soon after the court had been established at Valladolid, Charles and Eleanor considered how they might rescue their little sister from her lonely prison. The problem was to remove her in the quietest manner possible, with the least disturbance to the deranged queen, for there was no way out of the child's room except through her mother's.

It turned out that an old Flemish serving-man named Bertrand, who had come to Spain years before in Philip's suite, still lived at Tordesillas and enjoyed Juana's trust.[7] Bertrand agreed to take part in the rescue. He had noted that an unfrequented gallery of the castle ran outside one wall of Catherina's room. Here he worked quietly and secretly to make an opening large enough to admit a man, the hole hidden on the inner side of the room by a hanging.

On the appointed night Charles sent a stately company from Valladolid to receive his sister: an escort of two hundred gentlemen headed by a Knight of the Golden Fleece, ladies of the Burgundian court including his old governess, the Lady Anne de Beaumont, all of whom waited on a little bridge in the dark a short distance from the castle.

An hour after midnight old Bertrand, in doublet and barefoot that he might move noiselessly, stole through the opening into the little princess' chamber. Seizing the night-burning torch "such as is accustomed to burn in the apartments of princes and great lords," he awakened Catherina's servant. The woman started up, astonished and perplexed, but she did not cry out, for she knew Bertrand well.

He had come, he said solemnly, by order of the King:

It would be well to awaken Madame, our little mistress, very gently; then I will tell her in your presence what the King, our Sire, has commanded me to say.

When Catherina had been awakened, old Bertrand made her a low reverence, told her she must dress quietly and quickly, for her brother had sent his people to bring her to court, and even now they were waiting to receive her.

The little princess, with astonishing presence of mind for a child of ten, considered thoughtfully, then said:

Listen, Bertrand, I have heard you. But what will the Queen, my mother, say when she asks about me and cannot find me? Certainly I wish to obey the King, but it seems it would be better . . . if I waited secretly somewhere here in town, so that I can see if the Queen, my mother, is content without me. If she is content, then I will go to my brother, and if she is too unhappy, perhaps they may tell her I was ill, and the doctors have ordered me away for a change of air.

Bertrand replied that she must leave at once or disobey the King, "her very dear lord and brother." Thereupon the child began to weep for love of her mother, whom she had to leave without a farewell. She allowed herself to be dressed, and then, with two women servants, she was led through the opening in the wall and out to the royal company.

The child was still troubled; in the litter that carried her to Valladolid the court ladies spent the night singing to her and trying to cheer her.

In the morning they reached Valladolid, and Catherina was brought at once to her sister Eleanor's apartments. The faithful reporter Vital, listening outside the chamber door, soon heard the music of laughter and feminine chatter, and knew that all was well. *"La n'y avaient nouvelles que de rire et mener joyeuse vie."*

Quickly and delightedly her older sister and her ladies transformed the little girl into a princess. They took off the dress of gray homespun and put on her a gown of violet satin embroidered with gold. They loosened her hair from the tight pigtail and dressed it fashionably in the Castilian style, "which became her marvelously, for she was a beautiful girl," says Vital, "more beautiful than any of her sisters or any girl I saw there. . . ."

The following day, a Sunday, Catherina accompanied her brother and sister to watch a tournament that lasted through the day and by torchlight into the evening, after which the company danced.

Charles had, meantime, asked Bertrand to watch Queen Juana and to let him know if all was well.

On the same Sunday Juana sent one of her ladies into her daughter's room to fetch the child to her. The lady returned in great distress to say that the room was empty and the little girl gone. Through all the rooms in the castle Juana went then, weeping piteously and asking for her child. She would not eat nor drink nor lie down to sleep.

Bertrand waited, hoping the mad queen's sorrow would subside, and he spoke to her, begging her to take a little food.

Ha! Bertrand [she replied], don't speak to me again of eating and drinking. I cannot, my heart is so crushed with grief, and I will not eat nor drink until I have my daughter again.

There was nothing for it then but to borrow a horse and ride to Valladolid, and tell Charles exactly how things were with the Queen, his mother, "at which the King was not in the least happy."

It was plain that Catherina must return to Tordesillas. But this time at least, Charles determined, his sister would not live in virtual confinement. He selected for her a court of ladies and of young girls her own age who would remain with her from that time on, and he himself conducted her back to their mother's castle-prison.

He found Juana still plunged in bitter grief; when he had greeted her, he said:

Madame, I pray you, cease grieving; I bring you good news of my sister whom I have brought back.

He told his mother that Catherina must no longer live shut up in a back room in nearly complete solitude. She must live in company suitable for her age and station. She must be allowed to play and to roam freely out of doors, "as much for her pleasure as for her health." Else, he added bluntly, she would surely die.

Hardly more than a year later Catherina's small person was thrown, figuratively at least, into the great bribing contest that accompanied her brother's election as Emperor. She escaped marriage into the family of the Elector of Brandenburg, although he continued for some years after to demand her as part of the price offered for his vote.[8]

Eleanor, meantime, married to the Portuguese king, was widowed within a few months of the marriage. Prince John, the late king's son by an earlier marriage, mounted the throne; for a time there was thought of marrying him to his stepmother, Eleanor, a suggestion that bore weight with the Spanish ambassador, who pointed out to Charles that a second marriage to the son might save the cost of another dowry—the first had, in fact, never been paid.

In the end it was Catherina who was dispatched to Portugal at sixteen to marry the new young king, and her widowed sister Eleanor was saved for a more important political match.

There was a third crucial family meeting on that first journey across Spain in the autumn of 1517: Charles's first encounter with his brother Ferdinand.

Unlike the subdued and twilit meeting of Charles and his mother, the two Habsburg brothers met on the highroad in full sunshine with *éclat* and splendor, sun flashing on armor and lances, to the noise of hoofbeats and marching feet and the music of flute and drum. As

Charles and Eleanor took their way from Tordesillas toward the capital of Valladolid, Ferdinand rode to meet them in a great company of grandees, cardinals, men-at-arms.[9]

In many ways his younger brother Ferdinand presented the most delicate and vexing problem Charles was called upon to handle just then.

Instead of growing up as brothers usually do, in the scuffling, quarrelsome, affectionate bondage of family life, these two had never laid eyes on one another, had grown up far apart in different countries, speaking different languages, absorbing different cultures. As things stood now, fourteen-year-old Ferdinand was not only Charles's successor, he was also his most dangerous rival. Born on Spanish soil, carefully groomed for succession to the Spanish throne by his grandfather, King Ferdinand, who had hoped to displace Charles, the younger boy was exceedingly popular in Spain, where Charles was looked upon as a foreign prince surrounded by a company of meddling foreigners.

The councilors of both princes had certainly tried to sow dissension between them. Just before he sailed from the Netherlands, Charles had written his brother, warning him to pay no heed to those among his retinue who spoke ill of the elder brother—"*palabras feas y malas*," he wrote.[10]

But their meeting went off beautifully, and they seemed to take an instant liking to each other. From the moment Ferdinand had ridden up in his glittering company and had dismounted to make a low reverence to Charles, the brothers hardly left one another's side. That night it was Ferdinand who presented the hand-washing basin and napkin to Charles, and it was Ferdinand who sat at Charles's right hand at supper to taste for the first time in his life the famed Burgundian delicacies and sweetmeats. A little later Charles himself hung about his brother's shoulders the collar of the Golden Fleece. And in February, when all Charles's Spanish vassals swore the oath of fealty to their new king, it was Ferdinand who first knelt, placed his hands between the palms of the Sieur de Chièvres as Charles's deputy, and swore the most binding of oaths to his brother.

Even Charles's most prejudiced Flemish councilors could find nothing to criticize in young Ferdinand. Vital declared that the boy "was so nice and full of good nature, he comported himself so modestly and so openly with the King, his brother. . . ."[11]

Nevertheless all was not going so smoothly in Spain as might be wished. Many of Charles's Burgundian followers treated the Spanish with contempt and garnered a harvest of hatred in return.

Spanish priests in Valladolid had been evicted from their houses to make room for members of Charles's court; they retaliated by refusing to say Mass in the presence of the foreigners and even demanded their excommunication. The Spanish accused the Burgundians of drunken and lascivious conduct, declared they had to keep their women under lock and key. Charles's Burgundian courtiers often had the contents of a chamber pot flung down on their heads as they returned from court, "without even having been warned by a 'Guarda!'" It was a case of occupier and occupied, and incidents of bitterness and mutual recrimination grew and multiplied.[12]

Young and inexperienced, unable even to speak the language of his kingdom, almost completely under the management of his advisors headed by Chièvres, Charles was far from sure of his footing in Spain. He could scarcely help noticing that when he appeared in the *cortes* he was coolly greeted, while his brother was received with jubilant cheers.

It seemed best, on the whole, to do as his councilors urged, and dispatch Ferdinand at once to the Netherlands.

But it was with mixed feelings and troubled in his heart that Charles parted from Ferdinand in the town of Aranda in April of 1518. The brothers rode together a half league out of town to the crossroads; when the younger tried to dismount to make his farewell according to protocol, Charles would not permit it, and it was on horseback as equals, both with head bared in the other's honor, that they embraced and commended one another to God. Ferdinand turned seaward toward the port of Santander, and Charles turned slowly back toward town.

Still the parting seemed to trouble him. Charles summoned the Marquis of Aguilar, who had been chosen to head Ferdinand's household, and begged him to ride after Ferdinand with a last message:

> Marquis, my friend [he said], keep my brother company until he boards ship. Commend me to him and say that he will often have news of me, and I shall often wish I were with him hunting the fallow-deer, the roe and the coney in my park in Brussels . . . I have no doubt he will like it there. . . .[13]

Whether Ferdinand liked it or not, he accepted his destiny with grace. Never again did he set foot in Spain.

[7] Emperor Charles V, painted by Titian at the Diet of Augsburg, 1548.
(Bildarchiv des Österreichische Nationalbibliothek, Vienna)

[8] Archduke Ferdinand, later Emperor Ferdinand I, about age eighteen, by Hans Maler. (*Kunsthistorisches Museum, Vienna*)

[9] Emperor Maximilian II and his family about 1553, by Giuseppe Arcimboldo. The three children are Anna, later wife of King Philip II of Spain; Archduke Rudolf, later Emperor Rudolf II; and Archduke Ernst. (*Kunsthistorisches Museum, Vienna*)

[10] Don Carlos of Spain, by A. S. Coello. The painting of the tragic son of Philip II was sent to his cousin, Archduchess Anna of Austria, when marriage between the two was projected. *(Kunsthistorisches Museum, Vienna)*

[11] Queen Anna of Spain, fourth wife of Philip II, by Antonio Moro. After the death of Don Carlos, the blonde princess was dispatched to Spain to marry his father. *(Kunsthistorisches Museum, Vienna)*

3. A Momentous Election

> . . . A man who wishes to make a profession of goodness in everything must necessarily come to grief among so many who are not good. Therefore, it is necessary . . . to learn how not to be good, and to use this knowledge and not use it, according to the necessity of the case.
>
> Machiavelli, *The Prince*

CHARLES WAS with his court in Lérida in Spain when news of his grandfather's death reached him in the spring of 1519. He learned very quickly that the promises Maximilian had bought so dearly from five of the seven imperial electors the previous summer, to insure Charles's election to the throne of the Empire, had vanished in thin air. The prince-electors in Germany were wondering whether the young Habsburg Charles had not already accumulated far too much power, and whether they might, besides, get a better price for their votes.

In Rome, Pope Leo X remarked quite candidly that month to the Venetian ambassador that the imperial crown was to be put up for auction "and knocked down to the highest bidder."[1]

One thing is certain. From the beginning Charles determined that the imperial crown should be his, not merely because so many of his ancestors had worn it, but because it was clearly the only supranational symbol with which he could hope to bind his distant and disparate lands. He had to have it. "To win this election," he declared, "we're determined to spare nothing and to give everything for it, as the one thing in this world which we most have at heart."[2]

What had looked a few months earlier to be a peaceful contest turned suddenly into one of history's most bitterly fought elections. For on the throne of France young King Francis I made up his mind with equal stubbornness that Charles was not to win. Although the imperial crown had taken on of late a German identity, there was nothing in the Golden Bull governing the election that prevented any European prince from becoming a candidate. If Charles won, France would find itself dangerously surrounded by Habsburg power—to the north, the Netherlands; to the south, Spain; to the east, the Empire. Young, energetic, courageous, the French king threw himself into the election contest with all the forces of gold and propaganda at his command.

Nor was he to be Charles's only rival for the electoral votes. Across the Channel King Henry VIII of England, advised by his astute chancellor, Cardinal Wolsey, saw no reason why he might not extend English power—already possessing a foothold on the Continent at Calais—far into central Europe as well. Wolsey intended to win the Papacy for himself the next time a vacancy occurred, and with Henry on the imperial throne—what a swathe they two would cut in European affairs!

Besides the French and English kings, at least two others cast an eye at the imperial crown. Young King Lajos of Hungary, himself one of the seven electors, had been named Maximilian's coadjutor and adopted son in the famous marriage treaty of 1515, with at least half a promise of succession. And his uncle, King Sigismund of Poland, was seen from time to time by many shrewd observers as a likely candidate in case of an electoral deadlock.

Whoever won, it was perfectly clear that the outcome would affect all Europe for years to come. The luster and prestige of that crown would set one monarch above all others, and his sphere of influence would clearly be continent-wide. From London to Moscow that spring of 1519, little else was talked of in political and diplomatic circles save the hotly waged election campaign.

It must have given the prince-electors an exhilarating feeling of power to hold the fate of Europe in their hands for a few months. It was a circumstance that might not occur again in their particular lifetimes, and—with one exception—they were determined to make the most of it.

Charles, meantime, immersed in problems in Spain, could not take a very direct hand in the affair, but left the management of his electoral campaign in the capable hands of his aunt, Regent Margaret.

He was nervous about money. In spite of the vast extent of his realm, he had little actual cash, and he made his envoys promise to keep the bribes as low as possible.

His aunt, however, in her sensitive post as Regent of the Netherlands, kept a sharp eye on how things were going. She had no illusions about what moved men's souls—even electors'—and she declared bluntly, "There are two ways leading to the crown: one of money and one of force."[3] She was perfectly prepared to use either or both.

At first the advantages were all on the side of the French king. His mother, Louise of Savoy, was prepared to lay out her enormous fortune to buy the precious crown her son coveted so much. French ambassadors, perhaps the most highly skilled in Europe, went from one elector to the other, entertaining lavishly, spending grandly, whole mule trains of gold following in their wake. Rumor had it that Francis was prepared to spend between 400,000 and 500,000 ducats on each elector—a perfectly astronomical sum in that day. He said flatly that it was his intention "to draw ahead, and in the matter of gifts, honors, estates, and presents to surpass him [Charles]."[4]

Charles's delegates tried, as one of them said, "not to uncover our poverty" and drive the electors to the other side. One asked Margaret to use only code in writing to him, adding that if Charles did not soon send more money, "all our ardor and pursuit will go up in smoke, for where we offer a thousand, the French give ten thousand."[5]

As it turned out, the fate of the whole election lay in the city of Augsburg, where the powerful banking families of Fugger and Welser had their headquarters. When Margaret learned that the prince-electors preferred to deal through the Fuggers, whom they trusted implicitly, she immediately began to borrow from them—the bribes to be payable only after the election, and contingent on Charles's victory. She was cleverer even than that. She shrewdly forbade the merchants of Antwerp, where an important Fugger branch was located, to lend any money to any foreign power during the crucial months of the campaign. The Fuggers helpfully agreed to refuse to discount French notes during this period, which created enormous difficulties for Francis' agents.

The prices of the precious votes, meantime, went skyrocketing up and up. The whole thing, said one of Charles's agents, was a perfect "marché d'avoine"—a regular grain market; he had never, he said, seen people "so avid for money."[6] The Elector of Brandenburg was particularly greedy. He asked Jakob Fugger in February to tell him

in all confidence "how much gold [Charles] has sent to him and
to the Welser." When Fugger replied that the letters of exchange
Charles had deposited came to only 153,000 florins in liquid silver,
plus another loan of 126,000 florins, Brandenburg declared that "it
wasn't enough and he was going over to the French."[7]

And so he did: Francis promised to name him governor-regent of
Germany, should he win, and give him besides the French princess
Renée as a bride for his son, with a dowry of 200,000 florins. When
Charles's agent heard this, he offered Brandenburg the same amount
of cash, with the hand of Charles's young sister, Catherina—the little
sister of Tordesillas—thrown in the bargain. The French then doubled
the cash bribe—they could not, unfortunately, double the princess-
brides.

For week after anxious week, it looked as if the French king were
ahead. The Archbishop of Trier, traditionally in the French sphere
of influence, was declared to be for Francis. Archbishop Albrecht
of Mainz—who had purchased his own high office a few years before
and paid for it with those costly indulgences that had so angered
Martin Luther—was the brother of the Elector of Brandenburg, and
he too leaned toward the French king.

Everyone in Europe was by now taking sides, with almost as much
passion as if each held a vote.

The Pope made no bones about his feelings: he did not want
Charles to win. At first he tried to persuade himself that Charles's
election would be illegal, but he could find no valid reason against
it. He told the Venetian ambassador, Marco Minio, that he would on
no account have Charles win:

Do you know how many miles hence the borders of his territory
are? Forty miles![8]

The news that the Pope was supporting the French king aroused
the ire of the Swiss, who wrote to him angrily, accusing him of using
his spiritual influence in secular matters, and reminding him that he
was supposed to be their common father.[9]

Both sides, in fact, were crying "Foul!" The French protested that
the Swiss letter had been extorted by Charles's agents, while Charles's
ambassador in London complained bitterly to the English king that
the French were trying "to extort the imperial crown by violence
and tyranny," and that they had an army assembled on their borders,
and had lined up on their side "the Pope, the Signory [of Venice],

with a considerable force, the Florentines, the Genoese, the Switzers."[10]

At one point Charles's chances of winning seemed so dim that his aunt and some of the Habsburg adherents proposed substituting his younger brother Ferdinand as candidate. This suggestion Charles turned down instantly. His reasoning was as sound as it had been from the first: only the prestige of the imperial crown could give him the power to unite all his diverse lands, to keep the peace, to create a universal monarchy. He wrote to his brother warning him to stay out of Germany for the present, promising, however, that when the time came he would divide the realm as equitably as possible with him.[11]

Gradually, by late spring, a change of climate was discernible in the campaign. The votes were now reported to be split three and three, with the Elector of Saxony, Frederick the Wise, still refusing all bribes. Both sides claimed victory. In Rome on June 10, when the Venetian Minio visited the Pope, the Holy Father said that both French and Spanish ambassadors had been to call on him and each had bragged his king would be elected. The Pope added wryly, "One of the two will blush scarlet."[12]

The French ambassador in Rome, a man not without humor, boasted that King Francis had now got four votes promised him, a clear majority. He added:

We have four and [Charles's] people say they have four, so the electors must be eight in number.[13]

Meantime, in an atmosphere of tension and distrust, the seven electors gathered in Frankfurt to cast their votes. Nobody could say for sure what would happen—even war was not out of the question, for swords were rattling on all sides.

Margaret had got word that the French were concentrating troops along their borders. Thereupon she ordered her army to gather at Aachen near the Netherlands border. The two leading *condottieri* of Germany, Franz von Sickingen and Robert de la Marck, who in spite of the imperial law against such warring bands had each a sizable private army, declared first for the French king, then went for Charles. As the election day drew near they brought their mercenary troops within hailing distance of Frankfurt.

The Golden Bull clearly forbade the use of force during an election. Not only were all strangers required to leave the city of Frankfurt (which must have been a difficult rule to enforce), but no elector was permitted to bring a following of more than two hundred men to the city, only fifty of whom could be armed. According to the English ambassador, Pace, the electors were now very annoyed at sight of the German mercenaries and demanded to know of Charles's agents what was the meaning of these troops so close to the election scene. "They answered," says Pace, "that the army was not to use violence against them, but to resist such violence as the French king intended to use against them. . . ."[14]

The excitement in Frankfurt was at fever pitch. Pace wrote to Wolsey:

The French king has promised double what any other Christian prince will give for the empire.[15]

At the zero hour Pace was getting instructions from Wolsey to work for the election of King Henry VIII, on the assumption that he might win as a compromise candidate. He was told to work "as secretly as possible," but probably news of his efforts leaked out to Charles's agents, for Pace got thoroughly frightened.

He wrote home that if the English king did get elected, Pace and all his people would probably be killed before any help could get to them, and that one of Charles's people had boasted to him:

He had so much money and so many men that no Frenchman shall enter this country but upon speris and swerdis poyntes.

Pace added consolingly to Wolsey:

Besides, this nation is in such dissension that it is impossible for all the princes of Christendom to reduce it to good order.[16]

On this latter point Pace was probably right.

In the end, however, for all the cynicism and venality that went into the election campaign, neither money nor force really won out, but a factor that no one had counted on at all—the will of the German people. Though Maximilian's bribes had failed to carry over after his death, his image was fresh in people's minds, and the memory of a much-loved emperor, gay and chivalrous, full of humor and vitality, probably won the election for Charles.

On the eve of the election the English ambassador wrote home:

The Electors are in great perplexity and fear of the people, who all incline to the King of Castile [Charles].[17]

The last conversations of the electors took place on June 27. They had planned to postpone a decision even longer—perhaps waiting for yet larger bribes—but the pestilence had broken out in the city and they were understandably nervous that the hand of God might not altogether overlook their exalted persons.

On the morning of June 28 all seven—a proxy councilor had been sent as delegate for King Lajos—went on foot in a magnificent procession to the church of St. Bartholomew to hear the Mass of the Holy Spirit.

The town council of Frankfurt asked that when the great tocsin sounded three times that day every man would pray God to send his grace on the electors "that they might choose a king who would be useful to God Almighty, the Holy Empire and us all. . . ."[18]

The seven made their oaths on the Holy Evangel that their hands and hearts were pure and that no fraud would sully their free choice. They withdrew to the tiring room of the church and emerged not long after, wreathed in smiles, to announce that, inspired by the Holy Ghost, they had cast a unanimous vote for Charles, King of Spain.[19]

The day after the election the town fathers of Augsburg, home of the Fuggers, declared a public holiday and bore all the costs of the fireworks display.

Two days later, when the news reached Malines in the Netherlands, Margaret ordered bonfires lighted from one end of the country to the other, and feasts and *Te Deums* in honor of the election of her lord and nephew.

In Paris, in London, and in Rome the reception of the news was notably cooler. The Lord Mayor of London refused to permit the Spanish Embassy to light bonfires and illuminations, and threw several enthusiastic celebrants into the Tower. This, of course, was a grave diplomatic blunder, which the court belatedly repaired by having Cardinal Wolsey, swallowing his feelings, chant a *Te Deum*.

The Pope was not a bit pleasant about the whole thing. When the French ambassador upbraided him for supporting Charles at the end of the campaign, the Pope flew into a passion and declared "it was no use knocking one's head against a wall," and that besides,

I can come to terms with the Emperor *cum una spudaza* [with a mouthful of spit].[20]

When the official High Mass was sung in Rome in celebration of Charles's election, only two ambassadors showed up—the Spanish and the Portuguese.

A delegation headed by the Count Palatine Frederick brought the news of his election to Charles in Molino del Rey, where he had gone to escape the plague. What Charles said or felt on that momentous occasion is not recorded; there were certainly sour notes perceptible in the sweet chords of victory.

For one thing the Spanish were not at all happy to share their king with distant countries to whom they felt no common bond. They were even less happy when Charles appointed a foreigner—his own countryman and former religious mentor, Adrian of Utrecht—to rule over them as Regent in his absence. When Charles called the Castilian *cortes* together to vote a subsidy to pay his journey and coronation costs, they refused outright. Later, when enough deputies had been bribed to approve it, angry mobs attacked their houses; the money was never paid.[21]

In fact, when Charles set sail from Spain in the spring of 1520 for his coronation as world emperor, he found himself mortgaged to the hilt and facing a host of enemies. The election had cost him over a million gulden—possibly as high as $20,000,000 in today's currency. About half had gone for bribes, the rest for incidental expenses: propaganda, wages of agents, secretaries, couriers, payment of troops. The three archbishop-electors had got pleasantly large cash payments plus annuities; their entourages, even their valets, had been liberally tipped. The Count Palatine had raked in the biggest bribe—over 184,000 florin. Honest old Frederick of Saxony, who had asked nothing, found a debt he owed the Emperor canceled. The Marquis of Brandenburg, who had been so greedy and only voted for Charles at the very end, went away empty-handed. He was so angry at the way things turned out that he declared the whole election a fraud, and said he had cast his vote "out of very fear and not out of knowledge."[22] Nobody paid him the slightest attention. He insisted Charles owed him a bribe, and even attempted to collect the Infanta Catherina as part of the payment for his vote.[23]

In his whole lifetime Charles would never be freed of that burden of debt. Repeatedly he had to break his promises to repay the enormous loans from the Fuggers. Even when Spanish ships began to sail back from the New World, loaded with treasure, Charles's share hardly made a dent in his debt.

Nervous and fretful about financial problems, Charles would never get out of the habit of being careful with money, especially small amounts. He could not bear to see a ducat spent uselessly. He postponed buying new outfits for his pages, even when they became quite shabby; he noticed if so much as a handkerchief was missing from his wardrobe.

Later in his life a witness described Charles reviewing troops one day when it began to rain; the Emperor took off his new velvet hat and carefully put it under his cloak.

4. The Seamless Coat

> Sire, God has granted you this great grace . . .
> and you are now on your way to world sover-
> eignty and the gathering of all Christendom un-
> der one shepherd.
>
> *Gattinara to Charles V*

ON OCTOBER 22, 1520, Charles rode into Aachen for his coronation as King of the Romans. It was his first performance as central figure in Europe's greatest show—the public life of an emperor—and he acquitted himself admirably.

The ceremonial entry was designed to make perfectly clear to all Europe that the most suitable candidate had indeed been chosen for the imperial honor. There was no evidence of the impoverished state of his treasury: the Spanish had refused to pay the costs, and most had been borrowed from the rich city of Antwerp.

His procession took five hours to pass through the gates of the city. Hundreds of liveried servants and baggage wagons were followed by a thousand noblemen on horseback, as richly turned out as their purses would permit. Twenty-four pages in his livery—crimson satin with silver and gold facings—were followed by a company of musicians, kettledrums and trumpets, and a half-dozen equerries flinging gold and silver to the stampeding spectators.

A herald in gold-and-silver tabard bearing the silver-gilt staff sur-mounted by the imperial eagle walked grandly alone. Then came the prince-electors and the bishops, then the Lord Marshal of the realm bearing before him, point upraised, the great imperial sword.

Finally came Charles. He wore a coat of gold brocade over armor;

mounted on a prancing white steed whose hoofs scarcely seemed to touch the ground, he delighted the parade watchers with his practiced horsemanship. Behind him his bodyguard of archers bore on their coats in letters of gold his device: *Plus Oultre.*

The ancient coronation rite was celebrated the following day in the Church of Our Lady. The solemnity, the religious character of the service made a deep impression on the serious young king. Twice during the ceremony Charles had to prostrate himself in the shape of a cross on the pavement before the high altar, as a priest does during the rite of ordination. Laying his hand on the holy relics that had been found in the tomb of Charlemagne—the Book of Gospels and a casket containing earth soaked with the blood of Stephen the Martyr—he swore an oath to defend the Empire and the Holy Catholic Church.

The Archbishop of Cologne turned to the assembled throng in the church and asked:

Will you have King Charles as Emperor and King of the Romans, and will you be obedient to him according to the words of the Apostle?[1]

The watchers shouted *"Fiat!"* The three archbishops anointed him on the forehead, breast, back, and hand. They arrayed him in the imperial garments, girded him with Charlemagne's sword, handed him the scepter and the golden orb surmounted by a cross that represented the Christian sovereignty of the universal emperor.

From that day in Aachen the theme of Charles's life was chosen. He was resolved to restore meaning to the medieval concept of a unified Christian empire, and as its head he would lead Europe into peace.

How Charles appeared to watchers at approximately that time we may see from the portrait of Bernard van Orley: an angular, harsh-featured face under a velvet hat studded with jewels, a jutting, up-thrust chin, mouth ajar, intent blue-gray eyes—a young, smooth face, but impassive, self-contained, a face that gives nothing away. Over his furred cloak is suspended the collar of the Fleece.

It was just so that young Charles would have appeared to Martin Luther on an afternoon in April of 1521 in the great hall of the Diet of Worms.

Fresh from his coronation at Aachen, Charles had ridden south along the Rhine to Worms. It was the first time he had set foot on German soil; he did not even speak German; he was, in fact, once again a foreign prince in a foreign land. It had already been made quite clear to him that the aura of power he carried as Emperor was largely illusory and that the German princes were united in their will to curtail it. On the eve of his coronation he had signed the customary election capitulation—those promises by which an emperor must agree to abide—but his had been the most exacting any emperor had ever been asked to sign.

Green and inexperienced in the complex affairs of that puzzling, conglomerate Empire, twenty-one-year-old Charles appeared to preside at his first Diet, and was instantly plunged into one of the great crises of his reign—indeed, of all history.

When Luther had nailed his ninety-five theses on the door of the castle church at Wittenberg in October of 1517, Charles was still crossing the wild mountains of northern Spain on his first journey into his kingdom, and his grandfather, Maximilian, was still alive.

The immediate spark of the quarrel had been the sale of indulgences which the Pope had granted to Albrecht, younger brother of the Elector Joachim of Brandenburg. Ambitious Albrecht, already holding two bishoprics, coveted the vacant archbishopric of Mainz, which brought not only a fat income but the princely prestige of an imperial electorate. The Pope, intent on building a magnificent new church over the graves of the saints Peter and Paul in Rome, demanded an enormous installation fee for the archbishopric, and an additional sum for the irregularity of already holding two sees.

The actual bargaining for the archbishopric was carried out through the Fuggers, who were always glad to be helpful where large sums of money were concerned. Originally the Pope had demanded twelve thousand ducats, "for the twelve apostles," so the story went. Albrecht countered with an offer of seven thousand "for the seven deadly sins," and they finally compromised on ten, as one wag suggested, "for the Ten Commandments." Part of it Albrecht borrowed from the Fuggers. To raise the remainder the Pope granted Albrecht the privilege of selling indulgences, those handy little documents granting a remission of one's sins. A high-powered Dominican monk named Tetzel hawked the indulgences about Germany, traveling in the company of a Fugger agent who kept accounts and held the money boxes.

It was the offensiveness of this operation that had drawn Luther's indignation, though he at first intended his ninety-five theses only to engage some professor of theology in a lively debate. But his hammer blows awakened all the deep-rooted dissatisfactions that men in Germany—and elsewhere—had long been feeling about the power and abuses of the Church—and a Church that seemed to them "foreign," far away, headquartered in Rome. Overnight Luther became a celebrity with a cause on his hands. With a boldness born of his new popularity and self-confidence, Luther began to rain blows on the Papacy and the whole structure of the Church. During the following months he burned in public the papal bull condemning him for heresy, and he continued to preach and to write, fiercely, fiercely.

It was with the explosive problem of Luther that Charles had to deal in those first months as Emperor. On the one hand the Pope, whose support Charles needed—the spiritual arm of the universal Empire—clamored for immediate trial of Luther on charges of heresy, preferably with extradition to Rome. On the other hand, Luther had widespread support and sympathy within Germany, even among the prince-electors, and Charles was bound by the terms of his election capitulation to give native Germans a hearing in their homeland.

In response to Charles's invitation to "our noble, dear and esteemed Martin Luther," the fiery-tongued theology professor rode into Worms in a two-wheeled cart, escorted by a herald of the Emperor and bearing a safe-conduct signed by Charles.

On the afternoon of April 18, 1521, Luther appeared before a huge crowd gathered in the hall of the Diet. An official of the Archbishop of Trier examined him, and when he had finally pinned Luther down, demanding,

> I ask you, Martin—answer candidly and without horns and without teeth—do you or do you not repudiate your books and the errors which they contain?

Luther replied:

> Since then Your Majesty and your lordships desire a simple reply, I will answer without horns and without teeth. Unless I am convicted by Scripture and plain reason—I do not accept the authority of popes and councils, for they have contradicted each other. My conscience is captive to the Word of God. I cannot and I will not recant anything . . . God help me.

He may have added, "Here I stand; I cannot do otherwise."[2]

Late that night candles burned in Charles's room, where the youthful Emperor bent over, quill in hand, personally composing a reply to Luther's challenge. There could scarcely be a doubt where Charles would stand.

That the Church needed reform, he understood clearly, but reform must come from within through the medium of a council. Deeply influenced by Erasmus, who had been a member of his own council now for five years and had accompanied him as far as Cologne on his journey to Worms, Charles would for years embody the humanist approach, work for mediation, for conciliation. During his two eye-opening years in Spain he had seen what the gifted Spanish humanist Cardinal Ximénez de Cisneros had accomplished in reforming the Spanish church. But when Luther challenged the very foundation of the Church by questioning the validity of the Sacraments, and the doctrine of man's free will, there could be no question of compliance.

In his person Charles was the embodiment of the Establishment; his earliest oath to the Golden Fleece, and his latest oath at his crowning pledged him to defend the integrity of the Faith. He would not permit the severing of the one common bond that united all the peoples of Europe.

The following day, when he asked the electors for their opinion on Luther and they replied they were not yet ready to declare, Charles read his own statement aloud in French, his native language.

Proudly he recalled his cosmopolitan heritage:

> I am descended from a long line of Christian emperors of this noble German nation, and of the Catholic kings of Spain, the archdukes of Austria and the dukes of Burgundy. They were all faithful to the death to the church of Rome, and they defended the Catholic faith and the honor of God.

If Luther had spoken his fateful words with deep assurance, no less conviction rang in Charles's statement of his faith, his promise to hold to the unity of Christianity:

> I have resolved to follow in their steps. A single friar who goes counter to all Christianity for a thousand years must be wrong. Therefore I am resolved to stake my lands, my friends, my body, my blood, my life and my soul in pledge for this cause.[3]

For the following three days a committee met with Luther, attempting again to find common ground and to prevent an irreparable split. The Archbishop of Trier, who with Maximilian had uncovered under the altar of Trier Cathedral the seamless coat of Christ, begged Luther "not to rend the seamless robe of Christendom."[4]

Luther had gone too far to turn back. In the end the papal legate, Cardinal Aleander, drew up the edict that placed Luther under the ban of the Empire, charging him with sullying marriage, denying free will, making for "rebellion, division, war, murder, robbery, arson, and the collapse of Christendom."

At the end of the month Luther left Worms again in his two-wheeled cart; on the way back to Wittenberg he was kidnaped by servants of the Elector of Saxony and carried for safety to the great castle the Wartburg.

A little while after, when the Diet ended, Charles took his own way back to the Netherlands, to his childhood home.

He stood just then in a posture that would be a familiar one in his life: that of a man who has just leapt over a chasm only to find that a wider one yet has opened at his feet. In the same month of April in which he encountered Luther, he had confronted anxieties more troubling even than a single, stubborn, heretic monk.

Civil war had broken out in his kingdom of Spain, precipitated by the hostility the Spanish felt for the Burgundians Charles had left in charge. In the same month of April the royal forces in Spain had fought a decisive battle with the rebellious Spanish communes and had won a victory, though it would be weeks before the news reached Charles.

Ever since his election Charles had steadfastly tried to avoid war with France. In the same week as Luther's appearance in Worms, the French ambassador had left the city in a huff and King Francis declared war on Charles—the first of a series of wars that would flare up again and again through his whole reign.

Nor were civil war in his own kingdom and war against the old Habsburg enemy his only problems: there were also the Turks. A new and powerful young sultan, Suleiman who would be called the Magnificent, had just come to the throne. Charged with ambition and energy the Turks were driving up the Balkans. Before the end of summer of 1521 they would capture Belgrade, the gate of the Danubian plain and the very heart of Europe; before the end of Charles's reign the Habsburg crownlands would become the shield of Europe against Moslem invasion.

At Worms, moreover, Charles's closest friend and advisor, Chièvres, had died of plague. From this time on all decisions would be his own.

There had been family matters to see to as well. In the same week as his encounter with Luther, Charles had signed over to his brother Ferdinand the core of the Austrian crownlands; Ferdinand was also to be Regent of the Empire in Charles's absence. It was an important move in Habsburg family history, for out of that fraternal sharing was born the two-halved Habsburg realm. From Worms, Ferdinand had ridden southward to Linz on the Danube, where his wedding to

Princess Anna of Hungary was to take place, and where he would meet his young sister Mary for the first time in his life.

Charles had at first planned to attend those two family weddings—Ferdinand's and Mary's—and the accompanying festivities, but once again cares of state made him forego his own pleasure, and he returned instead to the Netherlands.

It was perhaps no accident that just that autumn the disciplined, self-contained Charles threw himself into a brief, passionate liaison.

Did someone have a hand in arranging it? Who knows? The Venetian ambassador reported a curious incident at Charles's dinner table in Brussels in September. A dish of meat was brought to the young Emperor, carefully prepared to his taste, but he did not touch it, and it was carried off to one of the lower tables, as was the custom. When the meat was cut into, it was found to contain "a small bladder filled with powder, hair and other mixtures . . ." Alarm and consternation throughout the palace and city. Charles's cook and three servants were immediately arrested on suspicion of poisoning. But those who knew, including Charles's physician, declared it was not poison but a love charm.[5]

Immediately after, Charles engaged in an affair with a Flemish girl, of whom nothing is known save her name—Johanna van der Gheenst of Audenarde. Out of the liaison was born a daughter, who was named for Charles's aunt, Regent Margaret, and given to faithful servants to rear as a royal lady.

From the Netherlands Charles sailed again to his troubled kingdom of Spain, where he was to remain for seven years.

5. *Years of Triumph*

IN THE DECADE that followed his coronation in Aachen, when the century and he were both in their twenties, Charles rose step by step to a dazzling pinnacle of world renown.

He had the good luck in that decade to put to rout all his enemies save one; even Machiavelli could not teach him how to deal with Martin Luther.

He wrestled with the French for control of Italy and won. At Pavia on Charles's twenty-fifth birthday the French were defeated and their king taken prisoner.

For nearly a year Francis I was imprisoned in Madrid while negotiations for his ransom and release dragged on. What Charles insisted on in his peace terms was the return of that portion of his grandmother's Burgundian lands which Louis XI of France had seized in 1477—the old core of Bourgogne and its capital of Dijon where the dukes of Burgundy lay entombed. For a long time Francis refused; then, ill and weary of imprisonment, he agreed and set his signature to the Treaty of Madrid in January of 1526. He agreed besides to join Charles in a crusade against the Turks, and as a seal of his faith, to marry Charles's sister, Eleanor.

Charles rode with the French king part way to the border. When he gave his hand in farewell he asked, "Do you remember all that you have promised?"

"Set your mind at rest, brother," replied Francis. "My intention is to keep it all, else you may call me a wicked coward—*lâche et méchant!*"[1]

A few weeks later Francis repudiated the treaty, declaring he had signed it under force. From his Madrid prison he had already smuggled out his ring with a message to the Sultan asking help from the Turk. Now he persuaded the new Pope Clement VII to join with the Duke of Milan, the Republic of Venice, the Swiss, and the English in a league against the Emperor.

Charles declared indignantly that Francis was no gentleman and offered to solve their differences by engaging in single combat. Reproachfully Charles addressed the Pope:

> Certain people are saying that Your Holiness has absolved the King of France from the oath by which he promised us to keep to what was agreed; this we do not wish to believe, for it is not a thing that the Vicar of Christ would do.[2]

The Vicar of Christ had, however, done just that.

Charles, meanwhile, as always short of cash, had been unable to pay his army in Italy. The winter of 1526–27 was a terrible one in northern Italy. Torrential icy rains fell; war and occupation had swept the country bare. The mercenary troops had long gone unpaid; they were hungry, in rags, barefoot, desperate. Near Bologna the imperial army mutinied, and when General Frundsberg, who had led the German mercenaries into Italy, offered what money he could scrape together with a promise of more, they went wild, threatened him with their lances, shouting, "Money! money!" The old general collapsed on a drum, was carried back to Germany, a dying man. Command of the imperial army fell on the Constable of Bourbon, a cousin of the French king who had defected to the imperial side. Bourbon tried to borrow money from the Pope to pay the troops. Unwisely the Pope refused.

Swelled by all the riffraff of the Italian peninsula, the imperial mercenaries swarmed south toward Rome, goaded by hunger, fury, greed, superstition. German followers of Luther saw in Rome the very enemy of religion, "the whore of Babylon," as Luther called it, the home of anti-Christ.

On the night of May 5, 1527, they came in sight of the Eternal City, just as the setting sun turned the myriad domes and spires to shimmering gold, gold enough to pay a thousand armies.

In the misty dawn of the following day, like a pack of famished wolves, the mercenaries swarmed over the walls into the world's most civilized city. The Constable of Bourbon was among the first to scale the walls. His white cloak made him an easy mark; a shot from an arquebus—Benvenuto Cellini claimed the honor of the shot—killed him instantly, leaving the army totally uncontrolled.

For ten days the soldiers raged through the city, pillaging, burning, raping, looting. Every convent, every church was ransacked; thousands upon thousands of citizens were killed in their houses, in the streets, in the churches where they had fled for sanctuary.

In the first hours of the invasion the Pope and the cardinals had tucked up their robes and fled across a secret passageway from the papal palace to the Castle of San Angelo. A day or two later a band of German mercenaries found the prelates cowering in a stable, half dead with fright. "They wept very much," remarked one of the Germans later, "but we all of us grew rich." One Bavarian captain dressed himself in the Pope's robe and triple crown, with the soldiers of his company in cardinals' robes and hats went frolicking through the city on donkeys.[3]

For ten months the imperial army occupied Rome. Plague followed in the ruined and desolate city. The invading army sickened too, and its numbers dwindled.

Charles was watching a tournament in Madrid when news of the sack of Rome reached him. Reports varied on whether he rejoiced or sorrowed; he certainly considered it an act of God visited on the Pope and the city of Rome for their sins. He had called the Pope "that poltroon of a Pope" not many months before,[4] and as his confessor Glapion once remarked, a forgiving heart was not among Charles's strong points. He permitted the Pope to languish in prison for seven months.

In the end they were reconciled; the Pope too was a politician. In February of 1530 Charles received the imperial crown at the hands of the Pope—not in Rome, however, for that would have been too bitter an irony, but in Bologna. In suitable humility Charles knelt and kissed the Pope's foot; the Pope drew him up and planted a kiss on each of Charles's cheeks. After the crowning, according to the medieval custom, the Emperor held the stirrup for the Pope to mount; side by side they rode through the wildly acclaiming crowd to the elegant and extravagant banquet. At the end of the banquet, in a delightful gesture of fiscal unconcern, all the gold and silver plate was tossed down as souvenirs to the crowds.

Charles was master of northern and southern Italy, as the medieval emperors had been.

The coronation was almost, but not quite, the moment of Charles's greatest triumph.

The Turks under Suleiman had been advancing steadily up the

Balkans, had defeated Charles's brother-in-law, King Lajos of Hungary, at the Battle of Mohács and finally reached the gates of Vienna in 1529. Just when it seemed the beleaguered city might fall, the Turkish army struck their tents and retreated, fearful of the coming winter.

In 1532 the Turks again advanced into the Austrian crownlands. Charles at the head of a great international army of Spanish, German, Italian, and Flemish troops marched to meet them. Back home in Wittenberg Luther composed his great hymn at this moment of Christian crisis, "A Mighty Fortress Is Our God." Once again the Turks withdrew without engaging in a major battle, and Charles entered the jubilant city of Vienna to receive a great welcome.

Three years later he assembled an international fleet in Barcelona and sailed for the African coast to put an end to the marauding Turkish pirates who, under Chaireddin Barbarossa of Tunis, were destroying Mediterranean shipping. At the personal head of his troops, in the intense heat of an African summer, Charles stormed and took Tunis. Some twenty-thousand Christian slaves were set free, clothed at his expense, and brought back to Europe, where they spread far and wide praise of the Emperor.

But already in the first brilliant decade of his reign, he was failing.

Immense distances and time, religious schism, churning nationalisms: all worked against the creation of a universal Christian imperium.

In vain Charles devised strategems to hold together a vast realm that had neither geographic nor ethnic nor linguistic cohesion.

His court was the most cosmopolitan in the world. Noble families of Spain and Germany, Italy and Burgundy sent their sons to serve as pages and as chaplains to the Emperor. A hundred German halberdiers, a hundred Spanish foot soldiers, a hundred Burgundian archers made up his personal bodyguard. He drew into the Order of the Golden Fleece not only Burgundians but noblemen of Spanish and German and Italian lineage. For chancellor he had an Italian, Mercurino Gattinara; for court marshal, a Spaniard, the Duke of Alva. A Burgundian served as shield-bearer, laced the Emperor's boots, and girded him in his armor.

His most potent instrument of unity was still his family. His aunt Margaret, Regent of the Netherlands, devoted herself heart and soul to his cause in that vital European crossroads, the Low Countries. His brother Ferdinand was his alter ego in the German-speaking lands. His sisters were queens of France, of Portugal, of Hungary and Bohemia, of Denmark, Norway, and Sweden. His aunt, Catherine of Aragon, his mother's younger sister, shared the throne of England with Henry VIII.

And yet the divisive forces were more powerful than those of unity.

6. The Padlocked Heart

> We have a pious Emperor. He has a padlock to
> his heart.
>
> *Martin Luther*

IN THE SPECTACULAR drama that was his life, Charles consistently underplayed the role of principle.

He had great style, but a style very different from the mercurial flash and brilliance of Francis I or the convivial aplomb and exuberant boldness of Henry VIII. A friend said of Charles, simply and with absolute certainty, "He was the greatest gentleman that ever was, or ever will be."[1]

Few kings in history have left behind so much in writing—minutes, notes, memoranda, orders, letters—yet the flavor of his personality eluded that mountain of paper. The memoir of his life which he wrote for his son Philip is dry and impersonal as a November leaf, set down in the third person in all the modest sobriety of unadorned nouns and verbs.

"It is not as I wished it," he wrote in a note attached in his own hand, "but God knows that I did not write it from vanity, and if he is offended by it, my offense should be attributed to ignorance rather than to malice."[2]

Pride he had, the Habsburg pride of race, worn like a plume in the helmet of his kingship; unlike most monarchs of his day, he did not, however, confuse the office with his person, and he was willing to credit his triumphs to God.

When the news of the victory of Pavia was brought to him, and he was told that the French king was his prisoner, he astonished the foreign ambassadors in Madrid by the restraint of his conduct. He went immediately into his oratory and remained for an hour in prayer. He would allow no celebrating, for, he said, "the victory was gained with the blood of Christian men." The next day he walked on foot to Mass, having asked the priest neither to eulogize him in his sermon nor to disparage the King of France.[3]

He described himself as "hard to weep."

Nor did he laugh often or easily; a faint smile might play about his lips at the antics of the buffoons who stood nearby to amuse him at dinner. He had wit, but it was cerebral, the dry ironic turn of a melancholy, introspective mind. Reading on the tombstone of a Spanish nobleman the epitaph "Here lies one who never knew fear," Charles remarked: "Then he never snuffed a candle with his fingers."[4]

Surrounded by flatterers from childhood, he could not endure flattery. Once he observed to the Venetian Contarini, "It is my nature to insist obstinately on my own opinion." The ambassador replied rather unctuously, "Sire, to insist on good opinions is firmness, not obstinacy." With a twitch of his controlled smile, Charles said, "I sometimes also insist upon bad ones."[5]

Out hunting one day in Spain, Charles lost his way and fell into conversation with an old peasant of whom he asked directions. The fellow, having no idea who Charles was, boasted that he had seen five kings reign in Spain.

"And who was the best of the five?" asked Charles curiously.

"Ferdinand," replied the old man promptly.

"And the worst?"

"The one we have now. Always gadding about abroad, instead of taking care of things in Spain where he belongs."

As Charles tried to defend himself without betraying his identity, one of his courtiers rode up and rebuked the old peasant for taking such liberties. "Fellow, you are addressing your king!"

The old man replied that if he had known he was talking to the King, he would certainly have spoken more plainly still. Charles was delighted and gave the old man a dowry for his daughter.[6]

His ministers addressed him as Sacred Caesarean Majesty. The Persian ambassador called him "the king who has the sun for a hat."

Everywhere he moved in Europe crowds were there to watch: when he rode, a glittering golden figure in the festive entries into one or another city; when he walked solemnly all in black, his court behind him, bearing tapers on Corpus Christi day; when he dined in public on a raised dais under a golden canopy, and anyone who wished might come to watch. ("He stuck his knife anywhere, and often used his fingers while he held his plate under his chin with the other hand," one witness, the German notary Bartholomew Sastrow wrote. "He ate so naturally and at the same time so cleanly that it was a pleasure to watch him."[7])

In the great street spectacles of the day—those most ephemeral of Renaissance art works—Charles was the central figure, the key actor. However wearisome the royal entries, the receptions, the festivals— the endless *tableaux vivants* presenting scenes of his triumphs, the throngs of angels presenting him keys to the city—still he accepted his part. Theater was part of the mystique of kingship; the public spectacle of majesty made it possible to govern.

But unlike his Burgundian ancestors Charles did not enjoy pomp and show for its own sake. His own tastes were neither extravagant nor ostentatious; he loved to hunt, but, according to the Venetian ambassador Cavalli, Charles did not "spend a hundred crowns on it." Cavalli added, "He does not consider it shameful to be surpassed in this, or dressing, or similar things." His one great indulgence were his musicians; music went with him on all his journeys.[8]

An emperor might have advisors; he was not likely to have friends. It was to his brother and his sisters, whose interests lay so close to his own, that Charles turned during most of his life for advice and companionship. Whenever they could they would meet—in the family palaces in the Netherlands, at the Diets meeting in Augsburg or Regensburg, in their grandfather's Innsbruck palace, from which they would ride out together to hunt. Charles would write Ferdinand, urging him to a meeting, "for I singularly desire to see you, and to enjoy the comfort and pleasure of your fraternal presence."[9] When they were apart their long, intricately detailed letters crisscrossed Europe by messenger, full of problems, of news, of advice.

On the last day before her death, in 1530, Charles's devoted aunt, Regent Margaret, did not fail to dictate one last letter to him, filled with fond and loving counsel:

Monseigneur, the hour has come where I cannot any longer write you with my own hand, for I feel so ill that I think my life may last now only a very short time. At ease in my conscience, and ready to receive what God sends me, without pain, except that I may not see and speak with you before my end . . .[10]

Roger Ascham said once of Charles that "nothing of him speaks except his tongue." Rare were those moments when tenderness broke through Charles's impassive demeanor like a chink of light through a shuttered window. He became very attached to his sister Ysabeau's boy, Johann. When he traveled to the Diet of Regensburg in 1532 his twelve-year-old nephew accompanied him. While Charles lay abed of an injury he suffered in a hunting accident, Johann sickened of a fever and died quite suddenly. Grieving Charles wrote his sister Mary the news:

I am deeply saddened, for he was the handsomest little boy of his age one can imagine. I am not less affected by his death than by that of my own son, for I knew him better and he was already bigger, and I looked upon him as my own child. . . .

It must be God's will, but I cannot help regretting that he should be taken from us. I could better have spared his father, God forgive me. Still, the little lad will be better off where he is. He died with so little sin to his account that had he had all mine to bear as well as his own, he could not have missed eternal salvation.[11]

His sister Mary grew closer to Charles than to anyone else as the years passed. She confessed to him once that he was—after God Himself—her "all in this world": *mon tout dans ce monde.*[12]

Yet Charles did not hesitate to use his family exactly as policy required. His sisters and nieces served to weave yet further the great dynastic net his grandfather, Maximilian, had flung over Europe.

Eleanor, called upon to seal with her marriage the peace treaty between her brother and the French king, could not have found life in the French court very happy. The French were consistently anti-Habsburg, and war between her husband and brother broke out again and again. Besides, King Francis' domestic attentions were fully engaged by a series of mistresses, culminating in the lovely Duchesse d'Étampes. He paid Eleanor only a modicum of attention and often took his mistress instead of his queen even on official journeys. All that might be expected in a royal match, and Eleanor knew it. But Dantiscus, the Polish ambassador in Paris, who had known Eleanor as a blooming, pink-cheeked girl in her teens, wrote in 1531 that she had quite lost her looks, had grown fat and her skin red and blotchy. He added that the King had apparently infected her with "the French disease" (syphilis) so that she was unable to bear children.[13]

The keenest of the Habsburg sisters, Mary, did not comply quite so docilely to her brother's plans. Widowed after the Battle of Mohács in 1526, Mary flatly rejected the second husband her brothers proposed for her—King James of Scotland—declaring that she intended to remain faithful to her first husband, King Lajos, even to death: *"pis in mein grub,"* she wrote.[14] Charles then prevailed upon her to take their aunt Margaret's place as Regent of the Netherlands.

A few years later, when he needed to pin down the loyalty of the unreliable Duke of Milan, Charles determined to arrange a marriage between the middle-aged duke and his twelve-year-old niece, Christina, daughter of his sister Ysabeau, Queen of Denmark, who had died in 1525. Little Christina had been living in the household of Regent Mary, in the Netherlands. Now Charles's spirited sister, who had herself been married as a child, fought angrily against the child marriage of her niece, writing her brother bluntly:

> It is against nature and God's laws to marry off a little girl who cannot yet in any sense be called a woman, and to expose her, herself a child, to the dangers of childbed.[15]

Charles's reply was curt and unequivocal: the interests of the Empire were to be served first. In June of 1533 the marriage contract was signed and the little girl dispatched to Milan. Christina was a widow before she was fourteen.

As for his own marriage, Charles had been betrothed over and over again during his childhood, to seal numerous alliances, with French, English, Hungarian princesses. In the end he chose for himself a sensible match based on money and politics. He wrote his brother with delightful frankness that he was marrying Princess Isabella of Portugal because she would bring a million ducats in her dowry, and because his Spanish subjects wanted no "foreign" queen, but a Hispanic princess who knew their language and their ways.[16] Isabella had certainly set her heart on the Emperor, for two years before her marriage, according to the Venetian envoy, she had chosen for her motto, *Aut Caesar aut nihil*—Caesar or nothing.[17]

Isabella proved a treasure of a wife, and the marriage founded on such a firm basis of ducats was thoroughly happy. In the paintings of Titian, Isabella appears a serene cool beauty, her golden blonde hair wound with strands of pearls and plaited above a fine brow. She had the same breeding, pride, and reticence as Charles. "Inward," the Spanish chronicler Santa Cruz described her; Charles too was "inward."

In March of 1526, just after he had signed the Treaty of Madrid and released the French king, Charles rode to his wedding in Seville. The young pair met in late evening in the great hall of the palace, and were betrothed and married at once. At midnight the Archbishop of Toledo read Mass, Charles and Isabella confessed and took the Sacrament, received the blessing, and were led to the bridal chamber.

In June, to escape the heat of Seville, they journeyed to Granada, and there in the enchanted palace of the Alhambra, among the drifting scents of orange and lemon trees, they passed a honeymoon summer.

The following May, Isabella bore a son whom they named Philip for Charles's father. Charles's joy was so great that he went out and celebrated with a *corrida*, killing a bull with his own hand.

A month before Isabella's delivery, Charles's aunt, Regent Margaret, had written from the Netherlands that she was praying "for a good and joyous delivery," and that it would be a fair young prince. She wished that she might be in Spain to assist in the accouchement, but since she could not, she was sending a most precious gift with her ambassador:

St. Elizabeth's own girdle, which is said to allay the pangs of childbirth of all pregnant ladies, and was sought out in Hungary by the late Emperor Friedrich, and given by him to his son, Emperor Maximilian, whom God absolve, who used it for the delivery of Madame, his good companion, on whom God give mercy.[18]

Whether the precious girdle aided the young empress, we are not told, but it was said that during the long and difficult hours of labor Isabella's attendants besought her to scream out her pain. She replied, "Die I may, but wail I will not," and asked only that her face be covered so that none might witness her suffering.[19]

The pleasures of family life were not for a world emperor. Again and again Charles's duty called him to the Netherlands, to Germany, to Italy and England and Africa. Departing for the Tunis campaign he wrote Isabella:

My dearest, beloved wife, I kiss this sheet of paper with the same tenderness and warmth that I would kiss your lips were I with you. . . .[20]

Again and again he left her weeping, to be away for months and years at a time, while Isabella maintained a careful, intelligent regency in his absence.

Crusades against the Turks were not half so perilous, however, as the occupational hazards of queens. Again and again delicate, fragile Isabella went into childbirth, bearing in all eight children, of whom three lived. In his memoir, Charles writes that the Empress was always *très-souffrante de ses couches*—that she suffered acutely in childbed. After the birth of their seventh child she lived in constant pain.[21]

Nevertheless in 1538, when Charles returned from a journey, Isabella immediately became pregnant again. She was so very ill during this pregnancy that Charles was constantly by her side. On April 20, 1539, she gave birth prematurely to a child who died almost at once. Isabella seemed for a time to be recovering, then a burning fever seized her and she died on the first of May.

Broken with sorrow, Charles knelt for hours at her deathbed, then withdrew to the monastery of the Hieronymite monks near Toledo, to hide his grief from the world. Not until many years later could he write:

> . . . it pleased God to call her to him, and we may be sure he did so out of his great mercy.[22]

7. The Seamless Coat Torn

AFTER THE DEATH of his wife the strain of melancholy, of pessimism, in Charles's personality deepened. He dressed only in black.

He had long suffered from gout, and now it tortured him increasingly. In vain he carried a blue stone to protect against it, and wore bracelets of gold and bone against the hemorrhoids. His doctor told him he would cure his gout only by shutting his mouth, but he had always enjoyed eating, and he continued to eat and drink a great deal, especially fish and game, oysters live and pickled, washed down with quantities of iced beer.

Of his gout he remarked ruefully that he was "unable to hope for any truce with it,"[1] and that "patience and a little screaming are a good remedy against it."[2] His health was ravaged by those incredible journeys across the face of Europe in all weathers, over the primitive roads, over snowbound Alpine passes and burning Spanish plains. Often he rode in excruciating pain, his gouty leg suspended in a sling from the saddle.

But the tenacious stubborn will held on.

For a quarter of a century he had been searching to find a way of conciliation in the religious quarrel, a *via media* on which Catholics and Protestants might again join. Somewhere, somehow, a solution could surely be found: if both sides, he thought, could simply agree on the ancient Articles of Faith, then men might be allowed to think as they pleased on questions of free will, predestination, justification by faith, about which they were so busy arguing now.[3]

But the extremists of both sides refused to give an inch. Through the twenty years since the first Diet of Worms, Lutheranism had spread widely in the German lands. The prince-electors of Saxony, Brandenburg, and the Palatinate had gone over to Protestantism; so had the Archbishop of Cologne. The Church was threatened not merely with a split, but with total fragmentation as a whole array of new sects sprang up.

Nor was it merely a doctrinal quarrel. The whole basis of civil authority was threatened with the seizure of church property, with such radical outbreaks as that of the Anabaptists at Münster.

Charles begged the Pope to call a church council to settle questions of doctrine and to instigate much-needed reforms. The Pope procrastinated. Charles's envoy, Loaysa, wrote him from Rome:

> When I pronounce the word 'council' in his presence, I might be speaking of the devil himself.[4]

Charles made a last great effort to heal the schism in the humanist way. He called the finest intellects, both Catholic and Protestant, to Regensburg in 1541: Cardinal Contarini came, Philip Melancthon, John Calvin. But Regensburg too came to nothing: both sides insisted on magnifying their differences rather than seeking links that would bind them together.

When the new pope, Paul IV, agreed to call a council to Trent in 1545, it was already too late. Both sides had decided on force.

Charles was forty-seven when he rode at the head of the imperial forces against the Protestant princes of the Schmalkaldic League, but he appeared far older. Prematurely aged, his face creased with pain and anxiety, tormented with gout, he had to be borne by litter part of the time, only with enormous effort drove himself on. Of his victory at Mühlberg he said, "I came, I saw, God conquered."

He had the illusion that he had won the peace, had settled the religious quarrel.

But gray as death, a doomed conqueror, he appears in the great painting Titian did of him in Augsburg that summer, in black armor, lance in hand, a specter-warrior in a somber, forbidding landscape.

8. Brothers' Quarrel

> So great a prince as you *must* only conquer.
> Defeat is the ultimate crime.
>
> *Mary to her brother Charles*

SINCE THEY HAD first met as boys on the road to Valladolid thirty years before, Charles and Ferdinand had managed their fraternal partnership smoothly. Together they had presided at imperial diets; together they had ridden out to battle the Turk; side by side they had knelt on Maundy Thursday to wash the feet of twelve paupers in memory of Christ's act of brotherhood. Back and forth across Europe their messengers had scurried, carrying the long, detailed letters to one another that made their joint rule possible. Since 1531, when Ferdinand had been crowned King of the Romans, he was his brother's official successor as well as Regent of the Empire.

Suddenly at Augsburg in the summer of 1550 the two Habsburg brothers faced each other in a bitter quarrel across the council table over whose son was to inherit the imperial crown. Both had sons, born within weeks of each other in the year 1527: Charles's son, the Infante Philip, in Spain, and Ferdinand's son, Archduke Maximilian, in Vienna.

When Charles believed he had successfully reconciled the two sides of the religious quarrel with his Interim agreement of 1548, he had turned his thoughts to a master plan for the future of the Habsburg realm. The core of the plan was to be the creation of a federation of German states, with the imperial crown a hereditary possession of the Habsburgs. Such a plan would give a degree of stability to the emperorship and to the *Reich,* which the venality of the election and the jealous power of the German princes had prevented.[1]

His own son, Philip, reared in Spain, a Spaniard through and through, was of course to inherit that kingdom. To bind his brother Ferdinand's family closely with his own, Charles planned to marry his elder daughter, the Infanta María, to Ferdinand's son, young Maximilian. It is clear from an early will that Charles originally intended to bestow the Netherlands on the young couple as a dowry.[2]

Gradually Charles changed his mind and his plans. Ever since his wife's death all his love seemed to be focused on this only son of his, a son who appeared to be all a father could want—agreeable, obedient, devout, well behaved.

Meanwhile, his nephew Maximilian had been living for some years at his court, and Charles did not like what he saw of him. Unlike Philip, young Maximilian was lively, gay, pleasure-loving, a bit wild in his ways, and he had showed far too frank a curiosity and interest in the heretical Protestant doctrines.

Gradually Charles concluded that Philip should get everything: not only Spain and its vast colonies, but Italy, Sicily, the Netherlands —even the imperial crown. Charles might marshal a host of logical arguments to back up his decision; the truth was that a father's blind love for his son moved clearly through the blueprint.

Maximilian was dispatched to Spain to marry his cousin María and to act as Regent of Spain in the absence of Prince Philip. Philip was brought north from Spain for a first acquaintance with his future realm. His journey through Italy, Germany, the Netherlands, was a long series of celebrations, of feasts, tournaments, entertainments, Joyous Entries. But the frail, unsmiling youth with the proud, cold bearing, who spoke little French, no Flemish or German, who had none of the easy bonhomie of his cousin Max nor his father's grave and perfect courtesy, failed to win many friends in the north. He had none of the Habsburg love of sports, nor the fine horsemanship that had always won for his father the quick acclaim of the crowd who judged a king by the way he rode. Wine made Philip sick; he was unhorsed by a too-rough jousting partner and knocked unconscious in the lists.

Neither his aunt Mary, Regent of the Netherlands, nor his uncle, King Ferdinand, was attracted to Philip.

So that, when Charles and Ferdinand sat down at the council table in Augsburg in the summer of 1550 to iron out the problem of the succession, it was almost inevitable that the discussion would end in catastrophe.

All his life Ferdinand had acquiesced to his elder brother, all his life followed gracefully and cheerfully where Charles led. Now, to Charles's intense anger and astonishment, Ferdinand balked, refused point-blank to sign an agreement that would pass over his own son, Maximilian, for the imperial succession.

Neither argument nor reason would move him in the slightest. Ferdinand had always assumed that the imperial crown would eventually pass from himself to his own son, who had grown up in the German lands, who spoke their language, knew their problems and their ways. When Ferdinand argued that Philip did not know the Germans and Germany, while Max was known and liked, Charles retorted that neither had Ferdinand known Germany when he had gone there in 1521, yet he had succeeded in making himself a popular ruler.

Behind the closed doors of the council chamber in the Fugger Palace the brothers' quarrel raged that summer of 1550. Recriminations flew back and forth between the two. Both, stubborn, certain of being right, held fast to their views. It was clear that the German princes backed Ferdinand's view; they disliked Philip and announced they would never again vote for a Spaniard.

Abruptly Charles broke off the discussions at one point, declaring that both had best reflect before speaking any further.

Ferdinand dispatched an urgent messenger to Spain to bring his son Max to Augsburg to lend his support. Charles sent to the Netherlands for his sister Mary to back his view:

For I can assure you [he wrote to her] that I can do no more without collapsing. And be sure that I have never so much felt nor feel anything that the dead King of France did to me or that this one would like to do as I have felt and feel in regard to the manner in which the King our brother deals with me.[3]

Mary responded as she had always responded to her brother Charles, to whom she gave the deepest loyalty of her life. A middle-aged woman, she did not hesitate to mount horse and, accompanied only by three dauntless ladies of her suite and with the Bishop of Cambrai to protect them, Mary made the journey across the wintry, snow-bound roads from Binche in the Netherlands to Augsburg, arriving in twelve days—a journey that ordinarily took a stout rider eighteen.

She arrived on New Year's Day of 1551 and plunged at once into the vortex of her brothers' quarrel. Young Max had meanwhile arrived in December to take his place by his father's side. Hour after hour, day after day, the debate raged behind locked doors. The two cousins,

Philip and Max, glowered at each other; the two fathers, Charles
and Ferdinand, refused to give in. Rumors of the Habsburg rift
spread through the town, though the family made a point of dining
together in public on Twelfth Night and hearing together a concert
by Ferdinand's famous choir.

The contrast of the two cousins, Philip and Maximilian, aroused
sharp comment among the onlookers—all in Max's favor.

In spite of all Mary could do to reconcile her brothers, the quarrel
continued through January and February. Charles was so angry that
he declared himself ready "to burst with rage"; he became ill with
a fever; he could not bear even to look at his nephew Max. Mary
used all her tact, all her gifts of persuasion to restore family harmony.

At last, in March of 1551, Ferdinand gave in and signed an agreement by which he promised to support Philip for the imperial crown,
after which Philip agreed to support Max to succeed him—an unlikely
event, since both princes were the same age. The crown was then to
rotate between the two branches of the house of Habsburg.[4]

Charles left Augsburg at the end of that summer of 1551, tortured
by gout, the dregs of the quarrel still bitter in his mouth.

The French envoy had described him not long before:

. . . creeping through his room, supported by a staff, with bent
back, snow-white hair, deadly pale, and with beardless lips.[5]

Now sunk in melancholy, he lay gout-ridden in the Innsbruck palace.
Sometime during that winter unpleasant rumors began to reach him
of treachery among his allies. From the Netherlands his loyal sister
wrote warningly that her spies noted ominous troop movements along
the French border; she had heard too that Maurice of Saxony had
turned traitor, allied himself with the French, and was even now pre-
paring to march against Charles.

In a deep inertia of depression and pain, Charles refused to believe
it. Suddenly word came to Innsbruck that the rumors were true, that
Maurice of Saxony was even now in Augsburg with his army, pre-
paring to swoop down on Charles.

Summoning all his strength, Charles set out with a handful of re-
tainers on the road to the Netherlands to gather an army to his banner
again. It was too late. A courier brought word that the enemy lay directly ahead, and Charles had to return in haste to Innsbruck.

On the night of May 19, a night of wild gale and rain, Charles was
forced to flee from the approaching Protestant army. He was in pain

too great to sit a horse. Accompanied by two gentlemen only, with a pair of servants and his barber, he was carried in a litter across the snowbound Brenner Pass. He recalled later that as he fled across the mountains that night he met two Protestant emissaries who promised if he would but heed their offer, all the Protestants of Germany would join him against the Turk until he entered Constantinople as the victor. Had he heard that siren promise earlier he might have listened. Now he replied that he wanted "no more realms, but only Christ Crucified," turned and plunged on into the night.[6]

A day or so later Maurice and the French entered Innsbruck, ransacked the imperial palace. "I have no cage big enough for such a bird," shrugged Maurice when he found the Emperor gone.[7] A little later, in Passau, Charles's brother Ferdinand signed the humiliating peace.

One last time Charles marched into battle. The French had seized Metz, the imperial fortress that had guarded the western borders of the Holy Roman Empire since medieval times, together with Toul and Verdun. Marshaling a last ounce of will power, Charles headed an army to retake Metz. He failed. Defeated and broken, he returned to the Netherlands in January of 1553.

He left his brother Ferdinand to deal with problems as best he could. The seamless coat was rent. At the Diet of Augsburg in 1555 a religious peace was made which gave each prince, great or small, the right to enforce the religion of his choice on his territory.

Charles roused himself for one last political and matrimonial *coup*. In England the elder daughter of Henry VIII, Mary Tudor, had become queen, and it was now Charles's plan to wed his son Philip to her and make him King of England as well as all else. To the plain and aging spinster Charles addressed love letters for Philip in his old gallant manner; his gout was so severe that his sister had to hold the pen. Philip agreed to the match though hardly with enthusiasm: "As a son ever obedient, it is not for me to have any other will," he wrote to his father.[8] He was provided with a dowry of sixty thousand pounds to sweeten the match for the English, and the wedding took place in London in July of 1554.

Not long after, Mary Tudor was announcing to the world that she expected a child, a miraculous heir who would save England for the Catholic faith. The child, however, refused to be born; it soon became clear that she bore within her no Habsburg heir but the seed of death.

9. *Exile*

A TERRIBLE SENSE of weariness, of impotence, of failure possessed Charles.

The Holy Empire, for whose keeping he was accountable to God, had been shattered. Two immense hostile camps confronted each other in a divided Christian world, while the Turks kept pressing farther into the heart of Europe.

At fifty-five Charles was an old man, worn out, in pain so great he could barely open a letter or sign his name. In those last years he would often kneel for hours in a room hung with black, or he would sit alone, silent, brooding, sometimes breaking into tears without speaking.

In May of 1555 word reached him in the Netherlands that his mother, that lost soul of Tordesillas, had died at last in Spain. Charles told friends that at the hour of her death he had heard her voice calling him. The strange bond that joined mother and son was finally severed.

He resolved now to lay down his crowns.

In October a respectful gathering assembled in the Hall of the Dukes of Brabant in Brussels, the very hall where Charles had knelt as a boy of fifteen, full of pride and hope, to take into his hands his first high office. Gathered here now were his Knights of the Golden Fleece, the nobles of the land, his faithful courtiers and servants, his son Philip, his sisters Eleanor and Mary, the widowed queens. His brother Ferdinand was not present.

Charles entered, leaning on the arm of a young friend, Prince William of Orange. His face was deeply lined, his hair quite gray.

His voice shook as he told those gathered to hear him that he had come to abdicate his thrones, to give away the kingdoms that had so long been in his keeping. He spoke of his weariness, of the interminable journeys he had made by land and by sea:

I have made frequent voyages—nine times to Germany, six times to Spain, seven times to Italy, ten times to the Low Countries, four times to France, in peace and in war, twice to England, twice to Africa—in all forty voyages.[1]

No other sovereign had journeyed so often, so far.

He declared that he had never willfully wronged any man, and if he had done so unwittingly he asked forgiveness. He had striven all his life, he said, "not with the ambition of holding yet more lands," but for the good of his states.

If I give way to tears, gentlemen, do not believe that it is on account of the sovereignty of which I am stripping myself at this instant. It is because I must leave the country of my birth and say farewell to such lieges as I had there.[2]

A sigh like the wind through a convoy of great sailing ships went over his listeners as he spoke those words no emperor had ever spoken before. When he finished speaking, the deep silence was broken from time to time by a stifled sob.

He asked that the imperial insignia be removed from the walls of his apartment. "The name Charles is enough for me," he said.[3]

Yet the last journey to which he now looked forward ardently had to be postponed, because there was not enough money to pay his servants and dismiss his household. At last in August of 1556 he took ship for Spain with his two sisters, Eleanor and Mary.

Freed at last from a lifetime of duty, he would try if there might yet be a drop of sweetness in the bottom of the cup. He had had a house built for himself close to the monastery of San Geronimo de Yuste in central Spain. It was difficult to reach. The old man had to be carried in a chair across the mountain passes:

I shall travel no other way in my life but the way of death [he said], and it is not too much that a place as good . . . as Yuste cost such a price to reach.[4]

The life he had chosen was not strictly ascetic; it was the self-exile of a contemplative, deeply spiritual man, but a prince too who had lived long in the Renaissance world. Precious Flemish tapestries hung on the walls of his pleasant house; deep-piled Persian carpets softened his footsteps. In his wardrobe inventory were listed sixteen quilted silken nightshirts. Mules brought fresh oysters and crabs packed in

nettles all the way from the Atlantic to his inland table. The Netherlands sent liver pies, partridges, smoked salmon.

He took his clocks and his astronomical instruments with him, and
his favorite books, bound in red velvet with silver corners—St. Augustine, Caesar, Machiavelli, and the charming romance, *Le Chevalier
Delibéré*, which Olivier de La Marche had written.

His strictly male court of fifty persons included his body physician,
his secretary, William van Male, who read aloud to him while he
dined, his jester, Perico, and his clockmaker, Juanello. It was Juanello
who visited him first each morning. After his devotions and breakfast
Charles would putter over his hundred clocks. Though he worked
for hours on them, he could never make any two run together for long.
"Clocks are like men," he muttered once to Juanello.[5]

In the last summer of his life a remarkable child came to perform
the duties of page for him, a lively boy of thirteen, with bright blue
eyes and an engaging manner. His name was Gerónimo—Don John in
history; he was the child of Charles's middle-age, born out of a casual
liaison in 1544 with a girl of Regensburg named Barbara Blomberg.
It may have puzzled the old Habsburg that this bastard child, with
only half the complement of kingly blood, had so much grace and
intelligence and high spirits—more, far more, than his single grandson
and legitimate heir, Don Carlos, child of Philip II and his first wife,
whom Charles had seen briefly in Madrid.

On the last day of August in 1558 Charles attended a requiem
service for his wife. He asked to have her portrait brought to him,
the one his friend Titian had painted, and he gazed long at the serene
face with its gray-green eyes and golden hair. Next he asked to see
his favorite Titian, the "Gloria," in which he and his wife and children were painted kneeling in clouds before the Blessed Trinity. Presently he turned to his physician, trembling, and said, *"Malo me siento"*
—I feel ill.

He did not leave his bed again. His last word was a sigh, in Spanish,
"Ay, Jesús!"

IV

Austrian and Spanish Cousins

1. Ferdinand's Family

FOUR MONTHS before Charles died at Yuste, his brother Ferdinand succeeded to the imperial crown.

Ferdinand had been conspicuously absent from the abdication scene in Brussels. The breach between the brothers had never really healed. A week after his abdication, however, Charles had written his brother an affectionate letter, telling him how painful it was not to have the consolation of seeing him again before his last long journey:

> But wherever I may be you will always find in me the same brotherly and warm affection that I have always felt toward you, joined with the inner wish that the friendship binding us one to another will continue between our children, which I will further so far as my strength avails; and I am certain you will do the same, not merely because blood kinship demands it, but because it will further also our common interests.[1]

The delightfully practical note of that last line would be the key to Habsburg policy for a century and a half; those common interests would shape European history. The two branches of the house of Habsburg—the Spanish branch founded by Charles and his son Philip, and the Austrian branch by Ferdinand and his sons—would straddle Europe like a dynastic colossus, the right leg in Madrid and the left in Vienna.

Cunningly, at the very end of his sovereignty, in those last days in Brussels, Charles's long slender hand reached out to manipulate the future of his clan.

He commanded his daughter María and his nephew, Archduke Maximilian, to journey from Vienna to Brussels in May of 1556, and there plans were made to betroth the couple's eldest daughter, Archduchess Anna, a child of seven, with Philip's son, Don Carlos.

It mattered not if the two fathers hated each other. Across the years, as Charles foresaw, the two Habsburg branches would subordinate personal feelings, their jealousy, suspicion, dislike, to maintain a close alliance, intermarry so often that only a genealogical map could trace the tangled net of familial relationships.

That bitter succession quarrel in Augsburg, like so many family quarrels, proved to be pointless: when the time came the electors would make their own choice.

Ferdinand, who stepped into Charles's place now as Emperor, was of very different temper from his elder brother.

Though his early childhood had been deeply enmeshed in his parents' somber tragedy, he showed no visible trace of it in his personality. He had been born in Spain in 1503, of his mother's distracted misery and deepening insanity. Juana had left him behind when she returned to the Netherlands; he had not seen either of his parents until 1506, just before his young father's death. A small boy of four, Ferdinand had gone along on that grim funeral journey across Spain behind his father's body, had lived for a time with his mother in the prison-castle of Tordesillas, until his maternal grandfather, the King, managed to spirit him away.

In spite of that somber beginning, Ferdinand had grown up a cheerful, sunny, outgoing child, with no discernible morbidity or melancholy in his nature.

Considerably handsomer than Charles, with fine, dark eyes, reddish hair and beard, he could still be recognized as a Habsburg by the prominent underlip and chin. Like the rest of his family he adored music, was a keen sportsman and hunter. Full of quick enthusiasms, curious, gay, fond of people, Ferdinand had much of his grandfather, the first Maximilian, in his temperament. Lacking Charles's patience and cool reserve, Ferdinand could flare up quickly; a contemporary called him "a powder keg that could explode at any moment."[2]

When Charles had appeared in Spain in 1517, Ferdinand had gracefully accepted a younger brother's place in the scheme of things and sailed away to the Netherlands to complete his education. The Spanish themselves had been less acquiescent; some of the rebels in 1521 demanded the return of Ferdinand, their native prince, to rule over them.[3]

When in that week of crisis in April of 1521 at Worms, Charles had divided his inheritance with his younger brother, Ferdinand had taken his way almost at once southward to Linz in the Austrian crownlands, for his marriage with Anna of Hungary. Though the lands

Charles had bestowed on him were somewhat less than had been promised, Ferdinand accepted the division equably; indeed, he was so pleased over everything that when he wrote his aunt, Regent Margaret, on April 17—momentous date in Protestant history—he did not even mention that Luther had appeared that day before the Diet, only that he had lands of his own now to rule and would set out soon for his wedding.[4] We may glimpse the eighteen-year-old Ferdinand as he appeared just then, merry and light-hearted, riding through the flowering Danube country in May to wed a princess whom he had never seen.

The two princesses, Anna of Hungary and Ferdinand's young sister Mary, the child brides in the famous Vienna wedding of 1515, had been waiting six years in Innsbruck to grow up and be claimed by their bridegrooms. Indeed Anna had not even known for sure to whom she was married until December of 1520, when an envoy appeared in Ferdinand's name, together with one from King Lajos of Hungary, to perform the proxy rite. The two princesses in jewels and glittering gala gowns had knelt dutifully in the Innsbruck church for a blessing, then lain down on gold-draped ceremonial beds in the great hall of the palace, while their husbands' ambassadors in velvet and satin, each with one leg bared, lay beside them in the cheerful symbolism of a marriage consummation.[5]

Now at last, at Whitsuntide of 1521, Anna and Mary had ridden to Linz to meet Ferdinand, and in Linz a true wedding took place. Ferdinand had intended to accompany his sister Mary to the Hungarian border, where she was to be met by her bridegroom, Lajos, but affairs of state drew Ferdinand back to the Netherlands, and Mary journeyed on alone to Budapest.

Ferdinand's household in Innsbruck—the family spent much time also, later on, in Prague and Vienna—was a gay and lively one, and that curiously chancy political marriage his grandfather Maximilian had engineered turned out beautifully. Ferdinand called Anna "after God my greatest and dearest treasure," and his marital fidelity in the Europe of Henry VIII and Francis I was the talk of courtly society. He took his wife along on most of his journeys. When one of his advisors remonstrated about the added expense—for, like Charles, Ferdinand was always short of money—he retorted that "it is better to spend money on one's lawful wife than on whoring."[6]

Ferdinand was away at the Diet of Speyer in 1526 when Anna awaited the birth of her first child in Linz. She wrote how miserable and lonely she felt when he was not with her, and how overjoyed when he sent word that she might join him as soon as she was well enough after the birth.[7]

Fifteen children were born to Ferdinand and Anna, of whom twelve—nine daughters and three sons—lived to grow up, a precious political capital unmatched by any other royal household in Europe. The cosmopolitan Habsburg heritage had a yet more international flavor, for Anna's mother had been a French princess and her father a Polish Jagellon.

The children were strictly and carefully brought up under their parents' watchful eyes. The cardinal legate Aleander called them "an angels' choir," declared they were all handsome, clever, and well mannered.[8] The boys might approach their father—who had been crowned King of the Romans in 1531—only with proper courtly etiquette, head bare, hat in hand, standing in his presence until he nodded permission to be seated. A note still remains in Anna's handwriting addressed to one of her daughters' governesses:

> Give them a piece of black bread . . . and let them bite on it, and if they are thirsty give them a sour wine or thin beer; if they do not want to drink it, bring them a pitcher of water.[9]

Ferdinand, whose education in the humanist vein had been supervised in Spain by the Cardinal Ximénez de Cisneros and in the Netherlands by Erasmus, took great pains with his own children's education. He insisted that his girls as well as his boys read the classics, and that all his children learn several languages. The throne heir, young Archduke Max, was particularly bright and had no difficulty in mastering seven.

The whole family enjoyed music together. The children were taught to sing and play instruments; Ferdinand's beautifully trained choir and orchestra traveled along on all the King's official journeys. Short as he might be of money most of his life, he never stinted on the wages of his *Cantorey knaben*, as the singing boys appear in court accounts.[10] Some of the family instruments—a beautifully carved cittern, and a group of curious dragon-shaped shawms that were probably used for masked balls—still remain in a Vienna museum.

And though daughters were an expensive commodity in any sixteenth-century household since they required dowries, Ferdinand was quick to defend his nine girls:

> Princes must welcome daughters [he wrote once] even more gratefully than sons; for sons may tear apart the family state, while daughters bring helpful friendships and in-laws.[11]

Ferdinand set to work promptly when the girls were barely in their teens to marry them off where such friendships would be useful—in Italy, in Germany, in Poland. The Regensburg Diet of 1546—with all Germany teetering on the brink of the first Protestant-Catholic war—must have been an anxious and solemn meeting in most respects. But for the Ferdinand family it was one long wedding feast; four daughters were betrothed or married off in that single summer.

2. The Turkish Scimitar

FROM THE DAY he took up his inheritance, Ferdinand's problems had been nearly as many and as vexing as his brother Charles's had been. He had come to Austria a Spanish prince with a foreign wife, speaking barely a word of German, surrounded by Spanish councilors who had not hesitated to line their pockets with Austrian money, as Charles's Burgundian advisors had done in Spain.

He was painfully short of money and experience. His grandfather, Emperor Maximilian, had left his Austrian lands saddled with debt; even his seven bastards had appeared on Ferdinand's doorstep demanding to be provided for.[1] Social and economic ferment, such as had sparked the *Comunero* and *Germanía* revolts in Spain, boiled up in Austria in the 1520s in a revolt of the Estates and in the Peasants' War.

But all these problems dwindled in importance beside the one overriding anxiety: the threat of Turkish invasion.

Immediately after his accession in 1520 Sultan Suleiman had declared war on Hungary, on the pretext that a messenger sent to announce his accession had been rudely treated by the Hungarian court. The summer of Ferdinand's marriage, in 1521, the Turks had moved swiftly up the Balkans, laid siege to Belgrade. With its capture the road to Hungary—and even Vienna—lay open to their onslaught.

While Ferdinand sent repeated warnings to his brother Charles, asking for money to raise an army, Charles—engaged just then in his first war against the French—had none to spare; instead, he besought Ferdinand to send troops to aid the imperial army in Italy.

The Turks, meanwhile, took time out to capture Rhodes, then turned once more to the invasion of Europe. In April of 1526, Sultan Suleiman set out from Constantinople again, this time with an army of more than a hundred thousand—"sufficient to exterminate the world," a Venetian merchant wrote home from Budapest.[2] In May the Turks took the great fortress of Peterwardein that guarded the Hungarian border; their grand vizier boasted that it was "a mere mouthful, just enough for breakfast."[3]

Ahead of the army rode squadrons of Tartar irregulars, tough, undisciplined horsemen who scoured the countryside like swarms of angry locusts, burning, looting, carrying off thousands as prisoners, to be sold in the slave markets of Asia and Africa. Again and again Tartars raided within the Austrian borders; in 1524 Ferdinand wrote his aunt Margaret that the Turks had just carried off four thousand persons from his lands.[4]

The backbone of the Turkish army were the spahis, the cavalry corps, and the janissaries—tough, well-disciplined troops made up of boys chosen for their strength and intelligence from captured Christian villages, and trained to be fanatic Moslems. A contemporary witness, Bishop Paolo Giovio of Nocera, writing to the Emperor Charles, declared that the Turkish soldiers were vastly superior to the Europeans because they were totally obedient, because they were fearless in the face of death, believing that the death of each man is already written in the stars, and finally "because they live without bread and wine, and often rice and water are sufficient for them."[5]

Hungary was ripe for disaster. Ever since the death of Matthias Corvinus, when the great Hungarian magnates had chosen as his successor the weak King Vladislav as "a king whose beard they could hold in their fists," the country had been tragically, fatally disunited. The greed and self-interest of the nobles was such that when Pope Clement VII sent money for Hungary's defense, one of the papal ambassadors wrote back to Rome that "if Hungary could be rescued by means of three guilders, it would be impossible to find three men willing to make such a sacrifice for their country."[6]

Rich as were the great magnates who owned most of the land in Hungary, the young King Lajos was so poor that, according to the Venetian ambassador, "sometimes there is nothing to cook in the kitchens . . . and the court sent out a servant to borrow fourteen ducats. . . ."[7] His Habsburg bride, Mary, had outfitted him with a decent wardrobe out of her own purse.

Now, with the Turks at their borders, there were no generals; there was no national army; there was no money to raise one. The most powerful of the magnates, János Zápolya, Voivode of Transylvania, who had set himself up as a rival to King Lajos, had gathered an army of his own.

Again and again Lajos wrote his brother-in-law, Ferdinand, begging for help. On July 15, 1526, he wrote again, reminding Ferdinand that should Hungary fall, the Austrian crownlands would be next.

In August, just as Ferdinand was appealing to the Diet in Speyer for help, a last messenger arrived from Lajos to say that his kingdom was in deepest danger. Ferdinand dispatched the messenger to Charles in Spain; since the road through France was closed because of war, the courier would have to travel first to the Netherlands, then by ship to Spain. Ferdinand begged his aunt to put the messenger on the earliest departing ship, "in which you will give the King of Hungary, the Queen and myself a singular pleasure," he wrote.[8]

In Hungary Lajos had gathered together a makeshift army, perhaps twenty thousand, and marched south to meet the Turks. In desperation he had named the leading clergyman of Hungary, Archbishop Tomory, commander in chief, though Tomory had begged the King with tears in his eyes not to saddle him with such a fearful responsibility.

On August 29, a perfect cloudless summer day, the Hungarians—mostly young, eager nobles, dreaming of great deeds of daring—drew up in battle order on the wide plain of Mohács. Deathly pale in his tent, Lajos stood while officers of his bodyguard set the gilded helmet on his head, helped him mount his heavy charger.

Drawn up in a thin, broad front on the plain, the Hungarian riders waited while the burning August sun beat down. At three in the afternoon the first Turks appeared. The Hungarian trumpets blew a huzza, and the troops raised their battle cry, "Jesus! Jesus!"

As the Hungarians rode boldly to the attack with their lances drawn, three hundred Turkish cannon chained together moved forward with deadly, impenetrable force. Behind the cannon, like a wall of steel, a Turkish army twenty times outnumbering the Hungarians, moved steadily on. In the slaughter that followed, nine tenths of Lajos' army lay dead on Mohács plain. In Hungary next day there were twenty thousand new widows—among them, the young Queen Mary, Ferdinand's sister.

Lajos had not even had the luck to fall in battle. As a heavy cloudburst drenched the blood-soaked battlefield, he had been persuaded to leave the massacre and flee under cover of the storm. His chamberlain had ridden to safety across a little stream, but as

[12] Emperor Rudolf II, by Hans von Aachen. (*Kunsthistorisches Museum, Vienna*)

[13] Emperor Ferdinand II. *(Bildarchiv des Österreichische Nationalbibliothek, Vienna)*

[14] Emperor Ferdinand III. *(Bildarchiv des Österreichische Nationalbiblio-othek, Vienna)*

[15] Emperor Leopold I, engraved after a painting by Daniel Preisler. (*Bild-archiv des Österreichische Nationalbibliothek, Vienna*)

Lajos started to follow, his wounded charger stumbled, reared up, and plunged over backward, burying the King in his heavy armor in the mud of the stream bed.

Wildly victorious the Turks fanned out over Hungary, setting village after village to flame, putting men to the sword, sending women into slavery.

Suleiman noted tersely in his diary for the day after Mohács:

Massacre of two thousand prisoners.[9]

Fleeing from Budapest, Queen Mary wrote hastily to one of her brother's ministers:

. . . unfortunately the Turk has totally defeated my lord and husband in battle, and many people have been killed, as regards his dear person, I am told that he got away. God grant that it be true.[10]

Only too soon word of Lajos' death reached her in Bratislava. Ferdinand wrote her consolingly from Innsbruck:

And I beg you, Madame, as a lady of great heart, comfort and console yourself, for in adversity does one know a person's virtue.[11]

He reminded her immediately of where her duty lay: according to the marriage treaty, that famous contract their grandfather had drawn up and sealed with the double wedding, both Hungary and Bohemia were to come to him if Lajos died without heirs. Ferdinand promised to put his body and his worldly goods at his sister's service, but she in turn must help him save what he could of Hungary.

Both countries were rightfully his—but they would be his only if he could seize and hold them.

The Bohemian Estates, according to an ancient privilege, elected their king; Ferdinand found himself facing powerful rivals for the crown of St. Wenceslas—the King of France, who had lately allied himself with the Turks and would do anything to circumvent an increase in Habsburg power, and the Duke of Bavaria. But Ferdinand got himself elected, and he was crowned in Prague in February of 1527.

Things in Hungary were more difficult to manage. János Zápolya, who had held his army aloof and intact during the disaster of Mohács, called together the Hungarian Diet, and, with support from the French king, got himself elected and crowned King. A meagerly attended rump Diet called by Mary elected Ferdinand; not until he took the field in July of 1527 and marched an army to Budapest without a shot being fired did the nobles and clergy give him their support.

Ferdinand was crowned King of Hungary, but it remained an empty title; for years Hungary was a bone worried by rival dogs.

In May of 1529 Sultan Suleiman set out again from Constantinople to penetrate Western Europe. He allied himself with Zápolya, retook Buda, and within days had set up his tents under the walls of Vienna. If the Viennese did not surrender, he promised to level the city and sow the site with salt and ashes.

All Europe waited with bated breath; if Vienna fell, no one knew where the Turks would stop. During that summer of the siege Tartar outriders—sackmen, the Austrians called them—reached nearly to Regensburg in their plundering.

Inside Vienna barely sixteen thousand persons defended it against a besieging army many times that number—estimates run as high as 250,000. For three weeks the city held out valiantly, while Turkish sappers tried to push their trenches and mines under the walls. Among the cannon turned against the Turks were the artillery pieces that Ferdinand's grandfather, the first Maximilian, had collected, called "his saucy wenches," nicknamed affectionately Fair Dido, Fair Helen, Fair Medea.

On the first day of the siege the Turks had sent the arrogant message: "On the third day we will breakfast within your walls." As the days passed, and attempt after attempt failed to breach the ramparts, the city commander, Count Niklas Salm, sent word: "Your breakfast is getting cold."[12]

Suddenly, almost miraculously, the Turks struck their tents and retreated. The next day, October 17, snow began to fall. Seven hundred miles from Constantinople, dependent on the countryside for food and forage for their horses, the Turks had not dared risk the coming of winter.

Three years later, in 1532, Suleiman once again came perilously close to capturing the Habsburg crownlands. Charles and Ferdinand prepared to lead an international army against him, but once again the Turks retreated back into the Balkans, leaving only the sackmen to carry on a ruinous, year-in, year-out border war against the Austrians.

In the end Ferdinand bought a truce of sorts, paying the Sultan a yearly tribute of 30,000 ducats.

3. *Heresy in the Family Circle*

IN OCTOBER of 1538, in Ferdinand's household in Linz, a small family drama took place that was duly reported by the papal envoy in Rome. Before the whole household gathered to hear the announcement of new appointments to the official staff, Ferdinand delivered a wrathful discourse that sent his servants away shaking in their boots. Should anyone, he warned, speak to any of his children about the Lutheran heresy, or try to lead them from the true way, off would go his head without so much as a hearing. Turning to his oldest sons— young Max, who was eleven, and Ferdinand, nine—their kingly father warned *them* that if they did not immediately report such a dreadful misdeed, they would get a sound thrashing. King Ferdinand was not a man to mince words.[1]

But apparently the damage had already been done. Only shortly before, it had been discovered that his sons' tutor, a German named Wolfgang Schieffer, was not only a Protestant but a pupil and friend of Luther himself, and that he had freely discussed the heresy with his young royal charges. Schieffer had been instantly dismissed, but no doubt he had left behind a seed or two in the bright, quick mind of the older boy.

The whole problem of combating the spread of Protestantism in the Empire had devolved chiefly on Ferdinand. The new sect had spread so rapidly throughout the German-speaking lands that already in 1523 Ferdinand wrote his brother in Spain that "scarcely anyone in the Empire had not been affected by it," and that he worked "from break of day until one hour of the night in council . . . to find a way to halt the great evils that I see appearing."[2] And a month or two later he reported sadly to Charles that in many parts of the Empire people had eaten meat throughout Lent, and in other parts of the Empire priests and monks had married.[3]

Yet on the basic questions of religious doctrine Ferdinand was even less intransigent than his brother Charles. He too was quite willing to work out a reasonable compromise, but he feared the political consequences of a split, especially in his lands—Austria, Hungary, Bohemia—which had neither a common language nor common traditions to bind them together. And he saw clearly that Lutheranism was used as a tool by the German princes to reduce the central imperial power.

He had already had a taste of heresy within the Habsburg family and had dealt with it swiftly. He and his brother Charles had been unpleasantly surprised to see their young sister Ysabeau take Communion "in both kinds"—both bread and wine in the Protestant manner—in Nürnberg in 1522. This was serious enough, but when their sister Mary not only entertained Lutheran discussion but had a book dedicated to her by Luther himself, Ferdinand reprimanded her severely. Mary defended herself, in the end drew back into the religion of her fathers; when she was appointed Regent of the Netherlands, she agreed to leave behind her in Austria nearly her entire court, for all were suspected of Lutheran leanings.

But far more serious was the case of Ferdinand's eldest son, the throne heir Archduke Maximilian. Young Max had a lively, inquiring mind; he was gay, friendly, fond of people. But he was also clearly an adolescent rebel, and the crop of wild oats he set about sowing drove his royal father nearly to the end of his wits.

He drank more wine than was good for him. He took up with an assortment of disreputable companions. He got with child a noble lady of his mother's suite, the Countess Anna of East Friesland, who bore him a daughter while he was still in his teens.[4] But none of Max's youthful peccadilloes could compare in gravity with his leaning toward Luther's doctrines. He read Lutheran books, he listened to Lutheran preachers, he had a whole circle of Protestant friends.

When Max was sixteen, he and his nearest brother, Archduke Ferdinand, were sent to the court of their uncle, the Emperor Charles, to take lessons in imperial statecraft, and to acquire some of the polish of the more cosmopolitan court. When the Schmalkaldic War broke out between the imperialists and the Protestant princes, young Max had the command of a cavalry detachment.

Quite obviously Max and his uncle had not got along very well. Emperor Charles, gout-ridden, irritable, worried, was in no state to overlook his nephew's errant ways, the less so since his own son Philip, far away in Spain, was from all reports thoroughly docile, agreeable, devoutly Catholic, indeed even believed to be chaste up to the day of his wedding.

Meantime, in January of 1547, Max's mother, Queen Anna, bore her last child, a little girl named Johanna. But Anna herself, no longer a young woman in the reckoning of that day, died in childbirth. The pitcher had gone to the well once too often, and Ferdinand, after twenty-six years of happy marriage, was left alone, a sorrowing widower, to cope with his whole array of family problems.

The free-and-easy life of an army camp was not designed to improve young Max's morals, and only a month after Anna's death King Ferdinand had to address to his son a letter full of the severest reproaches:

> Maximilian! [his father wrote in Latin] I hear with the greatest sorrow that you are not behaving well at the Emperor's court, and that you have kept few of the promises you made me with a handclasp when we made our peace together, that you would turn over a new leaf.

> . . . From what I hear you are drinking great quantities of strong wine, and have shown signs of drunkenness, and it appears that whenever you were free you have been most often drunk.

> My son, you know that you must keep away from this vice . . . and that it is harmful for your soul, your honor, your health. . . .

> I hear too that you frequent frivolous company, and that these people, and your bear, and your music are your whole surroundings.

Ferdinand scolded him for avoiding the company of honorable and upright persons, whose conversation would be edifying; he berated him for reading dangerous books. His bitter pain over his son's misconduct broke out in the last words:

> I am so afraid that after my death you may become dissolute and shameless. I warn you that you must avoid lewdness![5]

Another rebuke might have been added, had his father known. A few days earlier, when Max got word of his mother's death, he had stolen out of camp in the middle of the night, without anyone's leave, and started in the direction of home, only to be pursued and brought back by a chamberlain of his uncle.

On the whole it seemed best if the marriage planned between Max
and his cousin María was hurried along. Accordingly the betrothal
was announced in the spring of 1548 at the Interim Diet in Augsburg,
and Max was dispatched to Spain for the wedding. His uncle, Emperor Charles, had another reason for sending his nephew off; he had
arranged for Maximilian and María to act as Regents in Spain while
he brought his own son Philip north and presented him as his successor
in the Netherlands and the Empire.

Young Max was a far from eager bridegroom. That Interim Diet of
1548 was one of the gayest of the sixteenth century, as the notary
Sastrow testified: banquets, dancing, giddy goings-on in all the noble
houses until all hours of the night. Princes spent all their money entertaining and had to turn to the local bankers for loans.

It was with reluctance that young Max turned his back on the
frolicking and journeyed southward over the Alps, his only company
the strait-laced Spanish household his uncle had hand-picked to accompany him and report on his behavior. Both his father and his
uncle had lectured him sternly before he left. His father's warning
on chastity had the effect such parental lectures usually have. In the
town of Mittenwald on the way to Genoa to take ship for Spain,
Max stopped long enough to "capture several women," as a bill of
payment indiscreetly kept by one of his secretaries testifies.[6]

On board ship he sickened of what was presumed to be quartan
fever. Ill he remained through the autumn, and ill he stood up for
his wedding on the day of his arrival in Valladolid, September 13.

The cousins, Max and María, made a strangely assorted bridal
pair, and evidently things did not go too well at the beginning, according to Max's court marshal, who kept the Emperor Charles informed of everything, including the fact that there seemed to be a
delay in the consummation. María, like the daughters of many great
men, had the misfortune to inherit her father's looks. She was plain,
long of face, heavy jawed. She was exceedingly devout, deeply serious,
certainly not a very lively companion for Max. But María was clever
enough to study ways of making herself agreeable; by and by the
marriage improved. By spring word reached Charles that his daughter
was pregnant.

While Max dutifully attended Mass four times a week in Spain and
kept all the fast days, he was miserably homesick. Over and over
again he wrote his uncle from Spain asking for permission to come
home.

Meanwhile his father and uncle were involved in their bitter succession quarrel in Augsburg and by the end of the summer of 1550 had reached a complete impasse. In September Max got the urgent message from his father to board the first available ship and hasten back to Germany to lend his support in the family dispute. By December he had reached his father's side in the Fugger Palace.

There had never been much sympathy between Charles V and his nephew, Maximilian; from now on they hated each other thoroughly. Charles could not even bear to look at Max. The nephew declared later that if his uncle "could have drunk him up in a spoon he would have done so."[7] Bitterly Maximilian wrote his brother-in-law, Albrecht of Bavaria:

> God grant that His Majesty [Ferdinand] will one day stand up to His Imperial Majesty [Charles] and not always show himself so chickenhearted as he has hitherto. . . . My father will not see how unfraternally and how falsely His Imperial Majesty is treating us.[8]

Certainly relations between the two brothers and their families were strained to the utmost.

Smarting with disappointment over the outcome of the succession quarrel, Max took ship again for Spain in the summer of 1551 to bring his wife and children home. He wasted no time in Spain but collected his family and was on his way again within a month.

The young archducal family landed in Italy, and in the city of Trent found the Council in progress that was to have solved all the problems of the religious schism. Max and María were lavishly entertained in Trent; they crossed the Alps to reach Innsbruck and spend New Year's Eve with María's father, Emperor Charles.

It was only a few days after this, on a hunting party in the mountains with his brother-in-law, Duke Albrecht of Bavaria, that Max was taken violently ill, so ill that he thought himself on the point of death. He was certain that he had been poisoned, and he blamed it on a Genoese soup he had eaten in the palace of Cardinal Madruzzo in Trent, who, it was hinted, might have arranged it to please Max's cousin, Philip. Ferdinand lent credence to the rumor of poison by dispatching antidotes to his son in all haste.[9]

Not until late spring had Max recovered sufficiently to continue his journey. In April he made his grand entrance into the city of Vienna. It was clear that his sojourn in Spain had not been a total loss: the whole city turned out to honor the popular young prince, his Spanish wife and children, and to admire the procession of exotic animals he had brought with him—fine prancing horses, of a color and kind never seen before, beavers and wolves and bright-colored parrots, and, most awesome of all, the first live elephant seen in Vienna. For months after local poets were busy addressing odes to the Archduke's elephant.

4. Archduke Ferdinand and Philippina Welser

KING FERDINAND, having married off his rebellious oldest son, pondered various brilliant matches for his favorite, the middle son, charming and handsome Archduke Ferdinand. He sent an envoy to the English court in 1553 to query the possibility of a marriage with the new English Queen Mary, only to learn that a betrothal had just been arranged between Queen Mary and his brother Charles's son, Philip.

In the midst of his father's enthusiastic matchmaking, young Ferdinand showed a curious reluctance. The talk of princesses and queens and kingdoms made him uneasy and evasive.

The truth was that he had fallen passionately and irrevocably in love with a girl of common birth. He had met Philippina Welser in Augsburg during the Diet of 1548. Daughter of a wealthy banking family, Philippina was one of the legendary beauties of the century. She was said to be so fair that when she drank red wine it could be seen passing down her throat,[1] and of so modest and virtuous a disposition that many years later on her deathbed she "would not permit the least uncovering of her body, but drew her sleeves over her arms down to her wrists."[2]

Nothing could change, however, the fact that she was not of royal blood and no possible match for an archduke. They may have been married by a secret rite as early as 1548; it is known that in 1557 a private ceremony was performed by King Ferdinand's own court chaplain and witnessed by an aunt, Katherina von Loxen. Father Ferdinand—now Emperor—was in a towering rage when he got wind of it. He refused to recognize the marriage; he would not even see Philippina. When babies were born to the couple, they had to be whisked away by a helpful aunt, then deposited on the castle doorstep to be discovered by a servant, and raised by Philippina as foundlings.[3]

Some years later, in 1561, Philippina came *incognita* to Emperor Ferdinand's court at Prague. She gained an audience with him under an assumed name, and begged him to intercede with her harsh and unreasonable father-in-law. Moved by her beauty and her tears, Emperor Ferdinand promised to right her wrongs, whereupon she revealed herself as his own daughter-in-law and got his recognition of their morganatic union.[4]

That young Ferdinand held to Philippina devotedly, and that his family could not abide her, is clear from a happening in the Turkish War of 1566, when young Ferdinand led a troop of his own by the side of his brother Max. During the autumn, when the weather turned bad and plague broke out, young Ferdinand suddenly broke camp, unceremoniously and without warning; taking his own people with him, he departed, leaving his brother to carry on the war without him.

Understandably annoyed, Max wrote to his brother-in-law, Albrecht of Bavaria, that Ferdinand was certainly "bewitched," *verzaubert*. The trouble started, declared Max, when his brother got several letters from *der losen Brekin*—the bitch, as Max uncourteously referred to Philippina—

> . . . afterward he had no rest either by day or by night, only fell into a fit of melancholy, even into a fever. . . . So off he goes. . . . I wish the bitch were stuck in a sack and no one knew where. . . . God forgive me.[5]

Young Ferdinand inherited the province of Tyrol by his father's will. Happily and quietly he lived with Philippina in the Castle Ambras near Innsbruck, where he gathered together a wonderful collection of armor and the knightly weapons that were just then passing into disuse—perhaps the finest collection of its kind in the world today.[6] When he stood proxy at the wedding of his niece Elizabeth to young Charles IX of France, he got for his pains one of the most exquisite artifacts of Renaissance times, the famous golden salt cellar of Benvenuto Cellini.

Philippina collected too. In the National Library in Vienna today are two great folio volumes of her favorite recipes and medicinal remedies, mostly written in her own delicate hand: how to make an almond torte, how to cure the headache and stomach cramps, how to concoct an oil from May blossoms that is helpful in relieving the pangs of labor.[7]

5. Young Maximilian Gives In

THE RELATIONS between Emperor Ferdinand and his eldest son remained anything but peaceful. It was true that young Max had settled down into the role of respectable husband and father. Every year there was another christening in his household, just as there had been in his parents': María bore him in all sixteen children, of whom nine survived to grow up.

But his religious views continued to give his father constant anxiety and grief. Both father and son were hot-tempered, both stubborn; like many another father and son, neither could see the other's view, and each was perfectly certain he was right.

Elsewhere in Europe the religious temper had grown increasingly intolerant; both sides grew more rigid and harsh after the midpoint of the century. Before his death in 1546 Luther had cried that "Reason is the devil's bride." By 1558 Pope Paul IV had put all of Erasmus' works on the Index of forbidden books. The Calvinists condemned the free-thinking Miguel Serveto to be "burned with his book to ashes." Three hundred Protestant martyrs died in the 1550s under Mary Tudor.

Ferdinand was neither dogmatic nor harsh in his approach to religion, but he was first and last a politician. He had worked out the religious compromise contained in the Peace of Augsburg, but it was equally clear to him that the survival of the Holy Roman Empire depended on the strengthening and renewal of the Catholic Church. When his brother Charles had abdicated the imperial crown in his favor in 1556, the Pope at first refused to recognize it, and in 1558 declared flatly that he could not recognize as Emperor a man who tolerated heresy in his own heir.

With the division of the Habsburg inheritance, the Austrian branch remained for nearly a century the poor relation of the Spanish branch. To hold the Turks at bay, to maintain imperial strength, to pay the yearly tributes, required the financial and moral support of Catholic Spain. Ferdinand could not understand why his son Max did not perceive the political necessities of the situation.

In 1551 Ferdinand had invited monks of the new Jesuit order to Vienna, where Protestantism had made such inroads that half the pulpits were vacant. The smooth-operating Jesuits quickly found ways to appeal to the theater-loving Viennese. They founded an excellent school, and out of it a theater in which both religious and classical drama was performed on a stage so elaborate that twelve quick changes of scenery were possible. During successive epidemics of the plague the Jesuits were often the only physicians who remained in the city; the "Peruvian bark" they brought from Spain, the chief remedy against pestilence, was locally known as the "Jesuits' powder."[1]

But Max failed to be won by his father's arguments. He infuriated his father's confessor, a Jesuit named Canisius, by bringing his own Protestant preacher, Sebastian Pfauser, to Vienna, to preach even in that most imperial sacrosanct, the Augustiner Church adjoining the Hofburg. Pfauser's sermons, often two and three hours long, drew enormous crowds, who packed into the church so tightly that on one occasion when young ladies took fright, began to scream and to faint, the palace guards could not get through the crowd to help them.[2]

Young Maximilian continued to read Protestant books, to correspond with Protestant princes, even to choose as his children's tutors men who were doubtful Catholics.

Father and son were at constant swords' point. On Corpus Christi Day of 1558 Max refused to walk in the procession, excusing himself on the grounds that he was not feeling well and could not walk. Then, said his father, go on horseback. "I can't," said Max. "Go at least three or four steps for appearances' sake," demanded the father. "I can't," the son replied. "Why not?" asked the father. "Because I will not." "Why will you not?" "Because I will do nothing against my conscience, and in these ceremonies I find nothing to the honor of God."[3]

In the end neither father nor son walked in the procession.

In 1555 Ferdinand had added a bitter codicil to his will, addressed to his eldest son:

I would rather see you dead than that you should join the new sects.[4]

Cousin Philip, now King of Spain, did not help matters any by sending over a Franciscan monk to be his sister María's confessor and to report back to him all that went on in the Vienna palace. Max complained, not without reason, that his wife's Spanish household spied upon him. But when the Spanish ambassador approached María and suggested that she separate from her heretical husband, María flatly refused. She was a devout Catholic and Spanish through and through—in all her years in Austria she never learned to speak fluent German—but she loved her husband, had already at this time borne him nine children; she would not leave him.[5]

Matters finally reached a crisis. Ferdinand warned his son that he could not be elected King of the Romans except as a Catholic. He threatened to eliminate Max from the succession and pass the crown to his next son in line, Archduke Ferdinand.

Max bowed to political necessity. The Protestant chaplain Pfauser was dismissed; Ferdinand threatened to "throw him into the deepest well in Vienna" if he appeared on the scene again.[6] Max gave his oath in 1562 before his father and his two brothers that he would live and die in the Catholic faith. His peace was made. He was elected his father's successor.

On an evening in November of that year, 1562, father and son rode into Frankfurt for the coronation.

An English witness to the event declared it went off "wyth suche pomp and triumph as ys thought not to have ben done the lyke at any tyme synce the great Charles," and described the procession of forty thousand by torchlight into the city, princes, nobles, knights-at-arms, "everi man . . . a lyttel bugl horn about his neck hunterlyk and in his hat an oken branche wyth faded russet leaves as token of wynter."[7]

Afterward, at the magnificent state banquet in the town hall, Ferdinand and Max sat alone at the head table under a rich canopy, "no more persons but they two," says our informant, all other princes and nobles at lower tables, strictly according to precedence.

In the square outside a conduit ran white wine and red, free to all comers. "A mighti great ox rosted whole" offered a vast assortment of delicacies, the body stuffed with "dyvers sortes of other small footed beasts and fowles of sowndri kyndes, as falow deare, hare, kyd, lam, pygg, conye-squirrel, swan, goose, heron, mallow, phesant, pecock, capon, partridge, quayle, pigeon, woodcock, curlew, plover, snyt, blackburd, thrush, lark, greatest fowl to left unto the veari wren and tytmouse . . ."

6. *Last Days of Ferdinand*

IN THE END Ferdinand had won the succession quarrel against his dead older brother. His rebellious son had submitted too: he had Maximilian's oath that he would live and die a Catholic. Back in his palace in Vienna in 1563, Ferdinand might now take peaceful leave of the Empire.

If he looked back over his life in those last months, he might well have felt content. His had been a difficult reign as archduke, as Regent of the Empire, as King, as Emperor, harrowed by anxieties, galled by insoluble problems. But in the nearly half century since he had come from his boyhood in Spain to take up his rule in the German lands, his accomplishments had been remarkable, all considered. It was true that his nephew Philip held by far the greater and richer half of the Habsburg inheritance. But Ferdinand had the Austrian crownlands, Bohemia, Hungary—what he could hold of it. He had staved off the Turks from his lands, partly by arms, mostly by bribe. His daughters were usefully married in Poland, in Bavaria, in the Netherlands and Italy; three were in convents praying for his soul.

He had grandsons growing up in the palace he had built near the Hofburg for his son. With his sons and his sons' sons the Austrian branch of the Habsburgs would be firmly established in central Europe.

He had made Vienna his city, set his mark on it; it would serve Habsburgs very well as a capital. The threat of the Turks still hung over the city, shaped its thoughts, its plans, its destiny. Painstakingly the Viennese had rebuilt after the Siege of 1529, mended and strengthened the walls that girded the town like a mailed fist. Shut in by those walls, smaller far in area than sixteenth-century London yet nearly as densely populated, Vienna had grown upward—as high as one dared build in that day—and downward, where layer after layer of cellar honeycombed the city like a second, subterranean world.

Set in a ring of wooded and wine-terraced hills that sloped down to the Danube, the town would always keep a flavor of the country. "A garden of roses, a place of delight, a veritable paradise," the German Wolfgang Schmelzl, who came to teach at the Scottish monks' school, rhapsodized in 1550.[1] In every dooryard flowers bloomed; so many caged songbirds hung in the windows and in the arcaded courtyards that an Italian visitor, Antonio Bonfini, declared it was "like walking in an enchanted forest."[2]

Emperor Ferdinand too had had a Renaissance garden laid out near the palace, and every morning in summer fresh roses were brought to his bedside that he might smell them on waking. The Hofburg, a square block of stone with four bristling towers, built square against the city walls, more fortress than palace, had been refurbished after the Siege. Ferdinand had added a grace note in the bright red-and-gold Renaissance gate that opened on the inner courtyard. In the Gothic Court Chapel his Singing Boys performed the divine service like angels; his choirmaster, Christian Janssen Hollander, was a gifted composer. "No end of musicians and instruments here," Schmelzl had written of Vienna.[3]

In the great hall of the Hofburg, where his dead wife Anna as a little girl of twelve had curtsied to her first tentative bridegroom, Emperor Maximilian, in the famous wedding of 1515, Ferdinand entertained guests, carried on wit combats with his jester.

And in the treasure chambers he pored over his collection of beautiful and curious things. Everything interested Ferdinand; all sorts of things stirred his curiosity, as they had his great-grandfather, Friedrich III: the stars, numbers, the lines in people's faces, fossils, strange plants and animals. He collected fine sculpture and painting, rare jewels, antique coins, old manuscripts. In the treasure chamber lay the agate bowl believed to be the Holy Grail, that had come from Burgundy in his grandmother's dowry, and the unicorn sword of Charles the Bold. The Aztec treasures that Cortes first sent back from Mexico for the wondering eyes of the Spanish court, including the fantastic feathered headdress of Montezuma, had been presented to Ferdinand by his older brother.

Ferdinand had alerted his ambassadors to look for curious and precious things in their travels. The gifted Flemish scholar Ogier Ghislain de Busbecq, whom he sent as envoy to Constantinople, threw himself into his collecting mission with a fervor that must have delighted his imperial master. He sent back "whole wagonloads, whole shiploads of Greek manuscripts" for the imperial library in Vienna.[4] When he returned to Vienna it was with a tame ichneumon, six female camels, several fine thoroughbred horses, and the first tulips and lilacs seen in the Western world.

Ferdinand's three sons shared their father's passion for collecting, for music, for learning. Young Max had returned from his sojourn in Spain with a taste for exotic plants and animals and for the fine swift Spanish horses that had been bred for centuries in Andalusia from native stock mixed with Arabian and Moorish blood. Max had brought back some of those fine horses of Spain, and with his brother Karl established stud farms at Kladrub and Lipizza. A little later near the Hofburg he set up a riding ring where the Lipizzan stallions could be trained in the difficult disciplines needed to fight in the warfare of the century, when the life of a princely rider, even the outcome of a battle, might depend on the horse's ability to extricate his master from close fighting.

Within months after his son's coronation old Ferdinand sickened of a wasting fever. In his last illness Maximilian was the best of sons: he visited his father morning and evening, and sometimes during the day between meetings of the privy council, he slipped in to tell his father all that had passed. He arranged for musicians to come and play "sweet chamber music" in his father's rooms at certain hours, which seemed to be the best medicine for the old sick emperor.

The doctors had failed to diagnose his illness, which was consumption, until nearly the end; the court physician, whom everyone considered a fool, kept promising the invalid that he would be out of bed and riding out to hunt in no time.

Day by day Ferdinand grew weaker. On July 25, 1564, when his son Max came for his evening visit, he found his father so weak that he was persuaded only with difficulty to take two eggs in his soup. Young Max had hardly left his father to go to his own apartments when a servant fetched him back in all haste to the sick man's bedside.

He found his father's confessor leaning over the old man, speaking softly: "Ferdinand, my brother, fight like a true knight of Christ, and be true to your Lord even unto death. . . ."

Ferdinand died quietly, as he had wished, without any struggle. His councilor Zasius wrote to the Duke of Bavaria that the Emperor's life went "as a little candle flickers out in a lamp."[5]

By his testament the Austrian lands were divided among his three sons, instead of passing intact to the eldest, a division that weakened the power of the ruler, who had too little to support the estate of Emperor.

Ferdinand's fine collections of art and *curiosa* were specifically commanded not to be shared, but to remain in the treasury of the Hofburg and pass undivided to the eldest son.

7. A Spanish Education

THE AUTUMN BEFORE Ferdinand's death, the autumn of 1563, Maximilian's two oldest sons, Rudolf and Ernst, had been sent from Vienna to Spain to complete their education at the court of their uncle, King Philip II.

That their father had been reluctant about allowing them to go seems likely from the fact that he postponed their departure repeatedly. But the pressures had been great. Philip had invited, then urged their coming. Their mother, María, who remained a Spanish princess to the end of her days, joined with her brother in urging it—not only that her sons might taste the climate and culture of her own native land, but so that any taint of Protestant heresy they might have absorbed in Vienna could be effectively erased in the strict Catholic court of Madrid. Probably their grandfather, old Emperor Ferdinand, had urged it as well—but for dynastic more than religious reasons. Philip had only a single son, Carlos, and rumor already wafted to Vienna the news that Carlos was far from a sturdy, hopeful specimen of a throne heir. It was not impossible that all the vast Habsburg lands might once more be reunited under a son of Maximilian as they had once been under Charles V.

To accompany his two sons to Spain, Maximilian sent a trusted friend and advisor, Adam von Dietrichstein. His duty was not only to watch over the boys' welfare and studies, but to pursue in the Spanish court the long-projected scheme for a marriage between Philip's son, Don Carlos, and Maximilian's eldest daughter, Anna.

The Spain in which the young Austrian cousins passed the crucial years of adolescence was just then flowering into the great uncanny brilliance of the Golden Century. It was Spain at the pinnacle of world power, of Don John and the Battle of Lepanto. It was the Spain of St. Teresa and St. John of the Cross, of Cervantes and El Greco. Determined to crush heresy in his kingdom, Philip had firmly shut his country's door on dangerous outside influences, but within that narrow intellectual room thought and creation took fire with the color and intensity of the flames that were consuming heretics in the great autos-da-fé in Seville and Valladolid.

Young Rudolf, Maximilian's oldest son, was already a serious boy, inclined to fantasy and to melancholy. The years in Spain marked him deeply and for life.

From Barcelona where he met their ship, Philip took his nephews immediately to visit the somber Benedictine monastery on Montserrat, a wild and lonely mountaintop, where St. Ignatius Loyola, at the turning point of his life a few years before, had laid his soldier's weapons on the altar and changed his fine garb for sackcloth.[1]

The boys passed their first summer in Spain with their uncle and his pretty third wife, the French princess Elizabeth of Valois, at their enchanting summer retreat of Aranjuez. Philip was taken ill with fever; it was with Elizabeth and their aunt Juana that the boys rode out hunting. In the evenings Philip would have them come to his bedside to dance for him, or to show him their skill at fencing.

Of their cousin, Don Carlos, they saw nothing for some months. When Dietrichstein tried to press inquiries about the projected marriage of Carlos and the Archduchess Anna, the replies became evasive. Once someone dared whisper in his ear, "Better wait until you see him."[2]

But at the end of the summer, in August of 1564, Philip brought his nephews to meet his son; together the three young Habsburgs rode into Madrid.

What impression Rudolf and Ernst formed of their strange cousin is not recorded. Carlos was nineteen at this time; his manner toward his young Austrian cousins apparently was friendly enough. But the reports Dietrichstein sent back to the Viennese court on Carlos were ominous.

Philip's first wife, a Portuguese princess, had died giving birth to the boy, and Carlos had been deformed from birth. He was hunchbacked, pigeon-breasted; his whole right side was less developed than the left and the right leg considerably shorter. He spoke in a high-pitched, girlish voice, and stuttered badly. Probably he suffered also from tapeworm, for Dietrichstein wrote, "He has no desire or

interest except to eat, and he eats so greedily . . . that when he has
eaten he eats again from the start. . . ."[3]

Philip had given great care and thought to his son's education, but
it seemed to go for naught; in some way the mind was as warped as
the body.

The year before Maximilian's sons arrived in Spain, Carlos had
been established at Alcalá, near the great university, in the hope that
the fine intellectual air of the town would benefit his brain. In
Alcalá, however, he met with a serious accident. He had stumbled
down a flight of dark stairs—on the way, rumor said, to keep a
rendezvous with a gardener's daughter. He suffered a great gaping
wound in the head from his fall; erysipelas set in; he was bled again
and again. His head swelled to enormous proportions and he lost
his sight completely.

Philip hurried to his son's bedside in Alcalá, bringing with him the
gifted physician Vesalius, who could, however, do nothing for the
boy. A surgeon performed a trepanning, in vain. Philip called in
quacks, including a Valencian Moor with two magical ointments.
Carlos raved on in delirium.

Finally the Franciscan monks brought in their most precious relic,
the shrunken body of the holy Fray Diego who had died a hundred
years before, and still in its shroud the corpse was laid in the bed of
the sick prince. The body was declared to be in a most remarkable
state of preservation and even, according to the monks, exhaled at
this time "a most delicious odor." That night Carlos dreamed of the
blessed Diego, and from that time his pulse steadied, he gained
strength gradually from day to day.[4]

When he returned to Madrid, however, his conduct grew increasingly erratic. Combined with a kind of shrewd animal cunning was a
wild, unpredictable temper, and all sorts of rumors floated about of
acts of violence and sadism. He threatened courtiers with his dagger;
he had a fondness for beating horses and young girls. Of relations
with his father the Venetian ambassador reported succinctly, though
perhaps with dubious accuracy, "The father hates the son, and the
son not less the father."[5]

In his reports to Maximilian, Dietrichstein omitted rumor, reported
only his own observations and facts he believed to be true. When the
court painter Coello was commissioned to do a portrait of Don Carlos
for the prospective bride in Vienna, Dietrichstein noted carefully
that certain artistic liberties had been taken. In the portrait the
youth was cleverly posed so that the hump was disguised under his

velvet cloak, the legs do not appear to be uneven; only the strange wolf eyes gaze out of the long pale face with a kind of alert cunning and bravado.

While Philip's Austrian nephews bent over their schoolbooks in the Madrid palace, practiced their fencing, helped serve Mass on Sunday, the drama of the Spanish throne heir hurried to its tragic conclusion.

Carlos' probable impotence had long been a subject of discussion in the Spanish court. While Dietrichstein kept pressing for some definite word on the marriage of Carlos and Anna, Carlos underwent a "cure" at the hands of physicians and apothecaries, then a final "test," after which Carlos himself hurried to Dietrichstein to boast that he had passed the test, "and five times over."[6]

Plans moved ahead for the Austro-Spanish marriage. King Philip and Emperor Maximilian would meet in Innsbruck with their children, then proceed together to Brussels for the marriage. But a new Spanish envoy appeared in Vienna, there was further evasion and procrastination. Maximilian, exasperated, lost his temper completely, declaring that his daughter Anna "was not getting any younger," and that "from anger and disappointment" the girl "did not eat for a whole day."[7]

The last events of Don Carlos' life were closely bound up with the fierce revolt that had broken out in the Netherlands in the 1560s, where intransigent Philip was determined to stamp out the Calvinist heresy. Don Carlos dreamed of ruling over the Netherlands; he may have made overtures to leaders of the rebellion.

Philip apparently planned for a time to journey to the Netherlands himself, taking Don Carlos and his Austrian nephews. Ships were ordered and provisioned. But the spring of 1567 came and passed, and the summer. When the ships finally sailed, they carried, instead of a wedding party, twenty thousand troops under the Duke of Alva with orders to suppress the rebellion.

Don Carlos conceived wild plans to flee to the Netherlands. He sent out openly to borrow large sums of money, tried to enlist some of his father's friends, even his father's half-brother, Don John, in his plans.

Philip made one last trial of the boy's wits. He allowed him to preside over the state council in December of that year, 1567; Carlos turned all the business of the council upside-down. When one of Philip's gentlemen caught Don Carlos with his ear to the keyhole of his father's council chamber, he "got a fist in the face."[8]

Philip's apprehension for his son's sanity led him now to the most difficult decision of his life, and one of the most somber scenes in all history.

In January Philip returned from the Escorial, where he had spent Christmas, to Madrid, and went to Mass accompanied by Don Carlos, by his half-brother, Don John, and by his two nephews. It was remembered afterward that during that Sunday messages had flown back and forth between Philip and the Grand Inquisitor, Cardinal Espinosa.

That night as Don Carlos lay in bed an hour or so before midnight, the door of his chamber suddenly flew open. By the flickering light of torches shining down in his face, he saw his father all in black, with his intimate advisor, Ruy Gomez, and his confessor, all three somber and silent. Carlos started up crying, "Will Your Majesty kill me?" He perceived then that three servants had begun to nail fast the windows; his terror became greater; he fell on his knees and begged his father to kill him outright; he was only prevented by force from throwing himself into the fire that burned on the hearth.

From that moment the Spanish throne heir was dead to the world.

His young cousins never saw him again; his name was never mentioned in their letters. All through the courts of Europe the wildest rumors spread—that Carlos had threatened to kill his father, that he had been locked up for heresies. Philip announced briefly to the world that duty had forced him to take this painful decision.

To the Pope, Philip explained in a private letter:

> But since for my sins, it has been God's will that the prince should have such great and numerous defects, partly mental, partly due to his physical condition, utterly lacking as he is in the qualifications necessary for ruling, I saw the grave risks which would arise were he to be given the succession.[9]

In Vienna, where the news of Carlos' imprisonment had thrown the court into consternation, Emperor Maximilian said over and over again that he had "never in his life had such a desire to take the quickest way to Spain to visit the King and speak with him personally. . . ." He was certain, he said, that Philip could not refuse the proposals he would make.[10]

His brother, Archduke Karl, was dispatched to Spain, but before he had reached Madrid, the tragedy was ended.

In the burning heat of a Spanish summer, in 1568, Carlos was seized with a raging fever. He poured ice water on the floor of his prison chamber so that he might lie naked in it; snow was brought in great vessels to cool his bed. For days he ate only fruit, washed down with quantities of ice water. In mid-July he asked for a pasty; an enormous, highly spiced pie made of four partridges was brought to him, and he devoured it all. To quench his ferocious thirst he drank more than ten liters of water. He became violently ill; when the last Sacrament was administered, he vomited the Host. His last wish, according to Dietrichstein, had been to see his father; this was denied.

On July 24, 1568, it was announced briefly that the heir to the Spanish throne, the Infante Don Carlos, had "died of his own excesses."[11]

In the funeral procession his cousins, Rudolf and Ernst, walked behind the coffin where Don Carlos—"bones only under the garment" —lay wrapped in the Franciscan habit of his savior, Fray Diego.[12]

The rumor of poisoning—so frequent a rumor among sudden royal deaths in the sixteenth and seventeenth centuries—had much to feed upon in Don Carlos' case; people began to say openly that Philip had helped his son to death. More cautiously Maximilian wrote his brother-in-law, Albrecht of Bavaria, that one thing at least was certain: it would have been easy to prevent the death of a captive prince "by his own excesses."[13]

In Madrid one sorrow followed another. Philip's young queen, Elizabeth, grieved so bitterly over her stepson's death that the King had to forbid her tears. She was several months gone with child—a longed-for heir whose coming Philip hoped would replace Don Carlos. In early October she had swooning spells, was bled again and again, gave birth prematurely to a son. Mother and child died almost at once.

The Fugger correspondent in Madrid, relating this somber news to Augsburg, added the rumor already going the rounds in the Spanish court: that Philip would take the place of his dead son Carlos as bridegroom for his young Austrian niece, Anna.[14]

And so it turned out.

Two years later Archduchess Anna, a girl of twenty-one, "all milk and roses," married her uncle King Philip, more than twice her age.

Her two brothers, Albrecht and Wenzel, who were to change places with Rudolf and Ernst and in their turn receive an education in the Madrid court, escorted her to Spain. In Valladolid sister and brothers had a happy reunion with Rudolf and Ernst, whom they had not seen in seven years. On the same occasion Rudolf was betrothed to his tiny four-year-old cousin, the Infanta Isabella Clara Eugenia.

The following spring, when it became evident that a throne heir was on the way, Rudolf and Ernest were at last permitted to journey home to Vienna.

Years later Rudolf recalled that when word came to him that he might return home, "I was seized with such joy the following night that I could not bring sleep into my eyes."[15]

What effect Don Carlos' tragedy had on sixteen-year-old Rudolf is nowhere recorded; it is possible that his entire later life is a clue.

8. *Maximilian II, a* Via Media

MAXIMILIAN FOUND his young sons much changed after their long sojourn in Spain. He noted with deep misgiving the "Spanish humours" they had acquired, the air of supercilious gravity that so resembled their uncle Philip's, the cool and distant pride that did not promise to make the throne heir, Rudolf, very popular among the more sociable, free-and-easy German nobles.

The Venetian ambassador at the imperial court, Giovanni Corraro, declared that the Emperor Maximilian at once ordered his two sons "to change their bearing."[1] But a nineteen-year-old does not change his personality on his father's command; the "Spanish humours" remained. The Elector of Saxony, moreover, complained bitterly to Maximilian that "King Philip had administered an oath to his pupil [i.e., Rudolf] that he would always remain a good Catholic and after his father's death would persecute heretics with all his strength"[2]—a truth or a rumor hardly destined to win the friendship of the Protestant princes of Germany.

During the 1560s, while Maximilian's older boys had been absorbing the climate of their uncle's Catholic court, while religious attitudes all over Europe grew increasingly harsh and intolerant, in the lands under Maximilian's immediate rule, in Austria and Bohemia, the religious climate remained mild, astonishingly temperate.

In both the Austrian crownlands and in Bohemia, Protestants gained important religious concessions, to the alarm of his cousin, Philip, who had said that he would "rather lose all his lands than permit freedom of belief."[3] Once Maximilian explained to the papal legate—far from pleased with the young Habsburg's tolerant outlook —that he was "neither Papist nor Evangelical, but Christian."[4]

In fact Maximilian leaned toward Protestantism until the day of his death. He nearly succeeded in bringing about in his own domain that *via media* that his uncle, Charles V, had sought in vain; for a time in Maximilian's inherited lands there existed a degree of religious toleration not to be found elsewhere in Europe. The Venetian ambassador wrote in 1564:

> Here [in Austria] people have agreed to tolerate each other; in mixed communities the question is seldom asked whether anyone is Catholic or Protestant. . . . Protestants and Catholics intermarry without anyone being scandalized.[5]

Elsewhere in Europe violence was the order of the day. The Netherlands—which, but for Charles V's change of heart, might have come under the easy and tolerant rule of Maximilian instead of under Philip II—were torn now by the bitterest of civil strife, rooted in Philip's efforts to eradicate Calvinism. In October of 1568 the two great Dutch patriots, the Counts of Egmont and Hoorn, who only five years earlier had been guests at Max's coronation in Frankfurt, knelt on black cushions in the square in Brussels and laid their necks on the block.

And in Paris, a year or two after the marriage of Maximilian's pretty young daughter Elizabeth with the French King Charles IX, the streets ran with the blood of two thousand Protestants in the massacre of St. Bartholomew.

Maximilian could hardly bring himself to believe the news that reached him. In shocked disbelief he wrote to his friend August of Saxony:

> . . . it is neither right nor justifiable; religious matters will not be settled by sword nor by force but with God's word and by Christian agreement and justice.[6]

He got his son Rudolf crowned King of Bohemia, and, anxious over the imperial succession, called a Diet to meet in Regensburg. His health was deteriorating, though he was still a comparatively young man; he wanted to see his son crowned King of the Romans as soon as it could be arranged.

He had long suffered from gout, from heart attacks, from bouts of "kidney colic," quite possibly syphilis, that had been sweeping across Europe since the turn of the sixteenth century. His doctors advised him to dilute with water the strong Hungarian wines he loved to drink, in order to relieve the excruciating pains of the gout. "Yet it might still be borne," he wrote to a friend, "if only it did not grow worse."[7]

In the summer of 1576 Maximilian II set out for Regensburg with his wife and four of his children. On the way he was stricken ill—his doctors thought from eating too much fish, though a half-dozen doctors regularly stood by at each meal, watching every mouthful that reached His Imperial Majesty's mouth. In Regensburg he was ill again—this time, his doctors decided, from eating unripe fruit. He managed to open the Diet, to begin on the business of the meeting, when he suddenly fell unconscious—from the ice-cooled wine he had drunk in August, his doctors averred. He grew a little better, only to be taken sick again—from the pears and cherries he had eaten. His doctors were bewildered and dosed him with aloes.[8]

He failed to improve; a famous quack of Ulm named Magdalena Streicher brought a miraculous elixir she had concocted for the Emperor to try. What ingredients the wonder remedy contained were Magdalena's secret; it was probably not unlike the cure-all which the Danish astronomer Tycho Brahe prepared for Maximilian's son Rudolf a little later: to Venetian treacle was to be added "a single scruple of tincture of coral, or sapphire, or hyacinth, or a solution of pearls or of potable gold," the whole to be combined with antimony for all diseases curable by sweating.[9]

At first the Emperor seemed to grow better, then he took a grave turn for the worse. At the bedside of the dying man his whole family gathered to wrangle over his soul's health. His wife María on her knees at his bedside implored him to see the court priest; he replied that his priest "was in heaven." His sister, Ann of Bavaria, hurried to Regensburg to join in the pleas that her brother take the Catholic rites. His son Matthias, the papal legate, and the Spanish ambassador took turns arguing with the sick man. Maximilian replied that "he would think about it." The Spanish ambassador went even further and began explicitly, "I can see from your condition, Your Majesty, that it would be time—" Maximilian cut him short, "You are right, Herr Marquis, I have not slept well and would like to rest a little."[10]

He was forty-nine when he died. When the doctors examined his skull after death, they found it remarkably dry and warm, which they laid to his varied array of talents, "the great number of languages that he understood, the knowledge of so many things as well as the cleverness and skill that was so astonishing to everyone."[11]

Other sources declared that a "black substance as hard as stone was found in his heart."[12]

9. A Question of Breeding

THE MARRIAGE of Maximilian's favorite daughter, Anna, with the cousin he detested, Philip of Spain, had come about so that one more knot might be tied in the intricately looped cord binding Spanish and Austrian Habsburgs together for generations.

When they parted in autumn of 1570, father and daughter knew in their hearts they would never see one another again. In the company of her two younger brothers and of her father's gifted and entertaining friend, Ogier Ghislain de Busbecq, Anna journeyed to the Netherlands, thence by armed convoy to Spain.

Her marriage to the uncle more than twice her age took place in Segovia. At first it seemed that the whole frozen framework of Spanish court etiquette might melt under the impulsive, warmhearted good nature of the young Austrian bride.

The French ambassador wrote home indignantly of the informal manner in which the young queen had received him. She had not so much as offered him the upholstered stool that was his right by the rules of protocol, nor had she received him seated in dignity herself, but had chatted leaning casually against a wall.

And when the two small daughters of her dead predecessor were led in to be presented to their new stepmother, they had approached her as they had been carefully taught, to curtsy deeply and kiss her hands. Before they could perform the rite, Anna, who had grown up in a family full of younger brothers and sisters, snatched up both children and hugged them to her with kisses and sweet words. The little princesses were so astonished that they burst out "laughing and crying at once."[1]

For a time after Anna's coming there was brightness and frolicking even in the great palace-tomb, Philip's newly completed Escorial.

Anna romped with the two Infantas in the gardens, or sat conversing over fine needlework with her ladies. Or she might be glimpsed from time to time sitting beside her solemn, black-clad husband where he toiled over his mound of papers: Anna, the two little Infantas beside her, would be sprinkling sand on his signature.

Yet somehow, in the somber setting of the Spanish court, the radiance of youthful queens was too often quickly extinguished. Philip, not yet forty-five when he married for the fourth time, was elderly already, a dark suffering specter of a man, victim of gout and of the maleficent effects of a cure for gout he had taken.

His favorite pastimes were acts of devotion, especially the illumination of altars, when hundreds and thousands of candles and torches would be lighted at once to set one of the dusky Spanish churches glowing. Anna too began to devote herself to pious pursuits, especially to enshrining and honoring the relics of her favorite saint, Leocadia of Oviedo. On Holy Thursday, on the verge of a confinement, she "prostrated herself at the feet of the poor." Presently the French ambassador wrote to Catherine de' Medici—mother of the late queen—that Anna "hardly ever leaves her apartment, so that her court resembles a convent of nuns."[2]

Once—perhaps in a moment of compunction over the isolated existence of the young queen—Philip sent for the great Toledan actor Cisneros to perform for Anna and the young Infantas. Yet even that performance was not designed to bring smiles to their faces: Cisneros performed neither comedy nor the exciting cloak-and-dagger dramas of the day, but mystery plays based on the lives of saints.

In ten years of marriage Anna bore five children; four of the five children died one after the other, so that the young queen barely took off mourning before she must put it on again.

In 1580 occurred what was perhaps the very peak of Philip's life: the moment when he came into possession of Portugal and united for a last time the entire Iberian peninsula. Queen Anna, with the two Infantas and with her own little son, journeyed with her husband to the Portuguese border, where the ceremonies of union were to take place. In Badajoz the whole royal family became ill of a "grippe" that was just then epidemic; Anna was far gone in her sixth pregnancy; the court doctors dosed her with harsh purgatives and bled her mercilessly; the whole family recovered—save Anna. Her body was borne back to be entombed in the Escorial; Philip journeyed on alone to Portugal.

Anna's was neither the first nor the last in the series of intrafamilial marriages that wove so complex a mesh of relationships between the Austrian and the Spanish Habsburgs. Anna's grandfather, Charles V, had married his first cousin; Anna's father, Maximilian II, had married *his* first cousin. Indeed the inbreeding had begun long before, when on the Iberian peninsula the royal houses of Castile, of Aragon, of Portugal, ancestors of Charles's mother, the mad Juana, had intermarried closely to consolidate their interests against a common enemy—the Moors—and to insure a relatively peaceful succession.

And after Anna four more Habsburg brides married Habsburg bridegrooms within the space of a century. The pattern of those marriages was nearly always the same: the tearful farewell to home and family; the ceremonial journey across Europe in a glittering cortège of carriages, coaches, armed horsemen, baggage wagons; the *remise* or delivery at a border town into the hands of the bridegroom's people, and last good-byes to friends and country; and at last the ceremonial entry into her new country, and into the arms of a bridegroom she had never seen before.

One of the wisest men in Europe, Erasmus, in his *Education of a Christian Prince,* which became a guide in the training of young Habsburgs, argued against political marriages, urged his prince to seek a wife only "for her integrity, modesty, and wisdom." He railed against "the heartless effect on the girls themselves, who are sometimes sent away into remote places to men who have no similarity of language, appearance, character, or habits, just as if they were being abandoned to exile. . . ."[3]

Certainly life in the Spanish court—or in any strange court—must often have been intensely lonely for exiled princesses. And yet the tragedy of their lives was less that of their particular station and career than the tragedy of all women of their time: to lose children again and again to an early death, to succumb themselves, finally, to the mortal danger of childbirth. Of the five Habsburg brides who followed Anna, only one escaped death in pregnancy or childbirth.

The girl who followed Anna on the throne of Spain was again a kinswoman from Austria: Margarete, child of Maximilian's younger brother, Archduke Karl of Styria. Margarete crossed Europe in 1599 to wed Philip III, only surviving child of our Anna and Philip. From all accounts an attractive, lively girl like her predecessor, Margarete endeared herself quickly to her Spanish husband. In thirteen years of marriage she bore him seven children. Before the seventh birth she was beset by forebodings; her husband made light of them. She survived childbirth itself, only to be stricken with fever—probably the

deadly puerperal fever. Her doctors knew no other remedy save
bleeding. Margarete lost consciousness quickly, revived just long
enough to receive the rites for the dying, to speak to her confessor
of eternity. Weeping in his oratory, her husband cried out, *"Mi santa
muerta, yoç para qué vivo?"* My blessed dead one, what have I to
live for?[4]

Of the seven children Margarete left behind, one grew up to be
Philip IV; another, Maria Anna, crossed Europe from Madrid to
Vienna in a difficult, memorable wartime wedding journey to marry
the cousin who became Emperor Ferdinand III. *Their* daughter
journeyed back to Madrid a few years later, in 1649, to marry her
uncle, Philip IV. And finally *their* child, Margarita Teresa, the dark-
eyed, golden-haired Infanta who gleams out of the shadows in
Velasquez' great series of portraits, made the last Austro-Spanish
bridal journey from Madrid to Vienna in 1666, to marry *her* uncle,
Leopold I.

So far as may be judged from court gossip and from the observation of ambassadors, a surprising number of those marriages turned
out quite happily. Habsburg children were bred up to the expectation
of such a marriage of state; they knew nothing else and therefore
they made the best of it.

Within the context of sixteenth- and seventeenth-century power
politics, the Habsburg intermarriages were a logical, shrewdly planned
design of statesmanship. Their purpose, of course, was to insure that
the huge double realm would remain within the family; in default
of heirs on one side it could revert to the other. They were meant to
guarantee—as Charles V foresaw—the closest possible alliance between
two great areas of Europe which might otherwise have had no common bond: an alliance to fend off the Turk, to defeat heresy. They
meant, besides, that the two halves of the Habsburg realm would
continue to enclose France like a giant pincer.

So far as the possible consequences of inbreeding were concerned,
science as yet knew nothing to deter them. The Church, which forbade marriage within certain degrees of kinship, granted quick and
easy dispensations to princes. In fact the mystical belief in a divine
power of kingly blood—and the Habsburgs of all princely families
held most deeply to that assurance—meant that intermarriage among
them only intensified the potency of that precious ichor.

It is probably most astonishing that Habsburgs in both branches
survived so long that close concentration of genetic materials. In the
generation of Maximilian II two of Europe's great dynasties came to

an end: the Tudors and the Valois. Maximilian's sons had no legitimate heirs, and the crowns passed to his brother Karl's son. Still the Habsburgs held on and survived: in Spain until 1700, in Austria centuries longer.

10. The Court of Rudolf II

THE DARK HUMOURS from which Rudolf suffered since his return from Spain continued to deepen after his crowning.

The times too were strange, the skies as overcast and full of foreboding as the new Emperor.

In Vienna a mighty earthquake "shook the houses in the whole town and lifted the people bodily into the air." A lady of noble rank, being exorcised of devils by a priest in the Schotten Church, screamed out that she saw Luther burning in hell. There was terror in the city when a rain of blood fell near the Schotten Gate. (This turned out, however, according to the Fugger correspondent, to have been caused by a wicked servant cutting off an ox's tail to make him move faster.) The Jesuits drove a devil out of a poor maid, daughter of a witch, by giving her a drink of holy water. In the town of Dillingen a midwife named Walpurga Hausmännin confessed under torture that she had fornicated with a devil named Federlin, who required her to dishonor the Blessed Sacrament and to insult the Holy Virgin Mary, spitting in front of her and crying, "Shame, thou ugly hussy!" She had also slain many infants and used their tiny bones to produce hail.[1]

The smoke from the fires that consumed witches and heretics darkened the skies over all Europe. . . .

The plague came and went, and the Turks.

Rudolf rarely left the Castle Hradschin in Prague, withdrew more and more from the world. Taciturn, introspective, uncannily gifted in matters of art, of taste, of languages, he turned to the study of astronomy and magic, as his ancestor Friedrich III had done, and to the collecting of beautiful and curious things.

He gathered about him a fantastic assortment of astronomers, necromancers, artists, craftsmen, antiquarians. In his workshops skilled goldsmiths, enamelers, gem-cutters turned out artifacts of wonderful beauty.

In the imperial gardens the Danish astronomer, Tycho Brahe, set up his instruments for observing the stars—the most advanced astronomical instruments in that day—and set down with meticulous exactitude his measurements of the planetary movements. When Rudolf's heretic-hunting cousin, Archduke Ferdinand of Styria, banished Johannes Kepler from his province, Rudolf welcomed him and made him imperial mathematician. With Brahe's computations, named for their patron the Rudolfine Tables, Kepler laid down his theory of the elliptical movements of the planets, the basis of modern astronomy.

Strange tales drifted out of Prague, to be gossiped about the length and breadth of Europe. How tame lions and eagles and leopards walked about freely in the palace corridors. How Emperor Rudolf possessed a magic mirror that could foretell events in the future, and a magic magnet with which he could read the thoughts of persons even at great distances. How his mathematician Kepler planned a space ship to carry earth passengers to the moon.

Conjurers and alchemists stirred mysterious vats in the Emperor's magic kitchens, experimented with an elixir of life and with the philosopher's stone, with manufacturing artificial men and with resuscitating mummies. The English astrologer Doctor John Dee, who had set the date for Queen Elizabeth's coronation, came to Prague, and the sinister Edward Kelley, who was said to make gold "as fast as a hen will crack nuttes." He failed to produce gold for the Emperor, however, and was clapped into prison.

Rudolf's strange moods, his spells of anxiety and deep gloom, became more and more frequent during the 1590s and the early 1600s. Increasingly he was obsessed with the conviction that someone in his family planned to murder him. His friend, Tycho Brahe, who acted as all-around scientist to the Emperor, even prescribing for his gout, cast Rudolf's horoscope and assured him that a close relative would attempt to kill him, that it would be advisable not to marry.

Betrothed to his little Spanish cousin, the Infanta Isabella Clara Eugenia, before his departure from Spain, Rudolf postponed marrying year after year. His mother wrote from the court of Madrid begging him to marry, pointing out that her brother Philip's only son was exceedingly frail, and that the Infanta Isabella might be her father's heiress. Nothing mattered. One excuse after another Rudolf produced to procrastinate. In Prague he took as mistress the daughter of his court antiquarian, by whom he had a number of very strange children. At thirty-three the unlucky Isabella was finally wed to Rudolf's younger brother, Albrecht, with whom she ruled the Netherlands.

Although Rudolf had been betrothed to Isabella for twenty-nine years and had kept her waiting almost on the doorstep of the church for eighteen, he went into a frenzy of rage when he learned she had married his brother.

His brother Ernst died, and the next-younger brother, Matthias, became Rudolf's heir. Rudolf hated Matthias with a hatred that bordered clearly on the pathological.

Just after Rudolf had been crowned Emperor, Matthias had got himself involved in a deplorable international scrape. Ambitious but without gifts, Matthias had a perfect faculty for muddling everything he tried. In 1577, when the Netherlands was a wasps' nest of anti-Spanish intrigue, a group of Catholic nobles offered the regency to Matthias if he would come to the Netherlands. Without consulting his brother, Matthias threw himself into the plot with both feet. He let himself out of a second-story window in the Hofburg in his nightgown, so the tale went, blackened his face, and rode to the Netherlands disguised as a servant. But William of Orange and the group around him had not really wanted Matthias, but only to use the Habsburg name. Europe was treated to the not unamusing spectacle of an Austrian Habsburg intriguing against a Spanish Habsburg. The whole adventure ended in a fiasco. Matthias rode back to Vienna, his dreams of glory punctured, his pockets empty, to face his brother Rudolf's towering wrath.[2]

From that time on Rudolf took every opportunity to humiliate Matthias. While his other brothers were given responsible posts, Matthias was allowed neither money nor position, nor even given permission to marry. When he took a mistress Rudolf goaded him with his impotence because no children were born.

Meantime, around Rudolf in the Castle Hradschin the shadows of schizophrenia deepened. His melancholy, his withdrawal from the world, grew more marked. He moved in a nightmare world of fears. He kept his gold locked in chests; sometimes there was no food in the palace kitchens and even the servants went hungry.

Outside the imperial castle in Prague the world seemed to be whirling toward catastrophe. The Turks had again marched against Austria. In 1605 the Hungarians in Transylvania rebelled and set up their own kingdom under Stephen Bocskay. The Protestant-Catholic feud worsened; all Europe seemed to hover on the brink of war.

Rudolf paid little heed, went off to putter in his magic kitchen or pore over his collection of erotica. He refused to see foreign ambassadors, threatened one minister with a dagger, dismissed his faithful councilor Wolfgang Rumpf—who had been with him since his school days in Spain—and took as chief advisor one of his valets.

His own brothers had difficulty getting to see him on most urgent matters of state. Persons wanting an audience had to appear in the stables disguised as grooms; only there would Rudolf talk with a stranger. If anyone interrupted him at his work or his meditations, he would fly into a passion, smash everything at hand.

Once he tried to slash his own throat with a piece of broken window-pane.[3]

His brother Matthias had meantime gained an extraordinary ally in the person of the clever, fast-rising priest, Melchior Khlesl, who became his brain and hand. On Khlesl's advice the Habsburg archdukes, brothers and cousins of Rudolf, met in the Hofburg and bestowed the regency of Austria on Matthias, naming him head of the house of Habsburg. At the head of an army Matthias marched to the gates of Prague, forced Rudolf to sign over Hungary, Moravia, eventually Bohemia as well. Gnashing his teeth, Rudolf put his name to the deed of abdication, and hurled the pen to the floor.

He was given a generous pension, and left with possession of his castle in Prague and of the one crown nobody had the power to take from him: the crown of the Empire.

He died one morning in 1612 quite suddenly, just as his valet was handing him a clean shirt. It was said his heart had finally broken over the death the previous day of his faithful old lion and of the two pet eagles he had always fed with his own hands.[4]

His brother Matthias carried most of Rudolf's treasures back to Vienna, where one can see them in the museums today: the curious, surrealist-like paintings of Arcimboldo; the Bohemian crown jewels, marvels of the Renaissance goldsmith's art; exquisite vessels of amethyst, of onyx and chalcedony, of cunningly worked mother-of-pearl and gilded silver; beakers of rock crystal, one in the shape of a delicate long-legged crane; a bowl carved from an enormous twenty-six-hundred-carat emerald.

For a long time two of Rudolf's favorite possessions might be seen in the treasury of the Hofburg: the single fin of a mermaid, and a familiar spirit imprisoned in a bottle.

11. Matthias: Monarch of the Seven M's

AND SO AT LAST, in 1612, the despised younger brother arrived where he longed to be, Holy Roman Emperor, King of Bohemia, King of Hungary—an elderly man, nervous, insecure, gouty, determined now to do everything he had wanted all his life to do. He had come so tardily to sip the cup of power and pleasure—and it turned out he had so short a time to do so.

He had married the very instant he could arrange to do so, after Rudolf's abdication in 1611. Matthias had never even had enough pocket money, and now he spent lavishly. In the Hofburg he gave grand balls and banquets and festivals; musicians played, wine flowed, he danced too when his gout permitted. His wife—he had married a cousin, of course, Anna of Tyrol—was a serious, exceedingly pious woman, already past her first youth. She devoted most of her time to good causes, imported a new order of monks, the Capuchins, into Vienna, and with their help arranged a splendid crypt for herself and her husband, that extraordinary family tomb in the Kapuziner Church that holds the earthly remains of the Austrian Habsburgs. She kept a silver-tipped thong to lash herself for her sins, which could not have been many.[1]

No children were born to the imperial couple, nor did Matthias' younger brothers have children, so that the succession was to fall to a cousin, Archduke Ferdinand, son of Karl of Styria, the youngest son of old Emperor Ferdinand I.

Imperial power, in the meantime, was actually in the hands of Matthias' confessor and chief of counsel, the able and skillful priest Melchior Khlesl. As the Protestant-Catholic quarrel grew yet more bitter, two parties emerged close to the irresolute old emperor—a peace party headed by Khlesl, who counseled Matthias to move cautiously and leniently toward the dissident Bohemian Protestants, and a war party, headed by his cousin Ferdinand and his younger brother, Maximilian. When Khlesl opposed the choice of Ferdinand for the imperial crown, Ferdinand in a swift palace *coup* toppled the doughty cardinal. He was arrested on the stairs in the Hofburg itself, carried off through a secret passage to the city walls, and thence by a closed carriage to the Castle Ambras in the Tyrol.

Old Matthias, bedridden, helpless, was told of the downfall of his friend and favorite. At first he merely pressed the coverlet to his lips and said nothing. Later he was heard to mutter, "How much better if I'd been a happy private citizen instead of an emperor to whom nobody pays heed."[2] Two weeks later he gave a great family feast in the Prater and announced that everything was forgiven.

The storm in central Europe that had been so long a-gathering had broken even then.

A few months later, on a March morning in 1619, Matthias died in his bed in the Hofburg, as he was about to lift a cup of capon broth to his lips. His wife had died before him, and there was no one about except his valet. Everyone who was anyone was already busy paying court in the apartments of his cousin Ferdinand.

People were astonished and pleased to learn that Matthias' death had perfectly fulfilled the astrological prediction of the seven M's which Kepler had made for 1619:

Magnus Monarcha Mundi Medio Mense Martio Morietur. (A great monarch of the world will die in the middle of the month of March.)[3]

V

Habsburgs at Bay:
Protestant and Turk

1. Ferdinand II

> No now we are utterly, more than utterly laid
> waste.
>
> *Andreas Gryphius*

IT WAS a curious spark in a way that finally ignited the religious bonfire and set all Europe aflame; it happened in Rudolf's old castle in Prague on May 23, 1618.

After a particularly bitter altercation with Protestant leaders in Bohemia, two of His Imperial Majesty's Catholic envoys were treated to the old Bohemian custom of defenestration: they were flung out of a castle window nearly sixty feet into the dry moat below.

One of the victims, Baron Martinitz, screamed, "Jesu, Maria, help!" as he was shoved over the sill. The second envoy, Slavata, clung wildly to the sill shrieking to the Blessed Virgin before he was knocked senseless and fell too. One of the Protestant perpetrators leaned out of the window and called down after them, "See if your Mary can help you now!" A second later, in amazement, he exclaimed, "By God, his Mary has helped!"[1]

Quite miraculously neither envoy was seriously injured, their great Spanish cloaks having ballooned out with air and dropped them without serious injury on a heap of dung. Their secretary, a very polite fellow named Philip Fabricius, had been thrown out after them, along with their plumed hats. Philip fell on his master, Baron Martinitz, a grave breach of etiquette, but he had the presence of mind to beg His Excellency's most humble pardon before he even got to his feet. Philip was later raised to the nobility of the Empire under the delightful name of Baron von Hohenfall—Baron High Fall.[2]

On this *opéra bouffe* note one of Europe's most devastating wars began. Before it was over thirty years later, central Europe lay like a pockmarked graveyard; the German lands had lost a third of their population.

In 1618, when the Prague defenestration occurred, the war might have been, if not avoided, at least postponed. Emperor Matthias was still clinging to life, bedridden and ailing. His advisor, Cardinal Khlesl, counseled a policy of mildness and conciliation. It was at that juncture that Matthias' cousin, Ferdinand of Styria, stepped in boldly, had the Cardinal kidnaped and imprisoned in Castle Ambras. The war began.[3]

Ferdinand of Styria did not at all look the part of zealot in which history has cast him. A stout, friendly little man, with pinkish blond hair and freckles, his nearsighted pale blue eyes peered out at the world with habitual benevolence. He was careful and temperate in his habits, rose each day at six, and went to bed at ten. His kindness and generosity were proverbial. He was devoted to his family; his children were beautifully brought up. He shared the Habsburg love for music, theater, hunting.

Nor had he in the least a military turn of mind. When he was twenty-two he had ridden out to fight the Turks on the Hungarian border. On the way, according to the story, he spied a cloud of dust in the distance, either a stray band of spahis or a herd of bullock. He had immediately turned tail, and followed by most of his army, galloped pell-mell back across the River Mur, not stopping until he was safe within his own province of Styria.[4]

But where his religious convictions were concerned, Ferdinand had a spine of steel. He was the soul of the Counter-Reformation in central Europe.

He had been educated by the Jesuits at the University of Ingolstadt; like his godfather and cousin, Philip II of Spain, he had resolved very early to eradicate heresy from his realm. It was from Ferdinand's province of Styria that Kepler had fled to the court of Rudolf II in Prague. He would rather, he said once, leave all he possessed and go forth in the shirt on his back than give an inch to those who would damage the True Religion.[5] "Better a desert than a country of heretics," he once declared.[6]

In the uncompromising quality of his religious feelings, Ferdinand was, of course, no different from many—perhaps most—men of his age. Calvinists and Lutherans execrated one another as fiercely as they denounced Papists. Verbal if not physical violence was commonly preached in the pulpit. Force had long been the instrument of conversion to all three true faiths.

Ferdinand was particularly stubborn; the dogged tenacity of numerous Habsburg forebears had been reborn in him.

The following spring, as war broke out in earnest, Ferdinand's councilors and his confessor begged him to move out of Vienna to a safer post in the Tyrol. He refused. In June the Protestant Bohemian army of Count Thurn stood at the gates of Vienna. Shot poured into the windows of the Hofburg, hard by the city walls, and into the very apartments of the royal family. Without soldiers, without money, with even the citizens of his own capital only doubtfully loyal to him, Ferdinand went into the palace chapel to pray. Kneeling before the crucifix there, he heard, he declared afterward, very clearly the words, *"Ferdinando, non te deseram."* (Ferdinand, I shall not abandon thee.) God spoke to him quite correctly in Latin, the language of Hofburg diplomacy.[7]

A few days later, still besieged from without, Ferdinand found himself besieged from within as well. A deputation of Protestant leaders from the Austrian Estates entered the Hofburg and tried to force him to sign a grant of concessions. Exhausted by hours of harangue, he continued to refuse. A doubtful story has one of them grabbing the obstinate Habsburg by the buttons of his doublet and crying familiarly, "Nandl, you've got to sign!" At that desperate moment a blare of trumpets was heard, and the clatter of horses' hoofs in the palace courtyard. In rode a regiment of five hundred cuirassiers sent by his younger brother, Archduke Leopold, in the nick of time to save him.[8]

From that moment Ferdinand's fortune began to look up. By the end of the summer he had been elected and crowned Holy Roman Emperor. He appointed the Blessed Virgin commander in chief of his army; in November the combined forces of the Emperor and the Duke of Bavaria, his kinsman, defeated the Bohemian Protestants at the White Mountain and drove the young Elector Frederick, the Winter King of Bohemia, into exile.

In May of 1621 the death sentences of the Bohemian rebels reached Ferdinand's desk in the Hofburg for his signature. It was his duty as a monarch, an absolute monarch, to punish rebellion; blood must flow. But when he took up pen to sign, he could not. "Starting up from the council table he fled from the room mopping sweat from his forehead."[9] Not until the following day, when he had talked long with his confessor, could he bring himself to seal the death sentences. He went immediately to the shrine of Mariazell to pray that the condemned men be led back to the True Faith before they died. And when heads were falling on the execution day the following month at Prague, Ferdinand was on his knees in the Hofburg chapel praying for their souls. Their heads were spitted to the iron pickets on the Charles Bridge in Prague to remind citizens of what happens to a revolt that fails.

The *Majestätsbrief*—the charter of religious freedom which Rudolf II had granted the Bohemians—was returned to Vienna, where Ferdinand was said to have cut it to pieces with his own hands.

Ferdinand's crusade to exterminate heresy, to restore the Holy Roman Empire to Rome and unity, had barely begun.

Huge armies of mercenaries on both sides, chiefly outcasts of society fighting for wages and the chance to loot, swollen by camp followers who outnumbered the soldiers themselves many times over—it was said that six or seven infants were born each week in Bucquoy's army[10] —crisscrossed central Europe, fighting, pillaging, procreating, scourging the land bare as bone. Disease followed in their wake: plague, smallpox, scurvy, syphilis. A long series of crop failures in the 1620s added to the wretchedness of the population.

Twice, perhaps thrice, the terrible war nearly ground to a halt; each time a new motive, a new combatant sprang into action.

In the end the Thirty Years' War was no longer a religious battleground, but one more act in the long, bitter feud between the house of Habsburg and France.

2. A Wartime Bride

ONCE MORE, in the middle of the Thirty Years' War, the fate of the Habsburgs hung on the consummation of a single marriage. Once more the family future was staked on one of those precarious wedding journeys—this time across the face of a Europe convulsed with war. Whether they would indeed succeed in bringing the whole thing off remained for months—even years—a hairbreadth hope in the hands of a single determined courtier.

The old archduke uncles and cousins in the Austrian family had died one by one. Of the Emperor Ferdinand's two sons, the younger one, Leopold William, though he showed no glimmer of an inclination for the priestly vocation, had been dedicated as a child by his pious parents to the Church.

It was on the frail person of the elder boy, a third Ferdinand, and on his ability to produce heirs, that the fate of the dynasty hung. It astonished no one to hear, in 1626, that young Ferdinand would marry his Spanish cousin, the Infanta Maria Anna.

If the choice was not a surprising one, it was also not designed to throw the Viennese court into premature rapture. Maria Anna was still in Madrid—a world away from Vienna in time of war. She was said to be attractive, charming, intelligent, but she was also two years older than Ferdinand and something of an invalid; in fact, she had hardly stirred out of her chamber during the whole year preceding the betrothal. One could scarcely be overly optimistic about the prompt appearance of heirs.[1]

In Spain the family line was in as precarious straits as the Austrian branch. Philip II had murmured not long before he died, "God who has given me so many kingdoms has denied me a son capable of ruling them." And indeed indolent, pleasure-loving Philip III concerned himself largely with matters of etiquette. He had married the Austrian Habsburg, Archduchess Margarete, and died in 1621, leaving behind his heir, a fourth Philip, and the marriageable daughter, Maria Anna. (According to the witty comment of the French ambassador, Philip had died from the heat of a *brasero*—a pan of hot charcoal— because the proper court official appointed for its removal had not appeared.)

Once the betrothal had been made official, the Madrid court showed little haste in dispatching the bride. It was the difficult task of Ferdinand II's ambassador to Spain, Count Franz Christoph Khevenhüller, a superb courtier and the soul of tact and patience, to push the affair through, to plan, plot, prod, and maneuver until the wedding journey was underway.

The problems that stood in his way were of a complexity to tax the cleverest courtier's brain; in the last years of the 1620s the whole world seemed to conspire to prevent bride and groom from meeting.

The war was not going particularly well for the Habsburgs. In 1626, the year of the betrothal, a peasant uprising in Upper Austria had to be suppressed. While the imperial army fought the King of Denmark, a Protestant army invaded Silesia. While Spanish and Bavarians occupied the Rhineland, France sat astride the Val Telline, the vital Alpine pass between Austria and northern Italy. It was scarcely an auspicious moment for a wedding journey.

After the betrothal Khevenhüller betook himself back to Vienna to report and to receive the Emperor's instructions on the bridal journey. The marriage contract was signed on September 3, 1628; it was modeled after that of Maria Anna's older sister, the Infanta Anna, now Queen of France—except for one acutely important detail. Maria Anna did not renounce for herself or her children her rights to the Spanish inheritance.

Once the contract was signed, royal feet in Madrid seemed to drag intolerably over the departure of the wedding party. Evil gossips in the Spanish court had informed the Infanta that her future husband was ugly, deformed, and disagreeable, so that she herself could hardly have been overly eager to set out.[2]

Her brother the King, monarch of Europe's leading if waning power, insisted on dispatching his sister in suitable style, which meant with an accompanying retinue of several hundred persons.

But the Spanish were not very popular in Vienna, and the imperial court did not welcome either the expense or the complications such a migration would bring. It was Khevenhüller's delicate task to see that the size of the Infanta's wedding party was greatly reduced without offending anyone in the touchy Spanish court.

The imperial ambassador took pains to describe the dreadful winter climate in Vienna, so difficult for southerners, and the bitter homesickness that afflicted most Spaniards in Austria, and the difficulties of returning home during wartime. He arranged for Maria Anna's aunt, the Archduchess Isabella, Regent of the Netherlands (the same princess who had endured the long and futile betrothal with Rudolf II), to write her niece a letter overflowing with good advice for expatriate brides. Among other points she stressed the importance of traveling with as small a company of one's own countrymen as possible.

In the end Philip agreed that his sister might travel with a modest retinue of only two hundred Spanish. Heading this company—to Khevenhüller's dismay—was to be the Duke of Alva, an insufferably arrogant and difficult man, and constantly ailing; he was, nevertheless, Spain's top grandee, and he would have considered it an unbearable affront to be omitted. Khevenhüller had no choice but to assent.

His next problem was the bride's choice of confessor, tantamount in that day and in those royal circumstances to a privy councilor. Jesuits were *de rigueur* in Vienna, where the Emperor Ferdinand would scarcely lift a finger without consulting *his* Jesuit, Father Lamormaini. But Jesuits had fallen into disfavor in Madrid while the rival Capuchins were "in"; to Khevenhüller's helpless distress, Maria Anna chose for her confessor a Capuchin, Fray Diego Quiroga.

But by far the gravest problem of all was a shortage of money. It was up to the bride's family in such transcontinental royal weddings to bear the expenses up to the point of *remise* or delivery, after which the bridegroom's family assumed responsibility. The best estimates put the costs of the bridal journey from Barcelona to Genoa and thence to Trent in north Italy, where the *remise* was to take place, at a minimum of 600,000 ducats, a staggering sum to a treasury which had barely emerged from four bankruptcies in the space of a half century and was even now supporting huge armies in the Netherlands and the Rhineland.

While the Madrid court threshed out these worrisome problems, the court in Vienna fretted over the long delay and waited anxiously for some word on the bride's departure date. Communication was, of course, as slow as it took for a messenger to take sailing ship to Genoa and post horse across the Alps.

One or two morsels of good news had sweetened the long delay. Cardinal Richelieu in France found himself facing a Huguenot revolt at home and had to withdraw French troops from the Val Telline, which would open the transalpine route to the bridal party. The Emperor's army under Wallenstein had recaptured Silesia and occupied Denmark. The waiting bridegroom, the third Ferdinand, had been crowned King of Hungary and of Bohemia—which meant that the Infanta might soon be a queen; he had also taken the prize for lance-tilting in the accompanying festivities in Prague.

A date for the proxy wedding in Madrid was set for early spring of 1629. When the day rolled around, however, King Philip was sick with a fever, and the wedding had to be postponed. It took additional effort and persuasion on Khevenhüller's part to end the delay and arrange for a proxy ceremony to be performed in April at the bedside of the sick king.

Now it seemed the departure was really near and that nothing further could delay the journey. But Khevenhüller was reminded that nobody in Spain in his right mind travels in the heat of summer, and that the journey could only begin when the weather cooled but before the autumn rains set in.

It appeared, however, that Philip's queen found herself pregnant; Maria Anna could not dream of departing before her sister-in-law's confinement. The advent of a hoped-for heir to the Spanish throne was, of course, an event of world-shaking importance.

The news of the new delay was received in Vienna with no little bitterness and disappointment; it seemed that the Austrian branch must forever play second fiddle to the Spanish. Emperor Ferdinand dispatched a special envoy, Prince Cesare of Guastalla, ostensibly to carry a gift from the bridegroom, in reality to see what he could do to hurry things along. The gift was a diamond ornament bearing a miniature painting of young Ferdinand; it was hoped that a glimpse of the nice-looking prince, with his melancholy dark eyes, his curly hair and mustaches might encourage the Infanta to hasten her journey.

In October of 1629, amid great rejoicing, the Spanish throne heir, Balthasar Carlos, was born.

Winter had set in by the time the christening and attendant festivities were over. Since the proxy wedding Maria Anna had donned her new title of Queen of Hungary and Bohemia. Pressed now by Khevenhüller, she bravely agreed to set out the day after Christmas.

Her brother, the King, would accompany her as far as Saragossa. Brother and sister were devoted to one another—their affection for one another may well have been a factor in the long delay attending the Infanta's departure—and in the palace of Saragossa they spent a few

[16] Infanta Margarita Teresa, bride of Leopold I, from the studio of Velás-
quez. This was the last in the famous series of paintings dispatched to the
Vienna court to give them a glimpse of their future Empress. *(Kunsthistorisches Museum, Vienna)*

[17] The Great Siege of Vienna by the Turks, 1683, from a contemporary engraving. The print shows the final Battle of Vienna on September 12, when the imperial forces appeared to relieve the city. (*Bildarchiv des Österreichische Nationalbibliothek, Vienna*)

[18] The meeting of Emperor Leopold with King John Sobieski of Poland, after the Turkish Siege, 1683, from a contemporary engraving. In the background can be seen the city, the battlefield, and the Turkish encampment. Leopold is shown lifting his hat to the King and his son, which he did not in fact do. (*Bildarchiv des Österreichische Nationalbibliothek, Vienna*)

[19] *At right*, Emperor Charles
VI. *(Bildarchiv des Öster-
reichische Nationalbibliothek,
Vienna)*

[20] *Below*, Schönbrunn Palace in the eighteenth century,
painted by Bernardo Bellotto.
*(Kunsthistorisches Museum,
Vienna)*

[21] Maria Theresia at fifteen. (*Bildarchiv des Österreichische Nationalbibliothek, Vienna*)

last bittersweet days together. Both were under no illusion: their
parting would be forever. One day Philip arose before daybreak and
stole out of the palace before his sister was up to spare her the pang
of a last farewell.

But if Khevenhüller congratulated himself finally on a speedy ter-
mination to his years of work, it was premature. When the bridal
party reached Barcelona, they found the galleys ordered long before
were not yet ready; month after month they waited in the port before
the ships were provisioned and they could sail for Italy. Not until well
into June of 1630 did they land in Genoa.

Here new complications met them. War had broken out between
the French and Spanish over Mantua; plague had broken out in
Lombardy. Whether they would dare proceed northward over the
Italian Alps was the question. The Duke of Alva, nervous about his
health and responsible for the bride's safe arrival, refused, and proposed instead that they turn southward to Naples, take ship from
there around the heel of the Italian boot and up the Adriatic to
Trieste. The Viennese members of the suite protested.

In Genoa everyone waited while messengers posted across the
Alps to the Emperor's brother, Archduke Leopold of Tyrol, who was
to have received the bride in Trent. When he could not settle the
matter, couriers hastened to Emperor Ferdinand himself, who was
presiding at the Diet in Regensburg.

The Emperor had his hands full just then. At the Diet the German
princes were demanding that he sue for peace, that he dismiss his
doughty condottiere-general, Wallenstein, who had grown too big for
his boots, and reduce the frighteningly huge imperial army. As if
these were not difficulties enough, King Gustavus Adolphus of Sweden
had just landed with his crack army to bolster the Protestant cause.
Ferdinand sent back peremptory word to Genoa to get the precious
princess to Vienna by the safest and quickest route: he suggested
crossing the Apennines to Ferrara.

The bridal party proceeded to Naples; there, for reasons difficult
to discern, they lingered for three long months. It was not a peaceful
interlude. Alva quarreled with the viceroy of Naples, the Duke of
Alcalá; the Spanish lords of Maria Anna's suite quarreled with the
local nobility over questions of protocol and precedence, and whether
the latter might claim equal privileges with the Spanish, particularly
of appearing before the Queen with their hats off. In a huff the
Neapolitans stayed away from court altogether.

Beside himself with impatience, Khevenhüller was unable to prevail on the Duke of Alva to move on and to send the heavy baggage off by sea. In the end he and Alva were no longer on speaking terms, communicated only through their secretaries and in writing. After a time Alva did not answer Khevenhüller's messages at all.

Summer passed, the summer of 1630, and most of autumn. The icy rains of winter set in, when only the most foolhardy crossed the Apennines. In mid-December the wedding party set out, the ladies in great clumsy carriages not designed for such roads, behind them their mounted escort, their mules and baggage wagons. Cold rain poured down, the wagons mired in mud, the road often disappeared into a mere donkey track; often they must put up for overnight in the most primitive villages. It took four weeks to cross from Naples to Ancona on the Adriatic side. The delicate bride, who had been presumed to be a semi-invalid, survived in excellent health and spirits; it was the Duke of Alva who declared that he could not possibly go one step farther, that the bridegroom's uncle would have to fetch the bride from Ancona.

Once again everyone waited while a messenger rode northward across the Alps to the Tyrol and returned with Archduke Leopold's reply. It was an emphatic no. The Archduke declared flatly that it was out of the question for the honor of his house to proceed a single step farther than Trieste to meet the bride.

Khevenhüller racked his brain to solve the new impasse. The Duke of Alva could not be budged. The Austrian envoy begged the young queen to order her party forward with or without Alva. Maria Anna finally agreed, on condition that the Archbishop of Seville, the ranking prelate in the party, would replace Alva as journey master and preside at her *remise*.

Once more everything seemed in order, and the party made preparations to push on. Just then the Archbishop of Seville died. Khevenhüller was in despair. Finally the Duke of Alva was prevailed upon to proceed as far as Trieste.

The *remise* ceremony took place in Trieste on January 26, 1631. The bride became at that point officially a member of her husband's family; the final lap of the journey could begin.

Emperor Ferdinand had sent along a polite but firm command: because of the extraordinary costs involved and the state of the imperial treasury, only those persons officially appointed by the Vienna court might continue to accompany the wedding party. It was Khevenhüller's not unpleasant task now to pay off the Spanish members of the suite with suitably lavish gifts and send them on their way back to Madrid.

At the mountain pass of Semmering, high above the Danube Valley and Vienna, an escort of thirty gentlemen from the imperial court waited to greet the bride and conduct her to the capital. Royal bridegrooms were known to turn up in disguise somewhere along the route to catch a glimpse of the bride before the official meeting took place, so perhaps Maria Anna guessed that her betrothed would be among the troop of courtiers.

She recognized him instantly, she said, from the deep bow he made her, more reverent and courtly than any of the others; she returned it with her most graceful and ceremonious curtsy. Young Ferdinand was delighted to find that she really did resemble the blue-eyed blonde in the portrait Velasquez had painted; Maria Anna was so deeply relieved to find that her husband was neither ugly nor deformed nor stupid, as she had been told in Madrid, that she promptly fell in love with him. He spoke to her in Spanish, and though protocol would not permit them to dine together that night, he hurried back to her side as soon as he could to talk with her again before riding back to Vienna for the official reception.

At the next-to-the-last stop on the journey the bridegroom's stepmother, Empress Eleanor, and his two sisters waited to greet the bride. At the very last stop, at the summer palace of Ebersdorf, the Emperor himself waited in a splendid procession of fifty-six coaches, each drawn by six snow-white horses harnessed in tandem.

Ferdinand and Maria Anna were married on the same day she reached Vienna: February 26, 1631. The marriage had taken five and a half years to bring about, and nobody ventured to brook any delay in the consummation.

It was one of those political marriages that turned out nicely. While the war news grew more ominous, while the Swedish army marched southward and finally crossed the Danube, the Viennese court gossiped happily of the devotion of the newlyweds, how they dined together each evening when Ferdinand was not away at war. Maria Anna made an excellent wife, learned to speak fluent German, followed her husband on journeys, even when she was pregnant or nursing a child.

Five little Habsburgs appeared in due time, including a crown prince who would be the fourth Ferdinand. The couple's first daughter, named for her mother, was promptly and efficiently betrothed by long distance to her cousin, the small throne heir of Spain, Balthasar

Carlos, whose arrival had delayed Maria Anna's departure from
Spain. The Austrian ambassador in Madrid wrote that when news of
the little princess' birth reached Madrid, six-year-old Balthasar declared rather precociously that "he was very happy the Queen of
Hungary had given him a wife."[3]

Khevenhüller, that most loyal of courtiers, remained Maria Anna's
true friend. It was he who took charge of hurrying the imperial
children out of Vienna to safety when the city was threatened by the
Swedish army a few years later. And when Maria Anna, homesick
for her Spanish family, yearned to travel to Passau in 1634 to visit
her brother, the Cardinal Infante, when he was briefly there, Khevenhüller dipped into his own purse to help pay for the journey.

Maria Anna's father-in-law, Emperor Ferdinand II, did not live to
see the end of the Thirty Years' War, but he lived to see the German
princes choose his son King of the Romans at Regensburg in 1636.

Mortally ill, he took his way homeward to Vienna in late winter.
A letter still exists that he wrote along the way to his confessor,
Father Lamormaini, asking his help: he was accustomed, he said, to
praying for an hour each morning when he arose, but on this journey
it was so difficult, for he must arise at four each day to begin traveling,
and so what should he do for his prayers?[4] He died in Vienna, a week
later, holding in his hand the consecrated taper his confessor had
handed to him, murmuring the *Nunc dimittis*. . . .

In the palace in Linz on a day in May of 1646, Maria Anna, in
blooming health, awaited the birth of her sixth child. Without warning she suddenly went into labor and died. Her unborn child was
taken surgically so that it might be baptized. Her grieving husband—
now Emperor Ferdinand III—had the bodies of mother and child
borne on a boat down the Danube to Vienna and laid away together
in the Habsburg crypt under the Kapuziner Church.

As the Thirty Years' War ground to a conclusion out of the sheer
exhaustion and ruin of the participants, it seemed in many ways as if
the two Habsburg branches in Spain and Austria were reaching the
end of their road.

Spain's infantry, once the best in Europe, had been annihilated by
the French at the Battle of Rocroy in 1643. The Spanish treasury was
empty. The wife of Philip IV was dead. His only son, Balthasar Carlos,
the intended bridegroom of his cousin Ferdinand's first-born daughter, was dead of smallpox. Philip's only heir, as things stood now, was
the single daughter, María Teresa.

Matters were little better on the Austrian side of the family. The second and third Ferdinands, father and son, had not succeeded in reviving and uniting the Holy Roman Empire as they had hoped; the seamless coat was rent a hundred times over: dozens of princes, dukes, archbishops, bishops, and cities of Germany proclaimed their separateness. Nor had they purged the Empire of heresy as they had vowed. For the mystical seven in the electoral college a matter-of-fact eight had been substituted, with the addition of Bavaria, whose ruler had been granted a seat as a plum for fighting for the imperial cause.

Ferdinand's treasury was empty too; the crown jewels had been mortgaged again and again to provide funds for the war. When one of Ferdinand's ministers discussed the situation with one of his cousin Philip's, he made no bones about the state of the treasury, declaring that on some days "there was not enough money to set the Emperor's table."[5]

Worse yet, the old Habsburg enemy, France, was on the rise; determined to push her borders to the Rhine, she was even now gnawing away at the edges of the Empire.

And yet the Habsburg toughness would still be in evidence, as Habsburgs turned to uniting and strengthening their Danubian lands and creating an absolutist monarchy out of Austria. In their own lands Catholicism was preserved; Protestant nobility had fled or been converted. And there were again marriage plans in the offing.

The bells that rang in the Peace of Westphalia in October of 1648 rang in yet another Habsburg intrafamily wedding. The young daughter of Ferdinand III, his wife's namesake, Maria Anna, was to marry her aging uncle, Philip IV. In the young archduchess' wedding party went a few elderly Spanish ladies who had come from Spain with her mother years before on that difficult wartime journey.

Accompanying her also was her brother, the throne heir and fourth Ferdinand, a promising boy of sixteen. It was hoped he might also make a match in Spain and by marrying his cousin, the Spanish heiress, María Teresa, would provide a double insurance bond for the Spanish inheritance in case his sister's marriage was without fruit.

But when the bridal party had crossed the Alps to Rovereto, where the *remise* was to take place, a courier arrived from Madrid, rudely dashing those hopes. He brought explicit instructions that Archduke Ferdinand was on no account to continue the journey with his sister, and that he would not be received in Spain.

María Teresa was to marry Louis XIV; the Spanish court had decided to buy peace with France.

That particular Austrian-Spanish union would have been pointless in any case, as events soon proved; young Ferdinand died not long after of smallpox. His premature death broke his father's heart, and Ferdinand III did not long survive his son.

3. Leopold I: An Unwilling Emperor

> Truly I would rather live in desert solitude than
> in my Hofburg. But since God put this burden
> on my shoulders, I hope He will give me the
> strength to bear it.
>
> *Leopold to his confessor, 1680*[1]

THE YOUNGER SON who now succeeded to the throne had been
dedicated almost from birth to the Church, and the taste and
aptitude he showed for the priestly vocation had delighted his Jesuit
teachers. As a child he had used his toy blocks to build chapels, and
his favorite games were to decorate miniature altars and mimic the
serving of Mass.

Only when the bright and promising older brother died at twenty-
one was fourteen-year-old Leopold led out of his semicloistered
schoolroom, to be hastily fitted to a pair of crowns, and to stand
blinking and ill at ease under the sharp searchlight of the great world.

What the great world saw was not at all designed to impress it. He
was an undersized youth, excessively ugly, excessively shy, his teeth
broken by an attack of scurvy that had nearly killed him, so nearsighted that he needed a glass to see objects quite near at hand. He
had the grotesque Habsburg lip and chin in so exaggerated a form
from the double dose of genes in his cousinly parents that, like his
ancestor Charles V, he could not shut his mouth properly or speak
with any distinctness.

French wit made short and cruel work of Leopold. The Comte de
Grammont who met him in Frankfurt at the time of the imperial
election related in his *Mémoires*:

Having an unusually large mouth, which he always keeps open, he, whilst playing at ninepins with Prince Portia one day, complained as it began to rain, that the drops fell into his mouth. The Prince of Portia, his favourite, then taxed his ingenious brain, and, after having pondered for some time, advised his royal master to shut his mouth. The King of Hungary forthwith did so and found himself considerably the better for it.[2]

But, contrary to appearances, Leopold was not stupid. He was only without personal charm, and tortured by pangs of conscience and self-doubt. The chronic stomach-aches from which he suffered all his life stemmed no doubt from those tensions; so did his insistence on the strictest court etiquette that would serve to keep the world at a distance.

Leopold was really at ease only in his small family circle. This was a very special circle indeed, dominated by his clever and worldly Italian stepmother, Eleanor of Gonzaga, and by his gifted connoisseur-uncle, Archduke Leopold Wilhelm, who had brought back to Vienna from his regency in the Netherlands a collection of paintings chosen with fantastic perception and taste.

One of Leopold's pastimes, when he was not busy with his royal duties, was to play a game with these two elders, of improvising Italian sonnets, each one of the trio speaking a couplet, to be continued by the next one. At other times young Leopold might be found sorting through old manuscripts with the palace librarian, Peter Lambeck, or carving intricate delicacies into a bit of ivory, or bending over the vessels and retorts in his alchemical laboratory endeavoring to change silver into gold.

But the passion of his life was for music; it was music that made an uncomfortable life endurable. He himself played the flute; in his spare time he composed passable madrigals; he directed his court chapel and orchestra; he quite literally lived, breathed, ate, drank, prayed, and hunted to music, and his musical taste was of the highest order.

Left to his own devices Leopold would probably have turned into a learned, conscientious, dilettante cardinal. It was his ill luck to become a monarch, and yet greater ill luck to be pitted against the two most dangerous adversaries of his century: Louis XIV of France and Kara Mustapha, Grand Vizier of Turkey.

Unprepared by nature or by training to play either the diplomatic bravura passages or the military marches the times called for, Leopold somehow made do with his faulty equipment. In one of the longest reigns in Austrian history, and with what unfriendly historians usually ascribe to pure luck—plus the brilliant generalship of Eugene of Savoy—he turned Austria into a first-rank European power.

His first collision with France occurred in Frankfurt, whither he had gone in 1657 to get himself elected Emperor in his brother's place. Once more the French were on hand, under Mazarin's skillful manipulation, to cozen and bribe the electors against the accession of another Habsburg. For eighteen months the bartering went on before Leopold finally, stage-managed by his uncle Leopold Wilhelm, got the necessary votes and knelt to receive the crown. So narrow was the margin of victory that the capitulation he was forced to sign was the most limiting of any in history.

The next round, the battle of the brides, went to the French, when Louis XIV captured the elder and therefore more desirable of the Spanish Infantas, daughters of Philip IV. Leopold had to settle for the younger princess, his niece, Margarita Teresa. That nuptial defeat proved to be the most costly of his reign.

It was not, of course, that marriage in itself mattered much to Leopold. The Venetian envoy, Molin, declared in 1661, "He indulges in no excesses, for he doesn't know passion at all; it would tear him apart."[3] And the urbane libertine Grammont wrote that up to the time of Leopold's election as Emperor "he had never spoken to any woman but the Empress, his stepmother. . . ."[4] Grammont, of course, found Leopold's continence a delicious and amusing marvel for his time and station.

Leopold had, in any case, to wait for the younger princess to grow up to nubility, and in between he and his art-loving uncle could feast their eyes on the series of marvelous portraits Velasquez did of their princess and dispatched to the Vienna court: the Infanta at three in a rose dress laced with silver, the Infanta at six in golden curls and a gown of white brocade sewn with pink rosettes; the Infanta at eight in blue satin, holding an enormous sable muff far too big for her small person.[5]

In 1666 she was fifteen, pronounced ready for marriage, and sent off across Europe from Madrid to Vienna along that much-traveled bridal route that both her mother and her grandmother had taken. The city of Vienna and the court, sick to death of war and taxes and money problems, threw caution to the winds and spared no expense on the wedding.

Leopold built a magnificent theater adjoining his palace, and there, in celebration of his wedding, an Italian opera—the first opera north of the Alps—was performed. *The Golden Apple* was so elaborate that it involved sixty-seven complete changes in scenery, included spectacular battles with dozens of participants engaged in thrilling swordplay, cost 100,000 florins to produce (an astronomical sum in that day) and was the talk of Europe for years after.

The wedding festivities, in fact, lasted through the whole winter until the beginning of Lent. The Viennese enjoyed themselves thoroughly; there was something for everyone, even for pickpockets, for the palace accounts put down in the wedding costs "9000 florin for stolen plate."[6]

The pretty dark-eyed bride, with her husband's stepmother and sisters, watched the ballets and pageants and spectacular fireworks from the palace windows, sitting under golden canopies, leaning out over gold-cloth-covered sills. Leopold took a leading part in all the theatricals. Dressed in silver point lace and diamonds, he led the nobles of the court in an intricate equestrian ballet. At the climax of the mythological pageant, a huge star-spangled globe under a rainbow rolled across the palace square and opened to display a temple of immortality, out of which rode solemnly the figures of fifteen Habsburg emperors. At the end, ensconced in a car of glory shaped like an immense silver sea shell rode a figure of Leopold himself; beside him, an enormous shimmering pearl—a delicate pun, quite intelligible to the onlookers, who knew that the bride's name, Margarita, in Spanish means "pearl."

For the fireworks exhibition two artificial mountains sixty feet high representing Mount Etna and Mount Parnassus were built on the open space near the city wall. To open the charming and noisy pyrotechnical pageant Leopold leaned out of a palace window and lighted the symbolic nuptial torch of Mercury, whereupon five hundred fires rose representing "the universal blaze of triumph of the whole world." All sorts of ingenious and earsplitting fun followed: a cupid worked on ropes flew through the air to Mount Etna, forged the golden wedding ring, and flew back to Olympus. The nine goddesses of Parnassus made sweet music. From an Austrian castle a thousand rockets rose; from a Spanish castle a thousand rockets answered. At the grandiose climax 73,000 fireballs went off from the temple of Hymen, three hundred rockets followed, ten great mortar charges, thirty giant rockets—some weighted with a hundred and fifty pounds of powder each—trumpets blared and kettledrums thumped; over all floated in the heavens the magical acrostic invented by Leopold's ancestor:

A E I O U

Austria Erit In Omne Ultimum: The house of Austria will endure forever.

Certainly his enemies felt justified for some years in entertaining the gravest doubts about the eternity of Leopold's house.

Of the five children Margarita bore him, only a single daughter was left surviving when the young empress died in childbirth at twenty-two. Leopold married again, as soon as it was decently possible, another youthful cousin, Claudia of Tyrol, who died at precisely the same age as Margarita, and again in childbirth. There was still no heir.

His third and last wife, Eleanor of Neuburg, was a very severe, devout, and gloomy woman who thought a great deal about sin, wore bracelets with spikes that drew blood on her arms, and carried a book of Psalms bound like a libretto when she went with her husband to the opera so that she would not give her mind too much to frivolous things. She had hoped to enter a convent rather than marry; the story was that she had done ugly things to her skin so the Emperor would not have her. Nevertheless, in spite of the inclination both had for celibate lives, they collaborated on ten children, two of them future emperors.

"Things may get worse yet, but God will surely help," Leopold was fond of saying.[7] Things certainly got worse in those early years of his reign.

While he and his Jesuit advisors ardently pushed a program of Counter-Reformation in Hungary, the Protestant nobles of Hungary intrigued with the Turks, in 1670 fomented a conspiracy to overthrow the Habsburg regime. The plot was discovered in time, several went to their death, more to the galleys. As for Leopold, from that time on he went in deadly fear of Hungarians. Nor were his fears lessened when attempts were made to poison him, through a pigeon pie, and once—so the clever alchemist Borri claimed—through poison smoke from wax tapers to which Borri alone could produce an antidote.[8]

Fire nearly destroyed the newest and finest wing of the Hofburg. Plague struck Vienna in 1679, carried thousands to their death. France continued to be troublesome. Louis XIV invaded the Netherlands, attempted to push the borders of France east to the Rhine.

Against the buffeting of fortune Leopold showed a stubborn, phlegmatic patience, a dogged determination to fulfill what was expected of him.

When Halley's comet flashed into view across the heavens in 1682, Europe shuddered to think of what new trials it might be the omen. Emperor Leopold, who kept in constant correspondence with his confessor, wrote him then:

> May God will that I do nothing wicked, for I know myself as a great sinner, and just now it is high time to appease the godly majesty, who shows his anger, for we see a comet that to all pious-minded people is clearly seen as a warning to make atonement before our new sins are punished with a well-deserved lash. . . .[9]

The lash, when it came, was from a not unexpected quarter.

4. The Great Siege of Vienna

FOR HALF A CENTURY, since the peace of 1606, the Turks had been slumbering under a series of indolent and incompetent sultans. Suddenly, about the same time that Leopold came to rule, a family of ambitious and energetic grand viziers came to power and proceeded once again to goad Turkey into action. Once again Turkish armies rode out of the East; once again the Turk bell rang out in Habsburg lands, and people fell on their knees to pray for deliverance.

In 1664 the imperial army defeated the Turks at St. Gotthard, and with a gift to the Sultan of 200,000 thaler Leopold bought a truce of twenty years. As the end of the twenty years approached, Emperor Leopold, his attention fully occupied by the military advances of the French in the Rhineland and in the Netherlands, hoped to buy another twenty years from the Turks.

But in April of the year 1683 Leopold's ambassador in Adrianople watched appalled as a tremendous Turkish army of some 250,000 moved off up the Balkans, and the Grand Vizier Kara Mustapha announced to the world that he would not rest until he had stabled his horses under the dome of St. Peter's in Rome.

The nervous cardinals began to sell off their plate, offered to pay anyone who would fight the Moslem menace. The Pope promised indulgences, implored the Christian rulers to unite in another crusade —with only moderate success. The long, ruinous religious wars had wearied Europe unspeakably. And the picture was very confused. His Most Christian Majesty, Louis XIV of France, had been lobbying steadily in the Sultan's court for war against the Habsburg Emperor. And a whole array of Hungarian Protestant nobles, bitter over the Counter-Reformation policies of Leopold and the Jesuits, preferred to range themselves on the side of the Turk.

Leopold's ministers declared optimistically that the Turks could not possibly reach Vienna this year. A string of strong fortresses lay between Belgrade and Vienna, and it would require the whole summer to besiege them one by one. Instead, the Turkish army bypassed the fortresses and raced on up the Danube.

In the early days of July, 1683, the whole city of Vienna fell into panic. Refugees from the east swarmed into the city with news of the Turks' swift advance and of dreadful Tartar atrocities. From the outlying suburbs and villages frightened people poured in, children in their arms, bedding on their backs. The Turk bell tolled for prayers morning and night; the churches were filled with supplicants.[1]

On July 3 the Dowager Empress Eleanor, Leopold's stepmother, moved into the city from the summer palace of Favorita outside the walls.

The Emperor still spoke soothingly: the imperial army would protect them all; everything would yet be all right. Calmly he went out hunting on July 3 and on July 6. But with rising fear the Viennese saw the imperial treasure carried away and wagons being requisitioned left and right by the court. The price of horses rose astronomically.

Absolute terror struck the city on July 7, when a messenger rode in panting to say that the imperial army had suffered a defeat at the hands of the Turks at Petronell, that the whole vast army of the Sultan was but a few hours away. People streamed to the palace, where chests were hastily being packed. Clearly the sacred person of the Emperor, like the treasure, must be taken from danger, or at least so thought his chief ministers. The town council hurried to the Hofburg to ask the Emperor humbly that wherever he would be, he would keep the city under his protection. Leopold wept with them, promised that he would send help, permitted them to kiss his hands.

That night the road leading out of the city toward the west was jammed with the carriages of the fleeing court. The flickering torches of the couriers fell on a huge procession of vehicles, wheel to wheel, stuffed to the top with children, servants, jewels, rugs—everything of value that could be packed in. Against the night sky, causing the postilions to whip their horses yet harder, could be clearly seen the burning convent of the Carmelites on the Kahlenberg, fired already by advancing Tartars.

The lead carriages were the Emperor Leopold's, with his wife far advanced in pregnancy, and their children. People crowded about the windows of his coach crying mournfully, "*Ach*, Your Majesty, stay here! *Ach*, Your Majesty, don't desert us!" After Leopold's carriages came those of his stepmother, the Dowager Empress Eleanor, then coaches jammed with terrified ladies of the court who had pushed, scrambled, and clawed one another for a place. Coaches of noble families and well-to-do burghers, followed—every kind of carriage, wagon, cart, nag: everyone, in short who could find wheels and could flee. The road was so jammed that the Emperor's mounted guard had to force a passage through for his carriages. Courtiers and servants had fled so quickly that the doors of the Hofburg had been left open in their haste. All night long the exodus went on, wheels clattering over the cobbles and out through Redtower Gate and across the Danube Bridge. The number of those fleeing the city was variously estimated at between six and sixty thousand.

In the town of Korneuburg up the Danube, where the Emperor spent the first night of flight, such utter confusion reigned that the provision wagon could not be found, and Leopold and his family supped on a few hastily procured eggs, and slept outdoors on straw over which their pages spread mantles. The little crown prince, five-year-old Joseph, wept lustily and long. The following day the imperial travelers journeyed on to Linz, thence yet farther to the safety of Passau, where they put up at the episcopal palace.

Left behind in Vienna, crowds stared sullenly after the departing carriages. In the churches people prayed and wept, "Ach Gott! Ach Gott! What poor souls are we!" In every dwelling lights burned all night; people who had no means of escape ran back and forth in the streets trying to think what to do. They told and retold one another fresh horror stories of the Turks, refurbished now with new and vivid details recounted by arriving refugees from Hungary.

And while they recounted them, new tales of terror were being enacted a few short miles away. In the village of Perchtoldsdorf, as the Turks approached, the townspeople took refuge in the church, and turned the church tower and walled churchyard into a little fortress. The Turks burned the town, sent a courier into the church promising the citizens safety if they would surrender. A pasha came, sat on a red carpet laid out in what was once the town square, commanded that the keys of the church be brought to him by a maiden with long blonde hair and a wreath of flowers; she was also to bring a gift of six thousand florins. The bailiff's daughter, a girl of seventeen, was chosen to lead the procession out of the church. The men were taken to the marketplace and disarmed. The pasha himself then rose and slew the trembling girl; the men—thirty-five hundred— were killed; the women and children and the parish priest carried off to the slave markets of Constantinople. Local tradition has it that one returned home after fifteen years, without tongue or ears, and that the tale of the dreadful happenings of that sunny July afternoon were told only by a single survivor who had hidden himself in the well in the churchyard.[2]

In Vienna, as soon as the last carriage had departed and the last refugee had been admitted, the gates of the city were clapped shut and barricaded. Nobody would leave now, until—until what? Nobody knew.

Not everyone had deserted who could. There were foreigners who chose to stay in the city out of love for it, like the old French ambassador, Vignancour; there were nobles who might have left and stayed to perform deeds of valor. Most left.

Inside the city, after the first hours of dreadful panic, the sheer calm of necessity and endurance, the special camaraderie of deep danger pulled the besieged together. They were totally cut off from the world. There would be no more food, no more ammunition, no messages from the outside world, no way of knowing if help were on the way.

When Count Starhemberg, commander of the city, climbed the tower of St. Stephen's, he could see across the plains to the east a vast semicircle of smoke and flame: the villages burned by the advancing Tartars. A day or so later when he looked down from his window in the cathedral tower, the Turks were encamped beneath the walls of Vienna.

As far as the eye could see lay a huge, colorful tent city, Oriental in splendor, unlike anything a European would ever see again. The trumpeting of elephants, the neighing of horses mixed with the cry of the muezzin only a few feet from the counterscarp of the city. Not far from the central bastions were the brilliant pavilions of the pasha leaders: the Grand Vizier's of green silk shot with gold and silver and sewn with pearls and precious stones. Gardens were laid down around the Grand Vizier's pavilion, with baths and fountains and even a menagerie for his pleasure—the latter swelled by the addition of a fine ostrich snatched in passing from Leopold's own summer palace of Favorita.

Nearest the central city gates were encamped the crack janissaries. Most deadly dangerous to the besieged were the Turkish sappers, who, night after night, pushed their trenches, roofed over with timber and sod, right under the city walls to lay mines or to scale the bastions and get into the city.

The question was whether the walls would hold out. Built during the Middle Ages—according to tradition, out of the ransom money got from the English in exchange for the person of Richard the Lion-Hearted—the brick-and-earthwork bastions, several feet thick and higher than a house, formed a rough three-quarter circle about the city, with the last quarter closed by an arm of the Danube. Outside and below the walls lay a broad, deep ditch, partly filled with water, out of which rose on the far side a second defense, the counterscarp. Beyond the counterscarp lay an open area, the glacis, which served in time of peace as a parade ground for imperial troops.

Inside the city the besieged had gone to work frantically to repair the dilapidated walls, mount palisades on the counterscarp, strip shingles off the roofs to prevent fires, and store powder in the vaults of the churches. In the cellars near the walls basins of water and drumheads of dried peas were placed, to signal the approach of the nearly silent Turkish sappers.

In addition to an infantry regiment, guard troops had been hastily formed of all able-bodied men—butchers and brewers, bakers and shoemakers. Three companies of university students under command of their rector performed deeds of great daring: they sallied out at night and captured Turkish prisoners, once even stole from under Turkish noses several head of cattle much needed in the hungry city. The smiths forged a huge and terrible weapon: a scythe six feet long and very useful against scimitars.

All the bells of the city were silenced except the great bell of St. Stephen's that rang to signal an assault on the walls when everyone must rush to his post.

The Bishop of Vienna had fled with the Emperor, but Bishop von Kollonitsch of Wiener Neustadt, who as a youth had lived through the siege of Malta by the Turks, took charge of welfare problems, collected and portioned food and drink for the soldiers, visited hospitals, tended wounded, and saw that cesspools were dug and regulations made to prevent black-marketing.

Now, day after day, the Turks blasted away at the walls with a continual bombardment of cannon. As the summer wore on the assault increased in fury. Turkish sappers pushed their covered trenches perilously close to the walls, hurled fireballs and flaming arrows into the city, laid mines to blow up the walls. The bitterest fighting took place along the stretch of wall adjoining the Hofburg; time after time

the Turks broke through the counterscarp at that point, began filling
the ditch so that they might mount the inner walls. Each time they
were driven back only by fierce hand-to-hand fighting.

The bridge across the Danube nearest the city had been destroyed,
but now the Turks gathered all the river craft and fastened together a
bridge of boats, so that they might enter the city on the Danube side.
The boatmen of Vienna went out under heavy fire and broke up the
floating bridge.

Meantime the commander of the imperial army, Leopold's brother-
in-law, Duke Charles of Lorraine, had taken his forces up the Danube
to wait until help could join him. The Emperor's envoys were plead-
ing for allies in every Catholic court in Europe—except France. Leopold himself was asking troops at the Diet in Regensburg.

Leopold had made an alliance the previous March with King John
Sobieski of Poland, by which each agreed to come to the rescue of
the other if the Turks should attack. Now, to the Emperor's ambassador
the Polish king replied that he asked nothing better than to deserve
well of God and man, and that he would keep the word of his
alliance with the Emperor.

In the middle of August he rode out of Krakow at the head of
the Polish army, and the Queen and her ladies rode with him as far
as the frontier.

As Crown Chief General of Poland, Sobieski had won notable
victories, including the Battle of Chocim against the Turks ten years
before. He had finally been elected to the kingship. A man more
unlike the Habsburg Emperor would be difficult to imagine. A born
leader of men, Sobieski had the three qualities that make a successful military man—confidence, courage, luck. He was passionate,
proud, egotistical; he was both hero and child.[3]

By the time he rode to the Siege of Vienna, John Sobieski was no
longer a young man; at fifty-five he was so heavy that he had to be
helped onto his horse. But he had not lost his youthful vigor and
spirit of adventure; he was perfectly gay and composed, as if he
were riding out to hunt. Beside him rode his young son, James, whom
they called Fanfan. And around him swarmed that strange army of
his, like a huge pack of gypsies, ill-clad and with the most non-
descript of weapons—muskets, half-pikes, clubs, and swords.

When someone remarked to him on the rags of his men, King
John replied, "They belong to an invincible regiment that has sworn
to be clothed in nothing but the uniform of its enemies."[4]

Meantime, as Duke Charles of Lorraine waited up the Danube with the imperial army for reinforcements to reach him, and while Sobieski and his Poles made their way southward from Krakow, the beleaguered city of Vienna in the heat of August suffered the inevitable accompaniment of every siege—sickness and starvation. Not enough food had been stored, and in spite of the Bishop's rules, the price of flour quadrupled in two months; long lines of women stood outside the empty meat shops. Still the Viennese could make a joke; little boys chased cats and brought them home to their mothers to cook for a stew called *Dachshase*—roof rabbit. Soldiers and citizens fell sick of spoiled meat and ill-brewed beer. Dysentery took a heavy toll; convents and churches were filled with sick and wounded. The courageous *Bürgermeister* had died of fever; the rector of the university and the chief engineer of the city were dead, and hundreds of others. Count Starhemberg, the commander, twice wounded and sick with dysentery, had himself carried in a litter around the walls directing the defense.

But by the early days of September of 1683 the city was barely holding out. The people were worn with the unspeakable exhaustion that comes of living night and day with fear. The Turkish artillery had torn huge gaps in the walls. The outer defenses were a heap of rubbish. Ammunition was short; there were no more grenades at all, and the shells that fell into the streets had to be hastily collected and reused.

Each day Starhemberg made his way up the tower of St. Stephen's and anxiously scanned the horizon to the north. When he called for volunteers to pass the Turkish lines and bring word of the city's desperate plight to the imperial army, a man named Kolschitsky, who had been in the employ of the Levant Company and spoke fluent Turkish, came forward and offered his services.

Dressed as a Turk, Kolschitsky was let out of the sally port at nightfall, walked boldly among the Turkish tents singing. An aga called to him, invited him into his tent for coffee. Kolschitsky coolly chatted with the aga, passed safely through the Turkish camp, and swam the several arms of the Danube, only to come within an ace of losing his life when his own countrymen down the river at Nussdorf mistook him for a Turk and shot at him. But he succeeded in bringing to the Duke of Lorraine Vienna's last desperate appeal for help: *"Plus de temps à perdre, Monseigneur, plus de temps à perdre . . ."* (No more time to lose, my lord, no more time to lose.)[5]

In the daybreak hour of September 4 a tremendous explosion shook the whole city and destroyed part of the inner wall near the Hofburg. Several thousand Turks holding sacks of wool before them for protection tried to scale the wall crying, "Allah! Allah!" They were driven back finally, but not before they had planted two standards on the wall. Inside the city, people grimly brought out their mattresses, wine presses, even the doors off their houses to fill up the hole.

The smiths had already forged huge chains and put them in place for street fighting. The defenders were tearing the gratings out of their windows to pile them up for barricades.

The Turks were within days, perhaps even within hours, of capturing the city. Probably only the greed of the Grand Vizier, who insisted on holding out for total capitulation so that he might have all the loot rather than share it with his army, prevented Turkish victory.

But the relieving forces had already met—not only the Polish army but Saxons, Schwabians, Bavarians, Bohemians. The besieged within the city beheld with joy on the night of September 10 rockets set off on the nearby Kahlenberg, and the smoke of a thousand friendly campfires.

The battle for Vienna took place on September 12. King John Sobieski and his son had slept outdoors under an oak tree on the Kahlenberg. In the morning the commanders of the rescue army heard Mass, swarmed down on the Turks from the steep slopes of the Kahlenberg. The battle was sudden and swift; by early afternoon it was decided. The Duke of Lorraine had broken the weak Turkish right wing; King John and his Polish hussars routed spahis and janissaries in a brilliant cavalry attack.

The whole Turkish army collapsed, retreated pell-mell back down the Danube, covering in twenty-four hours a distance it had taken them eight days to make when they were advancing.

By nightfall King John was in the Grand Vizier's tent, writing the famous letter to his pretty French wife, Marysienka: "*Seule joie de mon âme, charmante et bien aimée Mariette . . .*" promising to bring her the golden stirrup he had found in the tent of the Vizier.[6]

The following day, September 13, Sobieski and the other commanders made a triumphant entry into the city. The haggard, joyful people pressed about, kissed his feet, touched his clothing and his horse. He said afterward that it was the happiest day of his life. A Mass was sung in the Augustiner Church in honor of the great victory. All the church bells, those sweet familiar voices that had been so long silent, rang out again, and there was a banquet in the palace of the commander, Count Starhemberg.

During the last stage of the siege the imperial family had moved down the Danube from Passau to Linz, and it was there that the Empress gave birth to her child. Leopold was on board a boat between Krems and Tulln when a messenger brought him a letter from his confessor, Marco d'Aviano, giving him the news of the great victory the day before.

Leopold wrote back immediately that the victory celebration was to await his arrival:

> It is true I have commanded that I must be first to enter the city, for I fancy that otherwise the love of my subjects for me would be diminished, and their affection for others increase.[7]

The following day, September 14, the Emperor made his entry into Vienna, to the thunder of cannon and brave words of welcome from the council. But the cream of the celebrating had been skimmed, and it was not quite the same as if he had been first. There was another *Te Deum* in St. Stephen's, there were formal speeches of greetings and welcome and thanks. But there was a coolness between Austrian and Pole, not lessened by the fact that the Poles had been the most successful looters, still less diminished by the celebrated meeting beween Leopold and Sobieski.

This took place on September 15 near the camp at Schwechat, where the Polish king had withdrawn because of the stench of rotting bodies, horses, and camels in the immediate vicinity of Vienna.

Emperor and King met on horseback halfway between the Austrian and Polish armies. Leopold apparently had inquired of court protocol how an elected king such as Sobieski should be received by an emperor. When he asked the question of the Duke of Lorraine, the Duke cried, "With open arms!"[8]

Leopold extended his thanks to Sobieski in a brief Latin address, but he clung to the precise rules of protocol and did not even touch his hand to his hat when the Polish king's son was presented to him.

John Sobieski replied in Latin, saying in effect, "I am glad, Sire, to have rendered you this small service."[9]

Soon after their meeting John Sobieski left Vienna. He and the Duke of Lorraine pursued the fleeing Turks far down into the Balkans and delivered another crushing defeat. The Poles went home then in mid-December, all that was left of the army of rescue—less than half the number who had marched to the aid of Vienna in August.

On Christmas Day in Constantinople the Grand Vizier was strangled with a bowstring and his head carried in to the Sultan on a silver dish.

The victors fared better; nearly everyone found some reward. The famished Viennese had fallen on the stores of food in the Turkish tents. The courageous messenger Kolschitsky asked for just one prize: the sacks of curious brown beans that turned up in one of the tents —the hungry Viennese had wondered whether they should be baked, boiled, or fried. With his reward Kolschitsky opened the first coffee-house in Vienna, the famous Blue Bottle in Singerstrasse.

VI

In a Baroque World

THE NEWS of the great victory over the Turks was a burst of music in the ears of all Europe; it was the first news in years over which Europeans could exult in common; it was a *continental* rather than a national victory.

And it was another turning point upward in the fluctuating fortunes of the Habsburgs. As the imperial army drove the Turks out of Hungary and far down into the Balkans, the Habsburgs wore again the aura of a dynasty divinely blest. It did not matter if the sword that hung at Leopold's side had never been used; he became Türkenpoldl—Turkish Poldy—and Leopoldus Magnus.

He was said to have wept when he first saw the devastation of his city. There was not even a decent chamber in the Hofburg in which he could spend that first night. He had to sleep in the Stallburg, which had lately been used to stable the palace horses, and then returned to Linz to wait until his palace could be put to rights.

For this task he called in Fischer von Erlach, a young Austrian architect who came to him fresh from the soaring poetry of Bernini's Rome. It was Fischer von Erlach who put together all those divergent bits and pieces that had been added to the Hofburg across the centuries, fused them into a composition that had unity and grandeur. It was Fischer von Erlach who designed Schönbrunn, newest of the Emperor's summer palaces, which was to rival Versailles as a royal setting. It was Fischer von Erlach who designed the audacious majesty of the Karlskirche, and the Plague Monument in the Graben, that improbable bit of airy fancy in stone.

Vienna itself was no longer a border city, an eastern outpost, but the thriving capital of central Europe. In the half century that followed the Siege the whole face of Vienna changed: out of the ruins and ashes of the crowded medieval town a gracious baroque city rose, hewn not merely out of native stone and Italian marble, but out of the joy and relief and exuberance of a people who had lived under the Turkish threat for a hundred and fifty years.

The new city was a marriage of Italian culture with a sturdier northern taste. With farsighted vision the artists—Italians and Austrians who had learned their skills in Rome—composed urban space, coolly and imaginatively, like an abstract artist dividing his canvas, laying out broad avenues straight as a die, ending in a carefully planned climax, a church, a palace, or simply a hilltop view; opened up serene squares that echoed the quiet elegance of a baroque church front. The churches themselves were invaded with a flood of mellow color so that they wear the lavish air of palace ballrooms.

The palaces of the great nobles gleamed white and crisply new, taller than the palaces of Paris or of Rome, so high indeed that one had to crane one's neck in the still-narrow streets of the Inner City to see where angels and earthly creatures broke the roofline in a wholly Italian manner. Outside the city walls, over the ashes and rubble of the devastated suburbs where the Turks had camped, a whole array of summer palaces sprang up, nestled in a delicious setting of formal garden, Italian again in spirit, with play of light and shadow, of air and sparkling water, of wall-like hedges of dark green yew and hornbeam against pale gravel walks and stonework.

It was the last great age of kings, the last apotheosis of monarchy before the Enlightenment. At the supreme pinnacle of Europe's courtly world was the Holy Roman Emperor. In a society where hierarchy was everywhere of passionate concern, the Emperor was first-ranking monarch; no matter how far afield the French king sent his armies, no matter how magnificent a palace he raised or how extravagant a court, his ambassadors had always to yield precedence to the Emperor's.

Quite literally from infancy on, all members of the Emperor's family were carefully trained in the august roles they would play. Leopold's heir, Archduke Joseph, was only two and a half when he made his first formal appearance at court on Twelfth Night of 1681, and people were admitted to kiss his hands.[1]

Leopold and his sons were meticulous about the rules of etiquette and protocol; Leopold's refusal to remove his hat at the meeting with Sobieski's son was perfectly in accord with the dicta of that etiquette.

When Archduke Joseph became Emperor, he refused to sit down at table with a mere prince, not even when he was traveling in that prince's country and was a guest in that prince's palace.[2] Leopold's younger son, later Emperor Charles VI, would not shake hands with the newly created King of Prussia, because he had formerly been a mere elector.[3]

And once Leopold was heard to exclaim, when he lay abed and his body physician was examining him, *"Eheu! hoc est nostrum membrum imperiale sacrum-caesareum!"* (Careful! that is our imperial sacred Caesarean member!)[4]

No one appeared before the Emperor without performing the "Spanish reverence," which meant bowing deeply three times and dropping on one knee. To leave the presence required again three bows, performed while backing out of the room. It was also decreed that when the Emperor's name was mentioned in public the words should be accompanied by a Spanish reverence. The Russian ambassador had created a certain diplomatic problem in 1687 by refusing to perform the Spanish reverence before the Emperor, on the ground that three bows were reserved for the Holy Trinity.[5]

Lesser members of the imperial family and upper ranks of nobility might be accorded the "French reverence," a half bow.

Exactly how many steps down a grand staircase the Emperor might go to receive a visiting ruler, whether he would or would not uncover his head, and what kind of salute he would give were all exactly prescribed in the rules of protocol.

When the Elector August of Saxony visited Vienna in 1695, Leopold and his son Joseph drove to the Danube Bridge to meet him, descended from their carriage, advanced a precisely counted ten paces, and stood still. It was for the elector to close the remaining thirty.[6]

Etiquette was useful too in communicating what could not be spoken. At the time of his election as King of the Romans in 1655, Leopold had waited at the top of a staircase to receive the prince-electors; when they began to climb the stairs, he descended three steps to greet them, took precedence on their right in ascending again. Only when the Elector of Mainz appeared, whose vote had gone to the French candidate, Leopold (either absent-mindedly or more likely by design) descended only two steps and waited, whereupon the Mainz prelate, furious, stopped dead-still at the bottom of the stairs, refusing to budge until a court official reminded Leopold that he owed the elector one more step.[7]

Against the elegant backdrop of the city, the Emperor and his court performed a kind of continuing day-to-day drama. An elaborate daily and seasonal ritual revolved around the person of the Emperor, based on the ceremonial of the Burgundian dukes, formalized and frozen in the Spain of Philip II, embroidered further by the Catholic Counter-Reformation in Austria.

Engineering that complicated ritual were hundreds of courtiers who comprised the *Hofstaat,* the imperial household. Besides the great official staff an army of *Handwerker* and servants performed the manual chores: served as goldsmiths and barbers, armorers and carriage makers, trumpeters, wigmakers, chamber-heaters, pastry cooks, button makers, and several score other useful palace trades.[8] There was not enough room in the Hofburg to house the throng of courtiers and servants; most were billeted in houses about the town as a kind of feudal duty. This circumstance, together with the compact geography of the walled Inner City, brought the court far closer to the ordinary life of the town than happened elsewhere as a rule. Nearly everyone in Vienna, in fact, made his living in one way or another off the court, and the whole ponderous charade of court life took place squarely under the eyes of the neighborhood. While that shoulder-rubbing intimacy did nothing to erase the boundaries of a rigidly stratified society, it profoundly affected taste and manners. Everyone copied the fashions and habits and diversions of the court. And in the vast theater that was the baroque city even the audience were called upon from time to time to perform some part on the central stage.

All the members of the Emperor's *Hofstaat* were bound by the solemnest oath when they entered his service, to be "loyal, obedient, attentive," to warn him of possible harm; they usually remained with him until his death.[9] The emperor cult that lasted until the end of the Habsburg regime had as its core those families with a tradition of courtly service; that *Kaisertreue*—emperor loyalty—was a very real element in holding together the Danubian monarchy against the centrifugal forces of nationalism.[10]

The Emperor's perfectly predictable life was regulated with severity and order. He rose each day at precisely the same hour, attended by his body servants, the Gentlemen of the Black Key, and his chamberlains, the Gentlemen of the Golden Key. He heard three Masses one after the other, kneeling on the pavement in the chapel, his books of liturgy spread out before him. Next he held audiences, with people admitted strictly according to rank; the poor and the lower ranks of clergy got a paper packet of golden ducats.[11]

An elfin figure in a great curled peruke, blinking nearsightedly at everyone, his glass in hand to peer at visitors, Leopold managed to achieve an air of immense majesty. He wore only Spanish dress, all black with red stockings and shoes and plumed hat. Courtiers likewise appeared in the Hofburg only in Spanish dress.

At one he dined, usually alone and in state, in the newly refurbished and gilded Leopold Wing; anyone who wished might be admitted to watch the Emperor dine. He sat on a raised dais under a red-and-gold canopy, talking to his pages and jesters or listening to music. The Italian artist Burnacini, who had designed the magnificent sets for Leopold's wedding opera, designed the glittering interior of the hall where the Emperor dined, quite as if it were another theater set.

Archers and halberdiers stood at attention, heads uncovered. The papal nuncio and the foreign ambassadors attended, bowing and retiring when the Emperor took his first sip of wine, poured by cupbearers kneeling. The Emperor kept his hat on while he ate, removing it only when his chaplain said grace, or when the Empress dined with him and raised her glass to pledge his health. The food His Majesty ate, brought up from the kitchens in the bowels of the palace, passed through twenty-four pairs of hands to reach him.[12]

No one save the Empress sat down with the Emperor when he dined in state—in court parlance, "on the Emperor's side." After the meal His Majesty remained seated while everything, even the cloth, was removed and a fresh cloth laid. Then the first groom of the plate-chamber appeared with a silver-gilt basin for hand washing, and the Lord Steward passed the napkin.

Supper, a much more informal meal, was commonly served in the apartments of the Empress, or "on the Empress' side." Guests might be invited then; there was gaiety, conversation, music. The Empress' maids of honor, twelve young ladies of noble family who lived in the Hofburg, waited on the supper table and passed the hand-washing basin. Though the Elector August of Saxony was a guest in the Hofburg for four weeks in 1696 without ever dining "on the Emperor's side," he was a guest at the Empress' table and as a special token of esteem was permitted to pass the napkin to the Emperor.[13]

After the dinner hour, on fine afternoons in spring, the Emperor and Empress might drive in the city, slowly and grandly, in a red-leather-covered body coach, attended by three hundred guards on foot or on horse and a train of black court carriages following. The Emperor occupied the main seat of the carriage alone; the Empress sat facing him, her back to the horses. In the country, where the rules of etiquette were relaxed, she was permitted to ride at his side. Or the imperial pair might ride out to hunt in the afternoon, or to a shooting match. Or the Empress might retire to her mirror room after the dinner hour, to play cards with her ladies.

In the evening there might be a concert or an opera or a ballet performed in the Court Theater, with the strictest etiquette again observed. The Emperor and Empress sat on velvet-covered arm-chairs on a raised platform immediately confronting the stage—as if, indeed, they were as much a part of the performance as the leading actors. Two pages with fans knelt to cool Their Majesties. The Elector August, who was seated in an ordinary chair some distance behind, was handed a fan with which he might, if he chose, cool himself.

Life at court had a seasonal as well as a daily pattern. Festival and gala days were fixed on the calendar long in advance. On the birthdays and name days of the Emperor and Empress, the court and diplomatic corps appeared in the Hofburg to kiss hands and to watch the Emperor dine.

On *Toison* days—the ceremonial anniversaries of the Order of the Golden Fleece—the knights of the order, in their crimson velvet uniforms embroidered with gold, heard Mass and Vespers in the Court Chapel, dined with the Emperor in the Hofburg—a rare honor.[14]

Not all events graced by the imperial presence were conducted with seemly decorum. On feast days of various patron saints, when the Emperor visited the appropriate church and dined afterward in the communal refectory of the adjoining convent, the whole place was often in an uproar. A huge crowd would gather; there was yelling, pushing, pulling, and trampling for a place to see. Relatives and friends of the nuns shouldered their way through the guards to beg favors of the Emperor. Often the crowd was so wild and unruly that the imperial guard was helpless, and the court officers bringing in His Majesty's food (which was always prepared and brought from the palace kitchens) could scarcely make their way through the mob.[15]

And however formal life was during much of the year, in *Fasching* —carnival season—all bars were let down; lèse majesté was the order of the day.

From Epiphany until Shrove Tuesday a round of frolicking, of

masked balls, *ridottos,* comedies, operas, sleigh rides, fireworks, concerts, and horse ballets entertained the court set. At palace balls
supper was served at two in the morning, and one danced until
daylight. For the sleigh rides hundreds of carts brought fresh snow
from the mountains to strew on the streets and squares of the Inner
City. Gentlemen of the party drew lots for the lady who would
ride and sup with them. In beautifully carved sleighs in the shape
of dragons and peacocks and swans, the party drove through the
streets, music playing, torches sparkling on the jewels of ladies and
gentlemen.

Favorite of the Habsburg emperors in baroque times was the
palace masquerade called a *Wirtschaft* or "tavern." The Hofburg was
transformed into a country inn, The Black Eagle, the Emperor and
Empress dressed up as peasant innkeepers; the court came costumed
as milkmaids, barbers, wigmakers, shepherds; there was a great deal
of hilarity and dropping of court manners. At a famous *Wirtschaft*
in the Hofburg during a visit of Peter the Great in 1698, the Czar
came dressed as a Frisian farmer, downed a prodigious quantity of
wine, kept on his feet till dawn flinging about in Cossack style his
pretty dancing partner.[16]

While the two seasons of carnival and Lent reflected the contraries
of human life, the opposite poles of need, so that one could not
exist without the other, it was the robust spirit of *Fasching* rather
than the spirit of Lent that prevailed in Vienna. It was an easygoing
city and a merry one. The wine terraces that surrounded the town
from ancient times, the turning dances banned as immoral in other
German-speaking lands and long popular in Vienna, the wealth of the
aristocracy and the comparatively comfortable life of most burghers,
all contributed to the gaiety of carnival, which the British ambassador,
Sir Robert Keith, likened once to "living six weeks in a kettledrum."[17]
For a people passionately addicted to theater and play-acting, the
Masken-freiheit—freedom of the mask—of carnival time gave everyone
the chance to play for once in the year the role of his choice. Even
the Habsburgs descended from Olympus to play *Amphitryon* for a
day.

But the instant midnight sounded on Shrove Tuesday, the music
stopped, dancing feet halted, stages darkened, feasting paused. The
French ambassador in Vienna, the Duc de Richelieu, wrote home
complaining bitterly that he and the court had to follow the Emperor
at his devotions "like a pack of valets," and that he had spent a

hundred hours on his knees between Palm Sunday and Easter—probably no exaggeration, for no fewer than eighty public devotions during
Lent required the attendance of ministers of state.[18]

Yet the Lenten observances too had the character of great theatrical
spectacles. Glittering processions unwound like spools of light through
the narrow streets of the Inner City, sparkling with music and color,
often led by the Emperor and Empress on foot. At street corners,
on improvised stages, the Jesuits' pupils acted out a part of the
chosen drama of the day. The Lenten "Play Processions"—the Palm
Sunday procession, the Descent from the Mount of Olives, the Good
Friday procession—enacted with costume and music and hundreds of
participants the story of Christ's Passion.[19] For the Hernalser procession, the Emperor, the Empress, and the whole court donned mask
and costume of Biblical characters, and, mounted on asses, led the
townspeople out to a Calvary in the suburb of Hernals, as an act of
atonement for the first Protestant sermon preached in Vienna. The
Hernalser procession, to judge from contemporary accounts, owed
more to carnival than to Lenten spirit, and the thickets and hedges
along the way were frequently the scene of highly secular amusements among the participants.[20]

On Maundy Thursday the Emperor and Empress knelt before the
court in the great hall of the Hofburg to wash the feet of twelve
paupers. On Good Friday the Emperor, the court, and the townspeople made a pilgrimage from church to church to visit the Holy
Tombs, which, like the manger scenes of Advent, were often the work
of the great artists of the day. In a famous, much admired tomb
scene in the Augustiner Church adjoining the Hofburg, the Tomb
was depicted in a realistic Austrian mountain setting, with live trees
in which birds both real and make-believe perched; a small boy in the
wings mimicked the birdsongs.[21]

On the Saturday of Holy Week a Resurrection procession returned
the Host to the altar of each church.

Immediately after Easter the Emperor and his household moved to
the country, usually to Laxenburg, for hawking, and for stag- and
boar-hunting. In midsummer, just after St. John's Day, a long procession of carriages moved the court back to another summer palace
nearer Vienna, the new Favorita. In October the imperial family returned to the Hofburg, the great nobles came back from their castles
and manor houses to their town palaces, and the dance of court life
began again.

The great cycles of ceremony revolved not only around the day of the Emperor, and the season, but around the rise and ebb of life itself. Christenings, marriages, coronations, funerals: all provided the occasion for the grand spectacle, the ceremonial gesture, the pageant in which theater and real life inextricably fused. The court was both spectator and participant. The great musicians of the day composed for the occasion; the great artists designed opera scenes, illuminations for the christenings, wedding festivals, coronation settings, and finally the catafalques on which the imperial corpses were laid out.

There was a protocol to dying as there was to living. The Habsburgs usually managed impressive deathbed scenes, surrounded by family, clergy, top court officials, the last words carefully inscribed for history. Leopold would expire to the sweet, tenuous sounds of the baroque music he loved with a passion; there is a story that his son, Charles VI, a stickler for etiquette to the end, reared up on his deathbed to demand why only four candles burned at the foot of the bed instead of the "Caesarean six" that protocol demanded.

Of all the spectacles of court life, an imperial funeral was perhaps the most impressive. When an emperor died, the body was opened and carefully embalmed; the heart was removed, placed in a golden urn, and solemnly brought to the Heart Crypt of the adjoining Augustiner Church. The entrails in a copper urn, blessed by the palace chaplain, were carried by coach to St. Stephen's Cathedral, where the Archbishop of Vienna blessed them again and deposited them in the catacombs beneath the church.

While the two little funerals of the heart and entrails took place, the body of the dead monarch, dressed in Spanish style, even to the plumed hat on the head, lay in state on a high ornate catafalque in the Hall of Knights in the Hofburg. The lying-in-state was an awesome thing to see. All the rooms in the palace were draped in black. In the somber Hall of Knights the only light came from the grove of flickering black tapers that burned at head and feet of the catafalque, glinting off the burnished jewels of the crowns, the scepter, the orb, the Golden Fleece. Court chamberlains in long black mantles formed a perpetual watch; Augustine and Capuchin monks chanted Masses, and at intervals choirboys from the court chapel appeared to chant the *Miserere* or the *De Profundis*. Outside in the silent city muffled church bells tolled day and night.

The funeral was at night. By the light of torches and tapers the long procession formed: all the paupers from the city's hospitals walked first, taper in hand, then the monks of the various orders, the palace servants, and the court officials, magistrates, clergy, Knights of the Fleece. Twenty-four gentlemen of the Golden Key bore the coffin, followed by the imperial family in deepest mourning.[22]

After prayers in the church of the Capuchins, the coffin was borne down a winding stair that led to the crypt, and here the Controller of His Late Majesty's Household performed a last service for his master. He knocked three times on the closed door, while a voice from within the crypt demanded:

"Who is there?"

"The Emperor Leopold," replied the Controller.

"I know him not," said the voice. The crypt door remained closed.

Again the *Hofmeister* knocked thrice on the iron-studded door. Again the voice from within:

"Who is there?"

"I, Leopold, a poor sinner."

The door was opened from within by the Capuchin prior. The coffin was unlocked one last time so that he might identify the person he was taking into his keeping, then locked forever with double keys.[23]

VII

Problems of Inheritance

1. A New King for Spain

IT WAS WELL that death was accorded all the punctilious ceremony courtly etiquette could summon, for it was a frequent visitor in the Hofburg in those years. Again and again the brilliance of court life was snuffed out in the dark grief of another official mourning. Beards went uncut, dwarfs and jesters were sent on holiday, opera and comedy were banned, the ladies of the imperial family went about in the Spanish mourning garb of nuns.

The new enemy was smallpox.

Again and again it altered the course of European history. The Queen of England died of it. The Spanish throne heir, Balthasar Carlos, had died of it. Leopold owed his throne to it. Unlike the plague which the rich could escape by flight and good fortune, there seemed to be no escape from the smallpox. Children sickened and died within hours; women went to bed angels and rose up hags.

> All my sons and daughters except the King of the Romans [Leopold wrote to his confessor in 1691] are down with the smallpox . . . my youngest daughter born only last year. This angel was well until suddenly the evil began. Barely three days was she sick and this morning early seized with such terrible cramps that her innocent soul winged its way to heaven. . . .

> As a man I suffer bitterly, for the little one was my daughter, but I console myself that I have someone now who will pray God for me, and I take it as God's highest grace that when He wanted to take a child from me He took her while she was still so small.[1]

A few years later he was again turning to his friend and spiritual advisor, Father Marco d'Aviano, for consolation:

I must tell you of my grief, that my daughter Maria Theresia sickened with smallpox a week ago. It seemed not to be so bad when suddenly there came a change for the worse and God called her to him. You may judge how very much I have suffered from this heavy blow, for my daughter was so good and clever.

I console myself in the hope that God allowed it to happen so that she might be freed of the dangers of this world. . . . As soon as she knew she was ill of smallpox she wanted to make a general confession and was not yet twelve years old.[2]

By a stroke of luck the son and heir, Joseph, escaped smallpox— for the time being—and his younger brother Charles suffered only lightly so that he had a lifelong immunity.

Of Leopold's sixteen children, only five survived him.

In this he was more fortunate than his nephew, Carlos II, King of Spain.

Carlos, only surviving child of that last intrafamilial marriage between Leopold's sister, Maria Anna, and the elderly Philip IV, had been ailing from birth. It seemed likely the last feeble twig on the Spanish branch would wither away without issue.

Contemporaries ascribed Carlos' illness and impotence to witchcraft, nineteenth-century historians to the long inbreeding process. Whatever the effects of inbreeding on Carlos' genetic structure, the description of the manifold ailments that afflicted him from birth— suppurating ulcers, diseased bones and teeth, nervous difficulties— strongly suggest congenital syphilis, the quite probable result of his father's frequent forays into the bordellos of Madrid.

For almost a quarter of a century, from the time of Carlos' first marriage with a French princess, the great powers of Europe had been engaged in bedchamber espionage, to ascertain when and whether a throne heir would be produced. The Spanish had finally accepted with fatal irony the royal heirlessness, celebrating it in a popular quatrain:

> Three virgins there are in Madrid:
> the library of our Cardinal,
> the sword of the Duke of Medina,
> and our lady the Queen.[3]

In the years just preceding Carlos' death a series of secret treaties among the great powers carved up Spain like an apple. French claims were based on the marriage of Louis XIV with the elder of Philip IV's daughters, Maria Teresa, the Infanta whom the Austrian court had tried to capture, first for Leopold's older brother Ferdinand, then for Leopold himself. Maria Teresa had, however, at the time of her marriage, clearly renounced all claims to the Spanish throne; French legal experts had to burrow deep in their bag of tricks to find an answer. Since the Infanta's dowry had not been paid in full, they argued, her renunciation was invalidated. Leopold's claims were, of course, based on the long intimate ties that bound the two branches of the family together; his mother was a daughter of Philip III, and his first wife, a daughter of Philip IV.

There was still a third claimant to the throne of Spain: the seven-year-old son of the Elector of Bavaria, whose mother was Leopold's daughter by his first wife, the Infanta Margarita Teresa. For a time it seemed that Carlos and his ministers favored the Bavarian child as a compromise solution; the little prince was waiting in the Netherlands to set sail for Spain when he caught the smallpox and died.

Behind the frail figure of the King, an intricate and desperate intrigue was played out among Spanish ministers, French and Austrian diplomats, for the world's highest stakes. The French sent their most fascinating ambassador to Madrid to entertain lavishly, to hold out to Carlos' presumptive widow the possibility of remarriage with the Dauphin of France.

Carlos grew steadily worse. His hair had fallen out, his teeth were nearly gone, his eyesight was failing. He was stricken with "paralytic distemper"; in the Corpus Christi procession of 1699 he walked "with a staggering gait," fell several times.[4]

In October of 1700 a new will was drawn up by his ministers and brought to his deathbed for his signature. On November 1 he breathed his last. Almost at once a huge crowd gathered in the anterooms outside the council chamber of the palace where his will was to be opened and read.

According to a French account,[5] the Austrian ambassador, Count Harrach, "wearing a look of triumph" and perfectly certain that one of Leopold's sons would be named heir, stood next to the French ambassador, Blécourt.

The crowd grew restless; the press was so great in the anterooms that there was actual danger of suffocation. Still the inner door to the chamber where the ministers were examining Carlos' will remained closed.

Suddenly the doors flew open, and the Duc d'Abrantès, one of the late King's ministers, "whose wit was pleasant but much to be

dreaded," made his way through the crowd. He was instantly surrounded and begged to reveal the contents of the King's testament.

The French ambassador stepped forward hopefully; the Duke
looked at him, then turned away and searching the sea of faces suddenly perceived the Austrian ambassador.

> A look of joy came over his face. He flung his arms about
> [Harrach's] neck and cried loudly in Spanish, "Monsieur, it is
> with much pleasure . . ." He paused to embrace him again.
> "Yes, Monsieur, it is with the greatest joy . . ." (Another pause
> for embraces) "and satisfaction that I take leave of you for the
> remainder of my life and bid farewell to the Royal House of
> Austria!"

With that he turned, dashed through the crowd, leaving the Austrian
dumfounded, while the crowd leapt after him like a pack of dogs on
the scent to learn at last that the inheritor was France.

When Blécourt's news reached France, it was greeted with as great
astonishment as it found dismay in Vienna: a Bourbon, not a Habsburg, would inherit the whole of Spain.

In Vienna, on a fine September day in 1703, Emperor Leopold drove
out to his new country palace of Favorita with his two sons, Joseph
and Charles, beside him. There in the presence of the court and the
family servants seventeen-year-old Archduke Charles was declared
of age and named rightful King of Spain. It was as simple as that:
Leopold and Joseph, the elder brother, signed over to Charles their
rights to Spain. In secret clauses a whole plan of family succession—
including succession through the female line—was sketched out.

A few days later, on September 19, Charles took tearful leave of his
family. His mother, Empress Eleanor, parted with him most re-
luctantly, calling it "a sacrifice for the public service." His older
sister, Maria Anna, who was especially close to Charles, called his
pet dwarf aside, gave him a golden watch that struck the hours,
and begged him whenever he heard it chime and was with her
brother to remind him of her.[6]

Off went young Charles across Europe in a great cavalcade of
spanking new coaches, all painted in the Spanish colors, yellow and
white, along with chamberlains, secretaries, surgeons, apothecaries,
pursers, wigmakers, stove-lighters, cooks, undercooks, cellarers, footmen, huntsmen, confessor, and—of course—musicians.

Nearly three years had passed since that momentous reading of

Carlos' will. Louis XIV had not delayed, but had briskly dispatched his grandson, Philip of Anjou, to Spain with the famous but probably apocryphal remark "There are no more Pyrenees!" In those three years Philip had ample time to entrench himself firmly in Madrid.

The maritime powers, in the meantime, had rallied to the Habsburg side. Leopold bought the support of the Elector of Brandenburg by raising him to the grander title of King in Prussia, and the support of the Duke of Hanover by making him an elector.

While Eugene of Savoy and the Duke of Marlborough battled the French for possession of Spain, two kings occupied the divided throne—Philip of Anjou in Madrid and Habsburg Charles in Barcelona. While Charles's position in Spain bettered, worsened, bettered again, the court in Vienna proceeded to find a wife for him.

The matter was doubly important, for his elder brother Joseph had no sons.

On his way to Spain, Charles had detoured at Weissenfels in Germany to look over a particularly attractive possibility, Caroline of Ansbach. Beautiful, intelligent Caroline quite captivated Charles; she had just one count against her—she was Protestant. Caroline's ambitious family, eager for a Habsburg match, welcomed the Jesuits sent to convert her. Caroline, however, sat with a Bible open on her lap, disputing theological questions amid bitter tears. In the end the whole project had to be abandoned; Caroline married Prince George of Hanover—and eventually became Queen of England.

Charles was deeply disappointed. To his old friend Count Wratislaw he complained that so far as his marriage was concerned, "they'd managed to spill the best soup, God forgive 'em, it was done."[7]

Presently another bridal possibility turned up, once more a German princess: Elizabeth Christine of Brunswick—again, alas! a Protestant. Charles sent his confessor from Spain to look her over, and Father Tönneman returned presently with a charming portrait and the promise of a prompt conversion. In the Vienna court, enemies of the proposed match whispered that the girl was sickly and might not be able to bear children in useful numbers.[8]

The Emperor's personal physician was sent to Wolfenbüttel to take lodgings near the palace, to watch the princess out walking, and observe her from behind a screen when she sat at table. Both her health and table manners apparently passed the test. Her conversion was more difficult; it did not proceed without tears and sighs, and months passed before her family could furnish the written guarantee.[9]

In the spring of 1708 Elizabeth Christine journeyed to Vienna for a proxy marriage, thence over the much-traveled bridal route to Spain.

Charles met his bride at the seaport of Mataró. After their first hours together, phlegmatic Charles noted in his diary:

Rode to Mataró. Queen very beautiful. Quite content.

Two days later occurs a yet terser entry:

Königin Nacht sehr lieb. (Queen night very sweet.)[10]

A slender ash blonde with sparkling blue eyes and creamy skin, Elizabeth Christine was certainly the prettiest Habsburg bride in years. Charles called her fondly his "snow-white Liesl."

Leopold did not live to see the end of the succession war, but died in the spring of 1705 of "dropsy of the chest," not long after the victory of Blenheim. The war dragged on and on, involving nearly all of Europe, seesawing from one side to the other for nearly twelve years.

It was a viral accident finally that brought the war and Charles's Spanish kingship to an end. As his brother, now Emperor Joseph I, sat at table in the Hofburg one day in 1711, he was suddenly taken ill. It was smallpox, the dread disease he had escaped as a child. Despite all the remedies his doctors tried, including the newest one of wrapping him tightly in twenty yards of English woolen, Joseph died.

He left two daughters, but no sons.

Charles was hastily summoned back to Vienna. He stopped just long enough in Frankfurt to be crowned Emperor Charles VI.

Now Charles's allies agreed with his enemies that a double empire would be too much for a single Habsburg. When the Peace of Utrecht was signed in 1713, Philip of Anjou kept Spain. Charles got the Spanish Netherlands and most of Italy—Milan, Naples, Sardinia.

2. Problems and Pleasures of Charles VI

CHARLES'S LIFE in the Hofburg, like his father's, was the very pattern of regularity and order. He rose each day at the same hour, heard Mass, sat in council, held audiences, dined in public with his beautiful wife, observed all the rules of courtly etiquette. He was a methodical man and he was careful to enter the events of each day in his *Tagebuch*.

The temperament of his more phlegmatic Habsburg ancestors seemed to have been reborn in Charles, the very figure of stately majesty in public. And yet he had a vein of homely, droll, very dry humor, and he delighted in using the most colloquial of Viennese dialect in contrast to the formal Italian and Latin of the court.

He took his wife to see Josef Stranitzky perform in the original Hans Wurst comedies, impudently funny and often very rude, in the Kärntnertor Theater a stone's throw from the Hofburg. And he could hurry back unexpectedly from a journey through the provinces, wrapping himself in a great cloak so that even the guards did not recognize him, rush into his wife's apartment all unexpected, and buss her roundly, which, it was faithfully noted, "put her into an exceptional joy."[1]

And to surprise her after a childbirth, he conducted an opera in the Court Theater in her honor, calling out onto the stage their little six-year-old daughter, Maria Theresia, to enchant the audience with her singing.

Music was his passion, as it had been his father's. In Vienna everyone and everything made music: chairs were invented that played flute solos when you sat down, musical clocks played melodies when the hours struck. In the Court Theater and in the garden of the Emperor's summer palace lavish operas were staged. Charles's musicians were paid more than colonels in the imperial army.

Before Elizabeth Christine had arrived in Spain, Charles had whiled away a good many pleasant hours with a particularly beautiful countess of Italian extraction, Marianna Pignatelli. After his own wedding, Charles saw that Marianna was married to one of his courtiers, Count Michael Althann—one of those little services a truly loyal courtier might be called upon to perform for his sovereign. Althann was rewarded with one of the highest posts in the imperial household, Master of the Horse; the Althanns returned from Spain to Vienna with Charles and were installed in an apartment of the Hofburg.

A terrible fear haunted Charles, sat in like a ghost at every council table, stared over his shoulder where he presided in the throne room, and left an increasingly dark shadow over his whole reign. This was the fear that, like his Spanish cousin Carlos, he might beget no male heir, the Habsburg line would be extinguished as it had been in Spain, and his lands plunged after his death into another fearful succession struggle.

For the first eight years of their marriage, no children appeared at all. At last in 1716, to the jubilation of the court and the country, Elizabeth Christine bore a son, Archduke Leopold. Unhappily that precious bit of Habsburg male flesh survived only six months, leaving his parents inconsolably stricken. He died either—as court gossip related—because his nursery governess got the wetnurse in a fury over insulting remarks and quite spoiled her milk, or—as Lady Mary Wortley Montagu wrote home to England from Vienna—because his nurses unwisely tried to wean him in the middle of winter.[2]

Even the birth of two little daughters, Maria Theresia and Marianna, in the ensuing years failed to allay the Emperor's grief and anxiety.

All kinds of remedies, both physical and spiritual, were applied in the hope of producing another male heir. The court physicians prescribed strong wines and liquors for the Empress, which turned her fair cheeks a flaming scarlet. There were pilgrimages to the shrine of Mariazell for her soul's health, and to Karlsbad for her body's.

According to a Bohemian superstition which may have reached Charles's ears, only a crowned and anointed king could beget a male heir.[3] Charles would no doubt have had himself crowned in any case, but perhaps the legend contributed urgency to his plans. In any case in 1723 the whole imperial family made ready to journey to Prague.

The tremendous negotiations involved in such a journey took months to prepare; when Charles and his family finally left Vienna on June 19, it was in a convoy of more than four hundred coaches, including a small, low, specially built carriage for the six-year-old archduchess and heiress, Maria Theresia, so that she would be readily visible to the crowds.[4]

The coronation date was set for September 5; the summer was to be passed in Prague in a series of public appearances, processions, operas, receptions, hunts, and balls, designed to melt away the bitterness the Bohemians still nurtured against the Habsburgs for their defeat in the Battle of the White Mountain—and the subsequent harshness in their treatment—nearly a hundred years before.

Everything went off smoothly; even the tricky question of which citizens were to carry the "heaven" canopy over the Emperor for his entry into Prague—a question over which a small battle raged—was happily resolved when a drenching downpour made it necessary for him to enter the city in a carriage.[5]

A month before the coronation, however, on August 7, Charles made a significant entry in his diary: on that day his wife informed him that she was four weeks pregnant.

The terse entry gives no clue to Charles's feelings; jubilation and consternation must have waged war in his heart at that moment. It was her first pregnancy in five years; the joyful hope of a possible male heir was renewed; but the problem of getting the Empress safely through the exhausting coronation ceremony and back to Vienna without mishap was enough to cause the Emperor and his councilors a long series of sleepless nights.

The coronation went off without mishap, but in the days that followed Charles confided his anxieties to his diary.[6]

The first problem was to decide when to depart from Prague. He called his ministers together to advise him; all urged him to hurry back to Vienna as soon as the formal ceremonies were concluded. But Charles could not bear to risk a miscarriage in the early weeks of his wife's pregnancy; he decided to set a date for the beginning of November, as soon as she had felt the child quicken.

There was the tricky matter of a conveyance that could be trusted to transport the Empress safely in her delicate condition. Vienna was some eleven days' journey from Prague in the best weather, and the roads of central Europe were incredibly bad. Even the eleven-mile trip between the Hofburg and the imperial summer palace in Laxen-

burg could be downright dangerous at times, and more than once
axles broke, carriages overturned, and members of the imperial
family came back battered and bruised, "quite sick and limping."[7]
While the highroad between Prague and Vienna had been put in order
in early summer expressly for the coronation journey, the passage of
hundreds of heavy coaches and laden baggage wagons had damaged
it, and the autumn rains had quite returned it to its primitive condition.

Even a mule-borne litter would not be gentle enough, it was
decided. In the end a special sedan chair was ordered from Vienna,
together with twelve of the most skillful bearers, six to carry and six
to rest in a wagon that followed behind.[8]

The approach of winter brought other grave risks on such a
journey. The daylight hours were shorter; few inns or castles along
the way could provide well-heated sleeping rooms. Even the horses
could no longer be left out of doors at night as in summer. Most of
all Charles feared for his little daughters, whose "tender youth," as
he confided to his diary, made them particularly susceptible to chills,
and out of such chills the dreaded smallpox might come.[9]

Orders were sent ahead to the inns and castles where the party was
to put up for the night that the chambers where the Empress and the
little girls slept might be well aired and heated "to dispel evil smells
and dampness."[10]

Finally, on November 7, the huge party started out from Prague,
rising each day at three to begin traveling at four, stopping to
breakfast along the way at nine, and making an early halt for the night
before twilight fell in the afternoon. The homeward journey was
attended too by official celebrations, by serenades and illuminations
and fatiguing ceremonies. "Weib so grandig . . ." Charles reported
one day in his diary, "Wife pretty cross . . ."[11] But next day she was
herself again and taking part in a target shooting, which she adored,
and at which she acquitted herself so well that she won the first
wreath.

All in all, luck was with them. The seventeen-day journey went off
well; they reached Vienna on November 23, and Charles could
celebrate his relief and joy with the two things he loved most: a hunt
and a serenade by his chapel choir.

Hopefully he had Elizabeth Christine's apartments in the palace
decorated with robust male figures in the belief that they might
influence the child's sex.

But in April of 1724, after the months of planning and worry, the

Empress was brought to bed—again with a girl child. The youngest archduchess, Maria Amalia, joined her sisters in the nursery; not for long, however—the little girl died at five.

Even before his daughters had been born, Charles had begun to make arrangements for the succession in case he had no sons. The Pragmatic Sanction of 1713 stipulated that in the absence of male heirs his eldest living daughter would succeed to the Habsburg lands; if he left no surviving sons or daughters, the daughters of his dead brother Joseph would succeed.

But the succession of a woman to the Habsburg lands was without precedent, had been considered impossible in Germanic lands under the Salic law. As it became increasingly clear that there might be no male heirs, Charles sought to win acceptance of his daughter's heirship by the important European powers. A number of other monarchs had, through marriage or ancient claims, tenuous handholds on the Habsburg inheritance if a daughter's succession could be disputed. Charles paid a heavy price for agreement to the Sanction. He gave up his great plans for Austrian participation in sea trade—the price of England's agreement—he took part in two luckless wars; he lost territory in the south, west, and east.

Nobody ever quite gave up hope of an heir. In 1732 the Empress again journeyed to Karlsbad to take a cure, and again to Mariazell in the hope that the miraculous Virgin there would show special favor to the Habsburgs, as she had in times past.

The two little archduchesses, meantime, had been growing up in the Hofburg, well-bred little girls of charming deportment, who sang nicely, played the spinet, danced with grace, laughed at the antics of their father's dwarf jester, Baron Klein, in cap and bells, giggled in naughty daring over the coffee their maid smuggled in to them in a bag with their prayer books. Their strict and sensible governess, Countess Fuchs—whom they called irreverently *die Füchsin*, the she-fox—put a good deal more emphasis on manners than on history. Even the heiress, Maria Theresia, bothered her pretty head very little over politics; to the end of her life she would spell abominably and seldom read a book.

During the famous coronation sojourn in Prague one small event had taken place that was quite overlooked by eager and curious foreign envoys. While Charles was out hunting one day, a handsome fourteen-year-old boy had joined the hunting party quite casually; shortly afterward the imperial chancellor announced the arrival in Prague of Franz Stephan, heir to the duchy of Lorraine.

The closest bonds of kinship and friendship bound the ducal family of Lorraine to the Habsburgs. It was Franz Stephan's grandfather, Duke Charles, married to a half sister of Emperor Leopold, who had led the imperial army in the famous victory over the Turks in 1683. Franz Stephan's father had been Charles's closest friend during his boyhood. The boy's appearance in Prague as if by chance stirred little comment.

But when the hoped-for throne heir failed to materialize the following spring, and when the gay young prince appeared presently, to be installed in a wing of the Hofburg under a carefully chosen set of tutors and to ride out daily hunting with the Emperor, word flashed from one capital of Europe to another that a bridegroom was in training for the Habsburg heiress.

The eventual betrothal of the two was not accomplished, however, without months and years of political juggling. Other claimants vied for the hand of the heiress. Prince Eugene, eying the growing military might of Prussia, thought that marriage with the Prussian Crown Prince Frederick might be a safer guarantee of her future; others urged marriage with a Spanish Bourbon prince.

As for Maria Theresia herself, her affections had been firmly fixed on the gay, attractive boy she had first seen in Prague. By the time she was fifteen everyone knew she was in love with Franz. The English ambassador Sir Thomas Robinson wrote home that:

> . . . notwithstanding her lofty humour by day, she sighs and pines all night for her Duke of Lorraine. If she sleeps it is only to dream of him, if she awakens it is but to talk of him to her lady in waiting.[12]

While her father and his ministers debated her marriage, while Franz Stephan entertained himself in the courts of France and England, Maria Theresia continued to press her father to yield.

There was a last perilous moment. The French king demanded that, in exchange for French agreement to the Pragmatic Sanction, Franz Stephan must surrender his duchy of Lorraine to France. He was to be given the duchy of Tuscany instead, but it was a difficult decision and the young duke quailed before it. When, at the very end, he was presented with the document he must sign forfeiting his family's lands to France, three times he took up the pen, three times threw it down in disgust. One of Charles's ministers reminded him bluntly, "*Point de renonciation, point d'archeduchesse.*" (No renunciation, no archduchess.) Franz signed.[13]

A remarkably handsome couple, Franz and Maria Theresia, they were married the following February of 1736, in the Augustiner Church adjoining the Hofburg.

There was a single slight delay even at the very end. The papal nuncio who performed the ceremony declared it was his right to remain seated during the service. Emperor Charles hastily promulgated a Bull elucidating that important matter of protocol. The nuncio stood before the Habsburg heiress.[14]

The last years of Charles's life were beset with troubles and disappointments.

Prince Eugene died; there were no able generals to take his place. Charles got himself embroiled in a needless war with the Turks, which ended in humiliating defeat and the loss of Serbia and Belgrade.

There were nagging financial worries; the wars had eaten into the whole financial structure of the state; the treasury stood nearly empty.

That baleful ghost of his life—the dearth of male heirs—continued to pursue him up to the end. During the first four years of her marriage, Maria Theresia bore three children, all girls. Distracted with worry, Charles asked himself, would there never be another male in the Habsburg family?

He himself was no longer well. He had grown very stout; his stomach gave him trouble; he suffered miserably from gout.

He could still enjoy his music and his hunting. In the autumn of 1740 he rode as usual to his hunting lodge on the shores of swampy Neusiedler Lake. He returned one day from hunting in an icy downpour, became violently ill, and was carried back to Vienna, where he died a few days later.

His humor did not fail him. According to one story, as his doctors conferred worriedly at his bedside, he suggested that one of them dispatch himself after the autopsy and bring him word in heaven as to exactly what had ailed him.[15]

VIII

The Great Empress

1. A New Queen

THE ICY WIND that blew over central Europe that autumn of 1740, freezing the vines and ruining the wine crop, chilling and killing the Emperor Charles, was a winter long remembered in Austria; it was the bitterest of Maria Theresia's life.

She was twenty-three years old and pregnant with her fourth child when her father lay on his deathbed. Her physicians would not allow her to bid him good-bye; in the last hours of his life the dying Emperor turned in the direction of his daughter's room and raised his arms in a gesture of benediction.

She needed that blessing.

In spite of all her father had done to buy the right of succession for her, his death was the signal to loose a great Europe-wide succession war. Frederick of Prussia—not yet Great—grabbed Silesia before the young and inexperienced queen had so much as put on her crown. In December he invaded Silesia; she would hate him all her life for it.

In her own country everything was at sixes and sevens. Provoked by cold and misery, people rioted in Vienna in the month after Charles's death. There was no army to defend the country, no money to raise one. Morale was at a low ebb. Her own ministers—old, old men, all except one in their seventies—hadn't the slightest bit of faith in the ability of a young and pretty woman to rule anything. The faces around her council table were long and doleful. The English ambassador Robinson wrote home:

> "Oh!" cryed the Chancellor to me, "were she but a man with the very same endowments she has!"[1]

In the desperate anxieties of that winter, Maria Theresia wrote her mother-in-law, the Dowager Duchess of Lorraine, that she did not know where to go to await the birth of her child in peace.[2]

Terrible personal anguish beset her. Only the previous June her eldest child, a bright pretty little girl of three, had died within hours, stricken with a mysterious ailment. "She is inconsolable," Robinson had written. Now, again within the space of a few hours, her youngest child sickened and died.[3]

It must have seemed that December and January that her whole safe and familiar world was breaking apart, and she herself helpless to stop it.

The crown of the Holy Roman Empire passed out of the hands of the Habsburgs, for the second time in centuries. No woman could wear that crown; Maria Theresia had wanted desperately to see it bestowed on her husband, Franz of Lorraine. Once again France intervened to support the rival candidate. The Elector of Bavaria, who was laying claim to the Habsburg hereditary lands, was chosen instead.

One by one all the signatories to those treaties her father had bought so dearly now abandoned her. The Prussians defeated the Austrian forces at Mollwitz. France and Bavaria prepared to carve up the Habsburg Empire. In Paris, Cardinal Fleury announced to the world, "There is no more House of Austria!"[4]

But they counted without the remarkable courage and energy of Maria Theresia: she had to learn quickly how to command. A born worker, she was in her cabinet or at the council table from daybreak until late at night, conferring, planning, dictating, maneuvering, almost literally holding together with sheer strength of will the breaking package.

In March she was in childbed; suddenly her whole country took on fresh hope. A boy was born, the first male in the family in a quarter of a century, and not a mere boy baby but a hulking great Hercules of a child, who was said to have weighed sixteen pounds at birth.[5] The birth was so easy that his mother announced cheerfully a few hours later that she would not in the least mind being in the sixth month of another pregnancy.[6] With pride and joy the father laid in the little archduke's cradle the collar of the Golden Fleece.

In June of 1741 Maria Theresia was crowned Queen of Hungary, rode up the Coronation Mount at Pressburg on a white charger, wearing the tattered mantle of St. Stephen, to defy with her saber the four corners of the earth.

That summer a Bavarian army threatened to invade Austria—with a French army on the way to join it. Maria Theresia had virtually no army to defend her country. She called the Hungarian Diet to

Pressburg, and she herself appeared to plead her cause before the magnates, men who bore bitter resentment against the Habsburgs for a century of harsh treatment since the Thirty Years' War.

Still in deep mourning for her father, the Queen's dark gown set off admirably her fair skin and pretty shoulders. Under the crown of St. Stephen her blonde hair fell in curls to her shoulders. When she rose to speak, her voice broke with emotion:

Agitur de regno Hungariae [she cried], *de persona nostra!*

At the end of her moving plea for help, when she burst into very real tears, the magnates could no longer contain themselves—her old friend Count Jean Palffy recounted the scene afterward—but leapt to their feet, "as if animated by one soul, drew our sabres and cried, *'Vitam et sanguinem pro majestate vostra!'* (Our life and blood for Your Majesty.) We wept as did the Queen, aloud, tears of loyalty, of affection, and of indignation."[7]

More important, they voted her six regiments.

The Bavarians were driven out of her lands. The French made peace. Eventually the Holy Crown of the Empire went to Maria Theresia's husband, Franz.

She embarked then on the two great themes of her reign: the unification of her multilingual lands—the theme, in fact, of all Habsburg history; and that revolution in European diplomacy, the Habsburg-French alliance.

She was a difficult rival for Frederick of Prussia. All her life she would manage to give the impression of victory, though she lost to him quite consistently.

2. *The* Landesmutter

THE PALACE NURSERIES simply burst with children. There were sixteen in all. During the first half of her reign, when Maria Theresia was plunged into that long series of wars and difficult diplomatic moves, when she had to cope with the reorganization of her army and finances and the administering of the most complex realm in all Europe, she was always either pregnant or nursing a child.

It was maddening that her archenemy, Frederick of Prussia, could ride at the head of his troops and move them about with lightning swiftness, while she had to direct things from home. "No one," she declared once, thinking of her dawdling Austrian generals, "would have prevented me from joining my armies myself, had I not been continuously pregnant."[1]

And yet she was a thoroughly feminine woman who believed that women's place was by the cradle and at their husbands' sides, as she told her own daughters time and again; *she* happened to rule because it was the will of God and her duty.

They were feminine talents she brought to her queenship: tact, compassion, human understanding.

The old, old men disappeared from her council table. She had an eye for the right person in the right job; unlike her father and grandfather, she was quick to recognize and reward talent.

For chancellor she got the shrewdest statesman in continental Europe, Count Wenzel Kaunitz. A clever Silesian, Count Friedrich Wilhelm Haugwitz, handled army reform; a Bohemian, Count Rudolf Chotek, reorganized taxation. She never found a general to match Prince Eugene, who had died three months after her wedding, but she made out with the best she could get—a Scotsman, Laudon, and an Irishman, Lacy. She herself saw that her soldiers were properly fed, clothed, blanketed.

Her ministers and generals gave her unswerving loyalty; she was like one of those shrewd, capable Austrian housewives whose servants stay with them a lifetime.

She hadn't a shred of intellectual brilliance; the Enlightenment was a fearful bogey on which she firmly shut her country's door. But she had three things even more important in a ruler: sound judgment, a generous spirit, and an enormous store of physical and spiritual stamina.

She worked indefatigably; she danced tirelessly; she simply could not bear to waste time. She would drive very fast out of the city to her summer palace of Schönbrunn, the windows of her carriage flung down, like the windows of her apartment, winter and summer, so that her ladies in waiting shivered and her own hair blew about her face. She would drive in the great gates between the slender obelisks, grandly tossing out a handful of gold pieces to her guards, drive across the courtyard that bustled with carriages, market women, dragoons on guard, barefoot friars—the Venetian Bellotto has left us a vivid painting of the scene. Jumping down lightly at the great front door, she would hurry inside and in a few minutes be bent over her desk, writing those interminable memoranda, orders of battle, letters to ambassadors, instructions to her children's tutors—all dashed off in a rapid scrawl with the most perfunctory attention to spelling and grammar.

Though her chamberlain, Count Silva-Tarouca, had to reprimand her delicately for her inattention to dress, she was a handsome woman and a regal one, and she understood perfectly how to create an imperial image. She could make a splendid appearance in the throne room, magnificently gowned, with the gift her husband had brought from the treasures of his lost Lorraine, the huge diamond called "the Florentine" sparkling at her forehead; or in her carrousel coach, shaped like an open seashell, in which, filled with fresh flowers, she rode through the streets of Vienna like a youthful Venus Anadyomene. As long as her husband lived she could give the impression of beauty, in itself a considerable talent. Even Count Podewils, the ambassador of her archenemy, the King of Prussia, had to admit that Maria Theresia was "a most charming and delightful woman."[2]

Perhaps what most captivated her admirers was her warmth and naturalness, and her immense capacity for enjoying herself: at gala evenings in the palace, on horseback in the Vienna Woods with her husband at her side, and in that wonderful canopied bed in the Hofburg, where her solemn duty to the Empire coincided so perfectly with her own inclinations. It is clear from contemporary accounts that she laughed a great deal. Until 1765 she masked and danced and played jokes in carnival. To the end of her life she never lost her humor.

When her mentor, Count Silva-Tarouca, thought she was enjoying *Fasching* too much and sent her an earnest reminder of her duties as a monarch, she returned the memo with a marginal comment, "Remind me again when Lent begins."[3]

Goethe describes how she stood on a balcony in Frankfurt watching her husband's coronation procession emerge from the church in 1745; when Franz raised his hands and gestured up to show her the old red-and-gold gloves, the orb and scepter, she had laughed and clapped her hands with delight, as she had once long ago as a little girl when she had first seen her father in his imperial robes walking past in the Corpus Christi procession.[4]

As for the formal court etiquette that had ruled the Hofburg for so long, Maria Theresia brushed it away with a wave of her fan and a laugh of high good-humor. Her father and her grandfather, both shy men who could not bear the world nudging at their elbows, used etiquette to keep the crowd at a distance. Maria Theresia neither needed nor wanted it. She made it perfectly easy for her subjects to see her. At her audiences each morning at ten, anyone who wished might speak quite freely, even whisper in her ear on a very private matter.

When the Mozart family made their first appearance in Vienna, Maria Theresia had them out to Schönbrunn where the two children, little Wolfgang and his sister, performed for the imperial family, and as Leopold wrote his wife:

> Their Majesties received us with such extraordinary graciousness that when I describe it, people will not believe me. Suffice it to say that Wolferl jumped upon the lap of the Empress, put his arms around her neck and kissed her heartily.[5]

When the Scottish philosopher David Hume, very fat in his older years, was presented to the Empress, and with his companions began to bow his way out of the long reception room of the palace, Maria Theresia called out cheerfully, "*Allez, allez, messieurs, sans cérémonie!* You're not used to it and the floor is slippery!" As Hume said afterward, they were all very grateful to her, especially his companions, who had been desperately afraid he might slip and fall on top of them.[6]

And when, later in her reign, her first grandson was born, that precious and terribly important heir to the Habsburg throne, a messenger brought the news to her where she worked one evening in her cabinet in the Hofburg. Dropping her papers, she went rushing through the corridors of the palace in negligee and out into the loge of the Court Theater where a crowd had gathered to hear an opera. Leaning over the imperial box she called down, "Children! children! My Poldy has a boy. And on my wedding anniversary!" The pit was electrified and burst into thunderous applause.[7]

One of the legends in Austria of Maria Theresia—which, like most apocryphal legends of the great no doubt contains its kernel of truth —relates that as she walked in the garden of Schönbrunn with her infant son Joseph and his nurse, they came upon a beggar woman holding a screaming baby to her empty breast. The Empress stopped at once to open her purse; the woman turned away with an angry gesture, saying bitterly that a gold piece would not quiet her hungry babe. Thereupon the Empress picked up the squawling child and put it to her own ample breast.[8]

3. Maria Theresia's Chastity Commission

THERE HAD NEVER been a doubt that her marriage, for all its political efficacy, was one of true love.

When she was thirty-two and had been married exactly thirteen years, Maria Theresia ordered her tomb to be built in the Kapuziner Church. On the lid of that necrophilic masterpiece the imperial couple recline gracefully, as they might have flung themselves down on a flowery hillside at Schönbrunn, youthful, ardent, about to make love. It was not at all the usual royal tomb portrait. The Empress' low-cut court gown displays her handsome shoulders and breast, and, as a contemporary English visitor wrote home delicately, "The Emperor's posture, it must be owned, is somewhat equivocal."[1] While an angel holds a wreath above their heads, they gaze into one another's eyes for all eternity.

The Empress must have said, "I will have it so, in marble, and forever."

The truth was that her husband's attention was straying.

Franz of Lorraine was by all accounts a delightful man and a kind one, good-looking, cultivated, charming. He hunted well, danced with grace, made love beautifully—he had, after all, learned at the court of France. His wife had got him crowned Holy Roman Emperor, that one crown that no woman could wear, and had hoped he would prove a military, or at least a diplomatic, genius. Franz was neither. Gradually the Empress stopped consulting him about matters of war and state; he had, in the end, nothing at all to do except to fulfill his functions as her husband.

That voluptuous shared bedroom in the Hofburg must have become irksome in the end. For years his wife was nearly always pregnant. Besides, she kept atrocious hours, rising at four in summer, at five in winter, working energetically through the day, going to bed at a decent hour so that she could rise again and work at dawn.

Before long gossip got about that the Emperor Franz was flirting, that there were private, very amusing supper parties with a pretty dancer attending. The Prussian ambassador wrote home with undisguised malice that the Empress wished to keep a *ménage bourgeois*, but that the Emperor was not being entirely cooperative.[2]

It was not a delicate age, and morals in Vienna were far from tidy. Flirting and gallantry accompanied all the diversions of the court set. A few years earlier Lady Mary Wortley Montagu had described the situation in Vienna:

> Men look upon their wives' gallants as favorably as upon deputies that take the troublesome part of their business out of their hands; though they have not the less to do, for they are generally deputies in another place themselves; in short, 'tis the established custom for every lady to have two husbands, one who bears the name, and another who performs the duties.[3]

Comedy both on stage and off was apt to be coarser and bawdier than either in England or in France. Lady Mary professed herself shocked at a performance of *Amphitryon*. Such an event as the birth of a throne heir could be greeted with exceedingly gross public utterances. Some of Mozart's songs, written for the amusement of his friends in merry evenings at home, are, like his scatalogical letters to his little cousin in Augsburg, scarcely printable, but not at all out of keeping with the age and place.

When Maria Theresia discovered that her husband was finding amusement elsewhere, she had time to be angry and jealous. Her decision was on a typically imperial scale: she would simply abolish vice throughout her realm. She was perfectly sure she could rule morals as efficiently as she had handled taxation and supplies for the army.

In 1753 she set up a Chastity Commission, its purpose simply to enforce virtue in public and private. Her trusted chief minister, Kaunitz, was put in charge; he must have kept tongue carefully in cheek, for he himself was a man of decided French tastes, with no small reputation for gallantry in the court of Vienna. Under him a force of regular state police functioned, plus a body of secret agents whose job was to ferret out hidden vice.

Chastity police were posted in theaters and ballrooms; they patrolled the streets with orders to arrest girls found walking alone. At the Austrian borders they ransacked the luggage of travelers, even went through diplomatic mailbags to extract naughty books—or the works of the French philosophers.[4]

Prostitutes were transported to southern Hungary, where a rather unique village was said to have been populated almost entirely with the banished ladies. Streetwalkers learned quickly to avoid arrest by walking demurely, head down, ostentatiously fingering a rosary.[5]

Chastity police followed up reports brought by jealous wives, and counter-reports by jealous husbands. Easygoing Vienna howled—first with dismay, then with amusement. It seemed that a new fillip was added to the normal allurements of sin. A crowd of fast young men about town organized an intriguing secret society called the Figleaf Brotherhood, with the avowed purpose of thwarting the Chastity Commissioners. Their feminine equivalent, the Order of Free Ladies, met with them for gay parties wearing, gossip reported, chiefly masks and pseudonyms.

Once when police raided a party of Figleaf Brothers, the offenders were sentenced to be shackled at the city gates to beg their food and drink from passers-by. But none of them had to beg, for citizens flocked to the gate bringing delicacies and sympathy.[6]

Casanova just then visited Vienna with a mistress on whom he had bestowed the gratuitous title of countess. They were surprised at breakfast the day after their arrival by a visit from the Chastity Police, and when Casanova admitted he was a bachelor he was forced to move immediately into separate quarters. Ruefully he wrote that there was plenty of money and plenty of luxury in Vienna, but that "the bigotry of the Empress makes Cytherean pleasures extremely difficult."[7]

Actually this was only because Casanova did not know the ropes. The great lords and cavaliers of the city who had formerly set up a pretty mistress in a little house in the country—a custom far too dangerous now—would arrange for her to be hired as an extra chambermaid by some elderly, respectable marquise of their acquaintance who had not forgotten her own youth. So that when the lord's coach stood half the night outside a mansion door, nobody thought a thing about it, least of all the Chastity Police. An occasional "chambermaid" was caught, of course, had her hair shaved off, and was stood in the pillory. On the whole, however, there was a great rush into the chambermaid market.[8]

Certainly the Chastity Commission did not deter in the least the

Empress' own husband. Two years after it had been established, Franz took as his mistress a gray-eyed beauty of the court, the Princess Wilhelmina Auersperg. It was an attachment that lasted until his death.

The princess was no ordinary rival. Daughter of a field marshal of the Empire, she belonged to one of the noblest families at court, had married into another; she was, besides, supremely lovely. Franz gave her a country house near the palace at Laxenburg, and began to devote more and more time to the chase. The princess presided at lively little supper parties at Laxenburg, with covers set for ten or twelve, and all ceremony banished. Like Franz she adored the gaming table; her imperial lover undertook to pay her enormous gambling debts.

In August of 1765 the imperial couple set out from Schönbrunn by coach for Innsbruck to attend the wedding of their second son, Leopold, to a princess of Spain. The Empress was unaccountably nervous; they were late starting out, and Franz made her very cross by turning the carriage back to give one more farewell kiss to his favorite little daughter, Maria Antonia, who was then nine years old.

The following week in Innsbruck, on his way to a gala performance of an opera, Franz suddenly staggered, put his hand to his head, collapsed, and died within minutes.

Although Maria Theresia was only forty-eight years old, in a blooming and vigorous prime, she never took off her mourning. The pale gold ringlets that had entranced the Hungarian nobles at Pressburg, threaded now with gray, were snipped off and combed flat back under a black crepe cap. She moved out of those joyous rococo rooms in the Hofburg that speak even today of earthly love on a monarchical scale, into a black-draped apartment on the third floor, with a trap door that opened so she could hear Mass from the chapel beneath. She never wore her jewels again, never masked again, nor danced, nor took a lover. She forbade the ladies of the court to rouge for the whole period of mourning.

A few days after Franz's death the court exchequer brought the Empress a note for 200,000 florins—a gambling debt of the Princess Auersperg, found among Franz's papers. The Empress ordered it paid.[9]

The Princess Auersperg was particularly bitter about the ban on rouge, declaring, "Is it possible one cannot be mistress of one's own face?"[10]

4. Absolutism in the Nursery

> And however much I love my family and my
> children, so much that I would not spare myself
> effort, trouble, anxiety, or work, yet I would have
> preferred to them the country's general good if
> I had been persuaded in my conscience that I
> could further it, or that the well-being of my
> subjects required it, seeing that I am the general
> and chief mother of my country.
>
> *Maria Theresia*[1]

THEY WERE a much-painted family. At Schönbrunn and elsewhere
the baker's dozen of blond, blue-eyed boys and girls gaze brightly
and hopefully out of the portraits, as if the future could hold nothing
for a Habsburg child but the sunniest of Schönbrunn summer weather.
Against the identical Schönbrunn terrace background the eight pretty
girls smile out of the pictures, in splendid gowns, all lace, brocade,
and satin bows, the five handsome boys in periwigs and velvet breeches,
quite the picture of the Ideal Ruling Family, even to the two small
puppy dogs frisking in the foreground.

No wonder they were the talk of Europe. No other eighteenth-
century court had anything quite like them. In Potsdam the hated
Frederick kept a strictly male menage, communicated with *his* wife
only by letter. In St. Petersburg the childless spinster Czarina Elizabeth
hired lovers to keep her company. At Versailles there was Du Barry
to amuse the aging Louis XV, and a batch of unattractive and unmarried daughters.

In the family portraits in Vienna Emperor Franz, his roving eye
subdued in the pictures, sits with grace and ease, the crown of the

Holy Roman Empire on a table beside him, at his feet on a tiny throne, the bonneted baby, Maria Antonia, who would one day be Queen of France. Maria Theresia sits opposite him, a trifle stout by now, a trifle florid, but quite majestic. She does not bother to smile, to strike a pose; she is the most self-assured woman in Europe.

There was little time to spare for her children. They might kiss her hand at certain hours of the day; occasionally she would hurry down to the schoolroom to see how one or another of the children was absorbing his lesson. Parents and children, of course, addressed one another with the formal *vous*. Mostly she communicated her wishes on their upbringing in writing—precise instructions to each tutor and governess, even to the prayers the children were to recite each morning and evening.

For years the nursery wing that occupied part of the ground floor of Schönbrunn bustled with activity, with the drone of children reciting lessons, the tinkle of harpsichord and soprano scales, the clink of little boys practicing fencing.

The nurses and governesses and *ajos* (head preceptors) were usually widowed countesses or retired court officials, chosen less for their understanding and experience with children than for their irreproachable piety and knowledge of court protocol. Besides the chief tutors and governesses—one for each child or two—a regiment of special teachers came and went to give instruction in dancing, music, languages, writing.

Discipline was strict; there was no permissiveness in the imperial nursery. Nor did a child have any privacy; a tutor or governess or chamberlain was watching every hour of the day. Their daily schedules were crammed as full as their mother's. Delicate, nervous Josepha, who broke too easily into tears, studied in the course of each day German, Latin, Spanish, Italian, history, grammar, religion, and writing. At four o'clock her dancing master came, after which she recited her Rosary "very loudly," then ate a simple supper: "soup and one other dish," her mother's precise instructions read. She saw her family only on Sundays, when she could join them for church and dinner. Josepha's governess had got a firmly worded message from the imperial mother that the girl's bad habits

> must be uprooted immediate and thoroughly. . . . I cannot flatter myself that I can be successful with her until the source of her trouble, her violent temper and her selfishness have been restrained. When she is even spoken to, she becomes so irritated that she is ready to weep with anger.[2]

The eldest boy, Joseph, showed great promise. He was not a quick learner like his attractive, mercurial brother Charles, but he had the kind of dogged mind that never loses what it has once grasped. *Der Starrkopf*, the stubborn one, his mother called him, and instructed his tutor:

> In the evening you are to leave the Archduke; if necessary one of the chamberlains is to join him. But you are to remain in the room to observe his manners, his postures, and so forth from a distance. You can then judge his deportment and correct him.[3]

Once Maria Theresia ordered that Joseph be punished by a whipping. When his chamberlains protested that no archduke ever got spanked, she retorted, "That's plain to see from their manners," but she rescinded the order.[4]

The Empress, like most mothers, worried about her children's eating habits. Firmly she directed the governesses:

> [My children] are to eat everything set before them without making any objection. They are not to make any remarks about preferring this or that, or to discuss their food. They are to eat fish every Friday and Saturday and on every fast day. Though Joanna has a repulsion against fish, no one is to give in to her. . . . All my children seem to have an aversion against fish, but they must overcome this.[5]

Periodically she wrote long, detailed letters to her daughters, reviewing their manners and conduct. To fourteen-year-old Caroline, who had requested a change of governesses, she wrote permitting the change but reprimanding her severely for saying her prayers carelessly, for being rude to her ladies in waiting and bad-tempered while they were dressing her:

> I cannot forget this rudeness in you and I shall never forgive it. Your voice and your speech are unpleasant enough as it is; you must therefore make a special effort to improve in this respect; you must never raise your voice.

How one prepared oneself for queenhood she explained explicitly:

> You are conscientiously to continue your exercises in music, painting, history, geography and Latin. You must never be lazy, for indolence is dangerous for everyone and especially for you. You must occupy your mind, for this will prevent you from thinking of childish pranks, from making unsuitable remarks and from longing for foolish amusements.[6]

As they grew older the children began to appear in court society. Throngs came to watch them dine in public with their parents in the gilded Hall of Mirrors under a gold-embroidered canopy. On birthdays and name days and other celebrations they appeared in private theatricals and ballets in the palace theater: the foreign envoys exchanged malicious smiles when poor shy Joseph fumbled and swallowed his words as he recited a poem one of the ladies of the court had composed in honor of his mother's birthday.

They are scarcely out of the nursery before their mother is juggling marriage plans. These thirteen children (three of the sixteen had died in infancy) represented an incalculable political capital. For twenty years their marriages absorbed a great share of the Empress' time and planning. Into them she wove the great political theme of her reign—alliance with Austria's ancient enemy, France, against the new enemy, Prussia; through them she made subtle reconquest of the Italian states, lost by her father's inept statesmanship.

The matter of heirs having top priority, Crown Prince Joseph was married first, to Princess Isabella of Parma, a granddaughter of the King of France.

Joseph was shy with women; he had not much ease of manner or small talk. But he had the rarest good fortune for a crown prince—to fall deeply in love with the wife his parents had chosen for him. Isabella of Parma was apparently a remarkable girl, pretty, intelligent, sensitive, and perfectly trained for her role of royal wife. In place of sentimental novels, she read Bossuet and John Law; her writings show a remarkably acute understanding of the political situation in her day.[7] She took infinite pains to charm her awkward young husband, to draw him out, to give him pleasure in her company. "One must tell him the truth in all things," she wrote once, "and always meet him gently and tenderly."[8] The whole family was enchanted with Isabella; Joseph, a serious boy deep in the French philosophers, succumbed completely.

But if she was the nearly perfect wife, still it was not Joseph who commanded Isabella's deepest affection, but his sister, Marie Christine, whom the family called Mimi. Exactly the same age, eighteen, the two princesses, the dark Italian and the blonde Austrian, walked together in the Schönbrunn gardens, exchanged endless confidences, sang and made music together, painted portraits of one another, and even when they met each day, exchanged long, loving, intimate letters. When the Empress spoke to Mimi of Isabella, she called her *"votre chère moitié"*—your dear other half.

To Mimi, Isabella would write:

> I am writing you again, cruel sister, though I have only just left you. I cannot bear waiting to know my fate, and to learn whether you consider me a person worthy of your love, or whether you would like to fling me into the river. . . . I can think of nothing but that I am deeply in love. If I only knew why this is so, for you are so without mercy that one should not love you, but I cannot help myself.[9]

And a little later:

> I am told that the day begins with God. I, however, begin the day by thinking of the object of my love, for I think of her incessantly.[10]

Together with that violent friendship, a deep melancholy laid hold of Joseph's pretty young wife; Isabella's letters reveal an increasing preoccupation with death. There is no evidence that Joseph noticed anything unusual, but to friends and to her lady in waiting Isabella declared that she would die soon, and added that the little daughter, Thérèse, whom she had borne to Joseph, would not long remain behind:

> Death is good [she wrote]. Never have I thought of it more than now. Everything arouses in me the desire to die soon. God knows my wish to desert a life which insults Him every day. If it were permitted to kill one's self, I would have already done it.[11]

And again:

> I can say that death speaks to me in a distinct secret voice. For three days I have heard this voice.[12]

Certainly she did not have to seek death out: it was never long absent from any eighteenth-century household. When she had been married just three years and was pregnant with her second child, Isabella sickened with smallpox. Joseph had been immunized by a childhood attack, and now he watched by her bedside in anguish as she grew worse each day. She died in November, 1763, at twenty-one.

To Isabella's father, Joseph wrote:

> I hardly know if I am still alive. I shall be unhappy all the rest of my days.[13]

The following spring when he traveled to Frankfurt to be crowned King of the Romans, he was perhaps the most unhappy young king who ever knelt for a crowning.

The official court mourning period was not yet over before his mother was broaching new marriage plans: it was absolutely essential for an anointed successor to produce heirs. Absorbed in his grief, the young widower at first refused, finally gave in, looking over with indifference the distasteful choices offered from among the few available Catholic princesses.

His second marriage to the Bavarian Princess Josepha took place at Schönbrunn in 1765. It was anything but gay, though the Empress tried her level best to make it so. Even the Viennese could not summon up a festive spirit. The bride was two years older than her husband; cynics would have it that the Bavarian king had swindled the Habsburgs and sent his aunt instead of his sister. Besides being awkward and not at all clever, Josepha was downright plain; her whole face and body were covered with scorbutic sores. The family ignored her, except for the Emperor Franz, who was kind to everyone.

As for Joseph, he simply couldn't bear her. He had the balcony connecting their two apartments partitioned off, and spent as much time as possible traveling. He wrote his mother:

> Excuse me for not writing my wife. There is nothing to say to her; wind and rain cannot fill up a page.[14]

He added furthermore:

> They want me to have children. How can we have them? If I could put the tip of my finger on the tiniest part of her body which was not covered with pimples, I would try to have children.[15]

Melancholy and chronically ailing, the unfortunate Josepha spent her days trying cures at the nearby spa of Baden. In the terrible smallpox epidemic of 1767 Josepha got the disease in its most malignant form and died within days. The Empress in pity for the girl sat by her bedside during her last hours. It was then that Maria Theresia herself contracted smallpox and lay so close to death that the last rites were given her. She recovered, however: it would take more than smallpox to kill her.

That decade of the 1760s was a terrible one for the Empress. Her favorite son, Charles, a charming boy of sixteen, died of smallpox, and gentle twelve-year-old Joanna. Both Joseph's wives had died of

the pox, and in the middle of the decade Maria Theresia herself
became a widow.

Yet amid her sorrowing she continued with her marriage plans.
The oldest daughter, Marianna, crippled apparently from birth,
was destined by her mother for a convent.

The second daughter, Elizabeth, was the great beauty of the family
and a born coquette. ("So long as she pleases someone, whether it is
a soldier on guard duty or a prince, she is content," her mother once
wrote Joseph.[16]) Everyone was certain that a brilliant match, probably with a ruling monarch, was in store for Elizabeth. The Empress
turned down a proposal from Stanislaus, ex-King of Poland, certain
that something better would turn up. When King Louis XV of France
lost his wife, it seemed possible that the new Franco-Austrian alliance
just arranged by Kaunitz might be cemented by a match between
the blooming, young Elizabeth and the elderly monarch. Elizabeth
danced at a palace ball in a domino embroidered with fleurs-de-lis.

In the autumn of 1767 Elizabeth too came down with smallpox.
It was said that as the girl grew ill she asked for a looking glass so
that she could look one last time at her pretty face.[17] Elizabeth did
not die, but when she held a mirror again, it was to a face horribly
ravaged, every trace of her beauty destroyed. Her suitors melted
away. The lecherous old King of France slyly sent a court painter to
do her portrait; the marriage overtures were dropped.[18]

Frantically Elizabeth called in doctors and quacks, tried medicines
and salves. When it became clear at last that she was doomed to
spinsterhood, Maria Theresia bestowed on Elizabeth the only life
possible for damaged princesses and youngest sons—the Church.
Titular head of an order for aged ladies in Innsbruck, Elizabeth
continued to live in the Hofburg, a bitter spinster, angry with the
world and with her fate.

Vivacious, attractive Marie Christine, called Mimi, the third daughter, was her mother's favorite; she could always contrive to wind the
Empress about her finger. Her parents wanted to betroth Mimi to the
French Duc de Chablais, but Mimi held out firmly for her own
choice of suitor—Duke Albert of Saxony, a younger son with neither
fortune nor prospect of a throne. She got her way; it was a deeply
happy match. Her husband, a man of cultivated tastes, was a devoted
husband and son-in-law.

There were, in the meantime, the younger children to plan for.
Little Joanna, who died at twelve, had been betrothed already to

Ferdinando, child-king of Naples, and younger son of the Bourbon King of Spain. Maria Theresia, determined not to let the central Italian kingdom slip from her, hastened to betroth another daughter, gentle and attractive Josepha, to take her sister's place.

Most disquieting rumors had already reached the Vienna court about the boy-monarch of Naples. Ferdinando's older brother was an imbecile, and Ferdinando himself of so unpromising a mentality that his father had decided not to submit him to the rigors of an education. He could barely read, spoke only Neapolitan dialect, cared for nothing but hunting and outdoor games.

If Josepha sulked over her prospective marriage, her mother saw her own duty clearly. To Josepha's governess she wrote firmly:

> I consider Josepha a sacrifice to politics, and if she fulfills her duty to her husband and her God, I shall be content. . . . I hope my daughter will not be selfish; she has a tendency in that direction.[19]

In October of 1767 the preparations for Josepha's departure had been made, her trousseau, including a hundred dresses from Paris, was in readiness, and Vienna was thronged with wedding guests. Josepha had been born on her brother Joseph's name day, and she was his favorite little sister. He had promised to accompany her on her bridal journey as far as the city of Florence. Among those who had come to Vienna for the wedding were Leopold Mozart and his little son Wolfgang, hoping to find some musical chores to perform.

A few days before the wedding, the Empress took Josepha with her into the Kapuziner Crypt to pay a farewell visit to the tombs of the Habsburg dead. Josepha had begged not to go; her attendants declared she had wept in the carriage that drove her to the church, shivered while she knelt praying in the chilly crypt. Within a few hours Josepha too lay mortally sick of smallpox; she died on the day she would have departed to be Queen of Naples. The whole court whispered that she had caught the disease in the crypt where the body of her sister-in-law, the unlucky Bavarian Josepha, had festered unembalmed since the previous May.[20]

Maria Theresia did not abandon her plans for the throne of Naples. As soon as decency permitted, she betrothed her next-to-the-youngest daughter, fifteen-year-old Caroline, to Ferdinando. Caroline was neither so pretty nor so docile as her sisters had been, but she was plump, pink-cheeked, dimpled, and she possessed a good deal of her mother's robust spirit.

Caroline plainly did not want to marry Ferdinando. Probably word had reached Vienna of the boy king's behavior the previous autumn when he got news in Naples of his second fiancée's death. Bored and sulky because he was not permitted to go hunting that day, he made life miserable for his attendants until a way was devised to amuse him. When the English ambassador arrived at the palace in Naples to pay a sympathy call, he found Ferdinando and his suite playing funeral, with a young gentleman of the court in the role of the Archduchess Josepha in funeral robes, his face daubed with chocolate to resemble smallpox, and a great deal of accompanying hilarity.[21]

In spite of her protests, Caroline was married by proxy in Vienna. It was reported that she wept as the bridal procession made its stately way over the Alps and finally across the border into the then large Kingdom of Naples. Her elder brother Leopold, Grand Duke of Tuscany, met her in Bologna, saw to it that she was delivered into the hands of Ferdinando's people at the formal *remise* ceremony. Although Leopold wrote his mother soothingly that Caroline was "a most amiable little Queen," he added that she had been seized by a violent fit of trembling during the ceremony, and that "not for a whole kingdom would I want to live through such a scene again."[22]

At first the sixteen-year-old Caroline who had been so carefully educated in the Vienna court to be a princess of cultivated tastes and exquisite manners, was bitterly homesick in the Naples palace. After a few months of marriage she wrote that life was "a martyrdom":

I now know what marriage is, and I have a deep pity for Antoinette who has yet to experience marriage. I admit frankly that I would rather die than be forced to live again what I have gone through. If I had not been taught by my religion to think of God, I should have killed myself, for it was hell to live like that for a week. I shall weep bitterly if ever my sister is in the same situation.[23]

And yet, in spite of everything, Caroline took her mother's words to heart, made the best of her lot, managed to improve her husband's manners a little, learned how to get what she wanted, and finally herself became the mother and grandmother of kings, queens, empresses.

When her brother Joseph visited her in Naples two or three years later, things were already better, and he assured his mother the pair were getting along nicely. The King wanted Caroline to display more bosom, but to this she objected.[24]

Ferdinando's amusements continued to be decidedly unregal:

Five or six court ladies, my sister, the King, and I [Joseph wrote] began to play blind man's buff and other games. Throughout these the King distributes blows and smacks the ladies' behinds without distinction.[25]

On their way to the opera, the King seized one of Caroline's gloves, pretended to hide it, actually threw it out of the window.

My sister behaved with great moderation, considering that a few days previously Ferdinando had also thrown her best muff into the fire.[26]

After dinner, while Caroline sang and played the harpsichord, Ferdinando invited the guests of honor to attend him on the close-stool.

Joseph asked his sister if there were "any truth to the tales he had heard about the King's punching and slapping her. She admitted that she had received a few kicks and perhaps a few punches, half in temper, half in fun, sometimes in bed, but that he had never been really violent."[27]

"*Er ist ein recht guter Narr*," Caroline remarked philosophically. (He's a pretty good fool.)[28] As for the King, he told Joseph over and over again that he could not be more contented with his wife.

There were just two marriageable sisters left in the Hofburg: Amalia and the youngest sister, Antoinette. Pretty twenty-two-year-old Amalia had been a decoration in court society for several years. She had a pleasant coloratura voice, danced with grace, and already had her eye on a husband: the Bavarian Prince Charles of Zweibrücken, an eminently suitable match.

By this time Joseph was sharing the throne with his mother; he had designs on Bavaria and he felt the marriage would be politically awkward. Perhaps he had personal reasons for wishing to see his sister marry his beloved first wife's brother, the Duke of Parma; it would mean, in any case, one more Habsburg sharing an Italian throne. Amalia had not the will power or the persuasive gifts of her sister Mimi; in the end she submitted to the marriage arranged for her. Unhappily the bridegroom turned out to be an immature boy of seventeen, a clear case of arrested development, and the marriage was far more disastrous than Caroline's. Within a year Amalia's conduct was the gossip of every court in Europe; she threw herself into love affairs and into political intrigues. Her mother's scolding letters had not the slightest effect on her. A few years later her brother-in-law, Duke Albert, on a visit to Parma found Amalia so changed that he scarcely knew her. He wrote:

No trace remains of the sparkle of that beauty which used to fill us with wonder.[29]

Soon after Amalia's marriage the Empress became totally absorbed in the grand climax of all her matrimonial plans: that of her youngest daughter, Maria Antonia called Antoinette, to the Dauphin of France.

By the time little Antoinette was born into an enormous family that already had grown-up children, discipline in the nursery had considerably relaxed, and, as often happens in such families, everyone took turns spoiling the child. Antoinette and her sister Caroline, nearly of an age, shared the same lessons and the same governess. Together the girls ran about the gardens of Schönbrunn, skipped their lessons when they could, enjoyed themselves thoroughly.

Antoinette was eleven when her betrothal to the Dauphin was officially announced. People began to bow and scrape and address her as Madame Antoine, and her mother began to wonder how she could squeeze into that pretty little head all the knowledge and common sense and good judgment she would need to make her way skillfully through the temptations and intrigues of the court of France.

She got a whole new set of teachers to improve her French diction and her knowledge of French history. But it was her earlier masters who left the deepest impression: her music teacher, Gluck, and most of all, her ballet master, Noverre. Under his direction she had danced in ballets in the Court Theater; that wonderful grace of movement that enabled her to outshine far more beautiful women at the French court was certainly part of his training.

The wedding was probably the most brilliant of a brilliant century. French and Austrian officials had labored over knotty questions of mutual protocol for a solid year and finally given up in despair. In the end the French ambassador, the Marquis of Durfort, stayed away from the wedding supper because the bride's brother-in-law, Duke Albert, was given precedence over him at table.

On the whole, however, everything went smoothly. There were the preliminary ceremonies—the solemn audience in the Hofburg on April 16, 1770, with the court in full dress, when the French ambassador asked the hand of Madame Antoine as consort for Monseigneur the Dauphin; the gala performance at the Court Theatre of a new comedy of Marivaux and a new ballet by Noverre; the Act of Renunciation in the Hofburg, when the Archduchess signed away all her rights to the Habsburg inheritance; the grand nuptial ball at Belvedere Palace when six thousand guests in mask danced away the night.

And finally the wedding itself, in the Augustiner Church, where the bride's parents and most of her sisters had been married, with the bride's brother Ferdinand standing in proxy for the groom.

Two days later, "bathed in tears," Marie Antoinette bade good-bye to her mother and set off in a splendid procession of carriages for Versailles, certainly with a lighter heart than either Caroline or Amalia had had, and with her mother's last instructions, several closely written pages of that famous *Règlement,* to guide her first steps in France.[30]

Of her bridegroom she knew far less than Caroline had known of Ferdinando, certainly had not heard the judgment passed on the future Louis XVI by the Austrian ambassador in France, Count de Mercy: "Nature seems to have denied everything to M. le Dauphin," who possessed, it seemed, "only a limited amount of sense."[31]

Her marriage and the production of little Habsburg-Bourbons was to be the very keystone in the great Austrian-French alliance, the happy conclusion of the centuries-long feud between the house of Austria and France. Well prepared by her mother in those intimate sessions in the imperial bedchamber of the Hofburg as to the exact meaning of marriage, the pretty little bride could scarcely guess that she would remain a wife in name only for some seven years.

5. *Last Letter to the Queen of France*

BACK IN VIENNA the golden palace of Schönbrunn had emptied.

The last marriage of all was that of Archduke Ferdinand with Beatrix, heiress of Modena: another valuable Italian throne brought into the family. The youngest boy, Maximilian, who had no inclination for marriage, took holy orders and became Archbishop of Cologne, one of the richest and fattest prelates in Europe, and of course, handily for future Habsburgs, a member of the electoral college.

There was a last bitter grief for the aging Empress. Her first little granddaughter, Thérèse, child of Joseph and Isabella, died just before Antoinette's wedding. It was said, cruelly, that the child had contracted her fatal pneumonia running about in her grandmother's chilly rooms. She had been a particularly merry and attractive child, "full of promise and charm," Maria Theresia had described her to a daughter-in-law, "the darling of her father, and his one source of relaxation . . ."[1] Joseph, doomed now to lonely and childless widowerhood, wrote the little girl's governess:

> To be no longer father seems more than I can bear. . . . I shall miss my daughter all the remaining days of my life. . . . One thing I beg of you, let me have the little white woolen dress with the embroidery of flowers that she has been wearing indoors, and likewise some of her attempts at writing, which I will keep with her mother's writings.[2]

It must have been a lonely household, suddenly without young voices at all, and not a great deal to laugh about.

The Archduchesses Marianna and Elizabeth, two aging spinsters, quarreled constantly, ate at separate tables, each waited on by her own servants. Elizabeth, with her ravaged, pock-marked face, would often be so angry at the world that she refused to speak to anyone for days at a time. When she had an ulcer in her cheek and the British ambassador paid her a visit of sympathy, she laughed at him and said, "Believe me, for an archduchess of forty years who isn't married, a hole in the cheek is an amusement. No event which breaks the *ennui* of my life is a misfortune."[3]

Since his father's death, Joseph had shared the throne as co-Regent with his mother. It was a stormy partnership. Both stubborn, strong personalities, mother and son were separated by one of the most intellectually volcanic generations in human history. Maria Theresia, child of baroque times, devout Catholic, represented the best of a dying order—the old conservative, paternalistic monarchy. Joseph had cut his teeth on the French philosophers, longed to enlighten and revolutionize a whole feudal empire overnight. "With the best will in the world, we do not understand one another," she wrote to him.[4] They clashed constantly when they were together in the Hofburg. To escape those quarrels, Joseph traveled, as much and as far as he could, to France and Italy, to Bohemia and Hungary, Poland and Russia.

He lectured his brother-in-law, Ferdinando of Naples, on the French philosophers; he persuaded his other brother-in-law, the French king, to undergo that little operation that would enable him to perform his duty as a husband. He annoyed his mother by visiting dangerous French radicals—Jean Jacques Rousseau in a Paris garret, the naturalist Buffon. And he dined with her bitterest enemy, Frederick the Great.

Maria Theresia, in the meantime, was growing stout and dropsical. She wore gaiters around her legs, used a glass to look at persons a few paces away. She had quite lost her looks. The smallpox she caught at her daughter-in-law's bedside left her deeply scarred. On a journey to Pressburg, driving at her usual breakneck speed, the carriage overturned and the Empress was flung out on her face in the loose gravel, an accident that cost her the last vestige of her beauty and, very nearly, her eyesight.

Her profile on the silver ducats of the last years of her reign looks like that of an old, tough Roman senator.

She kept her high color, was indeed always so warm that she rarely put down her fan, kept her windows open night and day. Joseph had to put on a fur coat to visit his mother's chambers.

She never lost her humor. When she stood chatting one day with her chamberlain, Count Sinzendorff, who was as old as she but thin as a rail and very rheumatic, she dropped a petition she was showing him and she motioned to him to pick it up.

"Hélas, Madame," he replied sadly, *"il y a vingt années que je ne suis courbé."* (I haven't bent over in twenty years.)[5]

Bursting into laughter at the plight of two old souls, one so fat and one so thin that neither could stoop, the Empress rang for a groom to come and retrieve the paper.

She still loved Schönbrunn; as soon as spring came she moved into the garden rooms on the first floor, painted with exotic landscapes in the eighteenth-century fashion. She had only to open her door and walk out by a graveled path to the Gloriette, the little Greek temple that crowns the hill behind the gardens, her dispatch box strapped about her waist.

On the eighteenth of every month, the anniversary of her husband's death, she went down into the Kapuziner Crypt to visit her dead, that growing company that quite fills the majestic tomb room she had built. On November 3, 1780, she wrote her last letter to Marie Antoinette:

> *A mon âge j'aurais besoin de secours et de consolation, et je perds tout ce que j'aime l'un après l'autre. J'en suis toute accablée.*
> (At my age I need help and consolation and I am losing everything I love, one after the other. I am crushed by it all.)[6]

She stayed at Schönbrunn as late as she could in the autumn of 1780; she too caught a chill in the cold vast rooms. When she moved back to the Hofburg in early November, she was ill already and breathing with difficulty.

She never went to bed but sat propped up on a chaise, in an old dressing gown of her husband's, giving last instructions to Joseph as if he were a little boy.

IX

Joseph II: The Poor Man's Emperor

He possessed a thousand fine qualities
which are of no use to kings. . . . .

Anonymous French courtier

1. Tastes of a Simple Man

THE FIRST THING Joseph did after his mother's death was to rid himself of what he called "this feminine republic" that had ruled so long in the Hofburg. He announced briskly that, except for the oldest ladies who could not be moved, all the women his mother had kept about her—elderly court widows, relatives, ex-governesses—were to leave during the summer before St. Michael's Day of 1781. He added in a letter to his brother Leopold, *"On crie beaucoup mais je ne m'en soucie point."*[1] They make a racket, but I couldn't care less.

His oldest sister, Marianna, was packed off to her favorite convent in Klagenfurt, the embittered sister Elizabeth to her foundation for ladies in Innsbruck. She left, Joseph remarked, laughing and crying at the same time. Marie Christine and her husband were dispatched to Brussels to be Regents of the Netherlands—this at his mother's express instructions; Joseph had no faith in the ability of the two to rule anything. In fact, Joseph did not care much for any of his sisters; perhaps he had been ruled by women too long.

He kept the same apartment in the Leopold Wing of the Hofburg, where he had lived for years, three rooms simply furnished, with a trap door to the Chancellery below, and a machine by which papers could be raised and lowered to his desk. For a special retreat he remodeled part of an old family palace, the Augarten, near the Danube, spent as much time there as he could. "I dine alone in my garden with great pleasure," he wrote Leopold. "Tranquillity reigns."[2]

The extravagance and frivolity of his mother's court had appalled Joseph. Waging war had been staggeringly expensive and the government was up to the neck in debt. Joseph proved himself a liberal with his purse as well as his mind—two vastly different things—and had turned over the entire fortune he inherited from his father, over twenty-two million gulden,[3] to the state.

Applying Reason to court life, he had simplified etiquette; he forbade genuflecting, allowed no one to kiss his hand. All the splendid gala days that had formerly studded the court calendar were done away with; Joseph left only one gala day—New Year's. He did away with the old formal court costume that had been brought to Vienna from Madrid in the days of Charles V and the first Ferdinand. "My Lord Chamberlain will faint when he sees this," Joseph remarked as he donned a military uniform for the first time for a court function.[4]

He created new nobles by the dozen; it was a handy way of replenishing the treasury. For a mere 6000 florin you could become a baron; for 20,000 florin, a count; and 500,000 florin would turn you into a prince. The older aristocracy regarded the new titleholders with utter contempt, called them "bagatelle nobility" and gave them the cold shoulder.

The nobles with rising indignation saw their old privileges whittled away and all the fun vanishing from court life. The Emperor abolished the gambling tables that had supported the French theater, sending it into bankruptcy, whereupon Joseph turned it into a German National Theater.[5] He deprived the Aulic councilors, the supreme war council of the Empire, of their old habit of taking bribes. He gave peasants the right to kill wild boars that ravaged their crops, which nearly spoiled the sport of boar hunting for the court set. Noblemen were no longer allowed to beget bastards in the lower ranks of society without assuming liability for their support. In fact, as the witty Prince de Ligne remarked, "Joseph expected noble-mindedness from his nobles."[6]

Joseph's own menage in the Hofburg was very simple, as befitted a philosopher-king. He wore a plain frock coat, slept on a bed of skins, ate and drank sparingly. Five dishes were brought up from the Hofburg kitchens for his dinner and piled one on top of the other on the porcelain stove in his study to keep warm. He ate alone usually, chatting with the single servant who waited on him, and quickly so that he might get on with his work.

By the time he came to rule alone, a widower of thirty-nine, he had begun to grow stout and quite bald. He wore a round toupee over the crown of his head as a minimum concession to vanity; the thin, straggly pigtail that hung down in back was his own. He had a cap made of oilcloth which he wore even to the theater. Visitors noticed with astonishment that the elbows of his coat were patched.[7]

He made himself readily available to his people by opening the lobby outside his rooms to the public. Every morning the so-called "Control Corridor" was mobbed with petitioners. He turned over the imperial hunting preserves, the Prater and the Augarten, to the people of Vienna for public parks. When one of his courtiers protested that soon Joseph would have no place left where he could go to be with his equals, the Emperor retorted, "To be among my equals, I would have to retire to the Kapuziner Crypt."[8] He took to walking unaccompanied in the public parks, and so as not to constrain people by his presence, he forbade anyone to salute him or even notice his presence when he was out walking.

His grandfather, Charles VI, had crossed Europe with more than two hundred horses, with priests, physicians, surgeons, secretaries, pursers, furriers, wigmakers, stove lighters, cellarers, cooks, under-cooks, butlers, valets, wine pourers. Joseph liked to travel incognito as Count Falkenstein, riding in public post carriages with a suite of perhaps six persons. When he visited his sister, the Queen of France, he refused to stay in the palace of Versailles, rented instead two rooms in an inn in the village.

His dry, cerebral wit was the delight of the Paris *salons*. In 1776 when all Paris was agog with the American Revolution, someone asked Joseph what he thought of it, and he answered, "*Monsieur, je suis par métier royaliste*." (I'm a royalist by trade.)[9]

He arrived in Rheims one day ahead of his suite and was mistaken for a servant. When the landlord asked what were his duties in the Emperor's household, Joseph replied with his flicker of a smile, "I sometimes shave him."[10]

When he was young he had made motions at being gay, had masked in *Fasching* and even put on rouge to dance in court ballets with his young sisters. Now the only disguise he enjoyed was king-into-commoner.

Once at a stage stop in France, Joseph arrived just as the postmaster was about to have a child christened, and the Emperor—unrecognized —was pressed to serve as godfather. When the priest asked his name he replied quietly, "Joseph."

"Surname?"

"Second."

"Occupation?"

"Emperor."[11]

Another time he came upon a carriage overturned in the road and offered the passenger a place in his own. As they jolted along, the stranger, to carry on a conversation, asked Joseph to guess what he had for dinner.

"Fricassee of chicken," guessed Joseph.

"No."

"Leg of mutton?"

"No."

"An omelet?"

"No," said the man, and patting the Emperor on the thigh in the friendliest fashion, said, "Roast veal."

"We do not know each other," Joseph then remarked, "and now it is my turn to make you guess. Who am I?"

"A soldier?" asked the stranger.

"Perhaps," answered Joseph, "but I may also be something else."

"You look too young to be an officer," the stranger said. "Are you then a colonel?"

"No."

"Major?"

"No."

"Commander?"

"No."

"Not a governor?"

"No."

"Who are you then?" The stranger smiled broadly and asked jokingly, "You're not the Emperor?"

Joseph patted the man on the thigh. "You guessed it."

Crestfallen and embarrassed at the liberties he had taken with the ruler, the stranger wished to leave the carriage.

"No, no," said Joseph. "I knew who I was when I took you in, and I did not know who you were. Nothing has changed; let us continue our trip."[12]

Aside from traveling, Joseph's amusements were modest. He went to the theater, opera, concerts, dropped in sometimes afterward at the Liechtenstein Palace to play a game of ombre with three or four elderly ladies of the court. He was nearly always home by eleven, worked still longer at his leather-topped desk, lighted by a single candle in a pewter holder. Then to bed so that he might be up at five in summer, at six in winter—the very hours his mother had kept.

He was fond of music, though not particularly gifted, played the pianoforte and cello, had tried his hand at composing. He appointed Mozart court composer, to replace Gluck, who had died, but at a far lower salary—Mozart too was a victim of Joseph's economy drive.

2. Changing the World

JOSEPH WAS LIKE a fanatically tidy housekeeper moving into an ancestral home that hadn't been dusted in a hundred years. He could hardly work fast enough to put things to rights.

Frantically, from sunrise until midnight, Joseph worked on, wearing out seven and eight secretaries in a day, writing dozens and dozens of new decrees, new changes in old laws.

He set about abolishing serfdom on the great estates of Bohemia and Hungary, established a single land tax—which meant that the Hungarian nobility would pay taxes for the first time virtually in history, taxation being a right hitherto reserved exclusively for the peasant class. The medieval penal code was revised and torture abolished; there would be no punishment more brutal, said Joseph, than flogging on the bare buttocks. Next he abolished the death penalty entirely, made dueling illegal.

He allowed Jews to abandon the yellow stripes and yellow sleeves that had hitherto been the identifying badge of their race, gave them freedom of worship, and even raised several Jews to the nobility.

Everything needed seeing to. Commissioners by the dozen, inspectors by the hundred, rode out in all directions from the capital to check on everything conceivable: whether roads were being cleared, whether houses were numbered, whether the army was behaving, whether preachers were delivering indiscreet sermons, whether the sale of contraceptives was banned, whether anyone was caring for blind, deaf, and crippled children.

He made education compulsory, even for women.

He abolished censorship of the press. Joseph's was, for a time, the only country in Europe that had complete freedom. The cafés of Vienna were filled with scribblers writing tracts and lampoons, large numbers of which were directed against the Emperor. But the public, instead of hurrying to buy the works of the French philosophers, as Joseph hoped, flocked to read hot off the presses such tidbits as *A Nun's Letters, Concerning Viennese Housemaids, A Wonderful History of an Old Virgin Who Remained Unviolated for Thirty Years,* and *Bawdyhouses Are Necessary in Vienna.*[1]

If Joseph alienated his nobles by taking the pleasure out of court life and making them pay besides for austerity, he angered the clergy even more. He granted religious toleration to dissenters, closed all monasteries except those of the teaching and nursing orders, confiscated their property and used it for schools, pensions, charities.

The Pope—it was the handsome Pius VI—in anguish packed up and journeyed to Vienna to plead with Europe's ranking Catholic monarch. It was the first journey any pope had undertaken to German-speaking lands in three and a half centuries.

The visit, on the whole, went swimmingly. The Emperor Joseph drove out of the city four post stops to meet His Holiness and conduct him to his quarters in the Hofburg. Wherever the Pope appeared crowds of the faithful gathered and knelt for a blessing; his slipper was carried about from one noble drawing room to another to be kissed. When His Holiness departed, Joseph drove with him as far as Mariabrunn, presented him with farewell gifts of a diamond crucifix and a traveling carriage. Immediately afterward Joseph suppressed the monastery at Mariabrunn and proceeded to carry out his other anticlerical measures.

No matter was too trivial to get the attention of the "People's Emperor." Girls attending boys' schools were forbidden to wear corsets. Housewives might no longer bake the beloved gingerbread cake called *Lebkuchen,* because the Emperor thought it bad for the digestion. Coffins should be made with flat covers only; the Viennese called Joseph's coffins "nose squeezers." Presently Joseph went further, decreed that no coffins at all should be used but the dead buried simply in a plain sheet or a linen sack. The protests over this measure were so deafening that Joseph had to revoke it, which he did, angrily. One can almost see the sparks fly out of his goose quill as he writes:

> Since a great many subjects do not want to understand the reasons for the regulations concerning the burial sacks, which, considering rapid putrefaction, were instigated out of regard for the health of the population; and since, moreover, they display so great an interest in their bodies even after their death, His Majesty no longer cares how they bury themselves in the future.[2]

It was quite true that almost nobody in his day understood what Joseph was trying to do. As his mother had discerned, his was a difficult personality, tactless and stubborn, with more than his share of Habsburg obtuseness. Besides, he attempted the impossible.

Yet no monarch in Europe ever took such a passionate interest in the underprivileged, the dispossessed. Once, when a peasant complained to Joseph that the tax collector had taken his last farthing, Joseph investigated and gave the peasant the tax collector's job. His angry nobility nicknamed him "the peasants' God."[3]

He founded an orphan asylum, a training college for army doctors, a school for the deaf and dumb, the world's largest lying-in hospital, and the huge General Hospital of Vienna that remained for a century and a half the medical marvel of the world. Yet an anonymous critic in Joseph's day carped that "the Emperor's greatest enjoyment was to go and watch the women in labor in the great hospital in Vienna, or to spend hours at the top of a tower overlooking a courtyard full of shrieking madmen."[4]

Joseph might have echoed the complaint of his friend Catherine the Great, that whereas Diderot could draft his fine schemes on paper she had to write them on the skin of human beings, a far less tractable material.

3. Making of a Throne Heir

AFTER THE DEATH of his second wife, the unhappy Josepha, Joseph flatly refused to remarry. The chancellor, Kaunitz, continued to press Joseph to marry, preferably with the French Princess Elizabeth. Joseph checked out the rumors on the girl's size and appetite (she was said to eat each year a hundred million francs' worth of meat and fish), and finally, on a personal visit to Versailles, wrote Kaunitz summarily:

. . . she has increased to a size you simply can't imagine.[1]

The desires of the flesh did not trouble Joseph unduly. The French minister in Vienna wrote home that Joseph regularly spent a half hour a day with a gardener's daughter, adding a Frenchman's judgment that the Emperor "showed by the brevity of the encounter that it was merely a matter of need."[2]

It was quite all right with Joseph if his brother Leopold, Grand Duke of Tuscany, would see to producing the Habsburg heirs—a task which Leopold fulfilled admirably, fathering in all sixteen children.

Now and again on his journeys Joseph looked in on the grand-ducal nurseries in Florence, made the acquaintance of his nephews, taught them how to play "The Wolf Game" and "Look in the Soup" while he was really examining them carefully. Afterward, in his businesslike way, he would dash off letters of advice to his brother, telling Leopold exactly how to raise his children.[3]

He took particular interest in his eldest nephew, Archduke Franz, who would one day inherit the throne. Leopold, like Joseph, was a son of the Enlightenment, and he started out rearing his children strictly according to Rousseau. He found out that in practice it didn't work out very well, and presently everyone had a finger in the throne heir's educational pie—the grandmother, Maria Theresia, Uncle Joseph, various other aunts and uncles, ministers, governors, tutors. Long messages about Franz passed back and forth between the Hofburg in Vienna and the Pitti Palace in Florence. Periodically the educational system would be revised and a new tutor added, a priest or a bishop or an army officer, depending on whether it was Franz's mental, physical, or moral development that seemed most lacking at the moment.

When Joseph visited Florence in 1784 he looked Franz over once more, decided he was much too thin, probably didn't eat enough soup and bread. In typical Joseph fashion he wrote out a lengthy critical document entitled "Reflections on the Subject of the Archduke Franz," which he presented to the parents.

As his own mother had for him, Joseph shopped about Europe, found a suitable wife for Franz, a wholesome young German princess, Elizabeth of Württemberg, brought her to Vienna, Catholicized her, had her teeth straightened, got a little more education into her, and watched with avuncular pleasure the development of her "very prettily arched breast," as he wrote to Leopold.[4] He became in fact very fond of the girl, for Joseph—a born manager—loved the role of Pygmalion.

Next he sent for the sixteen-year-old Franz to be brought to Vienna, installed him in the Hofburg with a new set of tutors, and set to work to make a future emperor out of the boy. He found the going hard, and he did not trouble to hide his profound disappointment. Instead of a brilliant, quick-witted, charming, and responsive teen-ager, Joseph encountered a shy, awkward adolescent, thin and small and quiet, not at all clever at sports, who could repeat the proper answers once they had been drilled into him, but seemed incapable of a single original thought.

In his usual forthright way Joseph took drastic steps. When Franz had been living in the palace two months, his uncle called him into his study on a Sunday morning after Mass, handed him a closely written document headed "Observations Concerning the Further Education of Archduke Franz."

His eyes full of tears, the boy stood in his uncle's presence and read about himself in the third person:

He is retarded in size and strength and backward in physical skills and bearing. . . . He represents, in short, a mollycoddle, a weakling, without ability, accustomed to being led, unfit for statesmanship. . . . He speaks indistinctly, uses coarse expressions, has a barking voice, and swallows his words, partly from indolence and carelessness, partly from a misplaced shyness.[5]

There was more, much more, in the same vein. Swallowing his tears, he bowed and thanked his uncle for the trouble he had taken.

Franz tried desperately hard to please; he simply could not come up to his uncle's expectations. Joseph shouted at him in public because Franz was timid on horseback. His manner was too stiff; Joseph commanded him to be merrier. "He must loosen up, chatter more, laugh more," Joseph instructed the boy's tutor.[6] Franz loved to dance; his uncle remarked pointedly, "Cadence and lightness are not among Franz's strong points."[7]

A few months later, in the middle of the carnival season of 1785, as Franz was hurrying (almost merrily) from a ball in the Ballhaus to a ball in the palace Redoutensaal, Joseph called him into his study again, analyzed his faults for him once more. His spiritual development, said his uncle, was that of a twelve-year-old; because of his backwardness his marriage to Elizabeth would have to be postponed for several years.

No blow could have been more bitter, for Franz, unlike his uncle, hadn't the slightest inclination to celibacy. From the hour he had met the attractive, pink-cheeked, blooming Elizabeth in the park of Laxenburg the preceding summer, he had liked her instantly and wholeheartedly. They had seen each other often, on carefully supervised meetings and outings, and their fondness for one another had obviously grown.

Now Franz redoubled his efforts to please his uncle. Fortunately just at that juncture Joseph's sister, Marie Christine, returned to Vienna for a visit. Without children herself, Christine was an adored Aunt Mimi to all her Tuscan nephews and nieces, on many a visit to Florence had thrown nurses and governesses into consternation by wild rompings with the grand-ducal children. Now she advised Joseph that he was far too harsh with Franz; after her visit the relationship of uncle and nephew did warm a little. At times Joseph even expressed mild satisfaction with Franz.

In January of 1788 he permitted the young people to marry, and the two lonely teen-agers, pushed and prodded for so many years by their anxious elders, literally fell into one another's arms.

Two months after the wedding Joseph took Franz away to the Turkish campaigns, so that the newlyweds had precious little time together.

During her young husband's absence Elizabeth wrote him every day, urging him to hurry back, telling him she would gladly join him if she weren't afraid of "a good scolding" from their uncle, the Emperor.[8]

And tenderly she would write:

Your bird sits on my shoulder every day. I take the best possible care of him, because I know how fond you are of him. I have sent my own pet birds away so that yours will not forget, because of their cries, how to sing his own special song. . . . It is not possible to love you more dearly, my angel, than I do, and I cannot find any comfort while we are apart. [March 16, 1789][9]

4. Epitaph for Joseph

In Joseph's empire, meantime, things were not going so well as one would have imagined. It was almost as if people did not care about being reformed and enlightened.

While Joseph's mother had used great tact and finesse in her policy of unification, allowing the different parts of the Empire to keep their own languages and customs, Joseph wanted to centralize everything immediately, make German—for convenience—everyone's language.

Earlier he had got the idea of exchanging the geographically distant, politically prickly Austrian Netherlands for lands nearer home—specifically, his neighbor Bavaria. For a time it seemed as if Joseph might even pull off the happy exchange; then a new Bavarian heir proved intractable, and Frederick the Great stepped in to defend him.

Next Joseph planned to conquer and divide with Catherine of Russia the remainder of Turkey-in-Europe; he himself rode into the Balkans to lead his army to victory. Heat and quartan fever laid a third of his army low; the war of conquest ended in panic and retreat.

There is nothing like a lost war to make for a bad press at home. After the Turkish campaign, people said bitterly that Joseph gave his officers the small cross, but his people the big one. The Lombards remarked tersely, "He does good with a cudgel."[1]

He lectured his sister, Marie Antoinette, on her frivolous behavior and advised her to stop interfering in politics; then later he wrote asking her to influence her husband in certain crucial matters involving the Netherlands.

Unwisely Joseph moved the ancient Hungarian crown of St. Stephen to Vienna—a dreadful breach of sentiment; the Hungarians declared that as the saintly relic was borne across the border lightning

flashed and thunder pealed out of cloudless skies. Angered chiefly at
Joseph's taxation program, the Magyar nobles rose up against the
Emperor.

Joseph found he needed spies, expanded his mother's Chastity Police into an internal security force. It seemed as if everyone, from one
end of the Empire to the other, found something to be unhappy about.

If he lacked his mother's adroitness in dealing with people, Joseph
missed too her robust constitution. His letters the last years of his life
are full of his failing health—the fever he had got on the Turkish
front, erysipelas, an eye infection from goodness knows where, a
liver obstruction, a dismal, unshakable cough for which he dosed himself with bark and asses' milk. He was plagued too with hemorrhoids
and a fistula, which his surgeons had difficulty cutting, because—as
he wrote his brother—those parts had hardened in the years he had
spent in the saddle.[2]

In the end Joseph lay dying in the Hofburg, and the whole Empire
seethed with revolt.

There was almost nothing in which he could take comfort save that
the future of his dynasty was promised: his nephew's wife, Elizabeth,
awaited the birth of her first child. In the early days of February the
girl came to pay him a farewell visit; the sight of Joseph's shrunken
skull on the pillow in the light of a single flickering candle was so
appalling that she fainted and had to be carried out. The following
day she went into a long and difficult labor, was delivered at last by
the newly invented forceps. In delirium she asked those about her
whether she had not been brave and whether Uncle Joseph would be
pleased with her. Toward the end she began to hemorrhage, went into
convulsions, and died. The daughter she bore, a mental defective,
brain-damaged perhaps during the difficult birth, lived only six months.

"Throw me on top of her!" Joseph cried in anguish when the terrible
news was brought to him.[3]

Two days later, in the early morning of February 19, young Franz,
numb and bewildered, watched his uncle die, and that evening followed his wife's coffin to its place in the Kapuziner Crypt.

Joseph had asked to have engraved on his tomb the most sorrowful
of all royal epitaphs:

"Here lies Joseph II, who failed in all he undertook."[4]

X

Wars and Waltzes: Napoleonic Times

[22] Empress Maria Theresia and her family, painted about 1752 by Martin van Meytens. *(Bildarchiv des Österreichische Nationalbibliothek, Vienna)*

[23] A scene from the private life of Maria Theresia and her family, a drawing by the Archduchess Marie Christine. The occasion is St. Nicholas Day, and three of the younger children have just discovered their shoes full of sweetmeats and presents. The little girl with the doll is Marie Antoinette, later Queen of France. The little boy in the foreground munching on cakes is Maximilian, later Archbishop of Cologne and patron of Beethoven. The older boy, wiping away tears because he has apparently been naughty and got only a shoe full of switches, is Archduke Ferdinand. *(Bildarchiv des Österreichische National-bibliothek, Vienna)*

[24] Emperor-brothers: Leopold and Joseph (later Leopold II and Joseph II) as young men, by Pompeo Batoni. *(Kunsthistorisches Museum, Vienna)*

[25] Emperor Joseph II instructs a peasant in the art of plowing; from a contemporary engraving, about 1769. (*Bildarchiv des Österreichische Nationalbibliothek, Vienna*)

1. The Short Reign of Leopold II

IN THE LAST WEEKS of his life Joseph had written his brother Leopold in Tuscany, begging him to come to Vienna, for he longed to see him before he died. He wrote again then, desperately, imploring his brother to hurry, for time was growing short.

Leopold wrote back that the unexpected news of Joseph's illness had shocked his "very sensitive nerves," and made him quite ill.[1] To his sisters he wrote secret letters in lemon juice declaring that Joseph had set spies to watch him. And to his son Franz in Vienna he wrote instructions on what to do the moment Joseph died: he was to lock and seal all the offices in the palace, pocket the keys, and write detailed descriptions of all personages in the government. When news of Joseph's death did reach Leopold he dispatched a courier telling Franz to proceed with the funeral arrangements, "so that all these lugubrious functions may be terminated before my arrival, for I do not have the strength to participate in them."[2]

The weeks that followed must have been the longest and loneliest of Franz's life. He listened to his uncle's ministers drone at meetings; each day at eleven and six he sat at his uncle's desk and set his signature on hundreds of state papers, adding after his name: "in the absence of my lord father." Between times he wandered about his apartments in the palace, appallingy empty of his cheerful young wife's presence.

At last in March, Leopold came up from Florence, and Franz and his tutor drove to Klagenfurt to meet him and ride with him into the capital. Presently Franz's mother and his thirteen brothers and sisters came too, filling the bleak corridors of the Hofburg with sounds that had been absent for years—the shouts of children's laughter, the comings and goings of tutors and governesses and nurses, of dancing and music and fencing masters.

Among that great brood of children were several who would appear in history; most gifted of the brothers, Archduke Karl, who would lead the Austrian forces against Napoleon; Archduke Johann, warm-hearted, intelligent, liberal; and the music-loving brother, Archduke Rudolf, Beethoven's friend and patron.

Leopold made it one of his first tasks to find another suitable wife for Franz. He chose Marie-Thérèse, eldest daughter of his sister, Queen Caroline of Naples. In September of the same year, 1790, barely seven months after Elizabeth's death, Franz's second wedding took place in the Augustiner Church.

The Habsburg genius for matchmaking had quite outdone itself this time. Not only was Franz united with his lively young cousin, but his next younger brother and sister were married at the same time to another daughter and son of the Neapolitan relatives. The three bridal couples were actually double first cousins, blood-related not only through Leopold and Caroline but through Leopold's wife, Maria Louisa, who was sister of Ferdinando, King of Naples. It was as cosy a collection of family genes as a papal dispensation could make possible.[3]

All three honeymooning couples set off merrily with a great train of carriages—parents, courtiers, servants—to watch father Leopold crowned Holy Roman Emperor in Frankfurt.

Leopold II had been a liberal and enlightened ruler in Tuscany, had even considered giving his people a constitution, a novel notion for a monarch in the 1780s. But now, in the wake of Joseph's drastic reforms, Leopold found the Empire in a state of violent disorder. It was clear to him, as it had never been to Joseph, that the whole bottle of medicine could not be forced down the patient's throat at once.

As fast as horse and carriage could take him, Leopold sped from one end of the country to the other, soothing angry subjects, quelling rebellion, revoking his brother's more unpopular measures. A shrewd and skillful diplomat, Leopold might just have been—had he lived—a brilliant emperor.

Meantime the French Revolution had exploded. His youngest sister, Marie Antoinette, was imploring his help in restoring her husband's throne. In the beginning Leopold apparently sympathized with the aims of the Revolution, made it quite clear that the King of France could not expect to restore his monarchy on the old terms.

Leopold did not hurry to the rescue of his sister's family but wrote her firmly:

We have a sister, the Queen of France. But the Holy Empire has no sister and Austria has no sister. I can only act according to the interests of my people and not according to family interests.[4]

In the summer of 1791, however, when the French royal family tried to escape to Montmédy and were recaptured and brought back to imprisonment in Paris, Leopold began to fear for their safety, and took steps to join with other European rulers in restoring order in France.

But in March of 1792, before he could effect the family's rescue, Leopold suddenly sickened and died, probably of a ruptured appendix. His doctors had diagnosed "stomach colic," applied four blood-lettings and eighteen clysters during the two days he lay ill.

In despair Marie Antoinette in the Tuileries got the news of Leopold's death, certain that her brother had been poisoned by agents of the Revolution.

Until very near the end she had hopes that her relatives and friends would rescue her. At her trial she conducted herself with more skill and courage than she had ever shown as Queen of France, and it was in dying that she proved to be her mother's daughter.

In October of 1793, as the Widow Capet, with cropped snow-white hair and the frozen old woman's face that David sketched as it passed in the tumbrel, Marie Antoinette went to the guillotine. By then nothing visible was left of her beauty or of her birth; in her last prison they had taken even the little gold watch Maria Theresia had given her daughter when she left Vienna as a girl of fifteen.

Witnesses to her execution recalled afterward that the dainty feet in the purple slippers ran up the ladder of the scaffold as lightly as a girl's; only at the top she had stumbled and trod on the executioner's foot. Her last words were, "Monsieur, I beg your pardon. I did not do it on purpose."[5]

2. Franz II* vs. Napoleon

> Das liebe heilige Römische Reich,
> Wie hält's nur noch zusammen?
>
> *Goethe*
>
> (The dear old Holy Roman Empire, how
> does it still hang together?)

FRANCE HAD ALREADY declared war on Austria by then, two old feuding dogs who had never really made their peace. That war would drag on for twenty-two long wearying years, involving all of Europe, bringing enemy invasion again and again to Austrian soil.

On the imperial throne and freed at last of all leading strings was young Franz: Emperor Franz II. A slight youth with long face, pale blue eyes, protruding lower lip, his public image was cautious, quiet, melancholy; in his portraits he is never seen with a ghost of a smile. In Franz seemed to be reborn the family trait of patient, enduring phlegm, that ability to bear misfortune, humiliation, defeat, to cut his losses again and again and wait out a change of fortune.

His self-confidence had certainly been sorely mauled during the painful process of his education; it is hardly astonishing if young Franz doubted his own judgment, preferred to leave the onus of decision-making to others. The education his father and uncle had planned for him was certainly enlightened enough; among his favorite books when he came to Vienna had been a copy of Montesquieu. But he had also been taught that a paternalistic monarchy was the happiest form of government, that a wise Providence had chosen him for the kindly role of father to his people. When he witnessed the

* Franz I of Austria.

chaos his uncle Joseph's well-intentioned reforms had brought, when he shivered through his aunt's execution and the subsequent Reign of Terror, he resolved to shut his country's door once and for all on the dangerous breath of revolution.

For himself he reserved a kind of chief clerk's role in imperial affairs. He had a fondness for detail; he would write out in his own hand hundreds of official notes dealing even in such matters as the food served his children and the morals of his servants.[1] When he enlarged the police and espionage force, he took pains to read their long detailed reports each day, even to interview personally some of the informers.[2]

As Napoleon took possession of the Revolution in France, one of the most curious duels in history succeeded, between the brilliant, energetic, decisive young general, and the cautious, evasive, lethargic emperor.

The two were scarcely a year apart in age. Both had been born in lands Italian in character—Napoleon in Corsica, Franz in Tuscany. They would meet in the most unlikely of places, end up in the most improbable of relationships.

As Bonaparte swept through Italy he toppled one ruler after another off his throne, sending refugee Habsburgs scurrying home to Vienna. At the end of that first lightning campaign Emperor Franz was left with nothing of Italy save the province of Venetia, and this he lost in the next round.

After the Battle of Ulm in October of 1805, the French occupied Vienna itself, and the imperial family, with treasure, archives, art collections hastily packed in carriages, took flight for the fortress of Olmütz.

In December the combined armies of Austria and Russia were defeated at Austerlitz, and Franz wrote to his wife the shattering news in a letter that is a marvel of understatement:

A battle was fought today which did not turn out well. I pray you consequently to withdraw from Olmütz to Teschen with everything that belongs to us. I am well.

Your tenderest Franz[3]

In a windmill near Austerlitz the Corsican upstart and the scion of Europe's oldest ruling family met face to face for the first time. Napoleon was in fine spirits. He bowed very low and said, "I regret, Sire, that I must receive you here, in the only palace I have entered for two months."

Franz replied dryly, "Your present quarters are so profitable to you, Sire, that I think they cannot fail to please you."[4]

By the Peace of Pressburg Franz lost not only Venetia but a most precious part of the ancient family crownlands, the province of Tyrol. At Maria Theresia's writing desk in Schönbrunn, Napoleon dashed off the decree evicting her daughter, Queen Caroline, from Naples. Presently Caroline, Franz's bustling, talkative, indiscreet mother-in-law, would appear again in Vienna, to join the growing throng of French émigrés and dispossessed monarchs.

When Napoleon had himself crowned Emperor of the French and when a group of German princes seceded from the Empire to form the Confederation of the Rhine as allies of Napoleon, Franz laid down the imperial crown and announced the demise of the Holy Roman Empire.

Its obsequies were officially pronounced in Vienna in the square Am Hof in August of 1806. The glittering crown of the Holy Empire, the medieval regalia and vestments, freighted with the dim magic of ten centuries of tradition, were locked away in the treasury of the Hofburg. They would never be worn again.

To the world Franz had become Emperor Franz I of Austria.

3. Domestic Life in Wartime

In SPITE OF defeats and disastrous losses, Emperor Franz's popularity mounted during the years of war; each time after an exile, a lost battle, a lost peace, he was welcomed back yet more warmly by the Viennese. The tide of national feeling was rising; it was during the early years of the Napoleonic Wars that Joseph Haydn composed the anthem "God Keep Emperor Franz"; it was sung in all the theaters of Vienna in honor of the Emperor's birthday on February 12, 1797.

Franz would certainly have preferred, if he could, to avoid history in the making, and to cultivate his own delightful garden.

Against the setting of those stormy times the imperial household wore a look of amiable domesticity. Whenever Franz could spare the time, he spent hours arranging and rearranging his collections of books, puttering in his workshop making lacquered boxes or cages for the exotic birds he raised among his tropical plants in the glass-houses adjoining the Hofburg.

His second wife, Marie-Thérèse of Naples, was a frivolous little creature who loved nothing better than inventing diversions for her husband and their friends. Her mother, Queen Caroline, had taken Viennese manners and amusements to Naples with her; her daughter imported them back to Vienna, with an Italian flair and invention. There were plays and burlesques, magic performances, Chinese shadow plays and *camera oscura* productions.

Fireworks displays in the park at Laxenburg nearly rivaled the appearance of the battlefields. In a "house of whims" glass bells rang unexpectedly, colored lights flashed on and off, water spurted out at visitors. In the middle of the little lake at Laxenburg, Franz built a medieval water castle, furnished in authentic Gothic, much of it

from monasteries his uncle Joseph had suppressed. In the romantic
dungeon languished a mechanical prisoner who could be made to
move his arms and clank his chains for the delighted shrieks of lady
visitors.

Sometimes for a joke the carp pond was stocked with amusing
things, and family and friends would cast in their lines and pull up
an astonishing catch, such as the dummy "babe in swaddling clothes"
which the stuffy old court physician, Dr. Stifft, once fished up to
everyone's amusement.[1]

The whole imperial family danced at Laxenburg—Emperor, Empress, adjutants, governesses, children. The minuet was dead as a
doornail; it was the faster, livelier polka, the schottische, and most of
all the two-step waltz that had captured the ballrooms. All Vienna
was, in fact, in the grip of a dance mania; the Viennese waltzed
their way straight across the revolutionary 1790s, across the war-
torn opening years of the new century. Thousands and thousands
whirled their way around the huge public dance halls, one of which,
the Apollo, was built quite literally out of war casualties.[2]

The Viennese with their taste for revelry found nothing at all
extraordinary in the appearance of the Empress, Marie-Thérèse, at
every carnival season, though she was pregnant twelve times during
her sixteen years of marriage. The Viennese, in fact, thoughtfully
made provision for pregnant women who could not be induced to
stay home during carnival season, by providing rooms "with all con-
veniences; rooms . . . in which a child could be brought into the
world if unhappily this should prove necessary."[3]

Marie-Thérèse enjoyed masking so much that she would often
change her costume several times during a single night in *Fasching*
to mingle with the street crowds, now as a pastry cook, now as a
pretzel vendor, or as a harlequin, or as the Queen of the Night.
Franz, without mask, wearing only his serious face, joined the *Fasching* crowds too. Now and again someone recognized the Emperor
and called out, "Franzl, how are things going?" Once someone shoved
him very hard by mistake against a wall, and when his frightened
chamberlain cried out, "Please! Make way for His Majesty!" Franz
only murmured, "It doesn't matter; don't bother the people."[4]

For the Habsburgs and for Vienna they were richly musical years
as well.

In May of 1801 both of Haydn's great oratorios, *The Creation* and
The Seasons, were performed at court, with the Empress singing the

soprano solos. She sang, remarked Haydn tactfully, "with much taste and expression, but with a small voice."[5] When *The Seasons* got its first public performance in the Burg Theater in the following year, it drew the largest crowd in the history of the theater and stirred so much excitement that the Viennese barely noticed the Russian army of Suvarov passing through the city on their way to do battle with Napoleon.

The whole imperial family made music together; Franz played the violin, his wife the bass viol, their eldest daughter, Marie Louise, the harp. More than one courtier was said to have owed his rise in the ministry to his ability to join in the Emperor's house quartet; Metternich later contributed a first-rate cello performance.

Franz was a born family man, and within the bounds of private life the grave and cautious emperor gave way to the devoted, even lively husband and father. Under the ancient beech trees in the Laxenburg park he was often glimpsed, trundling a wheelbarrow in which rode his epileptic and sadly retarded little son, Crown Prince Ferdinand.

When Franz was away from home his whole family wrote affectionate, cheerful letters to "Dearest Papa!" and "Dearest, best husband!" Like any burgher's wife Marie-Thérèse would write, begging him to have a dress and hat made for her while he was in Prague and enclosing her measurements.[6]

When his wife was ill and the doctor would not allow him to see her, Franz found life totally unbearable. He wrote her dolefully in 1797:

Dearest wife,

I am writing you . . . two lines to tell you that I was happy to hear of your improvement. . . . I have been unable to sleep because of agitation and ardor, and now I have a sore throat. This business of being alone is my greatest ailment, so that I am anxious to come to you . . . Try to find out how long the continence is supposed to last and write me about it, for if the time is too long I shall simply come to you. . . . Farewell and believe me to be throughout life

Your loving Franz

If possible arrange in whatever way for me to see you soon.[7]

In May of 1807, as she awaited the birth of her twelfth child, Marie-Thérèse sickened, probably with pneumonia, was stringently bled, gave birth prematurely, and died. Franz clung weeping to his wife's body, and had to be dragged away forcibly by his brother Karl.

Barely eight months later, in January of 1808, he married a third time, a beautiful young cousin, Maria Ludovica of Modena, who was only four years older than his eldest daughter, Marie Louise. Franz might have explained, as Mozart had to his father a few years earlier, "A bachelor in my opinion is only half alive."[8]

It was in honor of the Emperor's third wedding that the enormous Apollo Dance Palace was opened in Vienna; the carnival season that followed was one of the most brilliant Vienna had ever known.

The marriage, however, that began to the tune of a thousand fiddles and a hundred enchanting waltzes, was shadowed almost from the beginning by an undercurrent of deep tragedy. Doctors soon discovered that the lovely pale young empress was consumptive. She was forbidden to ride and hunt by her husband's side in the woods of Laxenburg—though she sometimes did. She could not accompany him on the day-long rambles in the mountains. She could not bear him any children. Carefully chosen ladies were provided to take care of the Emperor's more pressing needs.[9]

Maria Ludovica's devotion to Franz and her high sense of duty came into constant conflict with her failing strength; the bundle of letters preserved in the State Archives reveal that bittersweet relationship. From a spa where she was hopefully taking a cure she wrote him in 1810:

> And you would be doubly, triply kissed with tenderness if I could do so, but I can't hope to have the consolation of seeing you so soon; in one respect it is as well, for the way I look right now you might decide to sell me at the secondhand market and take Spintin into your grace as substitute.

A little later, in another letter, Maria Ludovica wrote:

> I shall try to get very plump for your pleasure and to overshadow the charms of the skinny Spintin. Have you had to see her again, you rascal?[10]

In 1809 Austria, encouraged by French difficulties in Spain, marched against Napoleon single-handed. Once again a French army swept across Austria, to be defeated at Aspern, that single brief sweet victory garnered by the Emperor's brother Karl against Napoleon.

Immediately after came the defeat of Wagram; Franz had watched it from a nearby hill. He said only, *"Jetzt können wir halt nach Hause gehen."* (Now we can, I think, go home.)[11]

The new peace between Austria and France was signed in October of 1809; at once the Apollo ballroom opened with a glittering ball, and two days later the famous fireworks artist, Stuwer, produced a sensational display of pyrotechnics in the park of the Prater.

Emperor Franz had in the meantime called to office as state chancellor one of the smoothest diplomatic hands in Europe, Prince Clemens von Metternich. Metternich set to work immediately to buy peace—not permanent peace, to be sure, but peace until a day of reckoning. He bought it with the hand of Franz's eldest daughter, Marie Louise, who was to marry the divorced Napoleon and produce for the Corsican upstart a legitimate heir.

Habsburg daughters had always been trained for political marriages. The affections of the girl were already engaged; she was halfway in love with the younger brother of her stepmother, Maria Ludovica. Her father assured her he would not force her, but Napoleon himself put the whole matter bluntly, "May princesses fall in love? Why, they are nothing but political merchandise."[12]

Marie Louise complied dutifully; when Napoleon sent Marshal Berthier to woo her, she and her father showed him the sights of Vienna—including the Apollo Dance Palace.

The proxy wedding on a rainy March day in 1810 was not a joyous affair, and the Viennese who lined the streets to watch the bridal procession depart were not pleased to see a Habsburg archduchess delivered over to the man who so recently had been called "the Corsican ogre." While Metternich wrote his wife complacently, "For this I'll have the Fleece!" the girl's grandmother, old Queen Caroline of Naples, cried, "All that I needed to complete my misfortune was to become grandmother to the Devil!"[13]

Back in Paris, Napoleon, a bridegroom of forty with thinning hair and a thickening waistline, engaged his sister to teach him the Viennese waltz.

The second meeting between Emperor Franz and Napoleon—the only one after Austerlitz—took place in the Royal Palace in Dresden in May of 1812, with Napoleon on his way to conquer Russia.

The French emperor was exceptionally gallant to his frail young mother-in-law, walking beside Maria Ludovica's sedan chair as she was borne through the long corridors of the palace.

But for the first time in history another monarch took precedence over a Habsburg emperor. Napoleon entered the banquet hall first, sat at the head of the table, kept his hat on. Franz, dumfounded, exclaimed, *"Das ist ein ganzer Kerl!"*[14]

4. Family Reunion

THE NEXT TO LAST scene of the Napoleonic epoch in Vienna was a kind of glorious *tableau vivant* in the gardens of Schönbrunn. The year was 1814, the season summer.

The Battle of Leipzig was won. Emperor Franz had returned to Austria like a hero, a somewhat meager St. George victorious over the Corsican dragon. Wherever he went, his path was strewn with flowers, flags waved, bands played "God Keep Emperor Franz." The dragon himself, his claws pulled, had been safely banished to Elba.

In Schönbrunn the Habsburgs were reunited: brothers, sisters, sons, daughters—and the single, astonishing grandchild.

Emperor Franz's eldest son, the twenty-one-year-old Ferdinand, was not very promising. An army of tutors came and went, trying to stuff some learning into the huge vacant head. The second boy, twelve-year-old Franz Karl, while not a retarded epileptic like the Crown Prince, was not particularly bright.

Franz's eldest daughter, Marie Louise, was back in Vienna too, still wearing her title "Empress of the French," and with the arms of Napoleon still emblazoned on her carriage.

Most vivid souvenir of her recent glory was her little son by Napoleon, who had been designated by his father, in imitation of the old Holy Roman imperial succession title, "King of Rome." The whole family admired the pretty fair-haired child, pure Habsburg in looks but with Napoleon's quick mind and imperious temper; the Viennese public came swarming into the Schönbrunn gardens to have a look at the dragon's seed. The little boy still spoke only French, except for the naughty word or two his young uncle, Franz Karl, had taught him to respond when his tutors scolded him: "*Scheissen!*"[1]

The oldest personage at the family gatherings that summer was the little boy's great-grandmother, Caroline, the old ex-queen of Naples and Sicily. Enormous applause greeted the last living daughter of Maria Theresia each time she made her appearance in the imperial box of the Court Theater. The Baroness du Montet, who remembered Caroline as a handsome young girl before her marriage long ago to the King of Naples, wrote of her appearance:

> How old she had grown! How bent and curved by the blows of sorrow! Her head, almost white, seemed hardly to bear the weight of her crown. . . . She seemed to be tenderly interested in the young archduchesses, her grandchildren, and in the Archduke Ferdinand, the Emperor's son: from time to time she urged him to salute the spectators, pushing him toward the balustrade, turning him to the right and the left.[2]

Despite her hatred of Napoleon, the doughty old queen, whose own marriage had been no bed of roses, did not believe her granddaughter should abandon her husband, now that he was defeated and banished. She advised Marie Louise to knot bedsheets from her window and run away in disguise to Elba. "That is what I should do in her place; for when one is married it is for life."[3]

She called Napoleon's little son *"mon petit Monsieur,"* played with him, brought him toys and sweetmeats. One evening in September of 1814, she tapped on the window of the Schönbrunn nursery and said to the little boy's governess, "Bring my great-grandson to me tomorrow morning; I have something that will amuse him."[4]

In the morning, however, when her servants went to waken her, the old queen was dead.

So that it happened when the Congress of Vienna opened on a brilliant September day in 1814, to divide up the spoils of the Napoleonic Wars, it began with a funeral; and in the person of this last child of Maria Theresia the eighteenth century was effectively laid to rest.

XI
Kings on Holiday:
The Dancing Congress

1. Opening of the Congress

THE AUTUMN of 1814 was exceptionally long, mild, and beautiful in Vienna, so that very late in the year Habsburgs walking in the gardens of Schönbrunn were astonished to see the leaves appearing again on rosebushes, and buds pushing forth again. On a golden September day the first distinguished guests arrived at what turned out to be history's most celebrated house party. While crowds lined the streets and leaned out of windows along the way for a glimpse of celebrities, the three leading monarchs of continental Europe rode into the courtyard of the Hofburg: Emperor Franz of Austria, Czar Alexander of Russia, and King Frederick William of Prussia.

In the weeks that followed, from every corner of Europe a hundred thousand visitors converged on Vienna. No fewer than two hundred fifteen heads of princely families with their relatives and servants arrived. Add to them their ministers, statesmen, diplomats, aides, and secretaries by the hundred. Besides these there were the lobbyists, place-seekers, artists, writers, inventors, philosophers, actors and actresses, dancers, acrobats, prostitutes, pickpockets, swindlers, reformers burning with a cause, political dreamers with magnificent constitutions in their pockets—all congregating on Vienna to see and be seen, to bribe or make money, to get back an old kingdom or acquire a new one: everybody, in short, who hoped to snatch some plum out of the rich pie of Europe, waiting to be cut up.

It was scarcely strange that an atmosphere of carnival reigned in the city, that when Congress visitors sat down years later, gray-headed men and women, to write their memoirs, they remembered Vienna as a glittering, whirling, music-lifted ballroom, unlike any other place in the world.

The air itself was the intoxicating air of victory and peace, the first real peace Europe had known in twenty-five years. An entire generation had grown up in Europe who remembered little except war and invasion and occupation and the threat of new war.

Now by day the streets were brilliant with the life and color of moving crowds, with the uniforms of all the armies of Europe, with the latest frocks and bonnets, with horses and sedan chairs, with carriages and vehicles of every color and kind, often preceded by the elegant figure of a courier in Turkish dress—a custom that still existed only in Vienna—bearing a silver-topped baton, who seemed, as one witness described it, to vault before the horses like a tropical bird.[1]

And at night the whole city glowed with a luminosity that was fantastic and unforgettable to a world that knew only the inky blackness of most cities at night in that pregaslight era. The light of a million candles shone in the windows of the Inner City—eight thousand burned in the crystal chandeliers of the Riding Hall alone each night the Emperor gave a ball there. A thousand torches lighted the narrow streets as carriages crowded end to end for blocks on their way to the great parties. And on festival nights the sky was shot full of rockets and flares and bursts of stars, and there were pyrotechnic conceits that painted the flags of the visiting monarchs and of the buildings of Berlin, Milan, and St. Petersburg in fireworks across the sky.

Everywhere there was music—in the streets, in the palaces, in the Prater, in the packed public dance halls. In the palace of the Czar's minister, Prince Rasumovsky, Beethoven's great new quartets were played for the first time. In the Riding Hall five hundred voices sang Handel's *Samson,* and the composer Salieri directed a concert of a hundred pianos—the audience was only astonished to find that a hundred pianos did not make music a hundred times more beautiful than one.

Besides the sparkle of light and color and music, there were the jewels and the wit. Necklaces and tiaras and decorations appeared that had not been worn since the Revolution, that had been carried precariously, hidden in carriages of families fleeing to exile. There was in that day no naïve modesty about exhibiting gems on one's person; men as well as women glittered from head to toe. Prince Esterhazy at the head of the Royal Hungarian Guard on the opening day of Congress quite dazzled spectators in his pearl-and-diamond-covered magnate's uniform, with an aigrette of gems nodding on his headgear, and huge pearl pendants bobbing on his boots. The delightful British admiral Sir Sidney Smith could not bear to omit a single decoration and he would appear with his breast quite covered with his orders.

In one of the inns of the city one might see each evening that astonishing mountain of flesh that was the old Russian Countess Protassov, intimate of Catherine the Great, who had performed for her sovereign the delicate chore of *éprouveuse*—testing the queen's lovers to be sure they were free of disease. Now in Vienna the Countess received her own little court, ensconced on a sofa, her head, neck, arms, and immense bosom loaded with jewels—tiara, collars, bracelets, buckles, portrait pins, girandoles in her ears that dangled to her shoulders.

The Czarina Elizabeth, wife of Russia's current sovereign, wore her famous pearls and diamonds more discreetly. One night at a theatrical performance in the Hofburg, as the curtain was about to rise, her collar of pearls broke and scattered in all directions. As the gentlemen nearest her hastily got to their knees to collect the gems, the Czarina, in one of the more magnificent of imperial gestures, smilingly commanded them not to bother, it was scarcely worth the trouble.

As for wit, the choicest conversation at the Congress was certainly not to be heard in the banquet hall of the Hofburg.

But at the big round supper table of the Empress of Austria tavern some of the most brilliant and amusing men in Europe gathered each night to drink wine, joke, talk political philosophy, and pass judgment on all the personalities and business of the Congress.

Most celebrated of Congress wits was the distinguished old Belgian émigré Prince Charles de Ligne, who had made Vienna his home for some years. It was he who coined the most quoted and misquoted of Congress epigrams, *"Le Congrès ne marche pas; il danse."*

De Ligne lived in a little house perched on the city walls near Beethoven's, a house so narrow there was but one room on each floor. He maintained a threadbare kind of existence, slept in his library, rode about the city in a battered old gray coach with broken springs, drawn by a pair of emaciated horses, and attended by a ferocious-looking Turk who had been presented to him by Prince Potemkin at the Siege of Ismail.

He was invited everywhere, for he was a delightful old man, a charming raconteur, accomplished in all the lost arts of the salon, and possessed, moreover, not only of wit but of heart.

He had passed his youth at Versailles, fled during the Revolution, fought in most of the great battles against Napoleon, been decorated by all the sovereigns, and received in all the best drawing rooms of Europe. He had known everyone who was anyone in eighteenth-century Europe—Voltaire, Rousseau, Goethe, Frederick the Great, Catherine of Russia—and in that day when one dropped names as gaudily as one flaunted one's jewels, De Ligne's conversation was studded with celebrities. All his stories were apt to begin, "As I recall writing to Jean Jacques Rousseau," or "That reminds me of one afternoon on the Empress Catherine's yacht."

The Prince de Ligne was in his eightieth year when the Congress of Vienna opened; in the first months he scarcely missed a ball or a festival or a masquerade. He found time too to drive out to Schön-brunn to visit the little fair-haired son of Napoleon, who still spoke only French. A young friend who accompanied him describes in his memoirs how the little King of Rome sprang from his chair and threw himself into his old friend's arms. Later, together on the floor, they set up a regiment of mechanical soldiers in battle array. While old De Ligne, a field marshal of Austria, cried out the battle orders, the little boy executed the movements with grace and aplomb.

One windy night that autumn the old prince caught cold waiting on the bastions for a lady who did not keep her rendezvous. (To a passing friend he remarked ruefully, "At your age I made them wait; at my age they make me wait; what's worse they don't come at all.")[2] He made his cold worse by going out without a cloak next night to see some ladies to their carriage after a ball. He grew very ill and could not leave his bed; he could still remark to a visitor that he would contribute to the entertainment of the Congress by providing a field marshal's funeral. And so he did, on a December day in 1814. More than one lady dressing for a ball that night could not suppress her tears when under her window the funeral procession passed, and she saw on the coffin the old, battered, plumed hat that had lain outside so many drawing rooms from Paris to St. Petersburg.[3]

2. Hofburg House Party

ALL THE REIGNING sovereigns with their families and servants were put up at the Hofburg, a feat of housekeeping that taxed that imperial establishment to the utmost.

Each night forty banquet tables were laid in the palace; each morning hundreds of stoves were stoked, hot and cold water carried to the rooms, chamber pots emptied, meals brought, linen washed.

All the royal visitors had their peculiar habits and needs. The Czar Alexander, blond, handsome, gracious, Europe's *rêve chevalier* of the moment, occupied the most elegant guest suite—the one in the Amalia Wing that still bears his name. He required a block of ice to be brought up each morning for his toilette; it was whispered below stairs that some of his servants were not even *stubenrein*—housebroken. The King of Württemberg was so enormously fat that a hole had to be cut in his dining table to accommodate his girth, and a specially built, wide, low carriage provided for his excursions.

Fourteen hundred horses and several hundred spanking new carriages waited in the palace stables to take the Emperor's guests wherever they wanted to go at any hour of the day or night.

Since the sovereigns did not take part in the actual work of the Congress, the argument and debate and horse trading that went on around the council table in the Ballhaus, they had plenty of time to amuse themselves.

For their entertainment Emperor Franz and Empress Maria Ludovica provided a fantastic array of diversions; day after day, night after night, they hosted festivals, hunts, balls, theatricals, musicales. And in that comic-opera setting of the Congress, the domestic tragedy of that unlikely imperial pair unfolded. Drawing on all her reserves of strength, the doomed young empress gave herself to planning fetes, appearing before her guests each day bright-eyed, pale, faultless in bearing. The French ambassador had remarked of her when she was married, "She was already an empress in her mother's lap."[1] Now mortally ill, Maria Ludovica played out the role for which she had been painstakingly trained.

She joined her guests in great hunting parties at Laxenburg—falcon hunts in medieval style, grand *battues* in which beaters drove hordes of game into a clearing and each monarch could kill to his heart's content, having four pages assigned to keep his guns loaded. Afterward there were sightseeing trips through the Gothic water castle in the lake, and finally a grand hunt ball and supper, with minstrels in medieval dress entertaining the guests.

At outdoor festivals in the public parks the monarchs could enjoy the novelty of rubbing elbows with common folk. In the Prater a great festival celebrated the anniversary of the Battle of Leipzig; such crowds came that ladies had their jewels stolen, their sleeves and skirts torn off. A festival in the Augarten honored veterans of the late wars, and His Imperial Majesty's soldiers got free dinner served at huge tables in the green. Acrobats, dancers, horse races, games entertained the mob; as a grand climax the famous aeronaut Kraskowitz made a balloon ascension, rising majestically in his airy bubble to unfurl the flags of all nations over the city.

When the marvelous autumn waned and winter came, Emperor Franz gave a sleighing party. Thirty-two gilded sleighs, lined with emerald or sapphire velvet, harnesses ajingle with silver bells, with horses decked in tiger skins, carried guests an hour's ride out to Schönbrunn. There the sleighs formed a half circle around the frozen lake to watch two pretty Dutch skaters dressed as milkmaids dance on ice, and a young attaché of the British Embassy execute intricate designs, ending up tracing with his skates the monograms of each of the empresses and queens. From gay little tents servants on skates brought hot drinks to the watchers. Finally everyone went inside the palace to see a performance of *Cinderella*, to dance, sup, ride back through a whirl of great falling snowflakes to the city. The next day Franz presented to the Czar the gilded sleigh in which he had ridden.

Everyone fell victim to the Viennese passion for the waltz; night after night throngs whirled in the ballrooms of the great palaces and in the public dance halls. Even austere Lord Castlereagh and his eccentric wife engaged a dancing master to instruct them every morning.

One evening Franz and Maria Ludovica gave a magnificent *bal paré* in the Riding Hall of the Hofburg. Guests entered through a fragrant avenue of blossoming orange trees; the whole Riding Hall shimmered in snow-white and silver; thousands of candles flashed in the crystal chandeliers and mirrors. Another evening they invited guests to a carrousel, in the manner of the old regime: young men of the court dressed as knights tilted lances at Turks' heads and performed marvels of equestrian skill with hairbreadth accuracy. Afterward the royal guests waltzed in the Redoutensaal of the Hofburg and supped off the golden service of Maria Theresia.

"One sees everywhere," Talleyrand wrote home to King Louis XVIII, "nothing but emperors and kings, empresses and queens, hereditary princes, ruling princes, and the like." He added with some disdain: "At these assemblies royalty undoubtedly loses something of the greatness that belongs to it; the presence of three or four kings . . . at the balls and tea parties of simple private folk of Vienna appears to me most incongruous."[2]

The spectacle of majesty in undress has always provided entertainment for the general public; the gossip of the Vienna Congress was relayed by letter and word of mouth the length and breadth of Europe.

How the Czar and the King of Prussia surprised Emperor Franz on his birthday while he was dressing, and brought him a sable-lined lounging robe and a silver bowl and pitcher from Berlin.

How the stolid King of Prussia (*"une figure d'arsenal,"* De Ligne described him) sat for hours in the drawing room of the most beautiful woman in Vienna, Countess Julia Zichy, regaling her with descriptions of the most recent changes in the Prussian army uniform.

How dowdy Lady Castlereagh, wife of the British delegate, stitched together her own costume for one of the masked balls, appearing as a grotesque vestal virgin, with her husband's Order of the Garter wound about her disheveled coiffure.

How the Czar bet the pretty Countess Wrbna that he could dress faster than she. They met in street clothes at Countess Zichy's, were put in separate rooms with witnesses. In five minutes the Czar appeared before the gathering in full court uniform, every order in place, complete to silk-stockinged calves and buckled shoes. But the Countess was already waiting in a French ball gown, hair powdered, high-heeled slippers, beauty spot, and fan. The Czar acknowledged defeat and presented the Countess as a prize a complete, exquisitely bound library.

Another tale recounted how Castlereagh's insufferably arrogant half brother, Lord Stewart, English ambassador in Vienna, got his comeuppance. Descending a crowded stairway at the theater one night behind a pretty young countess, Lord Stewart thought he could with impunity take a certain liberty with her person. The young lady, however, turned quickly and delivered such a resounding smack on his lordship's cheek as to bring instant applause from everyone about.

And while the Congress itself nearly broke up over the burning question of Saxons and Poles, the crisis that absorbed the court set was whether the handsome young Count Wrbna would agree to shave off his carefully tended hussar mustaches so that he could play the role of Apollo in a private theatrical. In the end the Empress herself had to intervene and exercise her powers of persuasion: that night Count Wrbna posed in the *tableau vivant* as Apollo, his upper lip bare as a girl's.

Of the uncountable flirtations and romances that went on that winter, most talked of was that of the Czar's sister, the Grand Duchess Catherine, with the Crown Prince of Württemberg. They were by no means youthful lovers. Sharp-eyed, snub-nosed, eccentric, the widowed Catherine moved through life like an imperious little tugboat. The Prince had known and admired her years before; he had, in the meantime, been married for purely political reasons to Princess Charlotte of Bavaria. Encountering Catherine again in Vienna, he quite lost his heart to her, applied to the Pope for a divorce on the grounds that his own marriage had never been consummated. Amid the revelry of the Congress, the pair of unlikely lovers might be seen deep in conversation in a drawing-room corner, sharing a sleigh or a carriage in the Prater. The Prince won his divorce and the two were married shortly after the Congress adjourned.

As for the virginal grass widow the Prince abandoned, there would be an even happier ending in store for her: she would one day rule the Hofburg.

3. *Disagreements and Duels*

IN THE BAROQUE Ballhaus, the chancellery building adjoining the Hofburg, the Council of Four—Austria, Great Britain, Prussia, and Russia—met and performed the actual work of the Congress. The touchy question of precedence—who would enter and leave the conference room first—was solved by cutting four doors, so that the delegates of all four powers could enter and leave simultaneously. Very early in the operations the soft-voiced old fox, Talleyrand, had talked his defeated country into a leading place at the peace table, so that it became a Council of Five.

As for the assembly of all the Congress delegates, it was postponed again and again; never, in fact, met until June, 1815, to sign the final act. As Gentz remarked, there never really was a Congress of Vienna.[1]

The sovereigns did not attend the conferences in person, but in late afternoon, in the hour before dinner, they would meet together in the Hofburg to talk over what their ministers had threshed out in the morning sessions. As often as not, like Penelope's weaving, the morning's work would be undone by their majesties, especially by the volatile Czar, so that the hard-pressed ministers had to begin afresh the next morning.

In spite of the unctuous smiles the delegates wear in those mellifluous portraits of the Congress which the painter Isabey has left us, it must have been one of the most maddening summit conferences in history. Talleyrand kept raising procedural points, and managing with the utmost finesse to drive a poniard between the allies. (He managed so well, of course, that the famous secret treaty was drawn up by Austria, Britain, and France.) Then there were the Russian delegates with their Czar's inordinate—and changeable—demands. There was the canny Prussian Karl August von Hardenberg, virtually stone-deaf, who never could quite hear at the precisely right moment. And there was the council chairman, Metternich, elegant, vain, the jewel of the Golden Fleece about his neck, remarkable not only for the subtlety of his diplomatic maneuverings but for the way in which he carried on concurrently all the various layers of his life.

Besides presiding over the meetings of the Council, Metternich found time to supervise court fetes, to rouge ladies for a tableau, to play the cello in the Emperor's family quartet, and to maintain more or less satisfactory relationships with his various mistresses—a full program that made him late more than once for a vital Council meeting. His diplomacy of confusion and mystification was remarkably successful, and in the end he got everything, or nearly everything, he wanted from the Congress.

The question was how to dispose of Poland and Saxony, the former coveted by Russia, the latter by Prussia, the King of Saxony having made the mistake of remaining loyal to Napoleon to the end, while the other monarchs had been foresighted enough to withdraw their allegiance at the right time. (As Talleyrand remarked cynically, it was a question of dates.[2]) And if, in the end, millions of Poles and millions of Saxons were exchanged across the council table as coolly as a pair of jewel-studded snuffboxes, still the final agreement was not reached without frazzled nerves, temper, scenes, and walkouts quite as violent as anything seen in international meetings since. At one point the wits at the Empress of Austria tavern were betting odds the whole Congress would break up and war be renewed on the morrow.

For three months the Czar and Metternich did not exchange a word. The Czar refused to go to a ball at the Metternichs', declaring he would rather fight the Austrian chancellor with pistols.[3]

The only duel actually fought by participants of the council table was between two Prussians—Hermann von Boyen, minister of war, and the delegate, Wilhelm von Humboldt.[4] Boyen had been highly insulted when Humboldt hurried him out of the room at a signal from Metternich just as a secret discussion was about to begin.

Boyen immediately sent a challenge to Humboldt, seconds were chosen, and the hour set. What proved to be difficult in crowded Vienna was to find a nice quiet spot to duel. The Prater was full of strolling lovers, the Kahlenberg of picnickers. The two finally found a deserted meadow by the Danube and marked off their paces.

As challenger Boyen had the first shot; whether by accident or by design the bullet went yards wide of its mark. Humboldt, who hated every moment of the affair and was quaking in his boots, tried to pull his trigger, found the pistol jammed. He pulled and pulled, could not get it to fire at all.

In the end the two Prussians, having satisfied their honor, sat down on the Danube bridge, talked about life and their country and the Congress, and drove home together in the same *Fiaker*, the warmest of friends.

One element of Emperor Franz's obliging hospitality did not contribute to the good fellowship of the gathering: this was the espionage activity of the secret police. All the most distinguished guests, and a good many of the undistinguished, were tailed by police night and day. Letters were intercepted, conversations reported on, waste baskets ransacked, boudoir intrigues peeped at; porters, coachmen, chambermaids, and couriers bribed. The whole police system in Austria was just saved from being intolerable by its total lack of efficiency. So that, while Emperor Franz might find the reports highly diverting, his police never uncovered anything of real political significance.

Bribery and corruption were everywhere rampant, much of it under the same gracious guise as political favor-seeking and gift-giving today. Lobbyists spent freely for every cause in Europe, plus a few in Asia, from civil rights for the Jews to the German book-publishing industry and the acquisition of a duchy in Italy.

The King of Saxony was said to have paid Talleyrand an enormous sum to defend his boundaries, while rumor had it that Friedrich von Gentz, as Secretary-General of the Congress, was lining his pockets by taking bribes from both sides on all questions. Baron von Humboldt, the Prussian delegate, prided himself on being above corruption and turned down some tempting offers. He did, however, cheerfully tote up the number of jeweled snuffboxes he was certain to be given by the various embassies, and wrote his wife that he would pry off the jewels and have something splendid made to ornament her person. Sensible wife that she was, Frau von Humboldt wrote back tartly that any jewels he acquired would be used to pay off their debts.[5]

4. End of the Dance

LORD CASTLEREAGH and Prince Metternich had thought the peace treaty could be written in the space of four weeks. As it turned out, it was nearly nine months before the final act of the Congress of Vienna was drawn up and signed, and the last guests took their departure.

Meantime, with so many royal toes underfoot in the Hofburg, it was inevitable that the cozy air of a perpetual house party would wear thin before the Congress was over. One can imagine what scenes took place below stairs, where the regular Hofburg servants rubbed elbows day in and day out with cooks, ladies' maids, coachmen, and valets of their Prussian, Russian, Danish, and other majesties—all quite as jealous of protocol and position as were their masters and mistresses.

Attendance at the nightly imperial dinner parties began to fall off; the royal guests took to dining alone in their own suites. The King of Prussia declared pettishly that he would eat only food prepared by his own cook, because—so Humboldt reported to his wife—"the imperial cuisine and wine are said to be horrible."[1] The King's estrangement was probably more political than gastronomic, for it occurred during the quarrel over the Saxon-Polish question.

The King of Württemberg went home in a huff right after Christmas. He had been attending a conference at which the touchy question of the rights of nobles as opposed to the rights of sovereigns was under discussion. At a crucial point the fat king jumped to his feet to make a statement, his embonpoint caught the conference table, which had not been cut out to accommodate his girth as had the banquet table in the Hofburg, and over it went with a tremendous crash, sending papers, books, and inkwells flying in all directions. The King hurried back to his suite, ordered his servants to pack, and drove off that very night for Stuttgart.

Even the Viennese public suffered from a jaded appetite. Talley-rand was right. Seeing emperors and kings and princes every day was like living on sugarplums through the twelve days of Christmas. In the jammed city, prices had skyrocketed; the cost of housing, food, and firewood had risen astronomically. Everyone wondered what new taxes would be levied to pay Emperor Franz's huge bills for entertainment, which were estimated at possibly a half million gulden a day.[2]

The witticism going the rounds of the taverns was: "The Russian Czar makes love for all, the Danish King talks for all, the Prussian King thinks for all, the King of Württemberg eats for all, the King of Bavaria drinks for all, and the Emperor of Austria—he pays for all."[3]

On the evening of March 15, 1815, the Empress Maria Ludovica had invited guests to her apartments in the Hofburg to watch a *tableau vivant* from *The Barber of Seville*. Those frozen scenes from mythol-ogy and from the lives of royalty, which required neither acting nor singing but allowed the pretty young women of the court to show off their charms, must have become excruciatingly tedious to the audience that winter, which was nearly the same night after night. On that particular night the orchestra struck up the opening music, the curtain was about to part, when an astounding piece of news suddenly passed from ear to ear—one suspects with a thrill not unmixed with pleasure: Napoleon had escaped from Elba, was even now gathering his old army about him to march on Paris.

Congress did not, however, break up at once with a clanking of swords and trumpet calls to arms. Patriotic songs were introduced into the concerts, and the Duke of Wellington took his departure. Na-poleon's letters to his wife were passed around the conference table. Napoleon's little son, the King of Rome, was moved from Schönbrunn to rooms in the Hofburg as a security measure, and his French govern-ess was dismissed.

A few days after the news arrived, Metternich cooked up a de-licious little joke on Secretary-General Gentz, who was absolutely terrified of Bonaparte. Metternich had a fake manifesto printed which purported to come from Napoleon's headquarters. It announced in bold-face type that the Emperor of the French would pay ten thou-sand ducats to anyone who would deliver to him his mortal enemy, Friedrich von Gentz, dead or alive, or even present proof of his mur-der. Metternich had the sheet delivered to Gentz at his bedside with his morning coffee. The poor man nearly died of fright, could not even down his usual three pastry pies for breakfast.[4]

Most of the monarchs lingered in Vienna until the end of May. In the fine spring weather there were *barouchades*—processions of little carriages each holding a cozy twosome that wound through the streets and out into the Vienna Woods, to return by pleasant lanes and by-roads to the city for supper and dancing.

Nine days before the Battle of Waterloo, on June 9, 1815, the final act of the Congress was drawn up and signed. Slowly Vienna began to simmer back to normal.

Nearly all the visitors went home with some little souvenir of the Congress. Among the last to leave was the delightful French dancer Mlle. Bigottini, who had enjoyed enormous success for her performance in the ballet *Nina*. She went back to France richer by far, and with an illegitimate child acknowledged by Count Palffy, director of the Theater an der Wien, who had injudiciously mixed pleasure with business, and ended up guaranteeing mother and child a fat annuity.[5] This was, however, the most extraordinary child begotten during the Congress festivities; gossip had it that the talented Bigottini got no fewer than three eminent princes to acknowledge paternity and arrange discreet payments that would follow her to Paris. All of which was not bad for the pretty ballerina, considering that she was a Frenchwoman who knew how to be careful with money and still had the nimblest legs in France.

There were Viennese too who had come off well during that protracted festival that was the Congress: the Hofburg servants had been lavishly tipped by the departing monarchs, and there were shopkeepers nearly rich enough to retire, including a certain pastry cook, Johann Baptiste Höfelmayr, who had sold so many airy creations of *Schlag* and marzipan that he could afford to buy the Apollo Dance Palace in 1819.

As for the Emperor Franz, when he returned from his triumph in Paris with Metternich's Holy Alliance in his pocket, he had done well enough, too: he had got back the Tyrol, and Salzburg, and the fine Italian provinces of Lombardy and Venetia. He also got peace of mind and a quiet palace, where he could retire when he liked to his glasshouses and fuss over his birds and tropical plants.

In autumn of that year, 1815, Franz traveled south to visit his newly won Italian lands, and—against the advice of her doctors—his young empress, Maria Ludovica, went with him.[6] She had never been more beautiful than she appeared at the festivals and balls that greeted their arrival in Venice, in her lavish brocaded gowns heavy with pearls and brilliants, her cheeks flushed, her dark head carried high and proud with the great victory that was theirs.

But all night long she could not sleep for coughing.

They journeyed on to Modena, where her family was restored to the throne. Maria Ludovica was no better. Surely, surely, in the warm Italian spring she would regain her health. But in spring, in the palace in Verona, she grew worse. The doctors bled her again and again, and, quite suddenly, in April of 1816 she died. She was twenty-nine.

Her body was borne back to the Kapuziner Crypt in Vienna, and once more Franz wandered about, lost and lonely, in the vast, high-ceilinged rooms of the Hofburg.

One day he remembered that she had asked to wear a certain favorite ring to her grave. The ring was not to be found. Finally it was discovered in the possession of a lady of the court to whom it had been given as a mourning token. Forthwith Emperor Franz ordered Court Marshal Trauttmannsdorff to descend to the crypt and replace the ring on his dead wife's finger. It was certainly an errand to try the loyalty of the Emperor's most loyal servant. Accompanied by disgruntled monks bearing torches, Trauttmannsdorff descended to the black and chilly crypt. The outer stone sarcophagus was opened, and the inner three. With difficulty the last hinges, already rusty in the damp crypt, were prized open, and the torch shone down on the changed features of the dead empress. He tried to lift her hand to place the ring, but it had been tightly bound by the embalmers. A reek of death and of embalming scents filled the eerie crypt. Hastily he dropped the ring in the coffin, motioned the monks to close and seal once more the coffins.[7]

XII

Mr. Biedermeier and His Times

1. Franz the Good, Ferdinand the Good-natured

BARELY SIX MONTHS after the death of Maria Ludovica Franz married a fourth time, a princess twenty-four years younger then he, Charlotte of Bavaria, the virginal grass widow divorced shortly before by the Crown Prince of Württemberg.

Charlotte was ugly, but pleasantly so; when Franz saw her sturdy and blooming good health, he murmured to his adjutant, "At least I won't have another corpse on my hands a few years hence."[1] Grateful Charlotte, who as Empress took the name Karoline, was at pains to please her new husband, and the marriage turned out nicely.

In his plain brown frock coat the Emperor might be seen driving his wife in the Prater in the plainest of barouches. Like a true Herr Biedermeier[2] he cultivated a thrifty simplicity in his dress and habits, enjoyed his hobbies, looked forward to more grandchildren, deferred always to Metternich, "my most loyal servant and my very good friend."

There was no fresh batch of children from the fourth marriage: the newest generation of Habsburgs were still the seven sons and daughters surviving from the Emperor's second marriage with his cousin, Marie-Thérèse of Naples.

The eldest daughter, Marie Louise, that awkward reminder of the policy of appeasing Napoleon, had been granted by the Congress the duchy of Parma. The comic-opera little country suited her perfectly; off she went, with a suite that included as aide Count Neipperg, hand-picked by Metternich. A dashing figure in his hussar's uniform, Neipperg had lost one eye to a saber thrust and wore a black patch over it. His remaining eye, the left one, had a particularly devilish way of looking at a woman. He made short work of the susceptible, placid ex-empress, who rather too promptly—for Napoleon was still living out his exile on St. Helena—had two children by him. Marie Louise, an indolent sensualist, found it just as impossible as her father did to live alone. Moreover, certain Viennese clergy had confused matters by circulating a document immediately after Waterloo, proving that Napoleon's divorce was invalid, and that the Emperor's daughter had never really been married at all.

News of the two dubious children in Parma was carefully kept from her father, the Emperor, and after Napoleon's death in 1821, Marie Louise hastened to legalize her ménage with Neipperg. It was when Neipperg died in 1829 that the morganatic marriage was made public, and Marie Louise addressed a letter to her father beginning, "It is time for me to confess."

Emperor Franz's reply is a rather nice one, considering the awkward circumstances an imperial father had to face:

> I cannot hide from you the profound sorrow which this situation causes me—a situation about which nothing can now be done but which should never have existed before God and man. . . . In the hearts of parents there is always more indulgence for their children's failings than children show of their parents' failings. . . . In conclusion I must say you have hurt me deeply. But I am your father, and my love for you absolves you of everything it can forgive you.[3]

The stepmother, sensible Empress Karoline, wrote Marie Louise that she must be careful not to show off the two children until "you can do so without giving rise to embarrassing calculations."[4]

Marie Louise's little son by Napoleon did not go along with his mother to Parma. Metternich and the restored Bourbons in France feared the child might be a rallying point for the Bonapartist cause in Italy and France; they preferred to keep him firmly in Vienna under a watchful eye. An attractive, bright, mischievous child, little Franzi—now rechristened the Duke of Reichstadt—was the only grandchild in the family. His great company of archducal aunts and uncles in the Hofburg doted on him; Marie Louise's younger sister Leopoldine took him in her special charge, calling him "Papa's darling and mine too." His tutor informed Marie Louise:

> Nothing is odder or more delightful than to see him in the midst of his aunts and uncles, either walking solemnly along or else darting in between them to get up to some prank or other.[5]

His uncle, Archduke Rainer, brought him a basset hound, and his grandfather, Emperor Franz, a man who loved children, fitted him

to a small uniform (Austrian, of course) and gave him lead soldiers
to play with in a corner of his study while he busied himself over his
interminable papers.

Metternich, who had arranged the match between Marie Louise
and Napoleon, went on playing royal marriage broker. A year after
Marie Louise departed for Parma, Leopoldine was betrothed to the
Portuguese crown prince, Dom Pedro, whose family had fled from
Napoleon to their South American colony of Brazil. Tomboyish
Leopoldine was not exactly pretty, pale of skin and hair and with
the protruding Habsburg underlip, but her eyes were a fine, deep,
clear blue, and she was an engagingly honest, warmhearted girl.

Leopoldine did not in the least look forward to an exile in Brazil.
She wrote to her sister just before her departure:

> Nothing remains for me to do except weep with you and curse
> the word politics for causing me so much suffering. Prince Met-
> ternich is accompanying me as far as Leghorn as my official
> escort; you can imagine how delighted I am!?!? . . . We unfortu-
> nate princesses are like dice whose happiness or unhappiness
> depends on the throw.[6]

When she landed in Brazil after her three-month sailing voyage,
Leopoldine was at first enchanted with her new country, wrote
home that her husband's family were "angel-good" to her, "especially
my dear Pedro," whom she found at first perfectly charming:

> I had a few hard days [she wrote home to "dearest Papa"] for
> I had to be in full gala dress from seven in the morning to two in
> the night, after which my beloved husband would not let me
> sleep, so that I am, truth to say, rather pale and have had stomach
> ache for two days.

As "dear Pedro's" wife, Leopoldine led a life which turned out to
be far from tranquil. Children arrived; that was to be expected;
Pedro wrote his father-in-law in Vienna about the first:

> My beloved wife began labor at five this morning; she ran all
> about the house and hung on my neck, and it was so, standing
> up, that she bore the child, and at half past five everything was
> over, and great joy, having given life to a daughter. . . .

But political events seethed in the palace in Rio. When Pedro's
father had returned to his throne in Portugal, Pedro threw in his lot
with a revolutionary group that declared Brazil's independence and
named him emperor. Leopoldine's pleasure in her new role was short-

lived; her husband installed a mistress in the palace, raised her to countess, then marquise, handed over the illegitimate child born of the liaison to Leopoldine to raise with her own in the royal nursery.

Humiliated, wretched, deprived even of the income promised her by her marriage contract, Leopoldine finally wrote out an ultimatum to Dom Pedro:

> Senhor! Since you have not slept at home for a month I ask you to choose one or the other of us, or else give me permission to return to my father.

Maria Leopoldine, Archduchess of Austria

A bitterly violent scene ensued; Dom Pedro stormed out of the palace, rode off to battle insurgents in Uruguay. Leopoldine collapsed, suffered a miscarriage, lay dying.

In December of 1826 she took the last Sacrament, bade her children an affectionate farewell—kissed the little son of her rival as well—and dictated to a lady in waiting a last letter to her sister in Parma:

> My beloved sister! In the most deplorable health, at the very end of my life, I have the sorrow not to be able to tell you personally all the griefs that have for so long afflicted me. . . . My sister! I shall not see you again! I shall not be able to tell you again how much I love you . . .

She implored her sister "not for revenge, but . . . for affectionate, sisterly help for my blameless children, who will either be orphans or will fall into the hands of her who was the cause of all my suffering. . . ."

Leopoldine died then, alone and uncomforted, a Habsburg child seven thousand miles from home.

Even with daughters married and gone, the family scene in the Hofburg was a lively one: carriages coming and going, bustling inroads of relatives and visiting royalty, great family dinners at which the whole clan gathered, including Franz's numerous brothers and sisters. Sometimes an artist was called in to paint such a group, as the artist Peter Fendi did in 1834: thirty-seven Habsburgs gathered together, including twenty-one children, some in diapers. "It was a sour piece of work," one of the archduchesses commented tersely.[7]

For the Emperor Franz there was a constant anxiety in those years: as yet no throne heir's heir.

His eldest son, Ferdinand, had not improved in body or mind over the years. Droves of tutors had come and gone in the palace, trying to instill sufficient knowledge in that huge vacant head. His favorite amusements were to wedge himself in a wastepaper basket and roll over and over like a ball. Or to stand for hours at his window staring down at passers-by. His conversations were stammered repetitions of things he had said before. His epileptic attacks were frequent and dreadful to see; he lived in mortal terror lest his father might be present and witness such a seizure. Yet for all his disabilities, Ferdinand was a sweet-natured youth, gentle and without guile.

He would not marry; doctors said it was not possible for him to beget heirs. Once, in a near-tragic hunting accident, he was wounded in the hand, apparently by his bright young nephew, Napoleon's son Reichstadt. For the gifted grandson who could never be Emperor, it was perhaps one of those Freudian death wishes; years later, on his deathbed, Reichstadt spoke anxiously of the "crime" he had committed.[8]

Clearly the job of perpetuating the family line must fall to Ferdinand's younger brother, Franz Karl. The latter, while neither epileptic nor retarded, was definitely not very bright. By great good fortune a brain was found for him: the attractive and clever Bavarian Princess Sophie, younger half sister of the Empress Karoline. In the tangle of royal relationships the two half sisters would share the Hofburg as stepmother-in-law and daughter-in-law.

It was not a marriage of love, nor even of semicompatibility. Sophie's husband was an insufferable bore; children—the one thing that could make such a marriage bearable—were long in coming. Even over the prospect of children hung the shadowy fear of epilepsy; to her mother Sophie wrote in horror when she once saw her brother-in-law Ferdinand in one of his seizures.

But Sophie was intelligent, clear-thinking, strong-willed; she would make the best of things. She insisted that her ineffectual husband, who had absolutely nothing to occupy his time, be at least admitted to the state council. She dreaded hearing of new failures, and when he returned at night to recount to her what had passed, she would shut her ears, she wrote to her mother, "for I was afraid of hearing something unpleasant."[9]

Sophie found ways to occupy her time: in studying court protocol and usage, in which she presently outshone her Habsburg relatives; in the theater, for which she had a passion and in which she could spend some of the pent-up romantic feelings that had no outlet in her life; and in her friendship for two young men far more attractive and amusing than her dull husband. The exiled Swedish prince, Gustav Wasa, came on daily visits to Sophie until court tongues began to wag.

The other friendship was for her nephew-by-marriage, the Duke of Reichstadt, six years younger than she, who was growing now into a charming, lively, promising young man—whom nobody quite knew what to do with. The Bourbons in France kept urging the Emperor to make a priest of the boy—which, they felt, would keep him safely out of the political scene. From faraway Brazil his Aunt Leopoldine —to whom he was always *Mein Schatz*—wrote to her father in protest. The boy's uncle, the kindly, liberal Archduke Johann, pressed the Emperor to emancipate the youth completely.

Meantime young Reichstadt laughed, joked, went to the theater with Sophie, and made boyish love to her, for which she reprimanded him. Sometimes he was ill with a high and unexplainable fever; Sophie came to visit him and made him take his medicine.

Whatever she did, Sophie would always know exactly on which side of the bread her personal butter was to be found. She knew very well how to shower her father-in-law, Emperor Franz, with all the warm little attentions of a pretty young woman that are so pleasant to an aging man. "I fell on his neck and kissed and hugged him so hard it's a wonder the good Emperor stayed in one piece," she would write to her mother.[10]

The good Emperor longed for the one piece of news that delayed long in coming: news of a throne heir. Tears stood in his eyes when he watched his ungainly son Ferdinand shuffle along palace corridors, pushed and pulled by aides, or when he heard him stammer out a few words from a mouth twisted out of shape by a seizure.

Sophie too longed more than anything in the world for a child, but it was not until six years after her marriage, in 1830, that her first son, Franz Josef, was born.

It was a cataclysmal event, that birth in Schönbrunn Palace. For the two days and two nights Sophie lay in labor, a crowd of relatives and courtiers filled the anterooms and bedchamber. In the chapel the Sacrament was exposed; prayers continued night and day. For two days and two nights nobody slept, except for naps caught from time to time on a sofa in one of the antechambers adjoining the bedchamber, from which could be heard the screams and the worried exclamations of the midwife. At last, on August 18, the heir made his appearance, the crowds could disperse, and Sophie's sister could write home:

> Good God, those were forty-three horrible hours, agonizingly fearful, and we are all totally exhausted! The christening will be at six today and we shall all look like ghosts in our gala.[11]

Twenty-one cannon shots thundered across the city to announce the news; the Emperor solemnly proclaimed that each time the child was taken out his carriage should be drawn by no fewer than six horses. From the day of his birth such throngs of relatives and courtiers milled through the nursery each day to see the child that his *aja*, a noblewoman of the Empire, had to retire behind a screen to dress in privacy. Only on rainy days was there a lull in the procession of viewers.

2. Biedermeier Romances

THE STORY IS TOLD that a few years after the Congress the court physician, Dr. Stifft, was examining the Emperor Franz, who had a severe cold on the chest.

"This cold, Your Majesty," said the old doctor, "although harassing, does not alarm me. There is, after all, nothing like a good constitution."

"What?" cried the Emperor. "We have known each other very long, Stifft, but let me never hear that word again! I have no constitution and will never have one!"[1]

Metternich echoed the sentiment. Although the kingdoms of Bavaria and Württemberg had got themselves constitutions, and the winds of change were surely blowing across all Europe, in Austria a kind of flower-sprinkled chintz curtain shut out any dangerous draughts of outside air.

If they had no constitution, if neither speech nor pen was free under the Metternich system, still the accommodating Austrians for some years made the best of it. In the narrow-walled intellectual room left for them, they created a special climate of *Gemütlichkeit*, of comfort and an artful way of life. There was also peace within the Empire: a commodity not to be underestimated by people who had suffered war for nearly a quarter of a century.

An air of perpetual nostalgia, of elegiac romance, suffuses that third of a century after the Congress, which came to be known as the Biedermeier age.

It was an age of small things, of dainty things, of the operetta, the sonata, the song, and the waltz; of the poem, the farce, the miniature painting; of chocolate cups of fragile Vienna porcelain painted with minuscule landscapes and gilded cupids; of embroidery and pleated fans; of tight little nosegays of pastel flowers encircled with a collar of lace.

Every house had a garden; flowers bloomed on wallpaper and materials. Little garden houses sprang up in the suburbs of Vienna, with espaliered walls and vine-covered pavilions. Inside the city, people still strolled on the walls or along the Graben, stopping to eat a pastry or an ice offered in a delectable range of flavors from violet, cinnamon, rose or chestnut through quince, cream, and punch. Viennese coffeehouses were on their way to their special glory: islands of peace where a man could go to smoke a quiet pipe, read a paper (albeit censored), talk of God and the world, scribble verses or a stanza of music, drink coffee served in fourteen different ways.

It was no longer the aristocracy but the middle class that set its stamp on society and on taste. Everything was *Bürgerlich*.

The first steamboat appeared on the Danube, the first gaslights on the streets of Vienna. (The gas company graciously offered to light up the Habsburg crypt in the Kapuziner Church with the newfangled device, an offer which Emperor Franz firmly declined; tapers would provide quite enough light for the eminent ghosts of his ancestors.)

If the plays that appeared on the boards—even Shakespeare—were carefully censored for political connotations, still music remained everyone's possession. Beethoven was admirably played in the taverns along the main avenues of the Prater; at "sausage balls"—modest festivities at which in place of champagne and pheasant, one drank beer and gobbled sausages—some of Franz Schubert's loveliest songs were first sung. A little later those musical evenings at home, called *Schubertiades* after the composer, were increasingly popular, with friends meeting to play impromptu music, to sing and frolic as Schubert's bohemian circle had done. And in a city of 200,000 persons, there were no fewer than sixty-five factories manufacturing pianos.

The passion for dancing had become a mania; during those years of the 1820s and 1830s all Vienna divided into two waltz camps to become passionate followers of smooth, sweet, romantic Josef Lanner, who conducted court balls at the Hofburg, or of heady, exciting, gypsyish Johann Strauss, who directed the orchestra at the huge Sperl ballroom.

Romance flourished too in the gentle air of Biedermeier Vienna, and it appeared in all sorts of forms and in highly unlikely places. There were notable mésalliances now in increasing numbers, between

the top ranks of society and the middle; the rigid lines of society
were blurring, and the old class demarcations fading a little.

Most popular of the Emperor's many brothers, Archduke Johann,
a convinced liberal and lifelong enemy of Metternich, astonished and
shocked court society by marrying—morganatically, to be sure—Anna
Plochl, the pretty daughter of the postmaster in the village of Bad
Aussee. In the end Emperor Franz, who of course never approved
the match, elevated Anna to the title of Countess of Meran. To
Anna's immense delight her first-born son had the unmistakable
Habsburg lip, which she pointed out proudly to everyone. "That at
least he has from his father," she said.[2]

But the mésalliance that set the court by the ears was the marriage
of Prince Metternich himself, that arch-snob and public upholder of
caste and legitimacy, with an exquisite little nobody named Antonia
Leykam, whose mother had been a dancer at the opera. Metternich
was a widower of fifty-four when he married Antonia in 1827; his first
wife, people remembered, had been the influential granddaughter of
the great Prince Kaunitz and had enormously furthered his career.

Metternich's idyl of true love lasted fifteen months; Antonia died
during her first childbirth, though her husband was said to have
offered doctors every treasure in the monarchy if they would only
save her life.

When he married a third time, a lady of suitable connections,
Countess Melanie Zichy, he continued to keep Antonia's portrait,
painted in a white dress with a bunch of violets in her hand, in his
study, facing the desk where he worked. The new Princess Metternich had her own portrait painted in a ball gown, with all her
diamonds, and had it hung on the wall behind her husband's desk.
Once, while he was away on a journey, she switched the two portraits. Metternich changed them back again as soon as he returned.[3]

It was Metternich who announced the most surprising marriage in
the imperial family.

In the spring of 1831, a few months after the birth of Franz Josef,
Metternich dropped the bombshell by announcing blandly that there
was no reason after all, why Crown Prince Ferdinand should not
marry, and that, in fact, a wife had already been found for him.
Sophie, who had been bending over the cradle of her small future
emperor, wrote home to her mother in shocked surprise.[4]

It was a cunning project. Old Emperor Franz, growing increasingly
feeble, certainly had not many years to live. Metternich reasoned that

if the throne succession were passed over the clearly defective Ferdinand, and the scarcely more capable Franz Karl, then it was not impossible that the Emperor's most able brothers and his own bitter enemies, Archdukes Karl and Johann, might come to power as Regents. This, Metternich was determined to avoid at all costs. Married to a suitable princess, Ferdinand might project to the world an image of a man at least passably normal and capable of wearing a crown.

Chosen as bride for the unfortunate epileptic was Princess Marianna of Sardinia, a conspicuously plain girl, very virtuous and humble —"so modest," explained her pretty married sister with alarming frankness, "that she hardly thinks she could satisfy a first-rate (*ausgezeichneten*) husband."[5]

Whether the girl really understood the conditions of the marriage is doubtful. She had never seen the bridegroom; a flattering miniature portrait of Ferdinand was prepared to be sent to her. When the brooch was passed around among the archduke uncles at a family party on New Year's Eve, it elicited such hilarity and rude comments that Sophie "blushed up to the whites of her eyes."[6]

Court circles awaited Marianna's arrival in some anxiety. When the pair first met in an inn outside Vienna, one of the ladies of the court reported to Sophie that "it went off better than she had hoped."[7] When the family gathered afterward in Schönbrunn, sharp-eyed Sophie noted that the bride was "white as linen," that she trembled perceptibly, her voice shook when she spoke, and whenever her eyes rested on the bridegroom they filled with tears. Even Emperor Franz was heard to murmur at the wedding, "May God have mercy."[8]

It was one of history's more tragic honeymoons. The bridal pair lived in a suite in the Hofburg like sick man and nurse. On Christmas night of that year, 1832, Ferdinand suffered twenty epileptic seizures of such violence his doctors abandoned all hope for him, and Marianna appeared in church next day "looking like a ghost."[9]

But Ferdinand miraculously recovered, held on to that stubborn strand of life, lived on year after year while his relatives died around him.

In the summer of 1832, while Sophie awaited the birth of her second child, young Reichstadt's precarious health took a turn for the worse. He was, in fact, dying of tuberculosis, while the blundering court physician, Dr. Malfatti, treated him for a liver ailment; toward the end he hastily applied leeches to the youth's throat and experimented with the most fashionable current cure, animal magnetism. Just after his twenty-first birthday Napoleon's only son died at Schönbrunn, in the same room where his father had slept after his victories at Austerlitz and Wagram.

Toward the end of the long severe winter of 1835, old Emperor Franz succumbed to pneumonia. When his testament was read, it was found he had named three men to act as Regents for Ferdinand: Prince Metternich, Count Kolowrat, and the youngest, most ineffectual of the Emperor's brothers, Ludwig. The Metternich system had another lease on life.

3. Revolution and Abdication

THE COURT of the Emperor Ferdinand—"the good-natured"—was certainly a strange one. Foreign ambassadors poked cruel fun at the unfortunate monarch. "What is the animal *implumis bipes* called Emperor?" Lord Palmerston demanded of his envoy in Vienna, and answered his own question: "A perfect nullity; next thing to an idiot."[1]

Ferdinand's public appearances had to be carefully stage-managed. Two or three servants pushed and pulled his shuffling, ungainly body down corridors and up stairs to a banquet hall. He could not appear at court balls, but his wife, Marianna, danced dutifully in his place. Sophie wrote to her mother that the Blessed Virgin dancing in her lifetime must have looked like Marianna, the same light, floating steps and lowered eyes, the grave humility and concern lest she might be giving herself too freely to worldly joys.[2] The comparison was apt in other ways as well.

In the Biedermeier world of the 1830s and 1840s Sophie's children —the eldest, Franzi (Franz Josef), next in line to the throne—grew up in an atmosphere of carefree happiness.

If the father, Franz Karl, had little to say about how things ran either at home or in the state, he accepted his role good-naturedly, enjoyed galloping about the nursery with little Franzi on his back, or taking him to the Prater to feed the deer, or helping him entice pigeons to the window sills of their apartment in the Hofburg. In the evenings Franzi and his brothers played "*Schnipp-Schnapp-Schnurr*" and "Black Peter" together, or they sat at their mother's feet while she read aloud from *Gulliver's Travels* and *Swiss Family Robinson*.

On birthdays and name days the whole Habsburg clan gathered in the Hofburg for family feasts and exchanging of gifts, and the younger members performed in carefully drilled ballets and playlets and recitations. Franz Josef's next-younger brother, Maxi, with his gift for mimicry, his fine singing voice and outgoing charm, was most often the star of these.

On Christmas Eve the whole family would gather outside the closed doors of the Emperor's apartments, the younger children trying to glimpse through the keyhole the Christ child leaving gifts. When the Christmas bells rang, the doors of the Red Salon were flung open. There stood the enormous lighted tree with truly imperial gifts: once a perfect child-size carriage, big enough to draw a pony, another time a palace guard in miniature, complete with sentry boxes, drums, and toy guns. All evening Franz Josef drilled his archduke uncles.

After Christmas, during carnival, there were the children's balls, tables laden with sweetmeats, and the gayest of waltzes and polkas. At the very end the grownups joined in the frolicking: even solemn, unbending old Uncle Ludwig would be dragged in to the dancing, though, as Archduchess Sophie observed, he must have planned to dance, for he had brought in his pocket a fresh pair of butter-yellow gloves.

After Easter, when fine weather came, there were long, sunny days for the children in the Schönbrunn gardens, riding about in a donkey cart, splashing in the *Schwimmbad,* playing in the Indian wigwam one of the gardeners had made for them, or visiting the whole array of strange animals their uncle, Emperor Ferdinand, had bought from a circus.

And there were such family jokes as that played by the children's father, Franz Karl, and pompous old Uncle Ludwig, when they came home very late one night to the Hofburg after an evening out and chanced upon the bell rope that dangled from the palace chapel belfry. They gave it a great yank and hurried off to their own rooms, while the chapel bell began to clang loudly. The whole palace awoke, the guards rushed to defend it against invaders, the servants to put out a fire, uncles and aunts, chamberlains and ladies in waiting in alarm and in night attire, wondering what in the world had happened. It was finally laid to the Hofburg ghost, the White Lady, who was known to make her appearance just before a member of the family died.

For Archduchess Sophie there was only one sorrow in those years. Her single little daughter, Anna, suffered from epilepsy, though the

DENKWÜRDIGE   ZUSAMMENKUNFT

Der Hohen Regierenden Monarchen und Deren Höchst bevollmächtigten hohen Amtsbeamten

[26] The monarchs and leading ministers at the Congress of Vienna, 1814. In the middle foreground clasping hands are Czar Nicholas II, Emperor Franz I of Austria, King Frederick William of Prussia. (*Bildarchiv des Österreichische Nationalbibliothek, Vienna*)

[27] Emperor Franz I of Austria driving near Schönbrunn Palace with his fourth wife, Empress Karoline Augusta, by J. B. Clarot. (*Kunsthistorisches Museum, Vienna*)

[28] Emperor Franz I of Austria in regalia, by Friedrich Amerling. The crown he wears is no longer the Holy Roman imperial crown, but the crown made in the Prague workshop of Rudolf II and used after 1806 as the Austrian house-crown. (*Kunsthistorisches Museum, Vienna*)

[29] Archduchess Sophie with her first-born, the future Emperor Franz Josef, painted in 1832 by Josef Stieler. (*Historisches Museum der Stadt Wien*)

older boys had apparently escaped. By the time little Anna was four her illness was so grave her hair had to be cut off and leeches applied to her forehead. She wept and wailed in terror; the treatment was to no avail; the child whom Sophie called her little mouse, her single treasure, the whole world's plaything, died before her fifth birthday.

Though always the firmest upholder of Habsburg custom and tradition, now Sophie adamantly refused the usual family death rite:

> We did not allow her body to be opened [she wrote to her
> mother] because I could not bear to have my child dismembered
> and parceled out in the city—her entrails in St. Stephen's, her
> heart with the Augustine monks.[3]

Archduchess Sophie was a strict and sensible mother, and for years she lavished her special attention and care on the education of her first-born, Franz Josef. As was usual with Habsburg sons, he was turned over to a governor and tutors at the age of six, to enter on an exhausting regimen of lessons. But Sophie continued to keep a close eye on her son, she sat in often on his lessons, supervised every detail of his life, went to watch him tilt lances at Turks' heads in the riding school, listened to him recite in French and Italian and Bohemian and Hungarian, often sat with him while he took lessons in the technique of governing from Prince Metternich.

It was his mother who took him by the hand on his thirteenth birthday and led him into the drawing room where he found, spread out among the heaped-up gifts, a shining new uniform of colonel and a patent appointing him to head a cavalry regiment. That night he could write earnestly in his diary that he had resolved never again to tell a lie or show any kind of fear.

To the end of his life Franz Josef showed the effects of his mother's careful training: the good boy, tidy, punctual, devout, and chivalrous.

Outside the schoolroom, events were something less than serene. The Viennese were genuinely fond of the gentle, kindly, less-than-bright emperor. But the Metternich government, with its rigid police rule, its iron corset of censorship and ubiquitous spying, had become intolerable.

When at last in March of 1848, fired by the Revolution in Paris, the long-suffering Viennese rose up against the Metternich government, it was at first a thoroughly middle-class revolution, led by university students who could shout the correct Latin subjunctive, "*Pereat* Metternich!" The Austrian revolution was not at that point anti-Habsburg, and the poster appearing on St. Stephen's proclaimed:

> Viennese! Liberate your good Emperor Ferdinand from the bonds of his enemies![4]

The Metternichs packed and fled hastily to England, where they bore with grim fortitude the miserable seaside weather at Brighton.

After their departure Ferdinand, Franz Karl, and his young son, Franz Josef, drove through wildly cheering throngs in the streets. Ferdinand, moved to tears by the demonstrators, promised them everything, even a constitution. The intoxicated mob detached the horses from the imperial carriage and pulled it back to the Hofburg singing Haydn's anthem "God Keep Our Emperor."

Things were by no means calm. In May, when demands were presented to the ministry for a constitutional assembly elected by universal suffrage, the imperial family took fright and fled to Innsbruck. The Viennese dispatched a petition signed by 80,000 citizens begging Ferdinand to return.[5]

Meantime the rising tide of nationalism brought revolts against Habsburg rule in the restless Italian provinces, in Hungary and in Bohemia. A triumvirate of generals crushed all three by force: Radetzky in Italy, Windischgraetz in Bohemia, the Croat leader Jellačić in Hungary.

The imperial family returned to Vienna, only to flee again in autumn when unrest flared again in the city, this time to the fortress of Olmütz in Moravia. When the hated Minister of War, Count Latour, dispatched a regiment of Austrian soldiers to help suppress the Hungarian revolt, a Viennese mob in fury lynched him, stripped his body, and hung it from a lamppost in the main square of Vienna.

The fate of the revolution was decided. Middle-of-the-road liberals were shocked out of their support. The army of Field Marshal Windischgraetz closed on Vienna and imposed an iron military grip.

Archduchess Sophie had watched the year's drama unfold, and had appraised the succession of events shrewdly. It was clear that gentle, feeble Ferdinand could not cope; he would have to go. It was equally plain to her, as it had been from the day of her marriage, that her husband was nearly as incapable of ruling as Ferdinand. But her son had just passed his eighteenth birthday; the day Sophie had been awaiting since the August morning in 1830 in the curtained bed in Schönbrunn had come at last.

To Ferdinand's apartment in the archbishop's palace in Olmütz all the Habsburg family, their court and servants were summoned for the early morning of December 2, 1848; all were told to appear in gala. Sophie's four boys dressed in their uniforms, she herself in a court gown of white moiré, in her hair a rose made of jewels, around her neck the necklace of turquoise and diamonds her husband had given her the day Franz Josef was born.

Ferdinand stood before the crowd in the deathly still room and in a faltering voice read the deed of abdication. Franz Josef knelt before his uncle and rose to become Emperor.

Ferdinand blessed the boy, murmuring, "Be good. God will protect you." Painfully Ferdinand scrawled his name to the deed of abdication; he had said once, "It is easy to govern, but what is difficult is to sign one's name."[6]

In his diary on the evening of his abdication day, Ferdinand wrote:

The affair ended with the new Emperor kneeling before his old Emperor and lord, that is to say me, and asking for a blessing, which I gave him, laying both hands on his head and making the sign of the Holy Cross. . . . Then I embraced him and he kissed my hand. Then my dear wife embraced and kissed our new master, and then we went to our room. Afterward I and my dear wife heard Holy Mass. . . . After that I and my dear wife packed our things.[7]

XIII

Franz Josef: A Long Reign Begins

1. Young Franz Josef

IMMEDIATELY AFTER the return of the imperial family to Vienna in 1849, Archduchess Sophie took things firmly in hand and soon had the Hofburg running again like clockwork.

Everything had got a little shabby and run-down during the non-reign of poor Ferdinand, and now the palace got a thorough refurbishing. The imperial apartments were repapered in silk, newly gilded and carpeted. The soldiers of the palace guard got new uniforms and silver helmets. When Sophie sallied out for her afternoon calls, it was in the smartest of carriages behind a young coachman in yellow spencer and black velvet cap, cracking a silver-mounted whip.

She saw to it too that her sons had plenty of fun and a chance to frolic, as was right for their age. Young Maxi built a snow slide in the Hofburg garden; all four brothers and their young adjutants had great sport sliding—even the Emperor, who went down holding his youngest brother, Bubi, in his lap.

Spiritualist séances were all the rage in Europe, and there were amusing sessions of table-tapping in the Hofburg. The banquet table where the older people sat did not budge an inch, but the long table about which the young people gathered with joined hands simply galloped through the banquet hall.

In the ballroom of the Hofburg and in the Great Gallery of Schönbrunn, Sophie arranged glittering court balls with Johann Strauss conducting and the prettiest of countesses for dancing partners. At the more intimate chamber balls and *thés dansants* Franz Josef and his brothers could have a fling without regard for ceremony; at one gay carnival ball tiny firecrackers were flung out on the dance floor to explode under the dancers' feet and make them skip about in wildest merriment.

Courtiers long remembered the magnificent ball given at the end of the *Fasching* season in 1851 in the Grand Gallery of Schönbrunn. For the opening cotillion hussar officers in scarlet uniforms formed a circle; girls in white ball gowns drew a larger circle about them. Uhlan officers formed a yet larger ring, around them circled girls in pink; and finally a great circle of *Kurassier* officers in white and gold uniforms closed the pattern—all dancing an intricately figured waltz. When midnight approached, the orchestra struck up a final polka, everyone in the palace from the oldest to the youngest joined in, the music grew softer and softer and faded away as the bells of midnight rang in the beginning of Lent. The dancers bade one another adieu; carnival was over.

Along with the general housecleaning of the palace, the remains of the Revolution of '48 were swept out.

The end had not, however, been quite painless. In Hungary the Habsburgs had been deposed and a republic set up, headed by the fiery rebel Kossuth. The Hungarians had, in fact, very nearly won the day; a decision had to be made, whether to withdraw troops from Italy and lose a portion, or to beg aid from the Czar of Russia, who was not ill-disposed toward suppressing revolutions. The latter course was chosen, Czarist troops helped restore the monarchy in Hungary, and the revolutionaries were punished with execution or banishment.

Archduchess Sophie had hand-picked her son's advisors and ministers, all from among the ultraconservative court set, with Prince Felix Schwarzenberg, a firm believer in absolutism, as prime minister.

In August, 1851, the young Emperor could write his mother in Bad Ischl, where she was holidaying:

We threw the constitution overboard and Austria has now only one sovereign! We have taken a great step forward!

In the margin of this letter in the State Archives, one may read in Sophie's excellent, strong hand: "God be praised!"[1]

By New Year's 1852 freedom of the press had again disappeared in Austria. The whole counterrevolution had been accomplished with a skill and speed that amazed even Metternich, who had returned from exile. The old prince had been received like a conqueror in Vienna. When he went to call on the imperial family in Schönbrunn, he found Franz Josef and his little brother Bubi at the window in gales of laughter. One of the storks in the Schönbrunn menagerie had got loose and wandered over to a dozing palace sentry, who had pulled himself together hastily, saluted and presented arms to the stork before he fully awakened and discovered his error.

To Archduchess Sophie and her son it seemed that an unreasonable and chaotic world had again been put to rights. With pardonable motherly pride Sophie watched the cool self-confidence and poise with which her son performed his duties. His manners were flawless, his bearing perfect; with consummate grace he managed his *entrées* at receptions and official gatherings, and the even more difficult *sorties de chambre*. He was tactful with everyone, and the soul of discretion; he went about the job of ruling as if at nineteen he knew all there was to know about governing an empire. It was not too much to believe that he would take on the image of his grandfather, old Emperor Franz, the kindly father-figure ministering to a nation of loyal subjects.

On February 13, 1853, Franz Josef left the Hofburg to stroll on the city walls with his friend and adjutant Max O'Donnell. As the Emperor leaned over the parapet near the Kärntner Gate to observe some troops drilling in the parade ground below, a man suddenly leapt up from a nearby bench, lunged at the Emperor with a long, sharp knife, wounding him twice in the neck.

The assailant, a little Hungarian tailor, was knocked down and disarmed by O'Donnell and a stout Viennese butcher who happened by. He had been waiting on that spot each day for nearly two weeks to kill the Emperor. The ubiquitous, ponderous, and gloriously inefficient secret police were, as usual, nowhere about when they were needed.

The Emperor's stiff uniform collar had impeded the blow, the wounds were not deep, and in a few days the young monarch was going about as usual.

His inner serenity, however, quite possibly never wholly recovered. In the whole long course of family history no Habsburg had ever been assaulted. With the exception of a possible poisoning now and then—and there was never any certain proof of these—the hand of violence had never fallen on a Habsburg son or daughter. The sole exception was Marie Antoinette, but this had happened at the hands of a French mob, of whom that sort of thing might be expected. Habsburg emperors and empresses had always gone about quite freely and without bodyguard in the streets of their capital, a thing that constantly astonished visitors from abroad. Archduchess Sophie had long harbored an anti-Hungarian bias; now she would certainly never forgive them.

Franz Josef gave his mother a diamond bracelet set with a large ruby, to allay a little bit the mental anguish she had suffered; under the ruby Sophie mounted a strand of her son's blood-soaked hair. The papal nuncio brought Franz Josef as a talisman from the Pope a tooth of St. Peter, which His Holiness had himself broken out of the skull of the apostle.

And Archduke Max, the Emperor's brother, took up a collection among citizens of the city to build a votive church near the spot where the attempt was made. There was to be a benefit performance of Wagner's new opera, *Tannhäuser*, to swell the building fund; the performance, however, was canceled at the last minute, when word came from the Hofburg that the work was deemed quite unsuitable, being both wicked and irreligious.

2. Empress Elizabeth

THE YEAR AFTER the attempted assassination, yet another event took place in her son's life over which Archduchess Sophie did not exercise the control she had wished: this was his marriage.

Sophie and one of her Bavarian sisters, Ludovica, had agreed that Ludovica's eldest daughter Hélène, a serious, docile girl, would make an excellent empress for Franz Josef. Accordingly, in the summer of 1853, the two ladies arranged to have the cousins meet at Bad Ischl. But events did not go quite as the mothers had planned, and Franz Josef proceeded to lose his heart to Hélène's prettier younger sister, Elizabeth, whom the family called Sisi.

Elizabeth was a charming fifteen-year-old, but she was far from grown up, completely unformed in Sophie's opinion, very shy, not even out in society. Franz Josef proved to be singularly stubborn, and his mother had to acquiesce. When Elizabeth was asked if she would have him, she answered, "Oh yes, I like him. If only he weren't Emperor!"[1]

In April of 1854 the pretty child sailed down the Danube from Linz in a flower-bedecked boat. Even before it was moored in a suburb of Vienna, the impatient bridegroom leapt aboard, to the delight of the onlookers, and kissed his bride. Elizabeth made the traditional entry of Habsburg brides into the capital, riding through the streets from the Theresianum Palace in the gilt-and-glass state coach, drawn by eight snow-white Lipizzaners, their manes and tails braided with silver, while young girls in white scattered roses in the street before the wheels. In rose-pink satin shot with silver, a diamond crown on her dark hair, the demure princess quite enchanted the susceptible Viennese with her astonishing beauty. But she was so shy that she could barely keep back tears at sight of the crowds pressing to see her.

Her husband's family showered her with gifts. Uncle Ferdinand and Aunt Marianna—the old ex-Emperor and Empress—had sent jewels. Franz Josef's stepgrandmother, Empress Karoline Augusta, gave her the Order of the Starry Cross in a garland of diamonds. From her mother-in-law Elizabeth got a tiara and necklace of opals and diamonds, and from her bridegroom, a new diamond crown to wear on her wedding day.

A little accident had befallen that crown. When the old Dowager Empress, Karoline Augusta, went to Schönbrunn to examine the displayed wedding gifts, a corner of her mantilla had caught the crown and pulled it off the table to the floor, breaking off two of the jewels and bending several points. A chamberlain rushed the crown to the court jeweler to be mended. Archduchess Sophie shook her head; was it, she wondered, an unlucky omen, that accident to the young Empress' crown?

On the evening of April 24, 1854, the pair stood in a forest of lighted tapers in the dusky Augustiner Church to make their vows—Franz Josef in a ringing voice, sixteen-year-old Elizabeth's assent barely whispered. The sermon was preached by Archduchess Sophie's close friend, Cardinal Rauscher; it dealt sternly with the duties of marriage and lasted so long that the Viennese promptly rechristened him Archbishop Plauscher (Gabbler).[2]

Afterward, on their thrones in the Ceremonial Room of the Hofburg, the bride and groom received the court and the diplomatic corps. Later on they drove with their families in an open carriage through the streets. The city was in gala; there was serenading everywhere; the palaces of the great families were decorated with lighted transparencies; in the Liechtenstein Gardens lighted balloons swayed like fruit in the branches of towering silver palm trees.

A quiet supper for the wedded pair followed in the Hofburg—not alone, of course, but en famille—after which Elizabeth's mother brought her to the imperial apartments to prepare for the night. When the bride was ensconced in the great bed, Archduchess Sophie led in her son, and the two mothers, beaming, bade the young pair good night.

Probably nobody enjoyed the wedding festivities more than the two mothers, Sophie and her sister, who had both endured miserably unhappy marriages themselves.

Archduchess Sophie had seen to everything. She had decorated the apartments the young couple would live in in the Hofburg. She had chosen suitable wedding gifts. She had also chosen Elizabeth's permanent attendants, elderly ladies of her own circle who could be counted on to keep a stern eye on the youthful bride.

Archduchess Sophie had made an emperor out of her son. She was determined now to make an empress out of her daughter-in-law. Even before the marriage she had begun to "form" Elizabeth—calling attention to her faults and her mistakes in etiquette.

There was, of course, no question about who ran the Hofburg. Attendance of the entire family at breakfast, tea, dinner, and Mass was punctually ordered; only when Archduchess Sophie was away did one dare appear late or not at all. Even on the morning after their wedding the newly wedded couple were expected to appear at the family breakfast table. Years later Elizabeth confided to a lady in waiting that she had fled from that table in tears, unable to endure her mother-in-law's scrutiny and pointed questions.[3]

Instead of honeymooning alone, Franz Josef and Elizabeth went on living among relatives, through exhausting days of public fetes, receptions, balls, parades, exhibitions. At the end of a wearying fortnight Franz Josef went off by himself to relax for a few days hunting the elusive *Auerhahn* (wood grouse) in the mountains.

Elizabeth found herself that summer in the common situation of royal brides—in a land of strangers, surrounded by people yet overwhelmingly lonely, without a single companion from her own country, from her own past, even her husband a virtual stranger. Now that she was Empress, she must appear flawlessly dressed at every hour of the day. Her life was no longer her own, her mother-in-law reminded her. When, eagerly awaiting her husband's return from the city, Elizabeth ran across the lawns of Laxenburg to throw herself into his arms, her mother-in-law reprimanded her sharply. An empress must always behave like one.

In the family castle in Bavaria, Elizabeth had grown up in exceptional freedom among a large family of brothers and sisters, a country princess devoted to the pleasures of the country. She loved to walk; she could walk for miles in every kind of weather, wearing out one lady in waiting after another. She rode beautifully and fearlessly, handling her horses with skill and understanding. She always had animals about her, birds and dogs—huge dogs, the bigger the better. ("She lives for her dogs," an elderly lady in waiting would complain, "always having some in her lap, at her side, or in her arms, and kills fleas at table and even on the plates!"[4])

Unlike Franz Josef, who seldom read any book except the *Army*

Register, Elizabeth read widely, in her room at night wrote poetry
—romantic verses about freedom and the sea. She was an incurable
romantic, natural, unaffected, and inclined to be dreamy. The spying,
the place-hunting, the hypocrisy of court life appalled her, as its
endless ceremony bored her unspeakably. Her shyness and fear of
crowds became so intense in the end as to make her physically ill.

The truth was that Elizabeth, for all her beauty and grace and
her bright, sensitive mind, was little suited either by temperament
or by training for the ruthlessly public job of Empress. While Franz
Josef had been reared from the cradle with the strictest sense of
imperial duty, Elizabeth had not the vaguest conception of her duty
either as wife or as Empress; all too often she behaved like a lovely,
willful, spoiled child.

The conflict with her mother-in-law was soon an open secret in the
Hofburg, the quarrel between the two women no less virulent for
being carried on in a palace and with the manners of royal ladies.
To her face Elizabeth called her mother-in-law *"Madame Mère";*
behind her back, *"die böse Frau"*—the wicked woman.[5]

When Elizabeth became pregnant, her mother-in-law's constant attention and advice became nearly unbearable. Archduchess Sophie
bustled into Elizabeth's apartment "to see what she was doing." Sophie
would write her son:

> I do not think Sisi should spend too much time with her parrots,
> for if a woman is always looking at animals, especially during the
> earlier months, the children are apt to resemble them.[6]

She urged Elizabeth to display her condition publicly to let people
see she had not failed in the first duty of an empress. Elizabeth, bred
in the nineteenth-century manner of young girls, shrank from those
public appearances.

When their first child was born, a daughter named for Franz Josef's
mother, the infant was installed in a nursery adjoining her grandmother's suite at some distance from the apartment of the young
parents. Archduchess Sophie chose the nurses, governesses, physician;
every day a procession of Sophie's friends passed through the nursery
to hover over the child, exactly as had happened with Sophie's own
first-born. It was, in fact, almost as if Elizabeth had not borne the
child at all, or so she thought. When a second little girl was born, she
too was whisked away to be brought up under her grandmother's
watchful eye.

In vain Elizabeth protested that she wanted to bring up her children herself. Franz Josef found himself in an awkward middle, when he longed only for domestic peace—torn between a young and beautiful wife, with whom he was deeply in love, and a capable, dominating mother who had always run his life—who had, in fact, put him on the throne.

Once Elizabeth got her way—with fatal consequences. Against her mother-in-law's advice she took her two little girls on an official journey to Hungary. In Budapest two-year-old Sophie sickened and died, probably of typhoid. To the young mother's terrible grief were added the unspoken reproaches of her mother-in-law. In vain for Elizabeth to remind herself that if the tragedy was anyone's fault, it was that of the bungling children's doctor, who had been chosen by Archduchess Sophie.

When at last a throne heir, Crown Prince Rudolf, was born to the imperial couple in 1858, and his father could proudly lay the chain of the Golden Fleece in his cradle, the boy too was soon established under his grandmother's surveillance.

By then it was whispered that things were not going well in the imperial menage. Soon after the child's birth, his parents moved into the apartments in the Hofburg that one sees today: Franz Josef's, plain, tidy, with their smack of Victorian *Gemütlichkeit*, the family pictures, the big comfortable desk, the iron bedstead and wooden washstand; Elizabeth's, cool and bright in white and gold, very bare now of her personality, paintings of her favorite horses on the walls of the small sitting room, the dressing room with gymnastic apparatus that kept her lovely figure in perfection, the bedchamber with its narrow bed, like a nun's, in the middle of a vast polished floor.

When Rudolf was two years old, in the autumn of 1860, Elizabeth developed the first of a long series of illnesses, half real, half imaginary, that would take her on journeys as far from Vienna as possible. Cynical Viennese called it "the Empress' ache"; after each journey Elizabeth would reappear, fresh and blooming and lovely.

Years later Elizabeth told her younger daughter, "Marriage is a nonsensical institution. One is sold as a child of fifteen and takes an oath which one does not understand but can never undo."[7]

3. Learning to Rule

THE YEAR 1859 was surely one of the loneliest and most bitter of Franz Josef's life. He faced, first of all, the loss of the Italian provinces.

That spring, in the early morning hours while the city still slept, he would ride out to talk to Metternich at his house in the Rennweg. The two would walk up and down in the gardens, the old prince at eighty-six a ghost of a world that was long since dead, stooped, wraithlike, skeletal. The hand he laid on his sovereign's arm was light as dust. "I am already counted among the dead," Metternich said, "but my nerves can still tremble. . . ."[1] And they must have trembled hearing in what straits the monarchy now found itself, after a decade of inept statesmanship and clumsy diplomacy. Austria, like the young Emperor, stood virtually alone; within and without the borders its prestige had fallen to a low ebb.

"God has willed that even now at the end of my days I bring order out of chaos. . . . I am a rock of order. *Je suis un rocher*," Metternich murmured once.[2] After Franz Josef had left, he would sit all day at his desk, trying to stir his old brain to compose on paper all the counsel needed to save the Empire.

In the Italian crisis he counseled patience, caution. "For God's sake, Majesty, no ultimatum! *Um Gottes Willen kein Ultimatum . . .*"

"It was sent yesterday evening," Franz Josef replied.[3]

War had broken out by then, Lombardy was in flames; Franz Josef left to join his army fighting the French under Napoleon III. When he returned to Vienna in August, after the defeats at Magenta and Solferino and the loss of Lombardy, Metternich lay in his grave.

The defeat in Italy had been a personal as well as a national one, for Franz Josef himself had taken part in the battle of Solferino. The Austrian army had been sadly managed, badly led. Prussian army headquarters, watching the movements of the Austrian forces in Italy, had commented tersely, "Lions led by asses."[4]

A still more humiliating blow was in store for Austria, aspiring to regain leadership in the German-speaking lands, lost with the lost crown of the Holy Roman Empire. No match for the resolute, hard-headed Prussian statesman Bismarck, Franz Josef allowed himself to be maneuvered into war with Prussia in 1866 and was swiftly, stingingly defeated at Königgrätz. The newfangled Prussian gun, the needle-loader, made short work of the clumsy, old-fashioned Austrian muzzle-loader.

In the fearful days that followed Königgrätz, the Prussians approached Vienna, as the Turks had two centuries before. There was panic in the city; the imperial library and the treasure were hastily packed and carried out; the Empress and the children took refuge in Budapest. In the streets of Vienna, Franz Josef heard people shout, "Long live Emperor Maximilian!"—a cry for him to abdicate in favor of his younger brother.

The Prussians were careful not to carry the humiliation of Austria too far. Their army withdrew, a peace was signed. Austria lost her last foothold in Italy—the province of Venetia. Even more bitter was the loss of the leadership of Germany. The ineffectual *Bund* designed years earlier by Metternich was dissolved; Prussia had a free hand to unify and to dominate Germany.

Franz Josef had come to the throne singularly ill-prepared for a revolutionary world. Slowly he began to learn. Slowly he began to revise the organization of the Empire.

The question he had never faced, and with which he would now grapple for a half century, was whether the accidental roof the monarchy provided for the dozen or so peoples of central Europe could survive the centrifugal forces of nationalism. In homogeneous lands that nationalism was a source of strength; in the heterogeneous complex that was the Habsburg monarchy it could lead straight to dismemberment.

The most complicated nation in Europe, the monarchy was in itself a little Europe, a microcosm of a continent, with a mélange of peoples and tongues and traditions, whose problems foreshadowed the problems of all Europe. Of its fifty million subjects, about one fifth were Germans, another fifth Magyar. Czechs and Slovaks comprised another large minority; the remainder were Poles, Serbs, Croats, Ruthenians (i.e., Ukrainians), Rumanians, Slovenes, and Italians.[5]

None of them could be sorted out with any precision into a single geographical area; all clung fiercely to national language, national heritage.

On the side of survival, however, was the powerful fact that the Danubian area constituted a viable economic entity, and a prosperous one. The Habsburg monarchy with its network of roads and railroads converging on the capital remained the largest free-trade area in Europe outside of Czarist Russia. What cement would hold it together, now that absolutism was out of date: this was the problem confronting the Emperor and his ministers.

Already after the loss of the Italian provinces, Franz Josef's government had taken the first faltering and unenthusiastic steps toward constitutional government. He wrote to his mother in 1860: "We are going to have a little parliamentary life, it is true, but the power remains in my hands."[6]

In the gloomy days after Königgrätz Franz Josef called to his side as Foreign Minister and chief advisor one of the smoother diplomatic hands in Europe, Count Ferdinand von Beust. An astonishing choice in many ways—Beust was not even a citizen of the Habsburg Empire, but in fact former prime minister of Saxony—it was an appropriate choice for cosmopolitan Austria. Beust himself explained with charming irony that he was "a sort of State washerwoman called in to scrub the dirty linen of the Austrian state."[7]

It was Beust who helped engineer the first step toward reorganization of the Empire: the Hungarian Compromise.

Hungarian liberal leaders had found the months after Königgrätz the psychological moment to press hard for Hungarian autonomy. The young and beautiful Empress Elizabeth had firmly supported their demands. She had felt herself increasingly attracted to Hungary, had learned to speak fluent Magyar, had chosen Hungarian ladies to replace the Austrian attendants the Archduchess Sophie had first placed around her, and had spent an increasingly large share of her time in Hungary.

The Compromise plan that was drawn up gave Hungary her own parliament and virtual autonomy; she would be joined to Austria only by a common army, a joint foreign office, and by loyalty to one emperor.

In June of 1867 the Compromise was officially consummated. Franz Josef and Elizabeth knelt to be crowned King and Queen of Hungary in the cathedral in Budapest.

The Compromise seemed to be one step toward the solution of the nationalities problem in the Empire. In fact it created nearly as many problems as it solved. The dominant Magyar aristocracy fought as bitterly against any further federalization of the Empire—which would give other national groups such as the Czechs a larger share in the government—as they did against granting their own minorities a share in the governing of Hungary. The Dual Monarchy that existed after 1867 resembled in many ways the situation in the United States after the Civil War: a large area, semi-feudal in character, had attempted to secede and had failed. Now a ruling oligarchy within that area consistently disenfranchised their own minorities, and successfully blocked all liberal moves within the Empire as a whole.

As the years passed Franz Josef came to possess a knowledge of the Empire that gave him an almost intuitive response to the pressures and problems of its various parts. Remote, stoical, chivalrous, with that incredible sense of duty, he may have possessed the only set of traits that could possibly hold it together: another Joseph II would have broken heart and brain in the trying.

4. Kaiserstadt

As FOR THE CITY of Vienna, the *Kaiserstadt,* it bloomed in the last half of the nineteenth century, a city of beauty and magic, where everything was now *Kaiserlich-und-Königlich*—imperial and royal, instead of merely imperial. The younger Johann Strauss ruled the ballrooms; it was in the days just after Königgrätz that "The Beautiful Blue Danube" was first sung at a concert in the Riding Hall for the benefit of families of the war dead.

The Vienna of Franz Joseph's boyhood insisted on changing; quite literally it had burst its seams. In 1857 the Emperor permitted the demolition of the walls (young Strauss forthwith dashed off a "Demolition Waltz")—those walls that had withstood the Turkish Siege of 1529 in the time of the first Ferdinand, the cannonade of Bohemians and Swedes in the Thirty Years' War, the great Turkish Siege of 1683, and the bombardment of Napoleon.

So steeply had land values risen that the strip of land outside the walls, the glacis, was sold for fifty million dollars, and the money used to build that most magnificent of boulevards, the Ringstrasse.

Inside the Ring the Inner City still hugged its baroque palaces and churches, its ancient houses and narrow cobbled lanes. Even though the population soared and the city spread far out beyond the old suburbs, it never quite lost the flavor of the country, and the horizon and the wooded hills of the Wiener Wald might still be glimpsed now and again from the city's center.

Behind spacious expanses of green lawn and borders of lime trees the Ring Boulevard was studded with opulent public buildings: the velvet-lined jewel box of the Opera, the Burg Theater, the twin Museums, Parliament, the Rathaus. The Hofburg, which had jutted on the old city walls and looked more citadel than palace, now had a final refurbishing. A new wing was added, and a new avenue led from the palace across a fine park to the Ring.

Along the Ring pranced the smartest carriages and the finest horses. The little Freuds out walking with their papa along the Ring of a Sunday could say instantly when a carriage emerged from the Hofburg whether it was the Emperor and Empress—who had fully gilded carriage wheels—or the Crown Prince, who got half gilding—or a mere archduke or archduchess, who had only quarter-gilded wheels. These latter the Viennese impudently nicknamed "shabbies."

Along the Ring one might see the handsomest uniforms in Europe: the brilliant red of the *Husaren,* the dark blue coats and sky-blue trousers of the Imperial Palace Guards; the Hungarian Life Guards in scarlet frogged with silver, lemon-yellow boots, the skins of leopard cubs flung picturesquely about their shoulders.

The imperial army was, in fact, one of the two great unifying forces in the Empire. The soldiers spoke Magyar, Czech, Bohemian, Croat, Serb, Polish, Ruthenian, but orders were given in German, and they swore a common oath of loyalty to the sword and person of the Emperor.

Most dashing and most arrogant were the cavalry; the cavalry officers rode the fastest horses, laid the wildest bets, fought the most daring duels, captured the prettiest girls. In barracks and drawing room, horses and horsemanship were the common topic of conversation. There were the exploits of the daredevil Count Zderko Kinsky, who had broken every bone in his body except his neck and his spine. And his even more audacious uncle, who had once driven a four-in-hand up the grand staircase into the banquet hall of one of the palaces.

And there was the famous wager of Major General Adam von Berzeviczy, who bet his fellow officers he could take his half-trained charger over all eight obstacles in the army riding school with his back to the horse's head. He was to be allowed one fall; even this proved to be unnecessary.

His feat won him the instant admiration of Empress Elizabeth, herself a fearless horsewoman. She appointed him Controller of her Household; he remained in her service until the end of her life.

5. Maximilian in Mexico

A FEW DAYS after the coronation in Hungary came news of the first of those tragedies of violence that very nearly put an end to the Habsburg family, lending to the last act of the dynasty's reign the air of an unfolding Greek tragedy. On a sunny hillside near Querétaro, Mexico, on June 19, 1867, Franz Josef's brother, the charming, lovable, impractical Maximilian, was shot as a traitor. He had reigned just three years as Emperor of Mexico.

The two brothers, Franz Josef and Maxi, only two years separated in age, had certainly been cradle rivals for their mother's affection. While the elder had all his mother's sober virtues—self-discipline, diligence, an acute sense of duty—Maxi was the born charmer, very gay, very poetic, easily led by the inclination of his heart. He sang a pleasant baritone, had the Habsburg fondness for music—of which Franz Josef had almost none—adored play-acting, was capable of such gestures as sending his mother on Christmas a bouquet of flowers seven feet in circumference.

He had married the attractive and ambitious Princess Charlotte of Belgium, a thoroughly happy match except for two circumstances: the pair had no children and no vocation.

Like many a younger brother or sister of a monarch, Maxi found little to do except to act as stand-in for the Emperor on official occasions. He had been sent down to Milan as governor-general, when the Italians were agitating for their freedom, but he was given little authority and it was far too late in the day to appease nationalist sentiment with the mere presence of an emperor's brother. He was fond of ships and sailing, had been made commander of Austria's modest fleet, but he alienated the military brass in the Ministry of War by proposing a larger navy and a separate Ministry of Marine.

Hints were dropped in Franz Josef's ear that it would be unwise to enlarge a service that acknowledged so deep a loyalty to his popular brother. Maximilian and Charlotte built themselves the delightful palace of Miramar overlooking the harbor at Trieste and waited for something worthwhile to fall into their laps.

In the early 1860s a group of wealthy Mexicans, émigrés of the recent Juarez revolution, Catholic and conservative in their political views, arrived in Europe looking for help in establishing a Mexican monarchy. They wanted money, troops, an authentic European prince. They got troops and a willing ear from Napoleon III of France, and encouragement from French financial interests.

As for the prince, they succeeded beyond their dreams in enticing an authentic Habsburg. Maximilian agreed to accept the crown they dangled in front of him.

The role of Franz Josef in the Maximilian affair remains somewhat equivocal. The brothers had often quarreled, rarely saw eye to eye in matters involving the monarchy. The Austrian foreign minister, Count Rechberg, opposed the Mexican adventure; so did Archduchess Sophie and numerous others at court. Franz Josef apparently let matters take their course. He promised no Austrian military support, and he insisted firmly that before Maximilian accepted the Mexican crown he must renounce all his succession rights to the Austrian. The brothers wrangled bitterly over that matter of renunciation; in the end Franz Josef himself had to go down to Trieste and secure his brother's signature on the document.

A few days later Maximilian and Charlotte set sail on the frigate *Novara;* they spent a sunny voyage writing up a protocol of courtly etiquette.

It was a preposterous affair from start to finish. The plebiscite that had been shown Maximilian as proof of "the yearning of the people . . . for a high-minded and noble prince to rule over them" had been a farce. In the primitive, semitropical country they found only a handful of supporters, besides the French army corps sent by Napoleon III, and a nearly bankrupt, debt-ridden government.

Maximilian tried desperately to win over the Mexican people, traveled about speaking bad Spanish, wearing a sombrero. He and Charlotte gave dazzling state dinners in their palace of Chapultepec, pinned dashing orders on the breasts of their followers, adopted a small Mexican boy as their "son"—he was later reclaimed by his real mother.

The affair moved swiftly to its somber denouement. Political pressures at home—especially the mounting fear of Prussia—forced Napoleon III to withdraw his troops from Mexico. Without money or a way of raising it, Maximilian appealed to the French emperor for a loan, was curtly refused. In the north, Juarez gathered his revolutionary forces, bided his time. Meanwhile Maximilian's letters home to the Hofburg were as rosy and cheerful as a boy's on holiday.

In the summer of 1866, in desperation Charlotte sailed back to Europe to seek help for her husband. Turned down brusquely by Napoleon III in Paris, she went on to Rome to plead the imperial cause with the Pope. In the Vatican, Charlotte collapsed, drifted away into a nightmare world of schizophrenia. Back in Mexico City, watching the French troops take their departure, Maximilian got the sorrowful news of his wife's insanity. Now at last he cabled his family in Vienna that he would doubtless return home before Christmas.

In Austria, meantime, the defeat at Königgrätz had enveloped the country and the Hofburg in the deepest gloom. Franz Josef's popularity was at the lowest point of his nearly seventy-year reign. There were rumors abroad that certain groups within the Empire would force Franz Josef to abdicate and bring Maximilian back from Mexico to rule as Regent during the minority of little Crown Prince Rudolf. Franz Josef could hardly have looked with joy on the prospect of his brother's return. Nobody in Vienna, however, dreamed at this point that delightful, easygoing Maxi was in any real danger. Archduchess Sophie wrote firmly that, much as she longed for his return, "I must still wish that you hold out in Mexico as long as you can with honor do so."[1]

Maximilian had already begun his journey home when, on the way to the port of Vera Cruz, he was dissuaded from giving up his throne by his Belgian and Austrian aides, including the sinister priest, Father Fischer, who had recently joined his entourage. He turned back, fatally. With only a small army of supporters he met Juarez in battle, was quickly defeated, captured, court-martialed, and sentenced to death.

A thrill of shocked horror sped from one capital to another. No one had dreamed that the romantic adventure could end in tragedy. Hastily wheels turned, pleas were sent, ministers made calls. Franz Josef appealed to American Secretary of State Seward to intervene, promised to restore Maximilian's succession rights.

Everything was just too late. On the sunny morning of June 19, 1867, Maximilian and his two Mexican generals were led out on the hill near Querétaro to be shot. "I could not have chosen a better day on which to die," he remarked. He presented each man on the firing squad with a gold piece, asking them to aim carefully at his heart. His last words were: "May my blood that is about to flow be for the good of this land."[2]

Not quite his last. The first volley did not kill him, and one of the bullets after all pierced his face. His last word—in Spanish—was a cry of pain and surprise. *"Hombre!"* The second volley finished him where he lay writhing on the ground.[3]

On June 30, just after Franz Josef and Elizabeth were crowned in Hungary, the terrible news of the execution reached Maximilian's family.

For days Archduchess Sophie could be heard walking back and forth in her room, in the Hofburg, crying over and over, "My dear, good son! Shot like a criminal!"[4]

Maximilian's last letters arrived in the Hofburg weeks later, as if they had been dispatched from the grave. To Franz Josef Max had written:

Dear brother,

Forced by fate to suffer a blameless and undeserved death, I send you these lines to thank you out of a full heart for your brotherly love and friendship.

May God reward you with fortune, joy, and blessings for you, the Empress and the dear children. For my mistakes, for any distress and pain I caused you in life, I ask your pardon with my whole heart.

One single request I make: that you will remember kindly the faithful Belgian and Austrian soldiers who served with devotion and sacrifice to the end of my course.

Maximilian
Querétaro   June, 1867[5]

Eyewitnesses to the last act of the Mexican tragedy drifted in to the Hofburg one by one—the Austrian consul from Tavera, with Max's last will; his old Hungarian cook, with Max's hat and blood-soaked handkerchief; and, one after another, his aides and soldiers, looking for imperial handouts.

Finally, in September of that year, three curious individuals appeared in the Hofburg who identified themselves as followers of Maximilian and gave their names as Archpriest Roccatani, Antonio de la Rosa, and Don José Maroto. They demanded an audience with

Franz Josef, declaring that they had a secret without price that could be confided only to him. This was their incredible offer: to Franz Josef, and the house of Habsburg, "as the last stronghold of legitimacy and the true religion," the three would demonstrate a secret formula for transmuting silver into gold; they would need five million gulden in pure silver from the mint to carry out their experiment. Franz Josef called in a professor of chemistry from the Polytechnic Institute to observe their experiments; the trio managed to milk 90,000 gulden from the imperial treasury before their swindle was unmasked.[6]

6. Family Life in the Seventies

THE PERIOD that followed their coronation in Hungary was perhaps the most serene in the lives of Franz Josef and Elizabeth. The year afterward, in 1868, their last child, a little girl named Marie Valerie, was born. Freed at last from the interference and domination of her mother-in-law, Elizabeth kept this child passionately for her own, lavished on her all the frustrated devotion she had been unable to give the older children. She took care that the little girl should be born in Hungary, in the palace of Gödöllö, where the imperial family now spent a portion of every year.

In the Hofburg too something like a normal family life existed for a time. Elizabeth strayed less often from home; she accompanied her husband to inspect garrisons, visit provincial capitals, open exhibitions —all those public duties that were so disagreeable to her. She even knelt in a long black gown on Maundy Thursday to wash the feet of paupers, and bore a taper in the Corpus Christi procession.

Of Christmastime in 1866 the Archduchess Sophie had written to Maximilian in Mexico:

> On December 26 Papa and I had our four grandchildren and their parents over to see the Christmas tree. Gisela and Rudolf adore spending Christmas with their small cousins [the children of Franz Josef's younger brother, Karl Ludwig] of whom they are both enormously fond; they were all very sweet and showed one another the toys they had brought along from their own trees.

> The Emperor, who can be so charming with small children, stuffed fat Otto into a Dutch sled and pulled him all over the place, after which Rudolf got a chance to give the others a ride. But Franzi [the three-year-old Archduke Franz Ferdinand]

picked himself the better part: he climbed up on the sofa and settled down by your sister-in-law Sisi, with whom he babbled at great length.[1]

Strikingly beautiful, Elizabeth could always, when she wished, captivate and charm, never lost her power over people as long as she lived.

The American ambassador John Lothrop Motley, presented to the Empress in 1863, wrote:

> She is a magnificent creature, moves with grace and dignity. . . . She is far handsomer than her photographs, which, of course, cannot convey the impression of youth and bloom, which is one of the effects she produces. Her figure is beautiful, her complexion that sort of mat white which is so brilliant in the evening. Her eyes are dark and her whole expression singularly gentle with even a shade of timidity. She spoke English to us, which she knows very well, in a very low voice.[2]

When the Shah of Persia came to visit the World Exhibition of 1873 in Vienna, he was far more eager to see the Empress Elizabeth, of whose great beauty he had heard. When he was presented to her in the Hofburg before dinner, he walked all around with his eyeglasses on, viewing her from all sides, muttering over and over—to the Empress' great amusement, *"Mon Dieu! qu'elle est belle!"*[3]

Even the Archduchess Sophie could be enchanted with her loveliness. On a Christmas Eve, when Elizabeth appeared in a gown of antique moiré the color of ripe strawberries, the Archduchess declared she looked like a piece of sugar candy; and when the Empress dressed for a *Fasching* ball in a white dress "like a cloud" with camellias in her hair, and diamonds and sapphires at her neck, she was, wrote Sophie, *"Zauberhaft* . . . enchanting, superb!"[4]

Though now she gave at least lip service to court formalities, Elizabeth continued to live much as she pleased. The older ladies of the court gossiped about the Empress' eccentricities, how she dieted carefully on beef juices and ices, exercised strenuously to keep her slender, erect figure, how one room of her apartment in the Hofburg was made into a little gymnasium where she exercised with apparatus, and took fencing lessons in a short coat of mail.

She rode constantly. At Gödöllö in Hungary she and the Emperor hunted. On yearly journeys to England and Ireland the Empress rode to the hounds, always appearing in graceful habits with flowing skirts and dainty hats—which, however, did not keep her from the hardest cross-country riding. In Vienna in the Riding Hall she took lessons from a circus rider—even, it was whispered about court, jumped through hoops!

She kept animals about her, as always, her enormous dogs; once, at Meran, a trained bear. At Gödöllö she allowed a pack of gypsies to camp on the palace doorstep. She brought a small Negro boy to the Hofburg to play with Valerie—to the horror of the ladies of the court.

She remained an incurable romantic.

One evening during the carnival season of 1874, when Franz Josef was away on a visit to Russia, Elizabeth put on a great auburn wig and mask and a long embroidered yellow domino. In the company of her friend and reader, Ida Ferenczy, she slipped into the great masked ball given by the Musical Society of Vienna.[5]

For some time the two ladies were content to sit quietly in the gallery, watching the dancers below. Presently, however, to add piquancy to their adventure, Ida Ferenczy, masked like the Empress and in a red domino, mingled with the crowds in the ballroom, and returned presently with a handsome young stranger on her arm.

The Empress, whom Ida addressed as her friend "Gabriele," chatted with the young man for a few minutes, then asked him, "You know I am a stranger here. . . . What are people saying about the Emperor? Are they content with his government? Are the results of the war quite healed?"

The stranger, who happened to be a young government official named Fritz Pacher, was struck by the bearing and the voice of the lady in the yellow domino, and puzzled his head to think who she might be. His replies were courteous and cautious.

"And do you know the Empress too?" she asked. "How do you like her and what do people say about her?"

He replied after a moment's hesitation, "Of course I only know the Empress by sight, from seeing her riding in the Prater. I can only say that she is a wonderful, gloriously beautiful woman. . . ." He added that some people criticized her for appearing so seldom in public and for spending too much of her time with her horses and dogs. "This is certainly an injustice," he added, "for I know that a passion for dogs and horses is a family trait. There is a story that her father, Duke Max, once said, 'If we had not been princes, we should have been trick riders!'"

The Empress laughed at this comment, and then she asked him, "Tell me, how old do you think I am?"

"You?" asked Fritz Pacher, using the familiar *du*. "You are thirty-six years old."

The lady in the yellow domino gave a start; it was in truth her exact age.

At first she had an impulse to dismiss the young man. Then she reconsidered and allowed him to escort her down to the main hall, where they wandered about, discussing religion and the world and Austria and poetry, until long after midnight. Fritz Pacher noticed how unaccustomed the masked lady was at being pushed about in a crowd; when people jostled her she began to tremble visibly. Sometimes people turned to stare after her; only once did someone seem to suspect her identity—Count Nicholas Esterhazy, Master of the Fox Hounds at Gödöllö.

As the evening drew to a close, Elizabeth asked the stranger to escort her to her carriage, but made him promise not to return to the ballroom afterward. "Your hand upon it!"

At the last moment he suddenly bent toward her and tried to lift the mask from her face. Her companion, in the red domino, screamed and threw herself between them. An instant later the ladies were in the carriage and driving off in the darkness.

The young hero of the Empress' *Fasching* adventure could not forget that evening. For days he wandered about the environs of the Hofburg and in the Prater, hoping to catch a glimpse of the Empress out riding. Once he stood close by when her carriage emerged from the Hofburg; for a moment her glance fell on him and her face changed. Moments later, when the carriage had passed, he saw the little flap at the back window raised and then fall back in place again.

A few days later he got a letter, postmarked Munich, and signed "Gabriele," directing him to write to her in care of the Poste Restante. A series of letters passed between them, but the assignation promised by the masked lady never took place. The following year he searched in vain at the Shrove Tuesday ball for the yellow brocade domino.

Franz Josef adored his lovely wife; his letters to her when she was away on journeys always began, "My dear heavenly Sisi," or, "My dearest angel," and ended, "Your lonely little husband," or, "Your faithful little husband."

Punctilious as ever in the performance of his duties, the Emperor was at his desk by five each morning, received public audiences twice a week, appeared in all the ceremonies and rituals of court life.

His tastes were simple, and he spent little on himself. A new valet taking over the imperial wardrobe was astonished to discover that the Emperor had, besides his uniforms, "hardly two usable lounge suits, a hunting outfit, and a single old-fashioned dress suit," and that His Imperial and Kingly Majesty's undergarments were in a shocking state, of cotton rather than linen, and not nearly so fine as the valet himself wore.[6]

Franz Josef was certainly a lonely man. In his whole life he seems to have had only one male friend—his cousin Albert of Saxony. Whenever the Emperor found he had a bit of time for a breather, he would dash off a note to Albert, begging him to meet him somewhere in the mountains for a round of hunting. "I have a longing," he would write, "for some good mountain air." Or: "I have hunger and thirst after the mountains." He kept careful track of his shooting prowess, recorded that between December 2, 1848—when he ascended the throne—and July of 1861, he brought down 28,876 pieces of game.

The Habsburg clan still gathered for the great family dinner parties in the Hofburg. But the older generation was vanishing one by one, the ancient archduke uncles who remembered the days of Napoleon; old Uncle Ludwig, last of Maria Theresia's grandchildren, died in 1865. The Dowager Empress Karoline Augusta, the last wife of Franz I, died in 1873, and in Prague the abdicated majesties, Ferdinand and Marianna, died a little later.

Franz Josef's father, old Archduke Franz Karl, still went out each day for a ride in his carriage-and-six, with footman and foreriders, and the Viennese, who were always attached to anything that had been around long enough, gathered along the curb to cheer and wave, so that, he would remark afterward to his wife, he could hardly put on his tall, old-fashioned top hat for the whole of the excursion.

As for Archduchess Sophie, she never really recovered from the sorrow of Maximilian's death in Mexico. One night in 1873 she returned to the palace from the opera, went out to sit on her balcony for a bit of fresh air, fell asleep, and was not found till morning, half frozen. Pneumonia set in, and she grew rapidly worse. She accomplished her death with all the dignity and decorum she could have wished, relatives and court officials gathered in her suite, and herself, breathing her last, the ancient Habsburg crucifix clasped to her breast.

XIV

The Tragedy at Mayerling

1. A New Throne Heir: Rudolf

> The government has changed and is a step
> nearer to the republic. Monarchy has lost its
> old power and clings to the trust and love of
> the people. . . . Monarchy is now a mighty ruin
> which may remain from today till tomorrow but
> which will ultimately tumble. . . .
>
> *Notebook of Crown Prince Rudolf,*
> *aged fourteen*[1]

MEANTIME, in the palace schoolroom, the Habsburg heir, bright, precociously gifted Rudolf, was learning a number of astonishing things.
During the years of his schooling some fifty tutors came and went in
the Hofburg, cramming his head with history and languages and a
dozen other subjects. Besides a study of Latin and Greek, he learned
to speak fluently French, Hungarian, Czech, Serbian. His education
was a matter of state; at intervals he was examined by a committee
of experts with his father and officials of the court attending. Rudolf,
who possessed a better intellect than perhaps any Habsburg since
Joseph II, could run to his grandmother after one of the ordeals, crying,
"*Der Papa* was terribly pleased with me!"[2] And indeed his father
would remark with pardonable pride that his son was learning "really
well, not just crown-princely well."[3]

A delicate, sensitive child, with a quick nervous temperament and
a look of high breeding, Rudolf resembled his mother far more than
his father.

The first few years of his life had not been happy; the early photo-
graphs as a small boy show a somber little face, a pair of dark worried

eyes, fixed at times in a positive scowl. The far from happy domestic scene, the conflict between his mother and grandmother, his mother's long absences from home, and his father's total immersion in affairs of state, together with his own frail health, no doubt contributed to the child's nervous instability and inner anxiety.

At the age of six he had been passed, as was the custom with Habsburg sons, into the hands of his first tutor, a peculiarly unhappy choice. General Gondrecourt, an old military hand, had been selected by Archduchess Sophie for his exemplary piety; he had little aptitude for child-rearing and small patience with a nervous little boy who cried easily and was afraid of the dark. Gondrecourt's first instructions were to do what he could to "harden" the boy.

One wintry morning Emperor Franz Josef heard the sound of army drill signals in the courtyard under his window; looking out he saw his little son undergoing the drill of an army private in the deep snow. Gondrecourt's other methods were even more drastic. Years later Empress Elizabeth remarked of Rudolf's first tutor to her lady in waiting: "It is madness to frighten a child of six with water cures and try to turn him into a hero."[4]

The following summer Gondrecourt locked Rudolf inside the enclosure of the big zoo at Lainz, ostensibly to teach him courage. He himself stood outside and shouted to the child that a wild boar was loose inside with him. Rudolf began to scream with fright, his tutor shouted all the louder, until the boy was beside himself with hysterical terror.

His mother had just returned from one of her long journeys. In that curious husband-wife relationship, where their two lives moved in formal, parallel paths in their separate palace suites, Elizabeth sat down and wrote a precise ultimatum to her husband: either Gondrecourt would go or she would. Gondrecourt was dismissed. In his place Count Latour von Thurnburg, a capable man of wide learning and decided liberal leanings, was engaged; he remained Rudolf's head tutor throughout his boyhood, as well as his closest friend.

Quite the opposite in mentality and temperament from the heir of the newly formed German Empire, Prince Wilhelm of Prussia, who was almost exactly Rudolf's age, Rudolf grew to maturity, thoughtful, curious, alert, and broad-minded, where Prince Wilhelm was a swashbuckling, narrow, and frivolous youth. The Seventies were liberal times in Vienna, and the liberal ideas that were debated in cafés, in the press, in parliament, found their way into Rudolf's schoolroom, to the dismay of such arch-conservatives as his father's old cousin, Archduke Albrecht.

At nineteen Rudolf was declared of age and given his own staff and the very same apartments in the Hofburg that had been presented to his great-grandfather, Emperor Franz, nearly a hundred years before by *his* uncle, Joseph II. Rudolf would have chosen to continue his studies at the University had this been possible, but tradition laid down the next steps for a Habsburg heir: training in the imperial army, marriage to a suitable Catholic princess.

Rudolf had grown up in the special isolation his rank and private education bestowed. He had no close friends his own age, nor even a confidant within his own family. His relationship with his father was a formal one; while he resembled his mother in temperament and taste, in his flair for writing, his fondness for travel and for animals, they had been separated too long in his early years ever to be companions. His tutor, Count Latour, had stood in the place of a father to him; now tutor and pupil parted. A few days later Rudolf's new court marshal, Count Bombelles, wrote Latour:

> I saw how he struggled with his tears and I said to him, 'Go on, weep, you need not be ashamed of those tears.' He wept and we talked of you, and his heart opened to me and it has remained. . . . He feels a great longing for you.[5]

Sons of the aristocracy traditionally served in the cavalry; probably by choice Rudolf joined the infantry, whose officers were nearly all from middle-class families. Rudolf did not bother to hide his contempt for the frivolous lives of most of the young Austrian nobility, including his own relatives. In 1879 he collaborated with one of his teachers, the economist Karl Menger, on an anonymously published pamphlet calling on the Austrian aristocracy to assume a responsible position in public life or lose their privileged status.

His family, in the meantime, pressed him to choose a wife. Of the few available Catholic princesses, the most practical match seemed to be with the Belgian Princess Stephanie, a pale, colorless child of fifteen, who had not yet reached puberty.

The wedding, postponed at Empress Elizabeth's insistence, took place in May of 1881. Stephanie's memoirs, written when she was an old and bitter woman, have nothing kind to say either of Rudolf or of her marriage, but they also reveal inadvertently a good deal of her own character; she was insufferably snobbish, self-centered, without an iota of warmth or humor. It was not a happy match. "My illusions were shattered by the dreadful experience of the wedding night," wrote Stephanie flatly.[6] They had even less in common than most royal couples. When Rudolf invited his wife to go with him to a *Heurige*, one of the little wine taverns on the outskirts of Vienna where he liked to go to listen to Viennese folk music, Stephanie did not enjoy herself:

> I dressed as a smart middle-class girl. . . . The air everywhere was stifling. There was a stench of garlic, burned fat, wine and tobacco. People danced, girls jumped upon tables and benches, singing again and again the same commonplace sentimental ditties.[7]

After the birth of a daughter, who was named Elizabeth, doctors expressed doubts that Stephanie could bear any more children.

Meantime Rudolf suffered from the fatal joblessness of emperors' sons. "I am condemned to be an idler," he wrote.[8] He was not invited to take any part in affairs of state, as he longed to do. After a brief flirtation with liberalism in the 1870s Franz Josef's government had moved steadily right under the leadership of shrewd, conservative Count Eduard von Taaffe.

But Rudolf remained an outspoken liberal. In 1881 he wrote out a "Memorandum on the Political Situation" addressed to his father, much as the youthful Joseph II had written for his mother a century before, and in which Rudolf argued for outright land reform, for heavier taxation on great estates, for increased rights for Slavic minorities. While Austrian foreign policy was moving closer to Germany after the Berlin Congress of 1878, Rudolf proposed closer friendship with France. "What is Germany in comparison to France?" he asked in his "Memorandum." "Nothing but a military state . . . only enlarged."[9]

To such courtiers of the old school as Count Taaffe, and the Habsburg cousin, Archduke Albrecht, who ran the imperial army, Rudolf's views were not only arrogant but dangerously radical. There is no record of any reply from his father.

Barred from any participation in government, Rudolf carried on a secret life of his own in the acquaintance of several, prominent, liberal journalists, particularly clever Moritz Szeps, editor of the *Neues Wiener Tagblatt*. Rudolf contributed regularly to Szeps's liberal paper, his articles appearing, of course, anonymously. Often after midnight Szeps was admitted by a back door in the Hofburg, conducted up servants' stairways into Rudolf's apartment, where the two sat for hours over a bottle of wine, discussing the state of the world.

During the eighties in Austria, as elsewhere in Europe, a right-wing, extremist group was emerging for the first time, flagrantly anti-Semitic in character, and in Austria fervently pro-German; its leader, Georg von Schönerer, was to become Adolf Hitler's inspiration. In the autumn of 1888, less than two months before his death, Rudolf was attacked simultaneously in the right-wing press in Germany, in France in a publication by the anti-Semitic Edouard Drumont, and in Austria by Schönerer—indirectly, for Schönerer did not dare attack the Crown Prince openly.[10]

Exactly what Rudolf's life was like in his last few months nobody really knows. His domestic life had become increasingly strained. He was pictured during his lifetime and after his death as a dissolute royal playboy. How much truth there was to scandalous rumors is not clear; he was certainly frequently confused with his notorious cousin Archduke Otto. There is a strong suspicion today that the whispering campaign against Rudolf may have had its roots at least partly in an attempt to discredit his political views.

The young prince was certainly frustrated, pessimistic about Europe's future, melancholy about his own. Police—evidently placed by Count Taaffe—were detailed to watch him and report his movements. He wrote to Szeps:

> They are becoming very watchful and suspicious of me, and I see more clearly every day what a tight circle of espionage, denunciation and supervision surround me.[11]

Stephanie declared later in her memoirs that in the last months of his life she saw a profound change in Rudolf, so grave that she discussed it with his father. Franz Josef shrugged it away. Apparently Rudolf began to drink heavily; there is no trustworthy evidence that he harbored long-time suicide thoughts.

On his thirtieth birthday, August 21, 1888, he wrote to Szeps:

> One must believe in the future. I hope and count on the next years.[12]

2. Mary Vetsera

A MONTH AFTER Christmas on Sunday night, January 27, 1889, the Emperor Franz Josef, with his son and daughter-in-law, Rudolf and Stephanie, attended a reception at the German Embassy in honor of the German Kaiser's thirtieth birthday. The Empress Elizabeth, who did not care for the German royal family and was anyhow bored by such events, stayed away.

For Rudolf the reception must have been a nagging reminder of all the things he liked least in his own life: he had passed his thirtieth birthday the previous August yet he had not the smallest part in affairs of state, while the former German Crown Prince Wilhelm, whom he detested, now ruled the German Empire.

At the reception was a certain Baroness Vetsera and her two daughters. The younger daughter, Mary, drew many eyes that night, and her mother, to whose ears had come rumors of the Crown Prince's interest in the girl, noticed with uneasiness the glances the two exchanged; and the Crown Prince, despite the presence of his wife, lingered near Mary all evening.

Mary Vetsera was seventeen, a beguilingly pretty little creature, with the kind of beauty that drew men's eyes like a magnet. She had a softly curved face and figure, dark-lashed blue eyes under white, sensuous lids. The Prince of Wales—later on Edward VII—who was certainly a connoisseur of feminine beauty, had visited Vienna two months earlier and pointed the girl out to Rudolf in a box at the Burg Theater. Later on he described Mary to his mother, Queen Victoria, as "one of the prettiest and most admired [girls] in Vienna."[1]

Mary Vetsera's mother, the widowed Baroness Helene, was half Greek; the family were newcomers to Vienna society and had never been received at court. Snobbish older nobility dismissed the Vetseras as climbers, but nobody could deny they were a lively, attractive and amusing family who spent money freely, entertained lavishly. Mary's uncles were gay blades, men of the world, knowledgeable about horses and women and racing. For all their easygoing sophistication families like the Vetseras were exceedingly watchful of pretty unmarried daughters; Mary's movements were always chaperoned—she never left the house without her maid or a hired *promeneuse*. After a woman married—well, that was something else again.

The Vetsera family expected that Mary would eventually marry some highly acceptable suitor, and they had smiled indulgently for a time over Mary's fatuous chatter about the Crown Prince, dismissing it as the kind of teen-age crush that half the girls in Vienna had on the handsome throne heir.

How Mary managed to meet Rudolf is not quite certain, perhaps through a letter she had indiscreetly written to him, probably through the offices of a cousin of Rudolf, Countess Marie Larisch, who took a leading and very dubious role in the whole affair. Marie Larisch was the daughter of a brother of Empress Elizabeth, by a morganatic marriage with an actress. She was also a friend of Mary Vetsera's mother; under the pretext of taking the girl driving or shopping or inviting her to tea, she arranged meetings with Rudolf, in her apartment in the Grand Hotel, in unfrequented allées of the Prater, in Rudolf's apartment in the Hofburg. With the connivance of her maid, Mary managed to escape sometimes in the evening, to find Rudolf's *Fiaker* waiting for her in the street outside the Vetsera mansion.[2]

It was a very brief and sad little affair that had begun only in November of 1888—a few stolen meetings, a few letters exchanged, of which no trace has ever been found.

Mary, however, confided everything in letters to a former governess of hers (later reprinted in her mother's tract):

> I cannot live without having seen him or spoken to him. I have two friends, you and Marie Larisch. You work for my soul's happiness and Marie works for my moral undoing.[3]

A bit later she wrote her friend:

> Today you will get a happy letter because I have been with him. Marie Larisch took me shopping with her and then to be photographed—for him, of course. Then we went to the Burg. An old servant was waiting for us; he led us up several stairs and through several rooms until we reached one in which he left us. At our entrance a black bird—some kind of raven—flew at my head. A

voice called from the next room, "Please come in." Marie introduced me, then he said to me, "Excuse me, but I would like to
talk to the Countess privately for a few minutes." Then he went
with Marie to another room. I looked around me. On his desk was
a revolver and a skull. I picked up the skull, took it between my
hands, and looked at it from all sides. Suddenly Rudolf came in
and took it from me with deep apprehension. When I said that
I wasn't afraid, he smiled.[4]

On January 13, 1889, seventeen-year-old Mary wrote to her old
governess:

I was with him last night from seven till nine. We have both lost
our heads. Now we belong to one another life and soul.[5]

Rudolph gave the girl an iron ring and a medallion to wear around
her neck which bore the mysterious letters *ILVBIDT*. When she asked
what they meant, he explained, *"In Liebe vereint bis in den Tod."*
(In love united until death.) With the help of Countess Marie Larisch,
Mary bought a golden cigarette case for Rudolf and had engraved
on it: *"Dank dem glücklichen Geschicke—13 Jänner 1889."* (Thanks
to a lucky fate.)[6]

The day after the reception at the German Embassy, a gloomy dark
January Monday, Countess Marie Larisch called at the Vetsera mansion and asked to take Mary shopping. The girl's mother kissed her
young daughter good-bye—and never saw her again, alive or dead.
    Years later, in the account of the fatal events of that day which she
wrote in defense of herself, Marie Larisch related that she drove in her
hired *Fiaker* directly to the little back entrance to the Hofburg that
opens on Augustinerstrasse. There Rudolf's valet Loschek met the
ladies, led them up rear stairs and back corridors and across a roof top
to the Crown Prince's apartment. Mary was left there, while Marie
drove to the shop where the golden cigarette box had been purchased,
then returned to the Vetsera mansion and sounded the alarm that
the girl had disappeared while she herself was inside the shop.[7]
    Mary Vetsera, meantime, had been sent by carriage to an inn on
the road that led to the Crown Prince's hunting lodge at Mayerling,
some twenty miles south of Vienna, in the foothills of the Vienna
Woods.
    In his rooms in the palace Rudolf wandered about restlessly. He had
not intended to go out to Mayerling until the following day, when he
had invited friends to hunt with him. However, he now ordered a

carriage for noon to take him to Mayerling, and told a servant that he would leave as soon as an expected letter and telegram arrived. When the servant brought the letter and, a little later, the telegram, he found the Crown Prince standing by the window gazing down in deep thought at the palace courtyard, his watch in hand. "He opened the telegram hastily, read it quickly, folded it up again, and as I withdrew threw it on the table exclaiming, 'Yes, it must happen. . . .' "[8]

A few minutes later he bade a hasty good-bye to Stephanie and his little daughter, and drove away toward Mayerling. The police officer detailed to watch his movements wired his chief that the Crown Prince had passed at 11:50 A.M. in the direction of Schönbrunn —the same road led to Mayerling.[9] Rudolf evidently found Mary at the inn where she was waiting, and they drove together to the hunting lodge.

In the deep January stillness of the Vienna Woods, with snow on the ground, they spent the rest of Monday alone together. An old servant of Rudolf's had gone out ahead to the manor to cook for Rudolf. The Crown Prince and Mary ate supper quietly alone by a wood fire, drank champagne, listened to Rudolf's devoted coachman Bratfisch whistle Viennese tunes for them.

Early the next day—Tuesday, January 29—Rudolf's hunting companions, Count Hoyos and Stephanie's brother-in-law, Prince Philip of Coburg, arrived by the early train. Rudolf appeared promptly and the three men breakfasted together. But Rudolf asked his friends to excuse him from hunting because he had caught a chill the day before. He was expected that night, together with Prince Philip, at a family dinner in the Hofburg, and later in the day he asked Prince Philip to take his excuses to the Emperor and Empress, saying that his cold would prevent him from going to the city.

That evening Count Hoyos appeared for supper with Rudolf; neither guests nor servants—with the exception of Rudolf's valet, Loschek, who slept in a room adjoining the Crown Prince's bedroom—slept on the premises, but in lodgings a few minutes distant. Hoyos and Rudolf supped that night in the billiard room on huntsmen's fare—goose-liver pie, roast beef, roast venison, pastry. Hoyos declared afterward that he never suspected the presence of Mary Vetsera in the room upstairs.

Over supper Rudolf discussed with his friend a political matter in Hungary, about which he had received three telegrams during the day. The Hungarian Parliament was just then debating a defense bill proposed by the Vienna government, providing for a joint Austro-Hungarian army in which Austria's treaty partner, Germany, would exercise considerable influence. The Hungarian Nationalists—who wished total separation from Austria—opposed the bill; a visit to the Crown Prince by his friend Count Pista Károlyi, a few days before had given rise to stories that Rudolf was supporting the nationalist cause in opposition to his father and Taaffe. Rudolf did not seem to be unduly disturbed by the matter; he ate and drank heartily, and, according to Hoyos, "exercised the entire spell of his personality."[10] At nine Hoyos bade the Crown Prince good night and left for his lodgings. Rudolf reminded him that they were to meet for an early breakfast, when Prince Philip was arriving again by the first train, and all three would go hunting.

On that same day, Tuesday, January 29, Mary Vetsera's family, in anguish over the second day of the girl's absence from home, had sought out the police chief, Baron Kraus. In an iron box in which her daughter secreted her most precious belongings, Mary's mother had found a photograph of the Crown Prince and a kind of last will and testament in the girl's handwriting. Baron Kraus, reluctant to mix in such a tricky matter as the amours of the Crown Prince, told the Baroness that the police had no jurisdiction over imperial residences. He advised her not to act hastily lest she damage her daughter's reputation. In her desperate anxiety Baroness Vetsera went directly to the Minister President, Count Taaffe, and begged his help in finding her daughter. Cynical old Taaffe dismissed the Baroness with scant courtesy.

That evening, while Rudolf and Hoyos supped at Mayerling, a reception was held at the House of Parliament in honor of the replacement of gaslights by electricity. While they waited for the newfangled electric lights to blaze on at seven o'clock, Count Taaffe and Police Chief Kraus chatted about the morsel of gossip that had come both their ways that day—of Mary Vetsera's disappearance and her probable whereabouts, of Baroness Helene's past reputation and of the beauty of her young daughter.[11]

At the same hour on Tuesday evening all the Habsburgs in Vienna gathered in the banquet room of the Hofburg. Rather late Prince Philip arrived with Rudolf's regrets, and dinner was served.

In Mayerling the next morning, Wednesday, January 30, Count Hoyos was about to leave his quarters to go to breakfast with the Crown Prince at the lodge when the Mayerling guard appeared with a message from Rudolf's valet that he could not awaken his master.

The guard added that the Crown Prince had been up at half past six, had gone into the anteroom fully dressed to tell his valet to awaken him again at half past seven, and to order his breakfast and the coachman with the carriage for the same hour. Whistling to himself, Rudolf had gone back to his bedroom. At half past seven Loschek had gone to awaken him again, had been knocking ever since, first with his knuckles, then with a stick of wood "without evoking any sign of life."[12]

Hurrying to the lodge, Hoyos found both doors into Rudolf's bedroom locked, and heard for the first time—according to his later testimony—that Mary Vetsera was with the Crown Prince.

A deathlike stillness hung over the whole manor. Instead of trying to force the door, Hoyos went downstairs to the billiard room to await the arrival of Prince Philip, and only when Philip arrived was Loschek ordered to break open a panel of the door with an ax.

> Loschek looked into the room and announced that both occupants were dead in bed. . . . Our horror and grief were inexpressible.[13]

Loschek reached through the broken panel, unlocked the door from the inside. According to Hoyos' testimony, he and Prince Philip did not enter the bedroom, but Hoyos sent the valet to ascertain whether there was life in the bodies—curious behavior, certainly, for a close friend and a close relative. Loschek reported that

> the Crown Prince was lying bent over the edge of the bed, with a great pool of blood in front of him, and that death had presumably been caused by taking cyanide of potassium, as was indicated by the hemorrhage.[14]

Leaving Prince Philip to guard the death room, Hoyos hurried downstairs, jumped into the carriage that was waiting at the door by Rudolf's orders, drove to the nearest railway station at Baden, and persuaded the stationmaster to flag down the Trieste-Vienna express, just then due.

An hour or so later he rushed into the Hofburg to break the terrible news, first to the Crown Prince's adjutant, Count Bombelles, then to the Empress Elizabeth.

The Empress was having her Greek lesson—she had lately become enamored of the Homeric world—and with the help of her little hunchbacked Greek tutor was reading the *Odyssey* in the original. When her lady in waiting knocked on the door and told her that Baron Nopcsa, Controller of Her Majesty's Household, wished to speak with her, Elizabeth answered impatiently that he should wait until her lesson was over.

"But he has important news, grave news from His Imperial Highness, Your Majesty!"[15]

Rising hastily and dismissing her tutor, Elizabeth heard what Nopcsa had to tell her, barely able to comprehend the staggering news of her son's death. Just at that moment a quick step was heard outside her door; it was her husband, the Emperor, come to pay a call. "Don't come in yet!" called Elizabeth, drying her tears and striving for composure. A few moments later Franz Josef entered with his brisk, elastic step. Witnesses said that he entered the room like a youth, and left, an old man.

Almost at the very moment when Empress Elizabeth was breaking the news of their only son's death to Franz Josef, Baroness Helene Vetsera, in her desperate quest for her missing daughter, had come as a last resort to the Hofburg. Even now she was waiting in the apartment of the Empress' reader, Ida Ferenczy, to ask for an audience with the Empress.

Elizabeth went in to her and firmly broke the news. "Baroness, gather all your courage; your daughter is dead."

"My child!" cried the Baroness. "My dear, beautiful child!"

"But do you know," continued the Empress, "that my Rudolf is dead too?"

The Baroness was dismissed with the words "And now remember that Rudolf died of heart failure."[16]

The terrible news had already raced, as bad news does, through palace corridors and out into the street. It had been heard in the environs of Mayerling and Baden; by late afternoon the whole city of Vienna was aflame with the news. Everywhere little knots of people gathered to talk in hushed tones. The *Neues Wiener Tagblatt,* for which Rudolf himself had written, announced the disaster in a black-rimmed box, that Crown Prince Rudolf, "the hope of the Empire, the darling of all the peoples of the monarchy is dead! A hunting accident has robbed Austria of its gifted, idealistic throne heir!"[17]

Already in the morning the court physician, Dr. Widerhofer, had hurried out to Mayerling. In the afternoon an official court commission had been sent out. They had found the two bodies apparently untouched: Mary's carefully laid out on the bed, a bullet hole in the brain, Rudolf's half-sitting on the edge of the bed, the side of his skull shattered. Suicide notes from both Rudolf and Mary had been brought to the Emperor, though none was addressed to him. And that night, after darkness had fallen, Rudolf's body was carried out of Mayerling, brought to Vienna, and laid out on the bed in his rooms in the Hofburg.

The day after the deaths the official *Wiener Zeitung* announced briefly that His Imperial Highness, Crown Prince Rudolf, had died suddenly of a heart attack the previous day in Mayerling. Telegrams bearing the same tidings were dispatched to all the chief rulers of Europe.

Wild rumors flew in Vienna. The Court Commission had been asked to sign an official report giving the cause of death as heart failure; this the doctors refused to do. On February 2 a corrected communiqué appeared in the *Wiener Zeitung*, stating that the Crown Prince had committed suicide while suffering from grave mental aberration. The autopsy report, purporting to show pathological symptoms in the brain, permitted the Crown Prince to be buried with Catholic rites, which, as a suicide, he could not otherwise have had. Even so the Vatican delayed in granting its permission.

In the somber days between January 30 and February 5, when Rudolf's funeral was held, there was no public mention of Mary Vetsera. Indeed, until the very end of the Empire, so far as official Austria was concerned, Crown Prince Rudolf died alone at Mayerling. Count Taaffe and Baron Kraus—certainly with the concurrence of Franz Josef and the Habsburg family—conspired to hide the double suicide, partly to assure a Catholic burial for Rudolf, partly to protect so far as possible the public image of the monarchy.

A cordon of police kept the curious away from the lodge at Mayerling. Mary Vetsera's family, who had been informed that Mary was dead but had as yet no idea of the circumstances under which she had died, were first told that she had poisoned the Crown Prince and had then taken poison herself. Her mother was warned to leave Vienna, in fact started on a journey to Venice, then in an anguish of uncertainty left the train and returned to Vienna.

The day after the Mayerling deaths, Mary's suicide notes were brought to her mother to read, on condition that they be returned to the Emperor. To her mother Mary had written:

Dear Mother, Forgive me for what I have done. I could not resist my love. In agreement with him I would like to be buried beside him at Alland. I am happier in death than in life.

Your Mary[18]

The girl had asked her sister to lay a camellia on her grave each year on January 13 and on the anniversary of her death. To her little brother she wrote:

I shall watch over you from the other world because I love you so much.

Your faithful sister[19]

On the same day, the day after the deaths, Mary's two uncles were sent out to identify the body and bring it to the monastery of Heiligenkreuz for burial. They were admitted to the hunting lodge after dark; in an upstairs linen room, sealed shut since the previous day, they found their niece's nearly nude body in a basket, covered with a heap of her clothes. On the wound in her temple the blood had congealed; her eyes were still open, and her stiff hands still held a small lace handkerchief. It fell to her uncles to wash the body, to dress her again in the clothes she had worn the day she went to Mayerling—a dark green suit, a fur coat, a small feathered hat.

The body was placed upright on the seat of the waiting carriage as if she were alive, and so, propped between her uncles, with a police officer mounted on the box beside the driver, the body of Mary Vetsera was brought to the monastery. The icy mountain road was treacherous, the carriage slipped this way and that over the frozen ruts, so that the coachman had to keep stopping to fix new caulks to the horses' shoes. It was not until midnight that the macabre procession—the two court commissioners following in another carriage—drew up before the gate of the cemetery of Heiligenkreuz. The grave was not yet ready, and though one of the policemen stood over the gravedigger egging him on to hack harder at the frozen ground, it was not until the gray light of Friday morning that a service was read and the body in a plain deal coffin laid in the ground.[20]

Rudolf too had left suicide notes—one for his mother and one for his sister, Marie Valerie. In the one addressed to his valet, he asked him to fetch a priest to pray over the bodies and added that they wished to be buried together.

However, Rudolf's body, the shattered forehead filled with wax and bandaged, lay in the Hofburg until February 5, when a state funeral carried him to the Kapuziner vault to lie among his ancestors.

He had left no farewell note for his father. It was for Franz Josef to carry himself stoically through the following days, to receive visiting dignitaries, to press through the arrangements for a Catholic burial, to

[30] A Habsburg family gathering in the Hofburg in 1835, by Peter Fendi. In the center background are Emperor Franz and Empress Karoline, and the unfortunate Archduke Ferdinand, later Emperor. Among the four children in the foreground is Franz Josef. (*Bildarchiv des Österreichische Bibliothek, Vienna*)

[31] Emperor Franz Josef, soon after his accession to the throne, by Franz Russ. *(Kunsthistorisches Museum, Vienna)*

[32] Empress Elizabeth, by F. X. Winterhalter. (*Bildarchiv des Österreichische Bibliothek, Vienna*)

[33] Crown Prince Rudolf in the year of the Mayerling tragedy. *(Bildarchiv des Österreichische Nationalbibliothek, Vienna)*

walk alone after the coffin on its way to the church, while the Empress and her daughter Valerie remained praying in a chapel in the Hofburg.

Only at the end he had broken down. He told his wife, "I held myself well, but in the vault it was not possible any more. There never was a funeral like today's."[21]

His son's black marble tomb bears only the six letters: *Rudolf*. But on the sunny hillside above the monastery of Heiligenkreuz, all among the graves of celibate monks who have died across the centuries, Mary's grave is marked with a cross and a stone on which is written:

Mary
Freiin Vetsera
geb. 19 März 1871
gest. 30 Jänner 1889

Wie eine Blume sprosst der Mensch
auf und wird gebrochen.
Job 14.2

(Like a flower man springs up and is cut down.)

3. *Conspiracy of Silence*

IN SPITE OF the iron hand of imperial censorship, news of Mary Vetsera's presence in the death chamber was soon known to the world at large. The Austrian press was securely muzzled, but foreign newspapers printing rumors of the double suicide were smuggled into Austria. On a single day, nearly a month after the tragedy, nearly five thousand foreign papers were confiscated by the police in Vienna. For forty kreuzer a Viennese could buy ten minutes' reading time in a forbidden newspaper kept under the seat of a *Fiaker* driver, or for the price of a glass of wine read another whisked out from under a café counter.[1]

Ambassadors in Vienna poked and pried, wrote home reams of hearsay and rumor. Queen Victoria implored her minister in Vienna, "Pray give all details you can gather, however distressing they may be."[2] The papal nuncio, on the excuse of praying on the death scene, got admittance to the Mayerling lodge and nosed about looking for a morsel of truth.[3]

The government of the All Highest remained adamant. Everyone who had anything to do with the last days at Mayerling was sworn to secrecy; nearly all witnesses kept their word. The bullets, the report of physicians and court commissioners sent out immediately to probe the tragedy, accounts of Rudolf's servants, suicide letters, love letters, even the personal belongings of the dead pair—nearly everything vanished from sight. Even the golden cigarette box that Mary had bought for Rudolf, which friends of the Crown Prince remembered seeing on his desk shortly before his death, disappeared.

The official file of Mayerling documents, probably kept in the possession of Count Taaffe, disappeared, possibly during a fire that swept his Bohemian castle a few years later.

Nearly every trace of Rudolf's personal and political affairs during the last months of his life has vanished as well. Even Dossier Number 25, containing documents relating to the Hungarian defense bill and to Count Pista Károlyi's last visit with the Crown Prince in January of 1889, was removed from the Foreign Office Archives four months after the death of the Crown Prince and never replaced.

So completely, so painstakingly, was every shred of truth, every concrete piece of factual evidence hurried out of public sight that even today, nearly eighty years later, the full truth of Mayerling continues to elude the searcher.

The truth could hardly have damaged the imperial cause more grievously than the tide of gossip, fantasy, conjecture, and rumor that swept over all Europe during the months that followed. Stories of Rudolf's dissolute life were revived and refurbished. It was said that he had compromised a girl of noble family, the Princess Aglaia Auersperg, had been challenged by her brother to an "American duel," the terms of which required the loser—he who drew the black bullet—to take his own life. Other rumors had him shot by Mary's uncle, killed in a duel with Count Hoyos, killed by masked assassins sent by his father to end a treasonous political embroilment.[4]

The rumor that Mary had poisoned her lover persisted, and the Vetseras found themselves ostracized from Vienna society. To defend herself and her daughter's memory, Baroness Vetsera wrote down what she knew of the tragedy, and printed in June of 1889 a little pamphlet containing the text of Mary's letters to her governess and her farewell letters. The police confiscated the pamphlet and it was not reprinted until 1919.

But on one point Rudolf's closest acquaintances and later biographers agreed: he did not take his life because of a frustrated love affair—though it was Mary Vetsera's romantic passion that led her into death—but more likely for political reasons that still remain obscure.

Stories current at the time and later suggested that Rudolf had applied directly to the Pope for a divorce, that the Pope had informed the Emperor, and that a bitter scene ensued between father and son just before the fatal events at Mayerling. But no factual evidence supports the theory.

If there was an open quarrel, it seems more likely that political events brought it on; it is significant that Rudolf left no farewell note for his father.

Of the suicide letters only the one to his wife has been reprinted;

all apparently were on the same theme—that his honor demanded his death. Crown Princess Stephanie published in her memoirs her husband's last note to her:

> You are relieved of my presence and vexation; be happy in your own way. Be kind to the poor little one; she is all that remains of me. . . . I approach death composedly; it alone can save my good name. I embrace you tenderly.
>
> Your loving Rudolf[5]

To his sister Rudolf declared, "I do not die willingly," and to his mother he wrote, "I know quite well that I was not worthy to be his son."[6]

What could the political crisis have been that led to Rudolf's suicide? Perhaps an affair involving Hungarian nationalists; perhaps a matter concerning leadership of the Austrian army—certainly Rudolf was at swords' point with his elderly cousin, Archduke Albrecht, who was Inspector General.

In any case, the price of imperial censorship in the Mayerling affair was enormously high. The secrecy in which it was cloaked left the Habsburg name gravely compromised, and the very foundations of the monarchy shaken.

In a sense the Empire came to an end that night of January 30, 1889.

XV

Hofburg Finale

1. Elizabeth in Mourning

FROM THE STUNNING blow of her son's death Empress Elizabeth slipped into a somber half-world of melancholy and loneliness from which she never again escaped. She had not been able to bring herself to attend the great state funeral, but a few days later, on February 9, she went to bed as usual, dismissing her lady in waiting and servants. A little later she got up, dressed, and slipped out of the palace by a back door, hailed a passing cab to take her to the Kapuziner Crypt in the Neuer Markt. There she roused the father superior to conduct her to the great iron crypt door and then bade him leave her alone in the dusky, ice-cold hall of the dead. By her son's coffin she called his name: "Rudolf! Rudolf!" Her voice echoed through the crypt, but there was no answer save the rustling of dead leaves outside the small high window.[1]

She vowed she would always wear mourning, and though for her daughter Valerie's sake she put on a light gray dress for a little while on the following Christmas Eve, she appeared only in black in public, without jewels. Her wedding ring she wore on a thin chain around her neck, together with a pair of lockets, one containing a lock of her son's hair, the other engraved with the Ninety-first Psalm:

Thou shalt not be afraid for any terror by night, nor for the arrow that flyeth by day.

The year after the tragedy Elizabeth's favorite younger daughter married and left home. There was nothing really to keep the Empress in Vienna any more. She took to wandering again, with a single lady in waiting in attendance, a proud, lonely, haunted woman, looking for an answer to life and to death without in the least knowing where to look for it. Her beautiful face, traced now by shadows of age, would be glimpsed under a white sunshade, behind a fan, shrinking from the public eye, here and there in European watering places, in Bad Nauheim, in Karlsbad, or in the islands of the Mediterranean. Her fantastic castle of Achilleion on the island of Corfu was finished in 1891; she stopped there briefly, but it gave her no pleasure and by 1893 she was already seeking to sell it.

She kept her slender, erect figure, ate little, often subsisting for days on beef juice or on violet-flavored ices and orange juice. She had had to give up riding; the Emperor exchanged two fine Lipizzaners for a pair of English cows, which usually accompanied the Empress on her travels. When he asked her once what she would like for Christmas, she wrote that she would like "a young royal tiger, or a locket, or a fully equipped lunatic asylum."[2]

Not long after Mayerling, newspapers began to print rumors of her insanity. Annoyed by the stories, she would show herself briefly in public at some ceremony by her husband's side; then she would vanish again from public sight for weeks or months or years.

2. A Friend for Franz Josef

IN THE LATE 1880s, some time before her son's death, Elizabeth had done a very kind thing for her husband. She had found him a friend, and an entertaining one, in a pretty young actress at the Burg Theater named Katharina Schratt.

Franz Josef had already admired Katharina Schratt on the stage, and she had been presented to him. Elizabeth helped things along by engaging a painter to do a portrait of the actress, and then taking the Emperor along to watch a sitting. Three days later Franz Josef wrote Frau Schratt, thanking her for permitting her portrait to be done and enclosing a small token of his esteem—an emerald ring.[1]

Frau Schratt was a thoroughly nice person, attractive rather than dazzling, cheerful, warmhearted, comforting and comfortable, a delightful woman with a full and engaging laugh. She was not a particularly good actress, for she always played herself, but it was a nice role and she had a very considerable following.

Franz Josef was fifty-five when the two met, and their very Viennese amour—temperate, autumnal, discreet—lasted for thirty years, until the day of the Emperor's death. In that day before the telephone supplanted the letter, the two wrote to each other nearly every day when they did not meet. Though in his letters to her Franz Josef confessed that he was "frightfully, eternally fond of" her and that "my longing for you is enormous," still he never addressed her except with the formal *Sie,* and for years signed his letters merely "Your most faithful Franz Josef" or merely "Your Franz Josef."

Sometimes Katharina went to early Mass in the palace chapel so that they might glimpse one another. Once, on an early morning in February, she fainted in the chapel, under the very eyes of the Emperor, who could not rush to her aid in that public place as an ordinary lover might:

How could you [he wrote her next day] come to church at that early hour and in that cold weather. You try to do much too much. . . . You certainly should not come to church so early at this time of year, and happy as I am to know you are there, for one cannot call it seeing in that pervading dusk, still I am more concerned about your health which you ought not risk.

Forgive me for not staying longer with you in church yesterday, but after I had made sure that, thank God, you were conscious again and able to walk, I wanted to avoid being observed and thought too that church was not the place for a longer conversation.[2]

Nor did the Emperor quite dare to seek her out at a ball in the Redoutensaal of the Hofburg:

I would have had to break through the crowd surrounding you, while people with and without opera glasses could stare at us from all sides, and everywhere the hyenas of the press waiting, to snap up every word a person says. . . . Besides, what could we have said to one another there? . . . I was afraid you would be angry that I did not approach you, and now your letter has set my fears at rest; a stone has fallen from my heart.[3]

Presently the actress was coming to the Hofburg two or three times a week, dropping in sometimes after a rehearsal at the theater to have *Jause*—a little supper—with the Emperor, or merely sit by his desk and chat while he ate his frugal meal. To show that her visits had the Empress' blessing, she would usually stop first in the apartment of the Empress' lady in waiting.

Franz Josef's daughter, Archduchess Marie Valerie, at that time not yet married, wrote in her diary that they were often four at dinner: her father, her mother, herself, and Frau Schratt. Valerie thought it very awkward; her mother called it *gemütlich*—cozy.

It was certainly one of history's most unusual palace triangles. The two women—the Empress and the actress—seemed genuinely fond of each other. It was almost as if they had switched roles in the Emperor's life: Franz Josef continued to adore his wife as a man might an elusive mistress, never quite assailable, never really possessed, while for Katharina Schratt he felt the affection a man feels for a dear and devoted wife.

She looked after him admirably, showered him with charming little attentions—a pot of four-leaf clover when he needed cheering, a bunch of violets on a chilly March day. She saw that he wore his bowler hat at just the right angle, kept him in the expensive Havana cigars that he loved to smoke but refused to buy for himself. She gave orders that champagne and a bite to eat were always waiting for him in his bedroom when he had been up late at some official function. She had a warm cloak made for him that hung just inside the door of the Empress' suite, for Elizabeth liked to have all the windows open winter and summer, and her husband always shivered when he entered his wife's rooms.

His friend listened to him talk and kept his secrets.

For his part he bestowed on the actress such favors as an emperor may. His financial arrangements with her were discreetly paternal; he gave her presents of money on her name day and her birthday, just as he gave his own children.

He wrote her during the carnival season in 1887:

Fasching is nearing an end, which requires beautiful clothes; they are expensive and you ought not run up bills, so I would be very grateful if you would take the enclosed small contribution in friendly fashion to defray the cost of your wardrobe. I hold you for an excellent and very talented woman, but I am not impressed with your financial skill.[4]

Presently Katharina was installed in a nice little villa near Schönbrunn Palace. When he was staying at Schönbrunn, Franz Josef would get up very early, let himself out of a little gate that opened onto Gloriettegasse, fetch her from her villa to walk in the park in the early-morning freshness. Sometimes he dropped in to her house for breakfast, or for tea to meet some of her amusing friends from the world of the theater, or in the evening to hear a quartet of *Schrammel* musicians play old Viennese airs. In the summer, when the Emperor went to Bad Ischl for a holiday, the actress had her own villa there near the imperial summer home; it was aptly named Felicitas.

It was Katharina Schratt who was waiting to see the Emperor at the very moment when the terrible news of his son's death at Mayerling was broken to him. Although she otherwise preserved all of Franz Josef's letters with care, two letters he wrote to her in early March of 1889—evidently concerned with the tragedy—have been torn in two and a portion destroyed.

Sometimes during his wife's long absences from home Franz Josef would wander through her apartment, touching the furniture wrapped in dust covers:

What I miss so much [he wrote to Elizabeth] are the moments
I spent with you during your breakfast and our evenings together.
I have already been twice into your rooms . . . and though all
the furniture is in covers, everything reminded me so mournfully
of you.[5]

At first Elizabeth made a point of spending Christmases at home; by
and by she stayed away for Christmas as well. Franz Josef wrote her
on December 25, 1891:

Today I want to send you my most heartfelt wishes, together with
a petition that you will be as kind and sweet to me during the
future which is in store for us—which may be only a short one—
as you have been more and more up to now. And I should like,
too, to put into words what I cannot do enough to show you—for
it would bore you if I were always trying to show it—how enormously fond of you I am. May God bless and protect you and
send us a happy reunion; we have nothing more left to desire or
hope for.[6]

In September of 1898 Elizabeth was on her way home to Vienna
from a cure at the waters of Bad Kissingen. She stopped off in
Switzerland for a few days, registering in a small hotel in Geneva
under the name Countess Hohenems. Nobody was fooled, however,
and the arrival of the Austrian empress was duly noted in the local
press.

On the morning of September 10, the Empress and a single lady in
waiting, Countess Sztáray, went shopping and bought a music box for
the Empress' grandchildren. At noon the two ladies left the hotel to
board the little excursion steamer that was to take them up the lake to
the village of Caux.

On their way down the street to the landing stage, a young man
ran up, pushed rudely against Elizabeth, and knocked her to the
pavement. Passers-by helped her to her feet, she staggered a bit,
pulled herself together, walked a hundred yards farther to the steamer.
There on the deck she collapsed and was dead within the hour; she
had been stabbed in the heart by a shoemaker's awl.

There was no particular meaning in the murder. The young Italian
anarchist named Lucheni who killed her had simply vowed to do
away with the first member of European royalty who appeared a
convenient victim.

When the telegram telling of his wife's murder reached Franz
Josef in the Hofburg, Frau Schratt was away on a holiday in the
mountains; she hurried back to be with him.

3. Uncle and Nephew

LIFE ON THE SURFACE changed little in the Hofburg after Elizabeth's death. She had been away from home so much for so many years; it must have seemed to Franz Josef that one day he would be handed a telegram again from Bad Kissingen or Geneva or Corfu telling him that Elizabeth was once more on her way back to Vienna.

He lived on in those austere rooms of his in the Hofburg, a dapper, elegant old man with bright blue eyes under bushy white brows, and carefully brushed side whiskers. He kept Elizabeth's portrait on an easel near his desk, the Winterhalter portrait in negligee, with her dark hair loosened on her shoulders. His valet often found him staring at the picture of the lovely woman who had somehow all her life eluded him.

With Frau Schratt he talked of Elizabeth, called her the Radiant One and the Unforgettable One. He wrote to his friend:

> I just discovered now the new, still very young moon out of my window and gave it a greeting, which made my thoughts linger with you and with our dear Radiant One.[1]

He continued to perform all his duties punctiliously, stood erect in uniform for hours reviewing parades on the Ring, rode at maneuvers, walked bareheaded carrying a lighted taper in the Corpus Christi procession. In the month of May his carriage led the procession of vehicles that wound their way out to the Prater along the avenue of pink horse-chestnut trees.

At court balls during carnival season, when guests had assembled in the ballroom of the Hofburg, the grand marshal would strike with his golden staff three times on the floor; there would be a moment of hushed silence. Then the orchestra struck up the notes of Haydn's anthem "God Save Our Emperor," the folding doors flew open, and the Emperor appeared, followed by members of his family and his aides. Slowly he would circle the ballroom, stopping to greet now one, now another, while the ladies he passed dropped their deepest curtsies. When he reached the end of the room, he would choose the highest-ranking lady and begin the first measured steps of the ball.

On Maundy Thursday in Holy Week, in his dress uniform with scarlet trousers and white-and-gold tunic, he washed the feet of twelve old men and served them their wooden bowls of soup.

The ceremony was carried off with precision and dispatch. The soup came first, but before the pauper-guests had tasted more than a mouthful, the archdukes who served were whisking off the plates, carrying away the table, while palace officials stripped off the right sock and shoe from each old man.

The Emperor removed his white gloves, knelt, and sliding briskly down the row of chairs, poured water from an engraved pewter canister over each outstretched foot while a priest caught the water in a silver basin. At the end of the row the Emperor rose to his feet, the chief steward poured fresh water over his hands and handed him a linen towel on a silver tray. Finally the Emperor hung about each old man's neck a white silken bag containing thirty silver crowns, and the twelve were led from the room.

It was an elderly court that surrounded the aging Emperor. By the year 1900 most of his own generation had died around him. His brother, Karl Ludwig, a painfully pious man, died of dysentery after drinking water straight out of the River Jordan on a trip to the Holy Land. Franz Josef's younger brother, Ludwig Viktor, who had evaded marriage, retired in a cloud of scandal to the castle of Klessheim near Salzburg. Franz Josef almost never saw him.

A deep pessimism about the future of the Empire shadowed Franz Josef in his last years. It seemed to him the qualities that had carried his family to power and sustained it there across centuries—their sense of divine election and of the privileges and duties of that election—had vanished. He hoped only to hold the Empire together, to pass it on undiminished to his heir. After his death—who could say?

Among the younger generation were numerous rebels, but none quite such an out-and-out *frondeur* as the Archduke Johann Salvator, son of the last Tuscan grand duke. Archduke Johann had had to be broken from his rank in the army for publishing in 1874 a tract highly critical of the Artillery. He had continually incurred the wrath of the

Emperor for one incident after another. He had attempted to gain the crown of Bulgaria; more recently he was apparently embroiled in a Hungarian nationalist plot—as Crown Prince Rudolf may also have been.

In the year of the Mayerling tragedy, Johann had left the country without the Emperor's permission (which was required of every Habsburg). From Switzerland he had written to renounce forever the title of Archduke and take the plain name of Johann Orth. He tried in vain to enlist in the Bulgarian army, then in the Turkish. Eventually he mortgaged his castle, bought a sailing ship in England, the *Santa Margherita,* and sailed for South America. In July of 1890 the *Santa Margherita* disappeared in a storm off Cape Horn, and in 1911 the court marshal of the Hofburg officially pronounced Johann Salvator dead.

Since Rudolf's death at Mayerling, Franz Josef's heir was his brother Karl Ludwig's son, Archduke Franz Ferdinand, a morose, choleric, humorless man with a prickly pride and a violent temper. Between uncle and nephew no love was lost. Franz Ferdinand totally lacked charm; he was simply not what the Austrians call *sympathisch.* He had, however, certain traits of mind and character that might one day prove useful to his country: he was not unintelligent, and he could be inexorably obstinate in pushing through his will.

Franz Ferdinand's stubbornness presently came to light on the question of his marriage.

While his family thought he was wooing a cousin, daughter of the wealthy Archduke Friedrich in Pressburg, Franz Ferdinand was actually courting a lady in waiting in the household, Countess Sophie Chotek. Though Sophie came from an old and titled Bohemian family, she was not considered of equal birth and not marriageable within terms of Habsburg family law.

One day Franz Ferdinand forgot his watch in Pressburg after a game of tennis, and a picture of the handsome Sophie was found ensconced within. The Habsburg family rocked with the news. Sophie was instantly dismissed from the Friedrich family's service. But Franz Ferdinand had no intention of giving in; he insisted on marrying Sophie.

Franz Josef was neither hardhearted nor totally intransigent. But tradition and law were the very keystone of the monarchy system, and a throne heir could least of all afford to flout them. Franz Josef had been trained to place duty above private happiness; he had seen the tragedy in his own family of those who failed to do so. He refused his nephew permission to marry.

But the ministers and archbishop sent to exercise their powers of persuasion on Franz Ferdinand did not move him in the least. "Your Excellency," he wrote in a note to Prime Minister Ernest von Koerber, "is aware of my unshakable intention; it is now a question of my life, my existence, and my future."[2] In the end he succeeded in wringing from the Emperor a reluctant consent to a morganatic marriage.

On June 28, 1900, before an assembly of his archduke relatives, his uncle's ministers and court, Franz Ferdinand was required to swear that his wife would be forever excluded from imperial rank, and that any children born of the marriage would be barred from the succession. Three days later he married his Sophie.

The summer of Franz Ferdinand's marriage Emperor Franz Josef celebrated his seventieth birthday at his summer villa in Bad Ischl. It was a sorrowful holiday. Katharina Schratt had made up her mind to end her friendship with the Emperor, and the two bade one another good-bye forever.

Tongues had wagged since Empress Elizabeth's death; that was to be expected. But Katharina felt herself plagued by slights from the Emperor's own family, by imagined wounds from him. She decided to end the affair and to leave Austria.

The two parted without bitterness, but both in tears. The next day Franz Josef wrote to her:

> Twenty-four hours ago I left my room to go to you for a last time, my dearly loved angel! After you had disappeared from my sight yesterday, I met a chimney sweep standing by the smithy. . . . You have always thought such fellows brought good luck, and for me luck is simply: to see you again.[3]

He was miserably lonely. A month or so later his court marshal, Prince Liechtenstein, wrote Frau Ferenczy:

> His Majesty is desperate and will hardly bear being cheered up. . . . His health, however, is excellent. . . . In Galicia he rode like the devil in front of his cavalry.[4]

The estrangement from Frau Schratt lasted a full year. In May of 1901 he was writing her from Hungary:

My mood is always sorrowful in my inconsolable loneliness, my age especially recently makes itself felt, and I am always tired.

I was so naïve as to hope that you would give me a sign, in memory of our true fifteen-year friendship, that you shared my sorrow over the death of my poor little great grandson. In that too I was disappointed, and that hurt me very much. One grief more or less doesn't alter things much, and one must bear it.[5]

At last, in August of 1901, when the Emperor was again in Bad Ischl for the holidays, Frau Schratt's old cook brought him a message on his seventy-first birthday. Would he call at the Villa Felicitas the following day? Would he call? Would he indeed? He sent word that he would be at her house at seven fifteen in the morning, for he must be back at the imperial villa by eight thirty to receive the formal birthday congratulations of his family.

For the remainder of his life the actress was the person closest to him—indeed, perhaps, the only person in his whole life who was really close to him.

4. Turn-of-the-century Vienna

SIGMUND FREUD'S SON Martin describes the early years of the century in Austria as "a golden age, a time when one could live in tranquillity and peace. Nothing like those years has returned for us."[1]

Stefan Zweig looked back on Vienna nostalgically:

> It was sweet to live here, in this atmosphere of spiritual conciliation, and subconsciously every citizen became supernational, cosmopolitan, a citizen of the world.[2]

Perhaps just because of its cosmopolitan character, its extraordinary racial intermingling, Vienna became in the first decade of the twentieth century the birthplace of the new, both the marvelous and the terrible.

Brahms was not long dead; at the dazzling new Opera House on the Ring, Gustav Mahler conducted, demanding perfection of performers and audience alike. Arnold Schönberg broke music apart and put it together again. While Gustav Klimt and others in the *art nouveau* circle painted ornamental elongated beauties in a highly colored dream world, an awkward boy from the provinces named Oskar Kokoschka wandered through the picture galleries on Sunday mornings. And all among the marble and gilded traditional of the new Ring buildings, Otto Wagner set his stark and controversial Postal Savings building, declaring firmly that "nothing that is not practical can be beautiful." Joseph Hoffmann and Adolf Loos designed buildings of astonishing, clean line, of austere, purposeful skeleton.

And in those years Sigmund Freud was unlocking the darker closets of the human mind. On Saturday nights he lectured in the psychiatric clinic of the General Hospital, next to the old Fools' Tower where Joseph II had pondered what he might do to help the insane. On

Wednesday evenings Freud gathered with his disciples around the long table in his patients' waiting room in Berggasse, to drink black coffee, smoke, and argue over doctrinal differences in the new religion of psychoanalysis.

Franz Josef's path and Sigmund Freud's had crossed just once. After a catastrophic theater fire on the Ring, the Habsburgs dedicated a new apartment building called the Sühnhaus, the House of Expiation; it was Freud's daughter Anna who won a gift from the Emperor because she was the first child born there.

It was in the cafés that the new ideas were germinating, among the journalists and philosophers and artists who gathered there to scribble and sketch and talk. In the Café Grienstadl the Young Vienna group of writers—Hermann Bahr, Arthur Schnitzler, Hugo von Hofmannsthal—had their headquarters. A brilliant group of journalists writing for the Viennese press wielded a profound influence throughout central Europe. At the top ranked the *Neue Freie Presse*—one of the great newspapers of the world in that day—of whose editor it was said jokingly, "Next to him the Emperor is the most important man in the country."

Already in the 1900s Vienna was plagued by all the social problems that have beset the twentieth century's great cities ever since.

In the forty years before 1900, Vienna's population had exploded 259 per cent—more than any other city in Europe except Berlin.

Housing was in dire shortage. The homeless poor flocked to the warming rooms, where they could sleep sitting upright on closely packed benches. Others took refuge from the cold in the sewers that ran parallel to the Danube Canal and the River Wien, where the iron doors could be forced open and space found inside out of wind and rain.

Nearly half the city's population were newcomers, among them thousands upon thousands of Jewish refugees from the persecutions of Czarist Russia. The great influx of *Ost Juden* inflamed existing anti-Semitic prejudice, and gave impetus to the politicians of the extreme right. Theodore Herzl, the brilliant *feuilleton* editor of the *Neue Freie Presse*, watching the slow poison seep through the veins of Europe, dreamed first of leading his co-religionists up the steps of St. Stephen's in a mass baptism to Christianity. He abandoned this plan as impractical and concentrated instead on the idea of a national home for the Jews, on which he based his tract, *Der Judenstaat*, the germ of modern Israel.

In the autumn of 1906—and again in 1908—a ragged youth from Upper Austria, rejected by the Academy of Fine Arts because he was without talent, wandered about the streets of Vienna. He slept in a hostel for homeless men, ate in a soup kitchen, listened to the harangues of demagogues of the extreme right. And he cursed the city for the very quality that Zweig called its peculiar genius:

> I was repelled [wrote Adolf Hitler in *Mein Kampf*] by the conglomeration of races which the capital showed me, repelled by this whole mixture of Czechs, Poles, Hungarians, Ruthenians, Serbs, and Croats—and everywhere Jews, and more Jews.[3]

Hitler called Vienna "the personification of incest"; the Habsburgs he damned as "cosmopolitan," terming them "the most degenerate, most guilt-laden dynasty that the German people ever had to endure."[4]

While the collapse of the multinational Habsburg monarchy continued to be predicted, chiefly outside the realm, within the country civilized Austrians liked to characterize the situation with humorous irony as "desperate but not serious."

It was true that a foreigner visiting a session of Parliament might think he had found himself in the Tower of Babel. In a single day one might hear passionate speeches in a dozen languages, of which most delegates might understand only one or two.

And there were occasions when all of Parliament erupted into violence, as happened in 1897 when the Badeni Language Decrees ordered that all civil servants in Bohemia and Moravia—down to postmen and street-sweepers—speak and write Czech as well as German. National feelings exploded all over the Empire; in parliament there was absolute bedlam. Inkstands were hurled through the air; filibustering went on far into the night; members engaged in fist-fights, desks overturned, whistles blew; one distinguished professor of Roman law from Prague noisily blew a fire-brigade trumpet.

The language laws were revoked, and things settled down once more. And when a huge Socialist parade was announced, to demonstrate on May Day for universal suffrage, and all good conservatives quaked in their boots, the affair went off in perfect decorum. A quarter of a million workers marched, waving banners in a dozen languages; not a policeman was needed to maintain order. Slowly the Social Democrats won a voice in the government; in 1906 Franz Josef agreed to their long-standing plea for universal suffrage.

Most citizens in all parts of the Empire continued to feel deeply loyal to the Emperor. Careful, conservative, slow to take action, wary of all that was new, but nevertheless fair-minded, Franz Josef trod a cautious line between hot and cold, left and right.

Grave problems remained to be solved, chiefly revolving around the participation of minority groups. But in Austria there was a cheerful optimism that these problems too would eventually be resolved, probably in that peculiarly Austrian manner called *fortwursteln*—blundering through—quite literally, to go on grinding out one's little sausages.

5. Twilight

BY THE TIME 1910 rolled around and Franz Josef reached his eightieth year, he was less a monarch than an institution to his people. There were Viennese who as children had watched him ride into the city that fine day in May of 1849, a fair handsome boy in a uniform that fitted like satin, had seen him turn into a grave, middle-aged monarch, performing every duty punctiliously, rarely heard to laugh out loud or seen to shed a tear in public, or reveal in any perceptible way the terrible blows that fortune dealt him as a man and as a monarch. Now they saw him in the early years of the twentieth century, a courtly old gentleman with silvery hair and side whiskers, a superb anachronism in a time to which he did not belong. To his Austrians he had become more endearing as he grew older, perhaps because his virtues had always been an old man's virtues: dignity, composure, propriety, resistance to change.

For years there had been rumors abroad that the Austrian Emperor was really dead, and that there existed in Vienna a kind of college that trained men to play his part in public.

He was, however, very much alive, and by no means ready to relinquish his power.

Each morning at precisely half past three his valet awoke him saying, "I am at Your Majesty's feet. Good morning."[1]

With the help of his washer the Emperor bathed in a portable wooden tub carried into his bedroom. He knelt to say his prayers, worked on his papers until breakfast, which always consisted of coffee, butter rolls, and ham except on fast days. He was not particular about what he ate. Once he found a cockroach baked in his breakfast roll, ordered the court baker's appointment canceled. Later on, though, when he learned the fellow had been nearly ruined, he reinstated him.

His washer gave him trouble too. The pay and the prestige of a functionary so close to the person of the All Highest were excellent; it was only the hours—three in the morning, winter and summer—that were dismal. The washer found it more convenient to sit out the night in a tavern near the Hofburg and appear for duty without going to bed at all. Unfortunately the wine he drank to keep awake began to tell increasingly, and one day when he all but fell into the tub with the All Highest, he had to be dismissed.

It was really in his study that Franz Josef lived out his days, at his big flat-topped desk from dawn till dark. He kept it meticulously neat. Behind the large standing calendar he kept a small brush and feather whisk, so that he might instantly brush off any ash and sand that remained when he dried the ink of his signature.

In the little anteroom off the study, on a small brick stove, water was heated for the imperial basin, and over a spirit lamp the Emperor's breakfast coffee was made. The Hofburg kitchens were so far away that lunch was carried up in two tin cases, with glowing embers in the bottom.

In his study the Emperor was shaved. When he had an aching tooth the dentist pulled it there, while the old man sat bolt upright and unflinching in his chair.

Each day at noon he left his desk to stand at the window and watch the changing of the guard in the palace courtyard.

When his grandchildren came for a visit he let them romp in his study, gave them used envelopes, and had them stay to lunch.

In the study he and Frau Schratt had cozy meals à deux, at a table his valet pushed into the center of the room. When his friend was coming for supper, the Emperor would order all her favorite dishes and his valet would see him repeatedly jump up from his desk, go into the adjoining bedroom, and brush his hair and side whiskers.

Katharina Schratt looked after the old man admirably. She bought him a warm shawl and a biscuit box, and a mechanical nightingale that sprang out of a little box and sang enchantingly when you wound it up. On his desk he kept a pocket mirror inscribed in her hand, "Portrait de la personne que j'aime."

To the day of her death she never betrayed that intimacy. Though she outlived Franz Josef for many years—she died only in 1940—she never wrote her memoirs, refused to allow herself to be interviewed or photographed for the press. A rare news picture taken unawares late in her life gives a glimpse of a sweet, rosy, grandmotherly face under a round black hat.

The new forces abroad in the world continued to shock and wound Franz Josef, as they had Queen Victoria, dead years before him. For a long time he refused to have a telephone installed in his study, or a typewriter. Telegraphing he liked; that was an invention of his youth and had had time to grow respectable.

He would not enter an elevator or a motorcar, and he wrote to Frau Schratt in 1907:

> That you have rented an automobile pleases me less, for it makes a person worry constantly.[2]

But he gave in with more or less grace:

> You seem to use your automobile in great style and for great distances. If, as I fervently hope, it brings no misfortune I will say nothing about it, but private [*heimlich*] the thing certainly is not.[3]

That same year King Edward VII came on a visit to Bad Ischl and persuaded Franz Josef to go for a spin in his motorcar. The two monarchs had their photograph taken, King Edward looking pleased with himself, Franz Josef exceedingly dubious, in the back of a high, old-fashioned touring car.

In 1908 the Empire celebrated the sixtieth Jubilee of Franz Josef's reign, and the whole Habsburg clan gathered at Schönbrunn to honor the old patriarch.

On the afternoon of December 1, just before the festival illumination of the city of Vienna, the Habsburg children presented a ballet in the little theater of Schönbrunn. First, however, the eldest daughter of Marie Valerie gathered the children about her to recount the fairy story of the king who wore so many crowns, "brave as a hero, strong and patient, even-tempered as the hand of a clock"—but underneath all the crowns was the one that no one saw: a crown of thorns. The longer he lived, the more deeply the thorns pressed into his brow. . . .[4]

The children's ballet, which had been planned by Franz Josef's nephew, Ferdinand Karl, a theater addict, presented the old-fashioned dances of Franz Josef's childhood, in Biedermeier costume. The old Emperor was delighted and less critical than the ballet master, who, perspiring over the rehearsals, had exclaimed, "My young lords, you dance like camels!"[5] At the end all the children marched up to the imperial box to present bouquets to the Emperor, whose eyes now were filled with tears, and to kiss his hand.

The next day the throne heir, Franz Ferdinand, gave the ceremonial address to the whole family, gathered in the Alexander Apartments of the Hofburg. There was a gala presentation in the Opera House with the entire audience rising to sing the "*Gott Erhalte.*" And in Prague that night Czechs and Germans quarreled angrily, the imperial flag was pulled down and trampled while a Czech patriot thundered, "What is the black-yellow flag? An anachronism and nothing else . . ."[6]

Between Emperor and heir apparent relations continued to be strained. It had been one of Franz Josef's gravest blunders with his own son, now again with his nephew, not to admit him to any real place in the government. There was, of course, something extremely disconcerting about having so palpable a *memento mori* as one's successor waiting impatiently in the wings for one to die. Franz Ferdinand called himself "His Majesty's most loyal opposition." In Belvedere Palace he gathered his own little court and cabinet of advisors, and made quite overt preparations against the day of his taking over.

Franz Ferdinand's marriage had proved to be a warm and happy one; Sophie was an affectionate, capable wife and an excellent mother. It was one of those marriages that can change a rather ordinary man into something several cuts above. "Soph is a treasure, I am indescribably happy," he wrote to his stepmother.[7]

Franz Josef had elevated Sophie to the rank of princess, then duchess; but court protocol still condemned her to a place far below her husband at official gatherings, and Franz Ferdinand smarted for the snubs his wife received. She sat in the very back of the imperial box at the opera instead of at his side; she was placed below all other Habsburgs at table; she walked behind the youngest archduchess during the grand entrances to the ballroom. It seemed likely to persons close to the couple that once he was Emperor, Franz Ferdinand would scrap his renunciation and make his wife Empress in fact.

Thinking ahead to the day when he would wear the crowns, Franz Ferdinand was already designing blueprints for a renewed and refurbished empire. He was determined to break the stranglehold the Magyars held on the Dual Monarchy. Favoring the Slavs, Franz Ferdinand apparently planned at first to add a third state of South Slavs, turning it into a Trialist Monarchy. Later on in his life he seemed to be veering toward a federalist plan of several states within the Empire, on the model of Switzerland and the United States.[8]

There had been one grave brinkmanship crisis in 1908, when Franz Josef's ministers blandly announced to the world the annexation of the Balkan provinces of Bosnia and Herzegovina.

The larger part of the Balkan Peninsula had won its independence from Turkey in 1877, with the help of Russia, but the great powers had stepped in to prevent total domination of the peninsula by the Czar. The two provinces of Bosnia and Herzegovina had been handed over to Austria-Hungary to administer at the Congress of Berlin in 1878.

Under Austrian mandate the provinces had, in fact, by colonial standards of that day, been well administered. Roads, schools, railways had been built; the crime rate in Bosnia and Herzegovina was the lowest in the Balkans. While the population was predominantly Serb, there were sizable Croat and Turk minorities.

The immediate cause of the annexation move was the Young Turk revolution in Constantinople in 1908, which, it was feared, might revive Turkish claims to the provinces. A more real threat, however, was the neighboring independent kingdom of Serbia, which hoped one day to expand and absorb the two provinces. By annexing the provinces, Franz Josef's government expected to relieve the internal pressures of Serb nationalist agitators; the provinces were promised a written constitution and autonomy in the near future. In fact the move was premature and unwise.

The repercussions from the annexation move were noisy and frightening to all Europe. Serbia threatened outright war. The Chief of the Austro-Hungarian General Staff, Conrad von Hötzendorf, who like most career army officers thought in terms of force as a solution to problems of state, urged an immediate "preventive war" against Serbia. Archduke Franz Ferdinand had opposed the annexation move; he sent peremptory word to Conrad to cease the sword-rattling. "War on two fronts! That will be the end of the song!"[9]

The crisis passed, to all appearances. But Serbia continued to promote nationalist agitation within the provinces, and the tensions grew rather than diminished.

In 1910 the old Emperor passed his eightieth birthday, and seventy-two Habsburg relatives appeared in Bad Ischl to help him celebrate.

It had already been a busy summer. He had journeyed to Bosnia on a state visit, a visit which passed without incident, although he had alarmed his entourage by leaving the planned route and walking coolly among the crowds.

But to Frau Schratt he wrote on New Year's Eve that year:

I long for you deeply, I miss your dear company, and I have felt myself in these last days very lonely and abandoned.[10]

A little later he admitted:

I am very tired, and the weaknesses of age are taking a toll; my mood is sad and dull.[11]

He was determined, however, to keep peace at all costs. As Conrad von Hötzendorf and the prowar group around him continued to urge military force against Serbia, Franz Joseph finally lost patience:

My policy is that of peace. To this policy all must adjust themselves.[12]

Two weeks later Conrad was forced to resign from his post. A little later he had to be reinstated; nobody had been found to take his place.

6. Sarajevo

EUROPEANS LONG AFTERWARD recalled the summer of 1914 as one of uncanny beauty and blissful sunshine. Holidayers flocked to the mountains and seashore. In the smart watering places of Austria and Bohemia ladies in white dresses sipped their cups and listened to Strauss waltzes in pavilions set on velvety green lawns. "Even today," wrote Stefan Zweig, "when I use the word 'summer,' I think involuntarily of those radiant July days in Baden near Vienna. . . ."[1]

Franz Josef had suffered a chill at Eastertime during a visit of the German Kaiser; it turned into a bout of pneumonia, and he was laid up for weeks in his iron bed in the Hofburg. In May, however, he was again at his desk and resuming his little walks with Frau Schratt.

In early June his nephew, Franz Ferdinand, appeared, to remind the Emperor that he would be leaving soon for the army maneuvers in Bosnia, to which he had been invited in his new capacity of Inspector General of the Austro-Hungarian army. For a number of reasons he felt somewhat uneasy about the visit. It promised to be a very warm summer; he was a stout man and the heat bothered him excessively.

"Do as you please about it," the Emperor told him.

Franz Ferdinand was well aware that the journey was not without danger.

Ever since the annexation crisis of 1908, and even more actively since the Balkan War of 1913, a Serbian terrorist organization known as the Black Hand, inspired by the Russian anarchist methods of Bakunin and dedicated to achieving a Greater Serbia through violence, had been actively agitating in Bosnia against the Habsburg regime.

While Austrian officials probably did not know of the existence of the Black Hand, they knew that acts of terror had already been perpetrated in the provinces.

As far away as Chicago, the previous December of 1913, a Serbian newspaper proclaimed:

The Austrian throne heir has set his visit to Sarajevo for next spring. Every Serb should remember it. If the throne heir wants to go to Bosnia, we'll defray the costs. . . . Serbs, seize every weapon you can, knife, gun, bomb, dynamite. Take holy revenge! Death to the Habsburg dynasty.[2]

But Franz Ferdinand had told a friend not long before, "I won't live in a glass case. We are always in danger of death. One simply has to trust in God."[3] He and Sophie left for Bosnia on June 24.

He might have been more anxious had he known that the very day after his interview with Franz Josef, on June 5, the Serbian minister in Vienna, Jovan Jovanović, had passed along to the Austrian Minister of Finance a warning of a plot against the Archduke, which he had just received from Belgrade. But the warning was couched in vague terms, and Jovanović contented himself with suggesting that it might be best to cancel the maneuvers. The matter got no further.

The truth was that during the spring of 1914 members of the Black Hand had definitely settled on the murder of Franz Ferdinand.

The brain behind the conspiracy, which apparently had Russian support, was the chief of military intelligence for the Serbian army, Colonel Dragutin Dimitrijević, known as Apis, "The Bee." Apis was experienced both in plotting and in murder, for he had taken part in the palace revolution in Serbia in 1903, and had helped assassinate Serbia's then-reigning king and queen.

Franz Ferdinand was to die not merely because he was the Habsburg heir and therefore abhorred by Serbian nationalists, but because his plans to create an autonomous South Slav state within the Empire could very well pacify the Serbs living in the two provinces and thereby end Serbia's hope of absorbing Bosnia and Herzegovina.

The visit in Bosnia went very well indeed. Franz Ferdinand attended his army maneuvers, and Sophie paid official visits to schools, orphanages, and churches—a chore she performed to perfection.

On the last night of their stay, after a farewell banquet in Ilidže on June 27, Sophie turned to the Croat leader beside her to declare radiantly, "Dear Dr. Sunarić, you were wrong after all. . . . Everywhere we have gone here, we have been greeted with so much friendliness."[4]

The next day, a Sunday and their last day in Bosnia—it happened also to be St. Vitus' Day and a Serbian national holiday—they were to attend a reception given by the mayor of Sarajevo and a farewell luncheon at the governor's house. By evening they would be on a train for Vienna and a reunion with their children.

Security arrangements for the day were peculiarly haphazard. A few suspicious persons had been rounded up; a handful of police only were deployed at wide intervals along the official route.

At ten in the morning Sophie in a white dress and a huge feathered picture hat, Franz Ferdinand in his bemedaled uniform and conspicuous green-plumed field officer's hat, climbed into the open touring car that would take them to the City Hall. As the procession of official cars drove slowly along the broad Appel Kai, one of the conspirators, a young typesetter named Cabrinović, hurled a homemade bomb at the Archduke's car. The bomb hit the hood and ricocheted off into the street, where it wounded several bystanders and an aide of the Bosnian governor riding in the car behind.

Franz Ferdinand was unhurt, only extremely angry. At the City Hall he exploded, shouting to the mayor, "Mr. Mayor, one comes here for a visit and is received with bombs! It is outrageous!"[5]

He calmed down presently and asked if the bomb-thrower had been arrested. When assured that he was safely in custody, the Archduke growled, "They'll probably be Austrian about it and give him a medal of merit."[6]

The mayor had learned his speech by heart and he proceeded to deliver it, though by now the words struck a somewhat ironic note:

> All the citizens of Sarajevo find that their souls are filled with happiness and they most enthusiastically greet Your Highnesses' most illustrious visit with the most cordial welcome.[7]

Later, when Franz Ferdinand tried to persuade Sophie to leave the city at once with one of his aides, she replied firmly, "No, Franz, I am going with you."[8]

Someone suggested canceling the remainder of the day's program. At that the provincial governor, General Oskar Potiorek, cried huffily, "Do you think Sarajevo is full of assassins?"[9]

As a matter of fact it was.

Once again the whole party climbed into the motorcars. They would proceed by way of the hospital to visit the wounded aide, Franz

Ferdinand decided, then to the National Museum, and then on to lunch as the program prescribed. Their route, however, would be somewhat changed from the announced route, for safety's sake. By one of those unlucky accidents that can change history's course, nobody remembered to alert the chauffeur of the car in which the archducal pair were riding, and instead of proceeding straight down Appel Kai, he turned right onto Franz Josef Street, as the earlier program had announced. The governor leaned forward and ordered him to stop and turn; the chauffeur braked the car, slowly backed it up, and brought it directly in front of one of the assassins, Gavrilo Princip, who had only to draw his pistol and fire point-blank at five feet away. It was perhaps the easiest assassination in history.

Neither Franz Ferdinand nor Sophie uttered a sound; both continued to sit bolt upright in the back seat, so that for a few moments nobody knew that either was wounded. Only when the frightened chauffeur stepped on the gas and the car lurched forward, a stream of blood spurted out of the Archduke's mouth. Sophie cried, "For heaven's sake! What happened to you?" At the same moment she collapsed across her husband's knees. One of the bullets had passed through her abdomen.

Franz Ferdinand cried out, "Sopherl! Sopherl! Don't die! Stay alive for the children!" His plumed hat had fallen off, and now as his aide tried to prop him upright he slumped over his wife's body, murmuring only one last phrase of well-bred politeness, *"Es ist nichts."*[10]

Franz Josef made no pretense of grief when the news of the double murder was brought him. He was silent for a moment, and then he murmured, as if to himself, "Horrible! The Almighty does not allow himself to be challenged. . . . A higher power has restored the order which I unhappily could not maintain. . . ." His daughter wrote in her diary that the event was *eine Aufregung*—an upsetting—for Papa.[11]

A little later, at Schönbrunn, a witness appeared to describe the exact manner of the deaths to the Emperor.

"And how did the Archduke bear himself?" Franz Josef asked in a low voice.

"Like a soldier, Your Majesty."

The Emperor nodded. "That was to be expected from His Imperial Highness."

There was a pause. It was broken by the Emperor in his normal voice. "And how were the maneuvers?" he asked.[12]

Within a month the chain reaction had begun. The long series of intricate treaties among European powers, the long piling of armaments, the unresolved hostilities, the revenge *motifs*—going back who knows how far in time—all had begun to interact beyond anyone's control, certainly beyond the control of the eighty-four-year-old monarch in the Hofburg.

Conrad von Hötzendorf and his war party had won the day. Austria-Hungary submitted an ultimatum to Serbia. Serbia rejected the ultimatum. Russia mobilized to support Serbia, Germany to support Austria, France to support Russia, England to support France. Gestures toward conciliation were offered—and brushed aside.

On the evening of July 25 the news was brought to Franz Josef in his villa in Bad Ischl that the Serbian reply to the ultimatum was not satisfactory and that diplomatic relations were now broken off. The Emperor stared at the young adjutant who brought the message; then he muttered, his voice so choked the words could barely be heard: "*Also doch!*"—So, then . . . in spite of everything . . .

The adjutant handed him the paper on which the message had been scrawled. Franz Josef took it, looked long at it, read it through again, and said as if he were talking to himself, "Well, breaking off diplomatic relations doesn't always mean war." And as if this thought gave him new hope, the old hands holding the paper shook a little bit less.[13]

7. *Death of an Emperor*

AFTER A TIME he did not leave Schönbrunn at all any more. He lived only for the dispatches that came each day from his ministers in the Ballhaus, with news from the war fronts, the enormous fronts that stretched from Poland across the Carpathians, into Rumania, southeastward deep in Serbia and Montenegro, and across the Italian Alps.

There were no more great family dinners at which the whole Habsburg clan gathered around the long banquet table. One ate black bread now, with the rest of Vienna.

The new throne heir, his grand-nephew Karl, paid official visits to the front in the Emperor's name. Franz Josef liked and approved of Karl. "I value Karl very highly. He speaks his mind frankly. But he also understands how to obey when I stick to my view."[1] Karl's wife, Princess Zita, and their children moved into the east wing of Schönbrunn. Sometimes too a pair of Franz Josef's great-grandchildren—his daughter, Marie Valerie, already had married children—came to play with their dolls in *Uropapa's* study, and it cheered the old man to hear their chatter.

For the most part he had drawn far away from the smaller affairs of the world. Marie Valerie wrote in her diary:

> It seems to me more and more as if a kind of veil lay between him and the outer world—a kind of deep weariness that gives way only where questions of great moment are concerned.[2]

In 1916 Franz Josef passed his eighty-sixth birthday.

There was that autumn in Vienna a feeling of exhaustion, of impending disaster in the air. The war was not yet going badly for the Central Powers. In the East the Russians had been driven far back. The German-Austrian armies were overrunning Rumania; Serbia was invaded and part of Montenegro. In the south they held the Italians back along the Isonzo and in the Dolomites.

But the Austrians had suffered appalling losses—450,000 men in the campaign in the north in June and July alone. The number of deserters in that polyglot army—especially Czechs, Italians, Ruthenians—had risen markedly.

The specter of war and famine haunted the city. The harvest that year had yielded only half the normal supply of grain; it was the Austrian half of the Empire that felt the pangs of hunger first. There was neither flour nor milk, nor potatoes, nor coal. Women stood in long queues before empty bakeries and food shops. The German ambassador in Vienna complained to Berlin in September of 1916 that attempts to make Austria-Hungary organize "after our example" broke down over their hopelessly dilatory habit of *fortwursteln*—blundering along.

One day there were food riots; shops were plundered; an angry crowd marched on Schönbrunn. The iron gates were locked and the guard doubled; the park that had always been open was closed to the public.

And then on October 21 the Minister President, Count Karl von Stürghk, was assassinated in broad daylight in a restaurant a stone's throw from the Hofburg. The murder was committed by a prominent socialist, Viktor Adler, in an effort to dramatize public need and to force a recall of Parliament.

A little later, in the early days of November, the old Emperor began to cough. Although he was feverish and in pain, he continued to work at his desk in Schönbrunn. It was true that he had no time to be ill.

The new Minister President, Ernest von Koerber, came to Schönbrunn to report to the Emperor on the grievous condition of the country.

Franz Josef's valet overheard the old Emperor reply, "If that is the case, then we must make peace—without taking my ally into consideration at all!"[3]

On November 19, the name day of the dead Empress, Katharina Schratt came to visit Franz Josef. They talked gently, as old people do, of the past and of the Radiant One.[4]

The next day his fever rose and fell and rose again.

His anxious confessor brought him communion and a special blessing from the Holy Father in Rome. His daughter, Marie Valerie, moved to Schönbrunn to be near her father.

A little after lunch on November 21 Dr. Kerzl found the Emperor sunk down in his armchair by his desk, his fever alarmingly high. But the stubborn old man resisted all efforts to put him to bed; he was still in the habit of giving the orders. He rested a bit in his chair, then returned to his papers.

His adjutant, Colonel Spányik, watched him through a mirror in the next room; he saw the Emperor rest his head first on one arm, then on the other, until at last the pen fell from his hand and he drifted into sleep. At four in the afternoon he awoke, pulled himself together, had his valet pick up the pen and put it in his hand again. He worked on. When he had signed the last paper in the pile, he straightened everything neatly, shut his portfolio.

He ate a little supper; when Marie Valerie tiptoed in, he told her that he felt better. She kissed her father's fever-hot hand and bade him good night.

Now the two doctors insisted that the sick man be put to bed. Two servants carried him, still in his armchair, to the prie-dieu by the bed. Franz Josef tried to kneel as his mother had taught him to do every morning and night, but he was too weak. *"Es geht nicht,"* he murmured. He said his prayers sitting in the armchair before the prie-dieu.

His valet, Ketterl, said, "Majesty, now it is time to lie down." "I still have work to do." But the protest was faint; he let his servants undress him. His doctors helped him into bed, and Ketterl asked as he did each night, "Has His Majesty any commands?"

Franz Josef replied as always, "Wake me tomorrow at half past three."

Slowly the chamber filled with people: his grandnephew, Karl, heir to the throne since Sarajevo; archdukes, archduchesses, councilors, ministers, aides, body servants. Everyone in the palace knew that the last hours of their sovereign were at hand.

"Too many people," murmured Marie Valerie when she entered the filled room.

The old monarch awoke and asked for something to drink; his valet raised the pillow and gave him a sip of tea. He fell again into a deep sleep.

At half past eight the palace priest came to administer the last rites. Marie Valerie held to her father's lips the ancient Habsburg crucifix that had consoled so many emperors in their last hours.

"My Jesus, mercy!" she prayed, and she put the cross into her father's hand and closed it within her own.

The Holy Office was ended. The old man's breathing became shorter, softer.

All the watchers in the room knelt; an unmeasurable span of time passed slowly by. In the room there was stillness, as in a chapel.

Suddenly a fit of coughing shook the body of the dying man. He half raised himself, sank back again.

"Is he breathing still?" his daughter whispered anxiously. The doctor leaned over and listened to the heart. "I can hear nothing more," he answered in a choked voice.

"*Et lux perpetua luceat ei!*" murmured the priest.

"Shut his eyes," someone prompted his daughter, and with a trembling hand Marie Valerie performed the last service. It was five minutes after nine in the evening of November 21, 1916.[4]

In Katharina Schratt's home the telephone jangled—that senseless instrument the Emperor had so despised. It was his court chamberlain, Prince Montenuovo, who gave her the sorrowful tidings.

She hurried to Schönbrunn. The room where the dead man lay was filled with important people, and for some time no one noticed where she stood quietly by the door. Then the new young Emperor Karl led her to the bed, and she laid her two white roses on the dead man's breast.

XVI

Curtain Fall for the Habsburgs

HOUR AFTER HOUR, patient, silent, two long queues of people waited outside the Hofburg gates in the cold, shuffling slowly forward until they were admitted to the palace precinct, to the chapel, and finally past the bier where the body of Franz Josef lay in his white and scarlet field marshal's uniform, in a forest of burning candles.

Many wore mourning for their own dead, for the dead of Lemberg, of Lutsk, of the San, of the interminable battles of the Isonzo, and the Karst, for men who lay dead in the Carpathians, in Galicia, in Montenegro, and on the frozen heights of the Dolomites.

The Viennese slowly filing into the palace were grieving less perhaps for this ancient Habsburg, who had lived so long like an old and precious relic shut up in his gilt-and-glass case of Schönbrunn, than for themselves, for a sunny, irretrievable world they had once known and would never know again.

Behind the funeral carriage drawn by eight black horses on November 30, 1916, a frail young man in a general's long coat led the walking mourners: the new Emperor Karl. Beside him, heavily veiled, his wife, Zita, a princess of the house of Bourbon-Parma; and between them their child, Otto, the new heir apparent—though to what no one could quite say—a dark-eyed, golden-haired four-year-old, almost illusory in his starched and princely perfection, glancing curiously at the crowds lining either curb.

At the grilled iron gate of the Kapuziner Crypt the ancient baroque funeral rite was performed one last time. The Lord Chamberlain, Prince Montenuovo, knocked with his golden staff, and a voice within demanded:

"Who knocks?"

"His Apostolic Majesty, our late Emperor."

"I know him not."

Again the golden staff rapped three times on the barred gate, while the mourners waited in a hushed cluster around the coffin. Again the voice.

"Who knocks?"

"The sovereign of Austria-Hungary."

"Him I know not."

And a last time the knocks sounded in the wintry stillness, and a last time the same query. This time the answer:

"Your brother, Franz Josef, whose sins were as many as hairs on his head."[1]

The door was opened and the coffin was borne into the shadowy crypt to join the great reunion of ancestors.

Ein guter Bursch—a good boy—his great-uncle Franz Josef had called young Karl, the inheritor, who found himself now, in the bleak winter of 1916 to 1917, holding the Pandora's box of family heirlooms that threatened to explode any moment in the heart of Europe.

Son of that proficient sower of wild oats, Archduke Otto, younger brother of Franz Ferdinand, Karl had been born in the year 1887, sufficiently far removed from the throne to be at first merely another junior archduke. But the death of his cousin Rudolf at Mayerling, the morganatic marriage of Franz Ferdinand, and the consequent barring of his children from the succession suddenly brought Karl to the heirship.

Had he been born in another age, in a time of peace and an era of kings, he would have been a very nice emperor indeed: gentle, kind, earnest, almost pathetically eager to do the right thing. A touch of the scholar, a touch of the saint: too frail, however, for the insufferable burden that now fell to him.

Even before his uncle's death, peace overtures had been begun by the Central Powers, Germany and Austria-Hungary, but the German tone had been highhanded, the terms were unspecific, and they were immediately rejected. The military situation at the moment was far from unfavorable for the Central Powers. The great fronts were holding, Rumania had fallen, Russia was about to bow out. Yet there were impelling reasons for Austria-Hungary to sue for peace, as Karl was fully aware.

In the early spring of 1917 Karl plunged into a conspiracy to make peace that became known in subsequent history as the Sixtus affair. Without the knowledge of his German allies, Karl began secret peace overtures with France, using as his instrument his wife's two brothers, the Princes Sixtus and Xavier of Bourbon-Parma, French citizens and officers in the Belgian army. To Karl's urgent invitation to come to Vienna, their sister added her plea: "Think of the men in the living hell of the trenches—hundreds of them killed every day—and come!"[2]

Smuggled into Austria from Switzerland, the two brothers appeared at the palace of Laxenburg in March. They had cleared their mission with the French government, had talked with President Poincaré and Prime Minister Briand, and brought with them France's basic demands.

In the chilly salon of Laxenburg on that March afternoon the brothers, their sister, and the new Emperor talked. Count Ottokar von Czernin, the Austrian Minister of Foreign Affairs—"tall, thin, and cold," Sixtus described him later—made an appearance. No solid agreement was reached, but a door was open for future negotiations, and Sixtus did in fact return to Austria in May. What Karl did, with or without Czernin's knowledge, was to give his brother-in-law a letter to take back to France, affirming his agreement in principle to French demands, including a promise to support their claim to Alsace-Lorraine.

"Peace absolutely must be concluded," he declared firmly. "I will have peace at any price."[3]

Karl was to attempt to persuade his German allies to agree to the terms, but if they refused, he would make a separate peace.

Tragically—both for Austria-Hungary and for the world—the peace maneuvers of 1917 foundered. Italy, which had changed sides and gone over to the Entente, demanded both Trieste and the Trentino as a plum. Karl refused to consider the surrender of his territory, especially of Trieste, which had been the Empire's seaport for centuries. The French government meantime changed hands, and the new ministers under Ribot, then Clémenceau, were less amenable to talking peace. So were the Germans, who had begun U-boat warfare. The United States entered the war; the Russians departed. The eastern front was relieved, and hungry Austria hoped for food from the Ukraine.

Now came the unsavory conclusion of the Sixtus affair. In an hour of incredible indiscretion the Foreign Minister, Count Czernin, bragged publicly that the French had initiated peace gestures and been turned down over Alsace-Lorraine. The new French premier, Clémenceau the Tiger, leapt to the defense of the truth and what he conceived to be his country's honor, revealing in the French press that the Austrian

Emperor himself had begun negotiations the previous spring, and had assented to the return of Alsace-Lorraine.

Now the fat was in the fire, and Austria-Hungary's German allies—just engaged in the *Kaiserschlacht,* the great western offensive of 1918 that was to win the war—demanded angrily to know if they had been betrayed by their partner.

Had Emperor Karl been utterly nerveless, of tougher fiber, he might have shouldered his way through the terrible dilemma in which a man of honor found himself. Czernin—who had created the dilemma—believed that Austria's only hope lay in German victory, and pressured Karl to deny the French claims of a "peace conspiracy." Arriving in Baden where the Habsburgs were staying, Czernin found Karl at the end of his rope, lying on a divan, compresses on his bursting head. Karl signed a bombastic telegram to Kaiser Wilhelm denying the peace moves: "Our answer is being given by my cannon in the west."[4]

Clémenceau published the text of Karl's letter to Sixtus, and the Emperor of Austria-Hungary stood revealed to the world as a liar.

From the beginning of 1918, things moved quickly toward un-mitigated disaster for the Danubian monarchy. The winter had been a severe one, and the food crisis had grown steadily worse. Nearly all available food was going to the army, the rationing system had broken down, black-marketing was widespread. A part of the Austrian navy mutinied; mutiny spread in the army. Presently mass strikes were halting the production of factories.

Parliament had been prorogued since 1914; Karl had recalled it in May of 1917, but it was far too late. Instead of meeting to solve the terrible problems in the land, Parliament broke down in the wildest disorder. Delegates of minority groups raised claims and counter-claims, shouted one another down, hurled inkpots and briefcases through the air of the stately marble hall.

On October 6, 1918, Karl published a manifesto setting up a federal state with complete self-government for the subject nationalities—a United States of Greater Austria, such as Franz Ferdinand had en-visioned. It was months and years too late. Hungary refused to have any part in it. Indeed, it was after the fact, for in Rome in April of 1918 a Congress of Oppressed Nationalities of Austria-Hungary had met and effectively concluded a dismemberment of the monarchy.

Mass desertions from the army crippled the fighting forces. Czecho-slovakia broke away, a new Yugoslavia was formed; Hungary too would presently announce complete independence. The trunk of Austria, all limbs amputated, an economic basket case, struggled to find a way to survive.

The Social Democrats gained control of the government; in the end they saved the life of the nearly mortally wounded patient.

In the early days of November, 1918, socialist leaders pressed for the abdication of the Emperor. Workers threatened to march on Schönbrunn, and Karl's remaining friends begged him to flee to a safe exile. On November 11 he signed—in pencil—a provisional abdication, promising to take no further part in affairs of state. That night, after darkness had closed in, two hired motorcars took Karl, Zita, and the children to their hunting castle of Eckartsau in the Marchfeld.

During that winter of 1918 to 1919, a terrible winter to the war losers, perhaps the bitterest in Austrian history, hundreds in Vienna died of hunger, of cold, and of Spanish influenza.

Karl too sickened of influenza and was slow to recover. Rare visitors found him huddled in an armchair, shivering under his wrapping of blankets. At Christmastime he was too weak to leave his chair, and it was wheeled into the room where the Christmas tree had been set up for the children. From the windows of the castle of Eckartsau he could look out over the plain of the Marchfeld where his ancestor, the first Rudolf, had fought King Ottokar and laid the foundation of Habsburg power. It might have seemed a kind of poetic justice that his family, which had risen out of the Terrible Times of the thirteenth century, now went down in the Terrible Times of the twentieth.

Presently all Habsburgs who refused the oath of allegiance to the new republican government were pronounced banished. Karl and his family moved on to Switzerland.

His exit was well mannered, temperate, and sad.

The Austrian revolution had been a mild one, without the eruption of fierce violence and horror that marked cataclysmic changes just then in Russia, in Germany. Now when Karl left his country by train, a cluster of loyal followers waved him good-bye from the station. He had done his level best to spare his countrymen further bloodshed.

Unwisely Karl and Zita tried to regain the Hungarian crown from their Swiss retreat, once in the spring and again in the autumn of 1921. Interned as peacebreakers, they were taken on board a British frigate and brought to the island of Madeira, where their children—seven now, with an eighth on the way—came to join them.

Pale, thin, prematurely gray, the ex-sovereign had no hope left, and only a very little cash. Faced with hotel bills he could not pay, he moved his family that winter up to a borrowed villa in the mountains, chilly, damp, uncomfortably crowded. Here he coughed his way through the last winter and succumbed to another bout of pneumonia in the spring. It was perhaps time to die.

Notes and Bibliography

Notes

HABSBURG NAMES

ALTHOUGH THE GERMAN or Austrian spelling of family names has usually been used, certain names, such as that of Charles VI, appear in the Anglicized form, because that form is so much more familiar to English readers. In some cases, where the same name appears in two or three or four individuals in the same generation, I have varied the spelling slightly to help the reader make a distinction.

A NOTE ON OLD CURRENCIES

Economists tell me it is impossible to establish today's monetary value of old currencies with any degree of accuracy. The following notes may be helpful to the general reader.

1 Austrian florin=1 gulden=60 kreutzer=$.50
1 gold ducat=4½ gulden=$2.25

One must multiply by at least 10, however, to secure a rough equivalent of sixteenth-, seventeenth-, or eighteenth-century sums in today's currency.

Some idea of the cost of living essentials can be gained from the quotation one of the Fugger correspondents gives of market prices in Vienna in 1594:

> 4 kreutzer for a small loaf of bread
> 2 kreutzer for a pound of meat
> 10 kreutzer for a bottle of old wine
> 5 kreutzer for a pound of candles
> 19 florin for a cord of wood

I. HABSBURG ANCESTOR

1. The name of the Habsburgs derived from their ancestral castle, the Habichtsburg or Hawk's Castle, lying in the Aargau near the River Aar in present-day Switzerland. The family's holdings in the time of the first Rudolf lay chiefly in Alsace and Swabia.

2. Matthias von Neuenberg, *Chronik*, quoted in Otto Frass (ed.), *Quellenbuch zur Österreichische Geschichte*, 2 vols. (Vienna, Birken-Verlag, 1956), I, p. 125.

3. Ibid.

4. Louis Leger, *History of Austro-Hungary* (London, Rivingtons, 1889), p. 109. The event may well be legendary.

5. Wilhelm Knappich, *Die Habsburger Chronik* (Salzburg, Verlag "Das Bergland-Buch," 1959), p. 20.

6. Ibid.

7. Ibid., p. 27.

8. Adam Wandruszka, *The House of Habsburg*, trans. by Cathleen and Hans Epstein (Garden City, N.Y., Doubleday & Co., 1964), pp. 35–36.

9. The crown of the Holy Roman Empire, together with the insignia and regalia of the Empire, is kept today in the Treasury of the Hofburg in Vienna. Scholars believe the crown was crafted in a German goldsmith's workshop for the coronation of Otto the Great in Rome in the year 962. The so-called Stone of Wisdom vanished from the brow plate sometime during the fourteenth century.

10. James Bryce, *The Holy Roman Empire*, 4th ed. (London, Macmillan & Co., 1904), footnote p. 263. The title of "Majesty" was officially conceded to the kings of England and of Sweden only in 1633, and to the king of France in 1641.

11. Karl Brandi, *Emperor Charles V*, trans. by C. V. Wedgwood (London, Jonathan Cape, 1939), p. 123.

II. HABSBURGS IN THE MARRIAGE MARKET: MAXIMILIAN I

1. The Wedding in Burgundy

1. Jean Molinet, *Chroniques*, 5 vols. (Paris, Verdière Libraire, 1827), LXXXV, p. 302.

2. Heinrich Fichtenau, *Der Junge Maximilian (1459–1482)* (Vienna, Verlag für Geschichte und Politik, 1959), pp. 11ff.

3. Frass, I, p. 201. The motto is also interpreted: *Alles Erdreich Ist Österreich Untertan* (the whole world is subject to Austria).

4. Fichtenau, pp. 13ff.

5. The lands of the dukes of Burgundy in the fifteenth century comprised the larger part of present-day Belgium, Netherlands, Luxembourg, together with a large portion of northern and northeastern France. The core of their holdings was the original duchy of Burgundy (Bourgogne), a

[34] Baroness Mary Vetsera. *(Bildarchiv des Österreichische Nationalbibliothek, Vienna)*

[35] Emperor Franz Josef in the last years of his life. *(Bildarchiv des Öster-reichische Nationalbibliothek, Vienna)*

[36] Karl I, the last Habsburg monarch, painted in 1917 by Viktor Krause.
(Bildarchiv des Österreichische Nationalbibliothek, Vienna)

[37] Funeral of Franz Josef, November, 1916. In the foreground are Emperor Karl, Empress Zita, and the four-year-old Crown Prince Otto. (*Bildarchiv des Österreichische Nationalbibliothek, Vienna*)

fief of the French king, and the county of Burgundy (Franche-Comté), a fief of the Holy Roman Emperor, to which had been added by marriage, inheritance, and conquest the counties of Flanders, Artois, Picardy, Hainault, Brabant, Gueldre, Holland, Luxembourg. It was the ambition of Charles the Bold to unite the southern portion of his lands, Bourgogne and the Franche-Comté, with the northern complex—the so-called *pays-de-par-deça* or "nether-lands"—by conquering Lorraine that led to his downfall.

6. Luc Hommel, *Marie de Bourgogne ou Le Grand Héritage* (Brussels, A. Goemaere, 1945), pp. 176–9. Eyewitness accounts of the Trier meeting are to be found in Joseph Chmel (ed.), *Actenstücke und Briefe zur Geschichte des Hauses Habsburg im Zeitalter Maximilian's I*, Part I of *Monumenta Habsburgica, Sammlung von Actenstücken und Briefen zur Geschichte des Hauses Habsburg in dem Zeiträume von 1473 bis 1576*, 4 vols. (Vienna, Aus der Kaiserlich-Königlichen Hof- und Staatsdruckerei, 1853–58), I–1, pp. 57ff.

7. Fichtenau, p. 28.

8. Hommel, pp. 286ff.

9. Karl Rausch, *Die Burgundische Heirat Maximilians I* (Vienna, Verlag von Carl Konegen, 1880), pp. 165ff. Also Chmel, I–1, p. 142, No. 39; p. 468, No. 177.

10. Chmel, I–1, p. 140, No. 37.

11. Ibid., p. 141, No. 38.

12. Ibid., p. 147, No. 42.

13. Hommel, p. 296.

14. Ibid., p. 299.

15. Olivier de La Marche, *Mémoires*, 4 vols. (Paris, Librairie Renouard, 1883–88), III, footnote p. 245.

16. Rausch, pp. 166ff.

17. Ibid., pp. 175ff.

18. Victor von Kraus (ed.), *Maximilians I. Vertraulicher Briefwechsel mit Sigmund Prüschenk, Freiherrn zu Stettenberg* (Innsbruck, Verlag der Wagner'schen Universitäts-Buchhandlung, 1875), p. 25.

19. De La Marche, biographical note preceding Vol. I, p. lxx.

20. Chmel, I–1, p. 157, No. 48.

21. Hommel, p. 307.

22. Ibid.

23. Rausch, pp. 177ff. Hommel, p. 308.

24. Rausch, pp. 161ff.

25. Chmel, I–1, pp. 159ff., No. 49.

26. Molinet, XLIV, p. 98.

2. *The Dowry*

1. Kraus, p. 28.

2. Chmel, I–1, p. 161, No. 49.

3. Philippe de Commynes, *Mémoires*, 3 vols. (Paris, Jules Renouard, 1840–47), II, p. 183.

4. Kraus, pp. 28, 31ff.

5. Ibid., p. 28

6. Hommel, p. 129.

7. *Flanders in the Fifteenth Century: Art and Civilization—Catalogue of Exhibition of Masterpieces of Flemish Art.* (Detroit, Michigan, Detroit Institute of Arts, and Brussels, Belgium, Centre National de Recherches Primitifs Flamands, published jointly, 1960), p. 322.

8. The agate bowl and the unicorn sword of Charles the Bold can be seen today in the Treasury of the Hofburg in Vienna.

9. Kraus, p. 28.

10. Ibid., p. 35.

11. Ibid., p. 27.

12. Ibid., p. 39.

13. Hommel, p. 114.

14. Kraus, p. 35.

15. For details on the early history of the order, see [Henri Marie Bruno] Baron Kervyn de Lettenhove, *La Toison d'Or* (Brussels, Librairie Nationale d'Art et d'Histoire, 1907).

Originally the name of the order was presumed to have come from the golden fleece of Jason and his Argonauts, but since Jason's virtue and integrity were both open to question, the symbolism was shifted to the Biblical Gideon. When the order was founded by Marie's grandfather, Philip the Good, on his wedding day in 1430, certain acid critics also interpreted the symbolism in the light of Philip's well-known amatory achievements, declaring that the twenty-four golden links represented Philip's twenty-four mistresses, and the fleece the beautiful golden hair of his favorite, Marie van Crombrughe.

16. Marian Andrews (pseud.: Christopher Hare), *Maximilian the Dreamer* (London, Stanley Paul & Co., 1913), p. 53.

17. Hommel, p. 337.

18. Glenn Elwood Waas, *The Legendary Character of Kaiser Maximilian*, No. 14, Columbia University Germanic Studies (New York, Columbia University Press, 1941), pp. 156ff.

3. Troubles and Glory

1. Jane de Iongh, *Margaret of Austria,* trans. by M. D. Herter Norton (New York, W. W. Norton & Co., 1953), p. 62.

2. In order to avoid the hazard of an interregnum, a custom had grown up during the Middle Ages of securing the election and coronation (at Aachen) of a successor during the lifetime of the Emperor. The heir apparent took the title "King of the Romans" until the death of the Emperor, when he acceded without further ceremony to the imperial crown. (Cf. Bryce, pp. 472ff.)

3. Molinet, XLV, p. 7.

4. Ibid., XLV, pp. 33–34.

5. Waas, p. 128.

4. Brides Lost and Won

1. Arthur May, *The Habsburg Monarchy, 1867–1914* (Cambridge, Mass., Harvard University Press, 1951), p. 6.

2. Frass, I, p. 259.

3. Traditionally the Holy Roman Emperor held his title only after coronation by the Pope in Rome. Friedrich III was, however, the last emperor to be so crowned. The Venetians refused to permit Maximilian to cross their territory in order to reach Rome, so he remained officially uncrowned. The Pope granted him the right to use the title "Emperor-Elect." Charles V was crowned by the Pope at Bologna, but his brother, Ferdinand I, who succeeded him, was never crowned by the Pope, who disputed his right, and from this time on the title "Emperor" was assumed after the Frankfurt coronation, on the death of the preceding emperor.

4. Michel Dugast Rouillé, Hubert Cuny and Hervé Pinoteau, *Les Grands Mariages des Habsbourgs* (Paris, G. Saffroy, 1955), pp. 31–32.

5. Julia Cartwright, *Beatrice d'Este* (New York, E. P. Dutton & Co., 1928), pp. 209ff. Also Anneliese Gatt, "Der Innsbrucker Hof zur Zeit Kaiser Maximilians I, 1493–1519" (unpublished doctoral dissertation, Leopold-Franzens Universität zu Innsbruck, 1943), pp. 78ff.

6. Cartwright, p. 219.

7. Waas, p. 61.

8. Andrews, p. 95. Kraus, p. 103.

9. Gatt, pp. 149ff.

10. Ibid.

5. Kaiser Max: His Image

1. Glenn Elwood Waas, in *The Legendary Character of Kaiser Maximilian*, already cited, studies in detail the legendary material that grew up around the Emperor during the century immediately following his death.

2. Friedrich Nüchter, *Albrecht Dürer*, trans. by Lucy D. Williams (Ansbach, Fr. Seybold, 1911), p. 22.

3. Molinet, XLV, pp. 76ff.

4. Karl Eduard Vehse, *Memoirs of the Court and Aristocracy of Austria*, trans. by Franz Demmler, 2 vols. (London, H. S. Nichols, 1896), I, p. 9.

5. Ibid., I, pp. 9ff. Also Knappich, p. 94.

6. Wilhelm Bauer (ed.), *Die Korrespondenz Ferdinands I* (Vienna, Adolf Holzhausen, 1912), p. 70.

7. Kraus, p. 48.

8. Vehse, I, p. 15.

9. Waas, p. 80.

6. The Spanish Marriage

1. Luc Hommel, *Marguerite d'York ou La Duchesse Junon* (Paris, Librairie Hachette, 1959), p. 289.

2. Ibid., p. 233.

3. Ibid., p. 235.

4. Ibid., p. 289.

5. Brouwer, J[ohannes], *Johanna de Waanzinnige, een tragisch leven in een bewogen tijd* (Amsterdam, J. M. Meulenhoff, 1949), p. 17.

6. De Iongh, p. 94.

7. Gertrude von Schwarzenfeld, *Charles V, Father of Europe,* trans. by Ruth Mary Bethell (London, Hollis & Carter, 1957), p. 129.

8. Brouwer, p. 40.

9. Schwarzenfeld, p. 133.

10. Brouwer, p. 41. Hommel, *Marguerite d'York,* p. 290.

11. Schwarzenfeld, p. 135.

12. Harry Tighe, *A Queen of Unrest. The Story of Juana of Castile* (London, Swan Sonnenschein, 1905), p. 199.

13. Schwarzenfeld, p. 137.

14. Tighe, p. 199.

15. Juana's most recent biographer, Johannes Brouwer, believes it "likely" that Philip was poisoned by his father-in-law, King Ferdinand, who would have benefited—in fact did benefit—greatly by his death. No proof is possible, adds this historian, and of course it remains possible that his death was due to natural causes.

16. William H. Prescott, *History of the Reign of Ferdinand and Isabella the Catholic,* 3 vols. (Philadelphia, J. B. Lippincott Co., 1870), III, p. 268.

17. Vehse, I, p. 35.

7. The Children of Malines

1. M. Le Glay (ed.), *Correspondance de l'Empereur Maximilien Ier et Marguerite d'Autriche Sa Fille, de 1507 à 1519,* 2 vols. (Paris, Jules Renouard, 1839), II, p. 380.

2. Ibid., I, p. 177.

3. Ibid., I, p. 293.

4. Ibid., I, p. 367.

5. Ibid., I, p. 383.

6. Ibid., II, p. 48.

7. Ibid., II, p. 37.

8. Waas, p. 139.

9. Le Glay, II, p. 257.

10. Troels Frederik Troels-Lund, *Dagligt liv i Norden i det sekstende aarhundrede,* 13 vols. (Kobenhavn, Gyldendal, 1908), IV, p. 167.

11. Jane de Iongh, *Mary of Hungary, Second Regent of the Netherlands,* trans. by M. C. Herter Norton (New York, W. W. Norton & Co., 1958), p. 35.

12. Le Glay, II, footnote p. 336.

13. Ibid.

14. De Iongh, *Mary of Hungary,* p. 28.

15. Leon Schick, *Jacob Fugger, Un Grand Homme d'Affaires au début du XVIᵉ Siècle* (Paris, S.E.V.P.E.N., 1957), p. 111.

16. Hans Ankwicz-Kleehoven, *Der Wiener Humanist Johannes Cuspinian* (Graz-Köln, Hermann Böhlaus Nachf., 1959), pp. 83ff.

17. Le Glay, II, p. 301.

18. Ibid., II, p. 300.

8. Dürer's Last Portrait

1. Great Britain, Public Record Office, *Calendar of State Papers and Manuscripts Relating to English Affairs Existing in the Archives and Collections of Venice and in other Libraries of Northern Italy*, ed. by Rawdon Brown (London, Longmans, Green, Reader & Dyer, 1867), II, p. 388. The *Calendar of State Papers . . . of Venice* is abbreviated in subsequent entries: *C.S.P.V.*

2. Schick, pp. 153ff.

3. Le Glay, II, p. 414.

III. THE ONE WORLD OF CHARLES V

1. Heir to the World

1. The famous Habsburg lip, which came to be an enduring family trait and appeared in members as late as the nineteenth century, undoubtedly stemmed from the marriage of Maximilian and Marie of Burgundy. As can be readily seen in his profile portraits, Maximilian already had a jutting prognathous jaw, while portraits of Marie's father, Charles the Bold, show a decidedly full lower lip. Tradition has it that Maximilian's jaw stemmed from his paternal grandmother, Cymburga of Masowia.

According to the chronicler Brantôme, Charles's sister Eleanor visited the tombs of the Burgundian dukes in the Carthusian monastery at Dijon and had the curiosity to have the tombs opened. Several of the bodies were well preserved, and on their faces Eleanor was delighted to see the advancing form of underjaw and lip. "Ha," exclaimed Eleanor, "I always thought our mouths were derived from those of Austria, but I now perceive them to be inherited from Mary of Burgundy and her progenitors." Quoted in William Bradford (ed.), *Correspondence of the Emperor Charles V and His Ambassadors at the Courts of England and France . . . With a Connecting Narrative and Biographical Notices of the Emperor . . .* (London, Richard Bentley, 1850), footnote p. 343.

Despite Eleanor's observation, however, the likelihood remains that the jaw came from the Habsburg side of the family, the prominent lower lip from the Burgundian ancestry.

2. Royall Tyler, *The Emperor Charles the Fifth* (Fair Lawn, N.J., Essential Books, 1956), p. 290.

3. Joseph Chmel (ed.), *Urkunden, Briefe und Actenstücke zur Geschichte Maximilians I und seiner Zeit* (Stuttgart, Bibliothek des Literarischen Vereins, 1845), p. 261.

4. Great Britain, Public Record Office, *Letters and Papers Foreign and Domestic of the Reign of Henry VIII*, ed. by J. S. Brewer (London, Longmans, Green, Reader & Dyer, 1867), I, p. 363, Nos. 3248, 3271. *Letters and Papers Foreign and Domestic* is abbreviated in subsequent entries: *L.P.F.D.*

5. Le Glay, I, p. 241.

6. Vital's complete journal of the voyage is given in Gachard et Piot (eds.), *Collection des Voyages des Souveraines des Pays-Bas* (Brussels, F. Hayez, 1881), pp. 1ff.

7. Ibid., p. 58.

8. Brandi, p. 171.

2. *Family Matters*

1. Ibid., p. 79.

2. Brouwer, p. 109.

3. Gachard et Piot, p. 135.

4. Ibid., p. 136.

5. Hommel, *Marguerite d'York*, p. 290.

6. Gachard et Piot, p. 140.

7. Ibid., pp. 237ff., for account of Catherina's rescue.

8. Bauer, p. 40.

9. Gachard et Piot, p. 146.

10. Bauer, p. 7.

11. Gachard et Piot, p. 147.

12. Ghislaine de Boom, *Les Voyages de Charles-Quint* (Brussels, Office de Publicité, 1957), p. 38.

13. Gachard et Piot, p. 270.

3. *A Momentous Election*

1. *C.S.P.V.*, II, p. 504.

2. Schick, p. 168.

3. Ibid., p. 167.

4. Ibid., p. 168.

5. Ibid., p. 172.

6. Ibid., p. 168.

7. Ibid., p. 173.

8. *C.S.P.V.*, II, p. 503.

9. Ibid., p. 514.

10. Ibid., p. 519.

11. Bauer, p. 11.

12. *C.S.P.V.*, II, p. 531.

13. Ibid., p. 514.

14. *L.P.F.D.*, III, Pt. 1, p. 115, No. 326.

15. Ibid., p. 114, No. 323.

16. Ibid., p. 115, No. 326.

17. Ibid.

18. Brandi, p. 111.
19. King Charles I of Spain became Emperor Charles V.
20. *C.S.P.V.*, II, footnote p. 545.
21. John Lynch, *Spain under the Habsburgs (1516–1598)* (New York, Oxford University Press, 1964), p. 39.
22. Brandi, p. 111.
23. Bauer, p. 40.

4. The Seamless Coat

1. Brandi, p. 123.
2. Roland Bainton, *Here I Stand: A Life of Martin Luther* (New York, Abingdon-Cokesbury Press, 1950), p. 185.
3. Schwarzenfeld, p. 74.
4. Bainton, p. 188.
5. *C.S.P.V.*, III, p. 180.

5. Years of Triumph

1. Schwarzenfeld, p. 115.
2. Ibid., p. 116.
3. Vehse, I, p. 56. Also Oscar Browning, *The Age of the Condottieri* (London, Methuen & Co., 1895), pp. 230ff.
4. *C.S.P.V.*, III, p. 401.

6. The Padlocked Heart

1. Tyler, p. 285.
2. [Joseph Marie] Baron Kervyn de Lettenhove (ed.), *Commentaires de Charles-Quint* (Paris, Firmin-Didot Frères et Fils, 1862), p. 4.
3. Brandi, p. 219.
4. D. B. Wyndham Lewis, *Charles of Europe* (New York, Coward-McCann, 1931), p. 68.
5. Vehse, I, p. 170.
6. Tyler, p. 278.
7. Bartholomew Sastrow, *Social Germany in Luther's Time, Being the Memoirs of Bartholomew Sastrow* (London, Archibald Constable, 1902), p. 230.
8. Mario Cavalli, "Relations of Venetian Ambassadors" in *Renaissance Reader*, ed. by James Bruce Ross and Mary Martin McLaughlin (New York, Viking Press, 1953), p. 303.
9. Bradford, p. 135.
10. Emil Schaeffer (ed.), *Habsburger Schreiben Briefe: Privatbriefe aus fünf Jahrhunderten* (Leipzig, E. P. Tal & Co. Verlag, 1935), p. 20.
11. Brandi, p. 324. De Iongh, *Mary of Hungary*, p. 160.
12. De Iongh, *Mary of Hungary*, p. 263.
13. Tyler, footnote p. 61.
14. De Iongh, *Mary of Hungary*, p. 130.

15. Brandi, p. 343.
16. Bradford, p. 136.
17. *C.S.P.V.*, III, footnote p. 374.
18. Karl Lanz (ed.), *Staatspapiere zur Geschichte des Kaisers Karl V, aus dem Königlichen Archiv und der Bibliothèque de Bourgogne zu Brüssel* (Stuttgart, Bibliothek des Literarischen Vereins, 1845), p. 34.
19. Sir Charles Petrie, *Philip II of Spain* (New York, W. W. Norton & Co., 1963), p. 34.
20. Schwarzenfeld, p. 20.
21. [J.] Kervyn de Lettenhove, *Commentaires de Charles-Quint*, p. 44.
22. Ibid., p. 52.

7. The Seamless Coat Torn

1. Brandi, p. 527.
2. Vehse, I, p. 165.
3. J. A. Froude, *Life and Letters of Erasmus* (New York, Charles Scribner's Sons, 1895), pp. 382ff.
4. Schwarzenfeld, p. 153.

8. Brothers' Quarrel

1. "Denkschrift über die Succession in der Kaiserwurde," probably written by the Bishop of Arras, in Lanz, *Staatspapiere*, p. 450.
2. Tyler, p. 174.
3. De Iongh, *Mary of Hungary*, p. 235.
4. Lanz, pp. 482ff.
5. Vehse, I, p. 164.
6. Tyler, p. 107.
7. Lewis, p. 189.
8. Jean H. Mariéjol, *Philip II, The First Modern King*, trans. by Warren B. Wells (New York, Harper & Bros., 1933), p. 26.

9. Exile

1. Schwarzenfeld, p. 264.
2. Lewis, p. 306.
3. Ibid., p. 82
4. Kervyn de Lettenhove, *Commentaires*, Introduction, p. vi.
5. Vehse, I, p. 150.

IV. AUSTRIAN AND SPANISH COUSINS

1. Ferdinand's Family

1. Schaeffer, p. 22.
2. Knappich, p. 121.
3. Lynch, p. 37.

4. Bauer, p. 12, No. 14.

5. De Iongh, *Mary of Hungary,* p. 55.

6. Knappich, p. 125.

7. Bauer, p. 400.

8. Viktor Bibl, *Maximilian II, Der Rätselhafte Kaiser* (Hellerau-bei-Dresden, Avalun-Verlag [1929]), p. 29.

9. Ibid.

10. Frass, II, p. 51.

11. Bibl, p. 29.

2. The Turkish Scimitar

1. Bauer, p. 70, No. 42.

2. De Iongh, *Mary of Hungary,* p. 96.

3. Ibid., p. 98.

4. Bauer, p. 130, No. 67.

5. Frass, II, p. 36.

6. De Iongh, *Mary of Hungary,* p. 90.

7. Ibid., p. 67.

8. Bauer, p. 435, No. 224.

9. Harold Lamb, *Suleiman the Magnificent* (Garden City, N.Y., Doubleday & Co., 1951), p. 99.

10. De Iongh, *Mary of Hungary,* p. 105.

11. Bauer, p. 444, No. 232.

12. Lamb, p. 127.

3. Heresy in the Family Circle

1. Bibl, p. 30.

2. Bauer, p. 37.

3. Ibid., p. 59.

4. Vehse, I, p. 203. A curious story is told of the marriage of Maximilian's natural daughter, Helena. When she had grown up to be a pretty and sensible girl, she was offered as a matrimonial prize to the winner of a wrestling match. A huge Carinthian nobleman, Baron Andrew von Rauber, won her by besting a Spanish lord of equal size, whom he tied in a sack and laid at the feet of the Emperor.

5. Schaeffer, p. 24.

6. Bibl, p. 46.

7. Knappich, p. 137.

8. Brandi, p. 630.

9. Bibl, p. 59.

4. Archduke Ferdinand and Philippina Welser

1. Vehse, I, p. 186.

2. Victor von Klarwill (ed.), *The Fugger News Letters,* trans. by Pauline de Chary (London, John Lane The Bodley Head Ltd., 1924), p. 46.

3. Bibl, p. 167.

4. Vehse, I, p. 187.

5. Bibl, pp. 153–4.

6. Now in the Kunsthistorisches Museum, Vienna.

7. "Symmicta Germanica de re coquinaria . . . Philippinae Welserae," in Manuscript Collection, Nationalbibliothek, Vienna.

5. Young Maximilian Gives In

1. Vehse, I, p. 183.

2. Bibl, pp. 71–72.

3. Ibid., p. 83.

4. Vehse, I, p. 182.

5. Bibl, p. 90.

6. Ibid., p. 92.

7. Anonymous, *A brief rehersal and discription of the Coronation of the hye and myghti Prince Maximilian Kyng of Romans . . . at the famus citie of Francford yn the year of owr Lord 1562. Newli prented yn Gaunte . . . 1565* (British Museum, reproduced University Microfilms No. 16578).

6. Last Days of Ferdinand

1. Richard Kralik, *Geschichte der Stadt Wien und ihrer Kultur* (Vienna, Adolf Holzhausen, 1926), p. 159.

2. Ibid., p. 130.

3. Ibid., p. 161.

4. *Letters of Ogier Ghislain de Busbecq to the Holy Roman Emperor Maximilian II*, trans. from the Latin text of J. B. Howaert by Robert Epes Jones and Bernard Clarke Weber (New York, Bookman Associates, 1961), p. 8.

5. Bibl, pp. 116ff.

7. A Spanish Education

1. Gertrude von Schwarzenfeld, *Rudolf II* (Munich, Verlag Georg D. W. Callwey, 1961), p. 22.

2. Bibl, p. 197.

3. Ibid., p. 198.

4. Charles De Moüy, *Don Carlos et Philippe II* (Paris, Perrin et Cie., 1888), pp. 66ff.

5. Bibl, p. 232.

6. Ibid.

7. Ibid., p. 208.

8. Ibid., p. 236.

9. Lynch, p. 179.

10. Bibl, p. 252.

11. Ibid., p. 255.
12. De Moüy, p. 333.
13. Bibl, p. 257.
14. Klarwill, pp. 7–8.
15. Schwarzenfeld, *Rudolf II*, p. 29.

8. *Maximilian II,* a Via Media

1. Schwarzenfeld, *Rudolf II*, p. 30.
2. Ibid., p. 34.
3. C. V. Wedgwood, *The Thirty Years War* (Garden City, N.Y., Doubleday & Co., 1961), p. 59.
4. Knappich, p. 132.
5. Vehse, I, p. 183.
6. Bibl, p. 298.
7. Vehse, I, p. 200.
8. Bibl, pp. 394ff.
9. Sir David Brewster, "Tycho Brahe" in *Martyrs of Science* (London, Chatto & Windus, n.d.), p. 180.
10. Bibl, p. 395.
11. Ibid., p. 30.
12. Vehse, I, p. 200.

9. *A Question of Breeding*

1. Ludwig Pfandl, *Philipp II* (Munich, Verlag Georg D. W. Callwey, 1951), p. 401.
2. H. Forneron, *Histoire de Philippe II* (Paris, E. Plon et Cie., 1882), pp. 401ff.
3. Desiderius Erasmus, *The Education of a Christian Prince,* trans. by Lester K. Born (New York, Columbia University Press, 1936), p. 243.
4. María Jesús Pérez Martín, *Margarita de Austria, Reina de España* (Madrid, Espasa-Calpe, 1961), p. 163.

10. *The Court of Rudolf II*

1. Klarwill, pp. 74, 107ff., 156–7, 208–9.
2. Schwarzenfeld, *Rudolf II*, pp. 44ff.
3. Ibid., pp. 146–7.
4. Vehse, I, p. 235.

11. *Matthias: Monarch of the Seven M's*

1. In the collection of the Sacred Treasury, Hofburg, Vienna.
2. Knappich, p. 154.
3. Vehse, I, p. 250.

V. HABSBURGS AT BAY: PROTESTANT AND TURK

1. Ferdinand II

1. Wedgwood, p. 79. Slawata's own account, "Der Prager Fenstersturz," quoted in Frass, II, p. 108.
2. Vehse, I, p. 243.
3. Wedgwood, pp. 81–82.
4. Vehse, I, p. 257.
5. Wedgwood, p. 59.
6. Knappich, p. 158.
7. Vehse, I, p. 262.
8. Frass, I, p. 109, for Khevenhüller's account from *Annales Ferdinandei zu 1619.*
9. Wedgwood, p. 139.
10. Ibid., p. 131.

2. A Wartime Bride

1. Grete Mecenseffy, "Habsburger im 17. Jahrhundert: Die Beziehungen der Höfe von Wien und Madrid während des Dreissigjährigen Krieges," Vol. 121, No. 1, of *Archiv für Österreichische Geschichte* (Vienna, Rudolf M. Rohrer, 1955), pp. 38ff. The account of Maria Anna's journey is largely drawn from this source.
2. Wedgwood, p. 228.
3. Mecenseffy, p. 44.
4. Schaeffer, p. 30.
5. Mecenseffy, p. 81.

3. Leopold I: An Unwilling Emperor

1. Schaeffer, p. 32.
2. Vehse, I, p. 423.
3. Victor von Renner, *Wien im Jahre 1683* (Vienna, Verlag von R. V. Waldheim, 1883), p. 4.
4. Vehse, I, p. 423.
5. Velasquez portraits of the Infanta Margarita Teresa, Kunsthistorisches Museum, Vienna.
6. Vehse, I, pp. 440ff.
7. Knappich, p. 177.
8. Vehse, II, p. 11.
9. Schaeffer, p. 32.

4. The Great Siege of Vienna

1. Eyewitness accounts of days preceding siege in Renner, pp. 218ff.
2. Karl August Schimmer, *The Sieges of Vienna by the Turks* (London, J. Murray, 1847), pp. 95ff.

3. *Cambridge History of Poland* (Cambridge, England, The University Press, 1950), pp. 537ff.

4. John Bingham Morton, *Sobieski, King of Poland* (London, Eyre & Spottiswoode, 1932), p. 186.

5. Ibid., footnote p. 178.

6. Ibid., p. 201.

7. Schaeffer, p. 33. Onno Klopp, *Das Jahr 1683* (Graz, Verlags-Buchhandlung Styria, 1882), p. 314.

8. Perhaps apocryphal. Klopp, p. 554, questions the veracity of the account, states it first appeared in the French account of Salvandy.

9. Klopp, pp. 321ff. Renner, p. 448.

VI. IN A BAROQUE WORLD

1. Vehse, II, p. 79.

2. Ibid., II, p. 82.

3. Ibid., II, p. 95.

4. Ibid., II, p. 12.

5. Ibid., II, p. 122.

6. Ibid.

7. Ibid., I, p. 424.

8. Rosina Topka, "Der Hofstaat Kaiser Karl VI" (unpublished doctoral dissertation, University of Vienna, 1954), passim.

9. Ibid., p. 133.

10. One of the more vivid instances of that *Kaisertreue* (recounted in Wilhelm Rausch, "Die Hofreisen Kaiser Karl VI," [unpublished doctoral dissertation, University of Vienna, 1954], p. 147) occurred in 1732, when Charles VI was hunting one day in Bohemia and had the ill luck to miss the deer and shoot instead his faithful friend and Master of the Horse, Prince Schwarzenberg. A surgeon was hastily summoned from Prague, but there was nothing he could do; the wound was clearly mortal. The Emperor was beside himself; he threw his hat and wig far from him and could not be calmed.

The dying man, however, asked the surgeon to comfort His Imperial Majesty, saying: "It is the fate of heaven that I have been shot by His Majesty. On my arrival in Heaven I shall ask God to send His Majesty a successor and beg for a long reign for him." Whether the words of the dying man were truthfully reported is perhaps of less significance than the fact that his contemporaries accepted them as perfectly credible, and that such loyalty in an imperial servant was not considered in the least extraordinary.

11. Vehse, II, pp. 1ff. Casimir Freschot, *Mémoires de la Cour de Vienne* (Cologne, Guillaume Étienne, 1705), p. 102.

12. Vehse, II, p. 128.

13. Ibid.

14. The Grand Mastership of the Order of the Golden Fleece had been held by the kings of Spain after Philip II. With the death of Carlos II and

the extinction of the Spanish line in 1700, it was claimed by Charles VI, who instituted the order at Vienna in 1713.

15. Freschot, pp. 135ff.

16. Vehse, II, p. 61.

17. Sir Robert Murray Keith, *Memoirs and Correspondence*, ed. by Mrs. Gillespie Smith, 2 vols. (London, Henry Colburn, 1849), I, p. 456.

18. Vehse, II, p. 125.

19. Therese Schüssel, *Kultur des Barock in Österreich* (Graz, Stiasny Verlag, 1960), pp. 107ff.

20. Vehse, II, p. 130. Freschot, p. 49.

21. Schüssel, p. 113.

22. P. Eberhard Kusin, *Die Kaisergruft bei den PP. Kapuzinern in Wien* (Vienna, Buch- und Kunstverlag Othomar Kloiber, 1949), pp. 71ff. Also Vehse, II, pp. 76ff.

23. Father Kusin doubts the existence of this particular portion of the Habsburg burial ceremony. Many accounts of Habsburg funerals describe it, however.

VII. PROBLEMS OF INHERITANCE

1. A New King for Spain

1. Schaeffer, p. 35.

2. Ibid., p. 36.

3. John Langdon-Davies, *Carlos, The King Who Would Not Die* (Englewood Cliffs, N.J., Prentice-Hall, 1963), p. 196.

4. Ibid., p. 238.

5. The account is that of the Duc de St. Simon, who, it must be remembered, was not present but drew his amusing version secondhand. Cf. *Saint-Simon at Versailles,* selected and translated from the *Memoirs* (of St. Simon) by Lucy Norton (New York, Harper & Bros., 1958), pp. 59ff.

6. Marcus Landau, *Geschichte Kaiser Karls VI als König von Spanien* (Stuttgart, Verlag der J. G. Cotta'schen Buchhandlung, 1889), pp. 147ff.

7. Ibid., p. 390.

8. Ibid., p. 391.

9. Ibid., p. 395.

10. Ibid., p. 485.

2. Problems and Pleasures of Charles VI

1. Wilhelm Rausch, "Die Hofreisen Kaiser Karl VI," p. 141.

2. Vehse, II, p. 142.

3. Ibid.

4. Wilhelm Rausch, p. 60.

5. Ibid., p. 64.

6. Ibid., pp. 88ff.

7. Ibid., p. 48.

8. Elizabeth Christine's green-upholstered sedan chair, a marvel of eighteenth-century traveling comfort—including even built-in plumbing facilities—can be seen today in the coach house of Schönbrunn Palace in Vienna. The silver-and-crystal travel service and portable stove used on journeys such as this one are preserved in the Silver Room of the Imperial Palace.

9. Wilhelm Rausch, p. 88.

10. Ibid.

11. Ibid., p. 90.

12. Mary Maxwell Moffatt, *Maria Theresa* (London, Methuen & Co., 1911), p. 49.

13. Margaret Goldsmith, *Maria Theresa of Austria* (London, Arthur Barker, 1936), p. 53.

14. Ibid., p. 56.

15. Ludwig Reiners, *Frederick the Great,* trans. by Lawrence Wilson (London, Oswald Wolff, 1960), p. 90.

VIII. THE GREAT EMPRESS

1. A New Queen

1. Moffat, p. 72.

2. Adam Wolf, *Marie Christine, Erzherzogin von Österreich,* 2 vols. (Vienna, Carl Gerold's Sohn, 1863), I, p. 5.

3. Moffat, p. 67.

4. Knappich, p. 215.

5. Moffat, p. 86.

6. François Fejtö, *Un Habsbourg Révolutionnaire, Joseph II* (Paris, Librairie Plon, 1953), p. 4.

7. Moffat, pp. 114ff. Nathaniel Wraxall, *Memoirs of the Courts of Berlin, Dresden, Warsaw and Vienna in the Years 1777, 1778 and 1779,* 2 vols. (London, T. Cadell & W. Davies, 1806), II, pp. 306ff.

2. The Landesmutter

1. Goldsmith, p. 95.

2. J. Alexander Mahan, *Maria Theresa of Austria* (New York, Thomas Y. Crowell Co., 1932), p. 229.

3. Moffatt, p. 145.

4. Knappich, p. 220. Moffatt, pp. 16, 163.

5. John Naglee Burk, *Mozart and his Music* (New York, Random House, 1959), p. 18.

6. Walter Horace Bruford, *Germany in the Eighteenth Century: The Social Background of the Literary Revival* (Cambridge, England, The University Press, 1935), p. 80.

7. Moffatt, p. 328. Vehse, II, p. 202.

8. Mahan, p. 238.

3. Maria Theresia's Chastity Commission

1. Wraxall, II, p. 319. The tomb was dedicated September 20, 1754.

2. Vehse, II, p. 206.

3. Lady Mary Wortley Montagu, *Letters and Works,* ed. by Lord Wharncliffe, 3 vols. (London, Swan Sonnenschein, 1893), I, pp. 295ff.

4. *Dr. Charles Burney's Continental Travels 1770–1772,* ed. by Cedric Howard Glover (London, Blackie & Son, 1927), p. 146.

5. Wraxall, II, p. 252ff. Vehse, II, p. 206.

6. Goldsmith, pp. 267ff.

7. Ibid., p. 168.

8. Walther Tritsch, *Metternich und sein Monarch* (Darmstadt, Im Holle Verlag, 1952), p. 192.

9. Goldsmith, p. 222.

10. Ibid., p. 223.

4. Absolutism in the Nursery

1. Wandruszka, p. 148.

2. Goldsmith, p. 151.

3. Ibid., p. 148.

4. Fejtö, p. 28.

5. Goldsmith, p. 150.

6. Alfred Ritter von Arneth (ed.), *Briefe der Kaiserin Maria Theresia an Ihre Kinder und Freunde,* 4 vols. (Vienna, Wilhelm Braumüller, 1881), III, p. 29.

7. Wolf, p. 13. Fejtö, p. 52.

8. Saul K. Padover, *The Revolutionary Emperor Joseph the Second* (New York, Robert O. Ballou, 1934), p. 37.

9. Goldsmith, p. 204. Fejtö, p. 52.

10. Goldsmith, p. 204.

11. Padover, p. 37. Fejtö, p. 52.

12. Mahan, p. 279.

13. Henry Vallotton, *Marie-Thérèse Impératrice* (Paris, Librairie Arthème Fayard, 1963), p. 186.

14. Padover, p. 49.

15. Ibid.

16. Ludwig F. Jedlicka (ed.), *Maria Theresia in ihren Briefen und Staatsschriften* (Vienna, Bergland Verlag, 1955), p. 30.

17. Moffatt, p. 311.

18. Mahan, p. 293.

19. Harold Acton, *The Bourbons of Naples* (London, Methuen & Co., 1956), p. 124.

20. Wraxall, II, pp. 323ff.

21. Acton, p. 126. Vehse, II, pp. 235ff.

22. Adam Wandruszka, *Leopold II,* 2 vols. (Vienna, Verlag Herold, n.d.), I, p. 207.

23. Goldsmith, p. 241.

24. Acton, p. 138.

25. Ibid., p. 139.
26. Ibid., p. 141.
27. Ibid., p. 137.
28. Ibid.
29. Wolf, I, p. 125.
30. Alfred Ritter von Arneth (ed.), *Maria Theresia und Marie Antoinette, Ihr Briefwechsel* (Vienna, Wilhelm Braumüller, 1866), pp. 1ff.
31. André Castelot, *Queen of France, A Biography of Marie Antoinette* (New York, Harper & Bros., 1957), p. 9.

5. Last Letter to the Queen of France

1. Moffatt, p. 327.
2. Ibid., p. 328.
3. Vehse, II, p. 237.
4. Jedlicka, p. 46.
5. Henry Swinburne, *The Courts of Europe at the Close of the Last Century*, 2 vols. (London, H. S. Nichols, 1895), I, p. 304.
6. Arneth, *Maria Theresia und Marie Antoinette, Ihr Briefwechsel*, p. 348.

IX. JOSEPH II: THE POOR MAN'S EMPEROR

1. Tastes of a Simple Man

1. Alfred Ritter von Arneth (ed.), *Joseph II und Leopold von Toscana, Ihr Briefwechsel von 1781 bis 1790*, 2 vols. (Vienna, Wilhelm Braumüller, 1872), I, p. 3.
2. Ibid., p. 28.
3. Padover, p. 49. The sum would represent a minimum of $11,000,000 in present-day currency.
4. Vehse, II, p. 124.
5. Padover, p. 107.
6. Vehse, II, p. 265.
7. Marcel Brion, *Daily Life in the Vienna of Mozart and Schubert*, trans. by Jean Stewart (New York, The Macmillan Co., 1962), p. 18.
8. Padover, p. 65.
9. An anecdote related by Thomas Jefferson, quoted in Padover, p. 120.
10. Vehse, II, p. 314.
11. Ibid.
12. Padover, p. 122.

2. Changing the World

1. Ibid., p. 217.
2. Ibid., p. 253.
3. Ibid., p. 192.
4. Castelot, p. 119.

3. Making of a Throne Heir

1. Adolf Beer (ed.), *Joseph II, Leopold II, und Kaunitz, Ihr Brief-wechsel* (Vienna, Wilhelm Braumüller, 1873), p. 102.

2. Padover, p. 98.

3. Walter Consuelo Langsam, *Francis the Good: The Education of an Emperor, 1768–1792* (New York, The Macmillan Co., 1949), pp. 52ff.

4. Arneth, *Joseph II und Leopold von Toscana,* I, p. 340.

5. Langsam, pp. 59ff.

6. Tritsch, p. 81.

7. Langsam, p. 67.

8. Ibid., p. 81.

9. Cölestin Wolfsgruber, *Franz I, Kaiser von Österreich,* (Vienna, Wilhelm Braumüller, 1899), I, p. 70.

4. Epitaph for Joseph

1. Padover, p. 389.

2. Arneth, *Joseph II und Leopold von Toscana,* II, pp. 270ff.

3. Langsam, p. 82.

4. Vehse, II, p. 305.

X. WARS AND WALTZES: NAPOLEONIC TIMES

1. The Short Reign of Leopold II

1. Langsam, p. 84. Arneth, *Joseph II und Leopold von Toscana,* II, p. 319.

2. Langsam, p. 86.

3. This marriage of double first-cousins apparently brought deleterious results in the offspring. The elder brother of King Ferdinando of Naples (of the Spanish Bourbon line), uncle of both Marie-Thérèse and Franz, was a complete imbecile, maintained in Naples with a keeper. (Joseph II, whose curiosity was unquenchable, went to have a look at the creature during a visit to Naples.) Of Franz's children, who could have inherited the strain twice over, five out of twelve lived to adulthood. The eldest, Ferdinand, was an epileptic of subnormal intelligence. One daughter, Maria Anna, was an imbecile who lived out her life at Schönbrunn with a keeper. Marie-Thérèse believed this daughter's defects were the result of a terrible fright she had received during pregnancy, when an orangutan got loose from the Schönbrunn menagerie and sprang onto her shoulder.

4. Tritsch, p. 103.

5. Castelot, p. 409.

2. Franz II vs. Napoleon

1. Langsam, p. 157.

2. Brion, p. 159.

3. Langsam, p. 159.

4. Emil Ludwig, *Napoleon*, trans. by Eden and Cedar Paul (New York, Boni & Liveright, 1926), p. 243. Tritsch, p. 205.

3. Domestic Life in Wartime

1. Langsam, pp. 162ff.

2. The Apollo was built by a clever surgeon, Dr. Sigmund Wolffsohn, who made a fortune from the invention of artificial arms and legs that moved—a great boon to the thousands of casualties of the Napoleonic Wars.

3. Heinrich Eduard Jacob, *Johann Strauss, Father and Son*, trans. by Marguerite Wolff (New York, Greystone Press, 1940), p. 24.

4. Langsam, p. 163.

5. Karl Geiringer, *Josef Haydn, A Creative Life in Music* (New York, W. W. Norton & Co., 1946), p. 157.

6. Langsam, p. 161.

7. Ibid.

8. Letter dated December 15, 1781, in *Mozart's Letters*, ed. by Eric Blum, (Harmondsworth, Middlesex, England, Penguin Books, 1956), p. 186.

9. Tritsch, p. 215.

10. Haus- Hof- und Staatsarchiv, Vienna, Sammelbände, Karton 43, Fass. 284, 1810, and pack 19, No. 103.

11. Tritsch, p. 223.

12. F. M. Kircheisen, *Memoirs of Napoleon I, compiled from his own writings* (New York, Duffield & Co., 1929), p. 126.

13. André Castelot, *King of Rome* (New York, Harper & Bros., 1960), p. 138.

14. Ibid., p. 64.

4. Family Reunion

1. Castelot, *King of Rome*, p. 195.

2. Acton, p. 616.

3. Castelot, *King of Rome*, p. 143.

4. Acton, p. 629.

XI. KINGS ON HOLIDAY: THE DANCING CONGRESS

1. Opening of the Congress

1. Comte A. de La Garde-Chambonas, *Souvenirs du Congrès de Vienne*, (Paris, Librairie Émile-Paul, 1904), p. 6.

2. Ibid., pp. 72ff., p. 204.

3. Frederick Freksa (ed.), *A Peace Congress of Intrigue*, trans. by Harry Hansen (New York, The Century Co., 1919), pp. 30ff.

2. Hofburg House Party

1. Tritsch, p. 214.
2. From "Letters of Talleyrand," quoted in Freksa, p. 315.

3. Disagreements and Duels

1. Harold Nicolson, *The Congress of Vienna* (New York, Harcourt, Brace & Co., 1946), p. 150.
2. Ibid., p. 164.
3. Ibid., p. 179.
4. Letter of Humboldt quoted in Freksa, pp. 204ff.
5. Freksa, p. 179.

4. End of the Dance

1. Ibid., p. 180.
2. Or a minimum of $250,000 in today's currency. Nicolson, in *The Congress of Vienna*, p. 167, estimates the total cost at "no less than thirty million florins." Talleyrand, quoted in Freksa, p. 315, estimated it at 220,000 gulden per day.
3. Emil Pirchan, *Fanny Elssler* (Vienna, Wilhelm Frick Verlag, 1940), p. 12.
4. Memoir of Countess Bernstorff in Freksa, p. 42.
5. Freksa, p. 119.
6. Tritsch, pp. 545ff.
7. Ibid., p. 547.

XII. MR. BIEDERMEIER AND HIS TIMES

1. Franz the Good, Ferdinand the Good-natured

1. Tritsch, p. 549.
2. The word itself comes from a fictitious character, Herr Biedermeier, a simple, good-natured Teutonic Babbitt, who appeared in a German journal, *Die Fliegende Blätter*, toward the end of the nineteenth century. In German-speaking countries the years preceding the 1848 Revolution—looked back upon as an age of Philistinism—came to be known as the Biedermeier age.
3. Castelot, *King of Rome*, p. 269.
4. Ibid.
5. Ibid., p. 195.
6. Siegfried Weyr, "Erzherzogin Leopoldine, das Leben einer Leidge-prüften," in *Neues Österreich*, (January 17, 1960, Vienna). The quotations from Leopoldine's letters that follow are drawn from the same source.
7. Egon Caesar Corti, *Vom Kind zum Kaiser. Kindheit und Erste*

Jugend Kaiser Franz Josephs I und Seiner Geschwister, (Graz, Verlag Anton Pustet, 1950), p. 94.

8. Corti, p. 17. Castelot, *King of Rome,* p. 365.
9. Corti, p. 15.
10. Ibid., p. 40.
11. Ibid., p. 26.

2. Biedermeier Romances

1. Vehse, II, p. 409.
2. Corti, p. 160.
3. Vehse, II, p. 377.
4. Corti, p. 33.
5. Ibid., p. 34.
6. Ibid., p. 35.
7. Ibid., p. 39.
8. Ibid., p. 40.
9. Ibid., p. 65.

3. Revolution and Abdication

1. Edward Crankshaw, *The Fall of the House of Habsburg* (New York, Viking Press, 1963), p. 14.
2. Corti, p. 156.
3. Ibid., p. 171.
4. Crankshaw, p. 26.
5. Priscilla Robertson, *Revolutions of 1848, A Social History* (Princeton, N.J., Princeton University Press, 1952), p. 224.
6. Horace Rumbold, *The Austrian Court in the Nineteenth Century* (London, Methuen & Co., 1909), p. 116.
7. Corti, p. 332.

XIII. FRANZ JOSEF: A LONG REIGN BEGINS

1. Young Franz Josef

1. Egon Caesar Corti, *Mensch und Herrscher: Weg und Schicksale Kaiser Franz Josephs I und seiner Geschwister Zwischen Thronbesteigung und Berliner Kongress* (Graz, Verlag Styria, 1952), p. 78.

2. Empress Elizabeth

1. Egon Caesar Corti, *Elizabeth, Empress of Austria,* trans. by Catherine Alison Phillips (New Haven, Conn., Yale University Press, 1936), p. 26.
2. Corti, *Mensch und Herrscher,* p. 145.
3. Corti, *Elizabeth,* p. 49.
4. Ibid., p. 172.

5. Ibid., p. 54.
6. Ibid., p. 53.
7. Ibid., p. 411.

3. Learning to Rule

1. Tritsch, p. 710.
2. Corti, *Mensch und Herrscher*, p. 223.
3. Tritsch, p. 709.
4. Karl Tschuppik, *Empress Elizabeth of Austria* (London, Archibald Constable & Co., 1930), p. 54.
5. May, *The Habsburg Monarchy*, p. 434.
6. Corti, *Elizabeth*, p. 90.
7. May, p. 33.

5. Maximilian in Mexico

1. Corti, *Mensch und Herrscher*, p. 381.
2. Egon Caesar Corti, *Maximilian and Charlotte of Mexico*, 2 vols. (London, Alfred A. Knopf, 1928), II, p. 822.
3. Ibid., p. 823.
4. Corti, *Mensch und Herrscher*, p. 397.
5. Ibid., p. 398.
6. Ibid., p. 404.

6. Family Life in the Seventies

1. Corti, *Maximilian and Charlotte of Mexico*, II, p. 771.
2. May, p. 151.
3. Corti, *Elizabeth*, p. 227.
4. Corti, *Mensch und Herrscher*, p. 285.
5. The *Fasching* adventure is based on the account in Corti, *Elizabeth*, pp. 238ff.
6. Eugen Ketterl, *The Emperor Francis Joseph I, An Intimate Study*, trans. by M. Ostheide (London, Skeffington & Son, n.d.), p. 27.

XIV. THE TRAGEDY AT MAYERLING

1. A New Throne Heir: Rudolf

1. Richard Barkeley, *The Road to Mayerling: Life and Death of Crown Prince Rudolf of Austria* (New York, St. Martin's Press, 1958), p. 27.
2. Corti, *Mensch und Herrscher*, p. 443.
3. Ibid., p. 420.
4. Corti, *Elizabeth*, p. 123.
5. Barkeley, p. 37.

6. Stephanie (Princess) of Belgium, Fürstin of Lonyay, *I Was to Be an Empress* (London, Ivor Nicholson & Watson, 1937), p. 113.

7. Ibid., pp. 153–4.

8. Barkeley, p. 181.

9. Ibid., p. 120.

10. Ibid., pp. 197ff.

11. Ibid., p. 117.

12. Ibid., p. 193.

2. *Mary Vetsera*

1. Ibid., p. 193.

2. Marie Larisch, *My Past* (New York, G. P. Putnam's Sons, 1913), pp. 224ff.

3. Baronin-Mutter Helene Vetsera, *Das Drama von Mayerling (Das Tagebuch der Baronin-Mutter Helene Vetsera)* (Reichenberg, Gebrüder Stiepel Gesellschaft, 1921), p. 15.

4. Ibid., p. 16.

5. Ibid., pp. 26–27.

6. Oskar Freiherr von Mitis, *Das Leben des Kronprinzen Rudolf, mit Briefen und Schriften aus dessen Nachlass* (Leipzig, Insel-Verlag, 1928), p. 395.

7. Larisch, pp. 299ff.

8. Barkeley, pp. 227ff.

9. *Das Mayerling Original. Offizieller Akt des K. K. Polizeipräsidiums—Facsimile der Dokumente der Authentische Bericht* (Vienna, Wilhelm Frick Verlag, 1955), p. 5.

10. Count Hoyos' *Memorandum*, deposited in the Haus-, Hof- und Staatsarchiv in Vienna, has been reprinted in Mitis' account, in *Das Mayerling Original*, and in part in Barkeley's account.

11. *Das Mayerling Original*, p. 19.

12. Mitis, p. 390.

13. Ibid., p. 391.

14. Ibid.

15. Corti, *Elizabeth*, p. 393.

16. Ibid., p. 395.

17. *Das Mayerling Original*, p. 79.

18. Barkeley, p. 239.

19. Ibid.

20. *Das Mayerling Original*, pp. 29–30.

21. Egon Caesar Corti and Hans Sokol, *Der Alte Kaiser: Franz Joseph I vom Berliner Kongress bis zu seinem Tode* (Graz, Verlag Styria, 1956), p. 129.

3. *Conspiracy of Silence*

1. *Das Mayerling Original*, p. 42.

2. Barkeley, p. 265.

3. Ibid., p. 271.
4. *Das Mayerling Original,* pp. 54ff.
5. Corti-Sokol, *Der Alte Kaiser,* facsimile of farewell letter, pp. 96–97.
6. Corti, *Elizabeth,* p. 397.

XV. HOFBURG FINALE

1. Elizabeth in Mourning

1. Corti, *Elizabeth,* pp. 403–4.
2. Ibid., p. 201.

2. A Friend for Franz Josef

1. Jean de Bourgoing (ed.), *Briefe Kaiser Franz Josephs an Frau Katharina Schratt* (Vienna, Ullstein Verlag, 1949), pp. 44–45.
2. Ibid., p. 55.
3. Ibid.
4. Ibid., p. 56.
5. Corti, *Elizabeth,* p. 440.
6. Ibid., p. 435.

3. Uncle and Nephew

1. Bourgoing, p. 421.
2. Joachim Remak, *Sarajevo* (New York, Criterion Books, 1959), p. 18.
3. Bourgoing, p. 401.
4. Corti-Sokol, *Der Alte Kaiser,* p. 264.
5. Bourgoing, p. 425.

4. Turn-of-the-Century Vienna

1. Martin Freud, *Sigmund Freud: Man and Father* (New York, Vanguard Press, 1958), p. 156.
2. Stefan Zweig, *The World of Yesterday* (New York, Viking Press, 1943), p. 13.
3. Adolf Hitler, *Mein Kampf* (New York, Reynal & Hitchcock, 1940), p. 160.
4. *Hitlers Zweites Buch, ein Dokument aus dem Jahr 1928,* ed. by Gerhard L. Weinberg (Stuttgart, Deutsche Verlags-Anstalt, 1961), p. 185.

5. Twilight

1. Ketterl, p. 39.
2. Bourgoing, p. 468.
3. Ibid., p. 469.

4. Reinhold Lorenz, *Kaiser Karl und der Untergang der Donaumonarchie* (Graz, Verlag Styria, 1959), p. 63.
5. Corti-Sokol, *Der Alte Kaiser*, p. 334.
6. Ibid.
7. Remak, p. 24.
8. Ibid., p. 27.
9. Corti-Sokol, *Der Alte Kaiser*, p. 331.
10. Bourgoing, p. 471.
11. Ibid., p. 473.
12. Corti-Sokol, p. 363.

6. Sarajevo

1. Zweig, p. 214.
2. Corti-Sokol, *Der Alte Kaiser*, p. 408.
3. Ibid., p. 409.
4. Remak, pp. 108–9.
5. Ibid., p. 130.
6. Ibid., p. 132.
7. Ibid., p. 130.
8. Ibid., p. 134.
9. Ibid.
10. Ibid., pp. 140–1.
11. Corti-Sokol, *Der Alte Kaiser*, p. 412.
12. Ibid., p. 414.
13. Ibid., p. 420.

7. Death of an Emperor

1. Ibid., p. 449.
2. Ibid., p. 445.
3. Ketterl, p. 247.
4. The account of Franz Josef's death is drawn from both the Corti-Sokol account (*Der Alte Kaiser*, pp. 464ff.) and from Ketterl's narration (*Emperor Francis Joseph I*, pp. 251ff.)

XVI. CURTAIN FALL FOR THE HABSBURGS

1. Hans Karl Zessner-Spitzenberg, *Kaiser Karl* (Salzburg, Salzburger Verlag für Wirtschaft und Kultur, 1953), p. 119.
2. Ibid., p. 137.
3. Arthur Polzer-Hoditz, *The Emperor Karl* (London, Putnam, 1930), p. 231.
4. Edmund von Glaise-Horstenau, *The Collapse of the Austro-Hungarian Empire*, trans. by Ian F. D. Morrow (London, J. M. Dent & Sons, 1930), p. 130.

Bibliography

HABSBURG FAMILY DOCUMENTS AND LETTERS

Arneth, Alfred Ritter von (ed.). *Briefe der Kaiserin Maria Theresia an Ihre Kinder und Freunde*, 4 vols. Vienna, Wilhelm Braumüller, 1881.
——*Joseph II und Leopold von Toscana, Ihr Briefwechsel von 1781 bis 1790*, 2 vols. Vienna, Wilhelm Braumüller, 1872.
——*Maria Theresia und Marie Antoinette, Ihr Briefwechsel*. Vienna, Wilhelm Braumüller, 1866.
Bauer, Wilhelm (ed.). *Die Korrespondenz Ferdinands I*. Vienna, Adolf Holzhausen, 1912.
Beer, Adolf (ed.). *Joseph II, Leopold II und Kaunitz, Ihr Briefwechsel*. Vienna, Wilhelm Braumüller, 1873.
Bourgoing, Jean de (ed.). *Briefe Kaiser Franz Josephs an Frau Katharina Schratt*. Vienna, Ullstein Verlag, 1949.
Bradford, William (ed.) *Correspondence of the Emperor Charles V and His Ambassadors at the Courts of England and France . . . With a Connecting Narrative and Biographical Notices of the Emperor . . .* London, Richard Bentley, 1850.
Chmel, Joseph (ed.). *Actenstücke und Briefe zur Geschichte des Hauses Habsburg im Zeitalter Maximilian's I*, Part I of *Monumenta Habsburgica, Sammlung von Actenstücken und Briefen zur Geschichte des Hauses Habsburg in dem Zeiträume von 1473 bis 1576*, 4 vols. Vienna, Aus der Kaiserlich-Königlichen Hof- und Staatsdrückerei, 1853–58.
——*Urkunden, Briefe und Actenstücke zur Geschichte Maximilians I und seiner Zeit*. Stuttgart, Bibliothek des Literarischen Vereins, 1845.
Frass, Otto (ed.). *Quellenbuch zur Österreichischen Geschichte*, 2 vols. Vienna, Birken-Verlag, 1956.
Haltaus, Carl (ed.). *Theuerdank*. Quedlinburg and Leipzig, Gottfr. Basse, 1836.
Jedlicka, Ludwig F. (ed.). *Maria Theresia in ihren Briefen und Staatsschriften*. Vienna, Bergland Verlag, 1955.
Kervyn de Lettenhove, [Joseph Marie Bruno Constantin] Baron (ed.). *Commentaires de Charles-Quint*. Paris, Firmin-Didot Frères, Fils & Cie., 1862.
Kraus, Victor von (ed.). *Maximilians I. Vertraulicher Briefwechsel mit*

Sigmund Prüschenk, Freiherrn zu Stettenberg. Innsbruck, Verlag der Wagner'schen Universitäts-Buchhandlung, 1875.

Lanz, Karl (ed.). *Actenstücke und Briefe zur Geschichte Kaiser Karl V,* Part II of *Monumenta Habsburgica, Sammlung von Actenstücken und Briefen zur Geschichte des Hauses Habsburg in dem Zeiträume von 1473 bis 1576.* Vienna, Aus der Kaiserlich-Königlichen Hof- und Staatsdrückerei, 1855.

——*Staatspapiere zur Geschichte des Kaisers Karl V, aus dem Königlichen Archiv und der Bibliothèque de Bourgogne zu Brüssel.* Stuttgart, Bibliothek des Literarischen Vereins, 1845.

Le Glay, M. (ed.). *Correspondance de l'Empereur Maximilien Ier et Marguerite d'Autriche Sa Fille, de 1507 à 1519,* 2 vols. Paris, Jules Renouard, 1839.

Schaeffer, Emil (ed.). *Habsburger Schreiben Briefe: Privatbriefe aus fünf Jahrhunderten.* Leipzig, E. P. Tal & Co., 1935.

Szeps, Julius (ed.) *Kronprinz Rudolf: Politische Briefe an einen Freund, 1882–1889.* Vienna, Rikola Verlag, 1922.

UNPUBLISHED MATERIALS

Franz II and his family, Letters of, in Haus-, Hof- und Staatsarchiv, Vienna.

Gatt, Anneliese. "Der Innsbrucker Hof zur Zeit Kaiser Maximilians I, 1493–1519" (unpublished doctoral dissertation, Leopold-Franzens Universität zu Innsbruck, 1943).

Rausch, Wilhelm. "Die Hofreisen Kaiser Karl VI" (unpublished doctoral dissertation, University of Vienna, 1954).

"Symmicta Germanica de re coquinaria Philippinae Welserae," Manuscript Collection, Nationalbibliothek, Vienna.

Topka, Rosina. "Der Hofstaat Kaiser Karl VI" (unpublished doctoral dissertation, University of Vienna, 1954).

LETTERS, MEMOIRS AND OTHER ACCOUNTS
OF CONTEMPORARIES

Ankwicz-Kleehoven, Hans (ed.). *Johann Cuspinians Briefwechsel.* Munich, C. H. Becksche Verlagsbuchhandlung, 1933.

Anonymous. *A brief rehersal and discription of the coronation of the hye and myghti Prince Maximilian Kyng of Romans . . . Don at the famus citie of Francford yn the year of owr Lord 1562. Newli prented yn Gaunte 1565.* British Museum, reproduced University Microfilms No. 16578.

Bertuch, Carl. *Tagebuch vom Wiener Kongress.* Berlin, Paetel, 1916.

Busbecq, Ogier Ghislain de. *Letters of Ogier Ghislain de Busbecq to the Holy Roman Emperor Maximilian II,* trans. from the Latin text of J. B. Howaert by Robert Epes-Jones and Bernard Clarke Weber. New York, Bookman Associates, 1961.

Campan, Jeanne Louis Henriette, First Lady of the Bedchamber to the Queen. *Memoirs of the Court of Marie Antoinette*. Philadelphia, John E. Potter, 1854.

Commynes, Philippe de. *Mémoires*, 3 vols. Paris, Jules Renouard, 1840–47.

Freksa, Frederick (ed.). *A Peace Congress of Intrigue: A Vivid Intimate Account of the Congress of Vienna Composed of the Personal Memoirs of Its Important Participants*, trans. by Harry Hansen. New York, The Century Co., 1919.

Freschot, Casimir. *Mémoires de la Cour de Vienne*. Cologne, Guillaume Étienne, 1705.

Gachard et Piot (eds.) *Collection des Voyages des Souveraines des Pays-Bas*. Brussels. F. Hayez, 1881.

Glover, Cedric Howard (ed.). *Dr. Charles Burney's Continental Travels, 1770–1772*. London, Blackie & Son, 1927.

Great Britain, Public Record Office. *Calendar of State Papers and Manuscripts Relating to English Affairs Existing in the Archives and Collections of Venice and in Other Libraries of Northern Italy*, ed. by Rawdon Brown. London, Longmans, Green, Reader & Dyer, 1867.

——*Letters and Papers Foreign and Domestic of the Reign of Henry VIII*, ed. by J. S. Brewer. London, Longmans, Green, Reader & Dyer, 1867.

Hitler, Adolf. *Mein Kampf*. New York, Reynal & Hitchcock, 1940.

Keith, Sir Robert Murray. *Memoirs and Correspondence of Sir Robert Murray Keith, Envoy Extraordinary and Minister Plenipotentiary at the Courts of Dresden, Copenhagen and Vienna, 1769 to 1792*, ed. by Mrs. Gillespie Smith, 2 vols. London, Henry Colburn, 1849.

Ketterl, Eugen. *The Emperor Francis Joseph I, An Intimate Study by his Valet de Chambre*, trans. by M. Ostheide. London, Skeffington & Son, n.d.

Kircheisen, F. M. *Memoirs of Napoleon I, compiled from his own writings*. New York, Duffield & Co., 1929.

Klarwill, Victor von (ed.) *The Fugger News Letters*, trans. by Pauline de Chary. London, John Lane The Bodley Head Ltd., 1924.

La Garde-Chambonas, (Auguste Louis) Comte de. *Souvenirs du Congrès de Vienne*. Paris, Librairie Émile-Paul, 1904.

La Marche, Olivier de. *Mémoires*, 4 vols. Paris, Librairie Renouard, 1883–88.

Larisch, Marie. *My Past*. New York, G. P. Putnam's Sons, 1913.

Das Mayerling Original. Offizieller Akt des K. K. Polizeipräsidiums—Facsimile der Dokumente der Authentische Bericht. Vienna, Wilhelm Frick Verlag, 1955.

Molinet, Jean. *Chroniques*, 5 vols. Paris, Verdière Libraire, 1827–28.

Montagu, Lady Mary Wortley. *Letters and Works*, ed. by Lord Wharncliffe, 3 vols. London, Swan Sonnenschein, 1893.

Mozart's Letters, ed. by Eric Blom. Harmondsworth, Middlesex, England, Penguin Books, 1956.

Polzer-Hoditz, Arthur Count. *The Emperor Karl*, trans. by D. F. Tait and F. S. Flint. London, Putnam, 1930.

Saint-Simon at Versailles, selected and translated from the *Memoirs of*

M. Le Duc de Saint-Simon by Lucy Norton. New York, Harper & Bros., 1958.

Sastrow, Bartholomew. *Social Germany in Luther's Time, Being the Memoirs of Bartholomew Sastrow*. London, Archibald Constable, 1902.

Stephanie (Princess) of Belgium, Fürstin of Lonyay. *I Was to Be an Empress*. London, Ivor Nicholson & Watson, 1937.

Swinburne, Henry. *The Courts of Europe at the Close of the Last Century*, 2 vols. London, H. S. Nichols, 1895.

Vander Linden, Herman. *Itinéraires de Marie de Bourgogne et de Maximilien d'Autriche*. Brussels, Maurice Lamertin, 1934.

Vetsera, Helene. *Das Drama von Mayerling: Das Tagebuch der Baronin-Mutter Helene Vetsera*. Reichenberg, Gebrüder Stiepel Gesellschaft, 1921.

Werkmann, Baron Charles von. *Tragedy of Charles of Habsburg*. London, Philip Allan, 1924.

Wraxall, Nathaniel William. *Memoirs of the Courts of Berlin, Dresden, Warsaw and Vienna in the Years 1777, 1778 and 1779*, 2 vols. London, T. Cadell & W. Davies, 1806.

Zweig, Stefan. *The World of Yesterday*. New York, Viking Press, 1943.

PERIODICALS

Andics, Hellmut. "Die Tragödie von Mayerling in neuem Licht." *Stern* (Vienna), January, February, March, 1964.

"Mayerling," (documentary series). *Grosse Österreich-Illustrierte* (Vienna), 1953.

Weyr, Siegfried. "Erzherzogin Leopoldine, das Leben einer Leidgeprüften." *Neues Österreich* (Vienna), January 17, 1960.

HISTORY, BIOGRAPHY, RELATED WORKS

Acton, Harold. *The Bourbons of Naples*. London, Methuen & Co., 1956.

Andrews, Marian (pseud. Christopher Hare). *Maximilian the Dreamer*. London, Stanley Paul & Co., 1913.

Ankwicz-Kleehoven, Hans. *Der Wiener Humanist Johannes Cuspinian*. Graz-Köln, Hermann Böhlaus Nachf., 1959.

Arneth, Alfred Ritter von. *Geschichte Maria Theresia's*, 10 vols. Vienna, Wilhelm Braumüller, 1875.

Bagger, Eugene. *Francis Joseph, Emperor of Austria, King of Hungary*. New York, G. P. Putnam's Sons, 1927.

Bainton, Roland. *Here I Stand: A Life of Martin Luther*. New York, Abingdon-Cokesbury Press, 1950.

Barante, M. [Amable Guillaume Prosper] de. *Histoire des Ducs de Bourgogne . . . 1364–1477*, 12 vols. Paris, Duféy, 1837.

Barkeley, Richard. *The Road to Mayerling: Life and Death of Crown Prince Rudolph of Austria*. New York, St. Martin's Press, 1958.

Bauer, Wilhelm. *Die Anfänge Ferdinands I*. Vienna, Wilhelm Braumüller, 1907.

Bibl, Viktor. *Maximilian II, Der Rätselhafte Kaiser*. Hellerau-bei-Dresden, Avalun-Verlag, 1929.

Boom, Ghislaine de. *Les Voyages de Charles-Quint*. Brussels, Office de Publicité, 1957.

Brandi, Karl. *Emperor Charles V*, trans. from the German by C. V. Wedgwood. London, Jonathan Cape, 1939.

Breitner, Erhard. *Maximilian I, Der Traum von der Weltmonarchie*. Bremen, Carl Schünemann Verlag, 1939.

Brewster, Sir David. *Martyrs of Science*. London, Chatto & Windus, n.d.

Brion, Marcel. *Daily Life in the Vienna of Mozart and Schubert*, trans. by Jean Stewart. New York, The Macmillan Co., 1962.

Brouwer, J[ohannes]. *Johanna de Waanzinnige, een tragisch leven in een bewogen tijd*. Amsterdam, J. M. Meulenhoff, 1949.

Browning, Oscar. *The Age of the Condottieri*. London, Methuen & Co., 1895.

Bruford, Walter Horace. *Germany in the Eighteenth Century: The Social Background of the Literary Revival*. Cambridge, England, The University Press, 1935.

Bryce, James. *The Holy Roman Empire*, 4th ed. London, Macmillan & Co., 1904.

Calmette, Joseph. *The Golden Age of Burgundy*. New York, W. W. Norton & Co., 1962.

——*Le Grande Règne de Louis XI*. Paris, Librairie Hachette, 1938.

Cambridge History of Poland, ed. by W. F. Reddaway et al. Cambridge, England, The University Press, 1941.

Cartellieri, Otto. *Am Hofe der Herzöge von Burgund*. Basel, Benno Schwabe & Co., 1926.

Carter, Charles Howard. *The Secret Diplomacy of the Habsburgs 1598–1625*. New York, Columbia University Press, 1964.

Cartwright, Julia. *Beatrice d'Este*. New York, E. P. Dutton & Co., 1928.

Castelot, André. *King of Rome*. New York, Harper & Bros., 1960.

——*Queen of France, A Biography of Marie Antoinette*. New York, Harper & Bros., 1957.

Catalogue of the Crown Jewels and the Ecclesiastical Treasure Chamber of the Hofburg. Vienna, Kunsthistorisches Museum, 1956.

Corti, Egon Caesar Count. *Elizabeth, Empress of Austria*, trans. by Catherine Alison Phillips. New Haven, Conn., Yale University Press, 1936.

——*Maximilian and Charlotte of Mexico*, 2 vols. London, Alfred A. Knopf, 1928.

——*Vom Kind zum Kaiser: Kindheit und Erste Jugend Kaiser Franz Josephs I und seiner Geschwister*. Graz, Verlag Anton Pustet, 1950.

——*Mensch und Herrscher: Weg und Schicksale Kaiser Franz Josephs I zwischen Thronbesteigung und Berliner Kongress*. Graz, Verlag Styria, 1952.

——and Hans Sokol. *Der Alte Kaiser: Franz Joseph I vom Berliner Kongress bis zu seinem Tode*. Graz, Verlag Styria, 1956.

Coudray, Helene du. *Metternich*. New Haven, Conn., Yale University Press, 1936.

Coxe, William. *History of the House of Austria*, 4 vols. London, Henry G. Bohn, 1847–53.

Crankshaw, Edward. *The Fall of the House of Habsburg*. New York, Viking Press, 1963.

Creasy, Sir Edward S. *History of the Ottoman Turks*. New York, Henry Holt & Co., 1878.

Dugast Rouillé, Michel, Hubert Cuny [et] Hervé Pinoteau. *Les Grands Mariages des Habsbourgs*. Paris, G. Saffroy, 1955.

Ehrenberg, Richard. *Capital and Finance in the Age of the Renaissance: A Study of the Fuggers and their Connections*, trans. by H. M. Lucas. New York, Harcourt, Brace & Co., [1928].

Eisenmenger, Victor. *Archduke Francis Ferdinand*. London, Selwyn & Blount, 1931.

Erasmus, Desiderius. *The Education of a Christian Prince*, trans. by Lester K. Born. New York, Columbia University Press, 1936.

Fauchier-Magnan, Adrian. *Small German Courts in the Eighteenth Century*, trans. by Mervyn Savill. London, Methuen & Co., 1958.

Fejtö, François. *Un Habsbourg Révolutionnaire, Joseph II*. Paris, Librairie Plon, 1953.

Fichtenau, Heinrich. *Der Junge Maximilian (1459–1482)*. Vienna, Verlag für Geschichte und Politik, 1959.

Fischer-Galati, Stephen A. *Ottoman Imperialism and German Protestantism 1521–1555*. Cambridge, Mass., Harvard University Press, 1959.

Flanders in the Fifteenth Century: Art and Civilization—Catalogue of Exhibition of Masterpieces of Flemish Art. Detroit, Michigan, Detroit Institute of Arts, and Brussels, Belgium, Centre National de Recherches Primitifs Flamands (published jointly), 1960.

Forneron, H. *Histoire de Philippe II*. Paris, E. Plon et Cie., 1882.

Freud, Martin. *Sigmund Freud, Man and Father*. New York, Vanguard Press, 1958.

Froude, J. A. *Life and Letters of Erasmus*. New York, Charles Scribner's Sons, 1895.

Geiringer, Karl. *Josef Haydn, A Creative Life in Music*. New York, W. W. Norton & Co., 1946.

Glaise-Horstenau, Edmund von. *The Collapse of the Austro-Hungarian Empire*, trans. by Ian F. D. Morrow. London, J. M. Dent & Sons, 1930.

Goldsmith, Margaret. *Maria Theresa of Austria*. London, Arthur Barker, 1936.

Gooch, G. P. *Maria Theresa and Other Studies*. London, Longmans, Green & Co., 1951.

Goodwin, Albert. *The European Nobility in the Eighteenth Century*. London, Adam & Charles Black, 1953.

Grimschitz, Bruno. *Wiener Barockpaläste*. Vienna, Wiener Verlag Ernst Sopher und Karl Bauer, 1944.

Hantsch, Hugo. *Die Geschichte Österreichs*, 2 vols. Graz, Verlag Styria, 1947–62.

Harding, Bertita. *Phantom Crown: Maximilian of Mexico.* Indianapolis, Bobbs-Merrill Co., 1934.

Holborn, Hajo. *A History of Modern Germany.* New York, Alfred A. Knopf, 1959.

Hommel, Luc. *Marie de Bourgogne ou Le Grand Héritage.* Brussels, A. Goemaere, 1945.

——*Marguerite d'York ou La Duchesse Junon.* Paris, Librairie Hachette, 1959.

Iongh, Jane de. *Margaret of Austria,* trans. by M. D. Herter Norton. New York, W. W. Norton & Co., 1953.

——*Mary of Hungary, Second Regent of the Netherlands,* trans. by M. D. Herter Norton. New York, W. W. Norton & Co., 1958.

Jacob, Heinrich Eduard. *Johann Strauss, Father and Son,* trans. by Marguerite Wolff. New York, Greystone Press, 1940.

Jacquot, Jean (ed.) *Fêtes et Cérémonies au Temps de Charles-Quint.* Paris, Editions du Centre National de la Recherche Scientifique, 1960.

Jenks, William A. *Vienna and the Young Hitler.* New York, Columbia University Press, 1960.

Juste, M. Theodore. "Charles-Quint et Marguerite d'Autriche," in *Mémoires Couronnés.* Brussels, M. Hayez, 1858.

Kann, Robert A. *The Habsburg Empire. A Study in Integration and Disintegration.* New York, Frederick A. Praeger, 1957.

Kervyn de Lettenhove, Baron H[enri Marie Bruno Joseph]. *La Toison d'Or, Notes sur l'institution et l'histoire de l'Ordre depuis l'année 1429 jusqu'à l'année 1559.* Brussels, Librairie Nationale d'Art et d'Histoire, 1907.

Kirk, John Foster. *History of Charles the Bold,* 3 vols. Philadelphia, J. B Lippincott, 1864.

Klopp, Onno. *Das Jahr 1683.* Graz, Verlags-Buchhandlung Styria, 1882.

Knolles, Richard. *The Generall Historie of the Turke.* London, T. Bassett, 1687.

Kohn, Hans. *The Habsburg Empire: 1804–1918.* Princeton, N.J., D. Van Nostrand Co., 1961.

Knappich, Wilhelm. *Die Habsburger Chronik.* Salzburg, Verlag "Das Bergland-Buch," 1959.

Kosáry, Dominic G. *A History of Hungary.* Cleveland, Benjamin Franklin Bibliophile Society, 1941.

Kralik, Richard. *Geschichte der Stadt Wien und ihrer Kultur,* 2nd ed. Vienna, Adolf Holzhausen, 1926.

Kretschmayr, Heinrich. *Maria Theresia.* Leipzig, L. Staackmann Verlag, 1958.

Kusin, P. Eberhard. *Die Kaisergruft bei den PP. Kapuzinern in Wien.* Vienna, Buch- und Kunstverlag Othomar Kloiber, 1949.

Lamb, Harold. *Suleiman the Magnificent.* Garden City, N.Y., Doubleday & Co., 1951.

Landau, Marcus. *Geschichte Kaiser Karls VI als König von Spanien.* Stuttgart, Verlag der J. G. Cotta'schen Buchhandlung, 1889.

Langdon-Davies, John. *Carlos, The King Who Would Not Die*. Englewood Cliffs, N.J., Prentice-Hall, 1963.

Langsam, Walter Consuelo. *Francis the Good: The Education of an Emperor, 1768–1792*. New York, The Macmillan Co., 1949.

Leger, Louis. *History of Austro-Hungary*. London, Rivingtons, 1889.

Leitich, Ann Tizia. *Augustissima: Maria Theresia—Leben und Werk*. Vienna, Amalthea-Verlag, n.d.

Lengyel, Emil. *The Danube*. New York, Random House, 1939.

Lewis, D. B. Wyndham. *Charles of Europe*. New York, Coward-McCann, 1931.

Lockhart, John Gilbert. *The Peacemakers*. London, Duckworth, 1932.

Lonyay, Count Carl. *Rudolf: The Tragedy of Mayerling*. London, Hamish Hamilton, 1950.

Lorenz, Reinhold. *Kaiser Karl und der Untergang der Donaumonarchie*. Graz, Verlag Styria, 1959.

——*Türkenjahr 1683*. Vienna, Wilhelm Braumüller, 1933.

Ludwig, Emil. *Napoleon*, trans. by Eden and Cedar Paul. New York, Boni & Liveright, 1926.

Lynch, John. *Spain under the Habsburgs (1516–1598)*. New York, Oxford University Press, 1964.

Mahan, J. Alexander. *Maria Theresa of Austria*. New York, Thomas Y. Crowell Co., 1932.

Marboe, Ernst. *The Book of Austria*, trans. by G. E. R. Gedye. Vienna, Österreichische Staatsdruckerei, 1948.

Margutti, Albert von. *Emperor Francis Joseph and his Times*. London, Hutchinson & Co., n.d.

Mariéjol, Jean H. *Philip II, The First Modern King*, trans. by Warren B. Wells. New York, Harper & Bros., 1933.

Martin, Percy. *Maximilian in Mexico*. New York, Charles Scribner's Sons, 1914.

May, Arthur J. *The Habsburg Monarchy, 1867–1914*. Cambridge, Mass., Harvard University Press, 1951.

Mecenseffy, Grete. "Habsburger im 17. Jahrhundert: Die Beziehungen der Höfe von Wien und Madrid während des Dreissigjährigen Krieges," Vol. 121, No. 1, of *Archiv für Österreichische Geschichte*. Vienna, Rudolf M. Rohrer, 1955.

Mitis, Oskar Freiherr von. *Das Leben des Kronprinzen Rudolf, mit Briefen und Schriften aus Dessen Nachlass*. Leipzig, Insel Verlag, 1928.

Moffatt, Mary Maxwell. *Maria Theresa*. London, Methuen & Co., 1911.

Morton, John Bingham. *Sobieski, King of Poland*. London, Eyre & Spottiswoode, 1932.

Moüy, Charles de. *Don Carlos et Philippe II*. Paris, Perrin et Cie., 1888.

Münch, Ernst. *Maria von Burgund nebst dem Leben ihrer Stiefmutter, Margarethe von York*. Leipzig, F. A. Brockhaus, 1832.

Newald, Johann. *Beitrage zur Geschichte der Belagerung von Wien durch die Türken im Jahre 1683*. Vienna, Verlag von Kubasta & Voigt, 1883.

Nicolson, Harold. *The Congress of Vienna*. New York, Harcourt, Brace & Co., 1946.

Nüchter, Friedrich. *Albrecht Dürer,* trans. by Lucy D. Williams. Ansbach, Fr. Seybold, 1911.

Padover, Saul K. *The Revolutionary Emperor Joseph the Second.* New York, Robert O. Ballou, 1934.

Pérez Martín, María Jesús. *Margarita de Austria, Reina de España.* Madrid, Espasa-Calpe, 1961.

Petrie, Sir Charles. *Philip II of Spain.* New York, W. W. Norton & Co., 1963.

Pfandl, Ludwig. *Karl II.* Munich, Verlag Georg D. W. Callwey, 1940.

————*Philipp II.* Munich, Verlag Georg D. W. Callwey, 1951.

Pirchan, Emil. *Fanny Elssler.* Vienna, Wilhelm Frick Verlag, 1940.

Polzer-Hoditz, Arthur. *The Emperor Karl.* London, Putnam, 1930.

Prescott, William H. *History of the Reign of Ferdinand and Isabella the Catholic,* 3 vols. Philadelphia, J. B. Lippincott Co., 1870.

Rath, Reuben John. *The Viennese Revolution of 1848.* Austin, Texas, University of Texas Press, 1957.

Rausch, Karl. *Die Burgundische Heirat Maximilians I.* Vienna, Verlag von Carl Konegen, 1880.

Reade, Hubert. *Sidelights on the Thirty Years War.* London, Kegan Paul, Trench, Trubner & Co., 1924.

Redlich, Joseph. *Emperor Francis Joseph of Austria,* New York, The Macmillan Co., 1929.

Reiners, Ludwig. *Frederick the Great,* trans. by Lawrence Wilson. London, Oswald Wolff, 1960.

Remak, Joachim. *Sarajevo.* New York, Criterion Books, 1959.

Renaissance Reader, ed. by James Bruce Ross and Mary Martin McLaughlin. New York, Viking Press, 1953.

Renner, Victor von. *Wien im Jahre 1683.* Vienna, Verlag von R. V. Waldheim, 1883.

Robertson, Priscilla. *Revolutions of 1848, A Social History.* Princeton, Princeton University Press, 1952.

Rumbold, Sir Horace. *The Austrian Court in the Nineteenth Century.* London, Methuen & Co., 1909.

Sauvigny, G. de Bertier de. *Metternich and his Times.* London, Darton, Longman & Todd, 1932.

Schick, Leon. *Jacob Fugger, Un Grand Homme d'Affaires au début du XVIᵉ Siècle.* Paris S.E.V.P.E.N., 1957.

Schimmer, Karl August. *The Sieges of Vienna by the Turks.* London, J. Murray, 1847.

Schüssel, Therese. *Kultur des Barock in Österreich.* Graz, Stiasny Verlag, 1960.

Schwarzenfeld, Gertrude von. *Charles V, Father of Europe,* trans. by Ruth Mary Bethell. London, Hollis & Carter, 1957.

————*Rudolf II.* Munich, Verlag Georg D. W. Callwey, 1961.

Sinor, Denis. *History of Hungary.* London, George Allen & Unwin, 1959.

Slocombe, George. *Don John of Austria.* Boston, Houghton Mifflin, 1936.

Steed, Henry Wickham. *The Habsburg Monarchy,* 4th edn. London, Constable & Co., 1919.

Stoye, John. *The Siege of Vienna*. London, Collins Sons & Co., 1964.

Strelka, Josef. *Der Burgundische Renaissancehof Margarethes von Öster-reich*. Vienna, A. Sexl, 1957.

Strieder, Jakob. *Jacob Fugger der Reiche*. Leipzig, Quelle & Meyer, n.d.

Taylor, A. J. P. *The Habsburg Monarchy: 1815–1918*. London, Macmillan and Co., 1941.

Taylor, Edmond. *The Fall of the Dynasties*. Garden City, N.Y., Double-day & Co., 1963.

Tighe, Harry. *A Queen of Unrest. The Story of Juana of Castile*. London, Swan Sonnenschein, 1905.

Tritsch, Walther. *Metternich und sein Monarch*. Darmstadt, Im Holle Ver-lag, 1952.

Troels-Lund, Troels Frederik. *Dagligt liv i Norden i det sekstende aarhundrede*. Copenhagen, Gyldendal, 1908.

Tschuppik, Karl. *Empress Elizabeth of Austria*. London, Archibald Con-stable & Co., 1930.

Tyler, Royall. *The Emperor Charles the Fifth*. Fair Lawn, N.J., Essential Books, 1956.

Ullmann, Heinrich. *Kaiser Maximilian I*, 2 vols. Stuttgart, J. G. Cotta'schen, 1884–91.

Valentin, Veit. *The German People*. New York, Alfred A. Knopf, 1952.

Vallotton, Henry. *Marie-Thérèse Impératrice*. Paris, Librairie Arthème Fayard, 1963.

Van Dyke, Paul. *Renascence Portraits*. New York, Charles Scribner's Sons, 1952.

Vehse, Karl Eduard. *Memoirs of the Court and Aristocracy of Austria*, trans. by Franz Demmler, 2 vols. London, H. S. Nichols, 1896.

Vernon, Katherine Dorothea Evert. *Italy, 1494–1790*. Cambridge, England Cambridge University Press, 1909.

Waas, Glenn Elwood. *The Legendary Character of Kaiser Maximilian*. No. 14, Columbia University Germanic Studies. New York, Columbia Uni-versity Press, 1941.

Wandruszka, Adam. *The House of Habsburg*, trans. by Cathleen and Hans Epstein. Garden City, N.Y., Doubleday & Co., 1964.

——*Leopold II*, 2 vols. Vienna, Verlag Herold, n.d.

Webster, Charles Kingsley. *The Congress of Vienna*. London, Oxford Uni-versity Press, 1918.

Wedgwood, C. V. *The Thirty Years War*. Garden City, N.Y., Double-day & Co., 1961.

Wolf, Adam. *Marie Christine, Erzherzogin von Österreich*, 2 vols. Vienna, Carl Gerold's Sohn, 1863.

Wolfsgruber, Cölestin. *Franz I, Kaiser von Österreich*, 2 vols. in 1. Vienna, Wilhelm Braumüller, 1899.

Zeman, Z. A. B. *The Break-up of the Habsburg Empire, 1914–1918*. Lon-don, Oxford University Press, 1961.

Zessner-Spitzenburg, Hans. *Kaiser Karl*. Salzburg, Salzburger Verlag für Wirtschaft und Kultur, 1953.

Zweig, Stefan. *Conqueror of the Seas: The Story of Magellan*. New York, Viking Press, 1938.

Index

Aachen (Germany), 3, 28–30, 88–89

Adrian of Utrecht (Pope Adrian VI), Regent of Castile, 86

Agate bowl, the, 21, 141, 416 *note* 8

Albert, Duke of Saxe-Teschen, (1738–1822), 244, 247, 248

Albrecht, Archduke, Field Marshal (1817–95), 355, 356, 370

Albrecht, Archduke, Regent of the Netherlands, 149, 161

Albrecht I, Emperor (1248–1308), 6

Aleander, Cardinal, 92, 122

Alexander I, Czar of Russia (1777–1825), 287, 293, 295, 296

Althann, Michael, Count, 218

Alva, Duke of, journey-master to Infanta Maria Anna, 173, 175, 176

Alva, Fernando Alvarez de Toledo, Duke of (1508–83), 98, 147

Amalia, Archduchess, daughter of Maria Theresia, wife of Duke of Parma (1746–1804), 247, 248

Anna, Queen of Spain, daughter of Maximilian II, wife of Philip II (1552–80), betrothal to Don Carlos, 119, 144, 145, 147; marriage to Philip II, 149, 154–56

Anna of Hungary, wife of Ferdinand I (1503–47), 52–59 *passim*, 94, 120–22, 131, 141

Anna of Tyrol, wife of Matthias (1585–1618), 163

Anne de Beaujeu, 28, 34

Anne of Brittany, 34–35

Anti-semitism, 356–57, 385–86

Apollo dance palace, 278, 280, 281; 433 *note* 2

Archduke, title of, 6

Arcimboldo, Giuseppe, court painter to Ferdinand I, Maximilian II, Rudolf II (1530–93), 162

Arras, Treaty of (1482), 28, 31

Aspern, battle of (1809), 281

Auersperg, Princess Wilhelmina, 237

Augsburg, 38, 39; Diet of 1519, 57–59; Habsburg quarrel at Diet of 1550, 109–11; Interim Diet, 132; peace of, 113, 137

Augustiner Church, 206, 207, 223

August of Saxony, Elector, 201, 203, 204

Austerlitz, battle of (1805), 275, 276

Austria, acquired by Habsburgs, 4; invasion by Matthias Corvinus, 9, 18, 28, 32; under Ferdinand I, 93, 119–21, 124, 140, 143; under Maximilian II, 151, 152; Turkish inroads, 125, 128, 161, 188–96; Matthias' regency, 162; as absolutist monarchy, 179, 183; during Napoleonic Wars, 274–85 *passim;* created empire, 276; rev-

NORTH SEA

ENGLAND

London

Amsterdam

NETHERLANDS

Bruges

Ghent

Brussels

Liège

AUSTRIAN NETHERLANDS
−1797

Cologne

GERMANY

Bremen

Hamburg

Berlin

ELBE R.

RHINE R.

Frankfurt

Sedan

Verdun

SEINE R.

MEUSE R.

Paris

LOIRE R.

FRANCE

−1801

−1805

DANUBE R.

+1779

Augsburg

SALZBURG
+1805

Linz

AU

SAÔNE R.

Bern

SWITZERLAND

Geneva

TRENT
+1803

Lyons

RHÔNE R.

LOMBARDY
−1859

Turin

Milan

Trent

VENICE
+1815−1866

Tries

Venice

PARMA
+1815−1847

Genoa

PO R.

ISTRIA
+1797

N

W   E

S

Marseilles

MODENA
+1814−1860

Florence

DALMA
+179

SPAIN

Barcelona

TUSCANY
−1860

ITALY

Rome

Napl

MEDITERRANEAN   SEA

0   Miles   200